The Qur'an

in easy English

❦ The Easy Qur'an ❦

Crenowned™

Crowned & Renowned

Title of book: The Qur'an in easy English (The Easy Qur'an)

Translator of book: Crenowned[TMK]

First published: January 2019

This edition: Updated Edition, April 2019

Version: HQC1.3b

Cover Version: HQC1.2bforHQC1.3b

Copyright © 2019, Crowned and Renowned Publications; Crenowned

1440AH/2019CE

crenowned@gmail.com

ALL RIGHTS RESERVED. This book contains material protected under all copyright laws and treaties. Any unauthorised reprint or use of this material is prohibited. No part of this book may be reproduced or transmitted in any form or by any means, electronic or mechanical, including photocopying, recording, or by any information storage and retrieval system without express written permission from the publishers.

Cover, design, typesetting and layout by:
Crowned and Renowned Publications (Crenowned)

Copyright © 2019, Crowned and Renowned Publications[TMK]
All rights reserved.
ISBN: 9781689612586

DEDICATED

to the guidance of all people

Contents

Contents	v
Notes to the Reader	ix
Surah 1. Opening (al-Faatihah)	1
Surah 2. Cow (al-Baqarah)	2
Surah 3. Family Of Imran (Aal 'Imraan)	42
Surah 4. Women (an-Nisaa')	64
Surah 5. Diningspread (al-Maa'idah)	88
Surah 6. Cattle (al-An'aam)	106
Surah 7. Heights (al-A'raaf)	126
Surah 8. Spoils of War (al-Anfaal)	147
Surah 9. Repentance (at-Tawbah)	155
Surah 10. Yunus (Jonah)	172
Surah 11. Hud	184
Surah 12. Yusuf (Joseph)	196
Surah 13. Thunder (ar-Ra'd)	208
Surah 14. Ibrahim (Abraham)	213
Surah 15. Valley of Rocks (al-Hijr)	219
Surah 16. Bee (an-Nahl)	224
Surah 17. Night Journey (al-Israa')	237
Surah 18. Cave (al-Kahf)	248
Surah 19. Maryam (Mary)	258
Surah 20. Taa Haa	265
Surah 21. Prophets (al-Anbiyaa')	274
Surah 22. Pilgrimage (al-Hajj)	282
Surah 23. Believers (al-Mu'minoon)	291
Surah 24. Light (an-Noor)	298
Surah 25. Criterion (al-Furqaan)	306

Surah 26. Poets (ash-Shu'araa') 313
Surah 27. Ants (an-Naml) 322
Surah 28. Stories (al-Qasas) 330
Surah 29. Spider (al-'Ankaboot) 339
Surah 30. Romans (ar-Ruum) 346
Surah 31. Luqman 352
Surah 32. Prostration (as-Sajdah) 355
Surah 33. Combined Forces (al-Ahzaab) 358
Surah 34. Saba' (Sheba) 366
Surah 35. The Originator (al-Faatir) 372
Surah 36. Yaa Seen 377
Surah 37. Those in Rows (as-Saaffaat) 382
Surah 38. Saad 389
Surah 39. Crowds (az-Zumar) 394
Surah 40. The Forgiver (al-Ghaafir) 402
Surah 41. (Verses) Explained in Detail (Fussilat) 410
Surah 42. Consultation (ash-Shooraa) 415
Surah 43. Decorations of Gold (az-Zukhruf) 421
Surah 44. Smoke (ad-Dukhaan) 427
Surah 45. Kneeling (al-Jaathiyah) 429
Surah 46. Sand Dunes (al-Ahqaaf) 433
Surah 47. Muhammad 437
Surah 48. Victory (al-Fath) 441
Surah 49. Private Apartments (al-Hujuraat) 445
Surah 50. Qaaf 447
Surah 51. Winds That Scatter (adh-Dhaariyaat) 450
Surah 52. Mount Tur (at-Tur) 453
Surah 53. Star (an-Najm) 455
Surah 54. Moon (al-Qamar) 458
Surah 55. The Most Compassionate (ar-Rahmaan) 461

Surah 56. Event (al-Waaqi'ah) 464

Surah 57. Iron (Hadeed) 467

Surah 58. Dispute (al-Mujaadalah) 471

Surah 59. Gathering (al-Hashr) 474

Surah 60. Tested Woman (al-Mumtahanah) 477

Surah 61. Rows (as-Saff) 479

Surah 62. Friday Congregation (al-Jumu'ah) 481

Surah 63. Hypocrites (al-Munafiqoon) 482

Surah 64. Being Defeated (at-Taghaabun) 483

Surah 65. Divorce (at-Talaaq) 485

Surah 66. Prohibition (at-Tahreem) 487

Surah 67. All Control (al-Mulk) 489

Surah 68. Pen (al-Qalam) 491

Surah 69. Truthteller (al-Haaqqah) 494

Surah 70. Pathways to Heaven (al-Ma'aarij) 496

Surah 71. Nuh (Noah) 498

Surah 72. Jinns (al-Jinn) 499

Surah 73. Wrapped in His Clothes (al-Muzzammil) 501

Surah 74. Wrapped in His Cloak (al-Muddaththir) 503

Surah 75. Resurrection (al-Qiyaamah) 505

Surah 76. Human Being (al-Insaan) 506

Surah 77. Those Sent Forwards (al-Mursalaat) 508

Surah 78. News (an-Naba') 510

Surah 79. Soul-Snatchers (an-Naazi'aat) 512

Surah 80. He Frowned ('Abasa) 513

Surah 81. Folding Up (at-Takweer) 515

Surah 82. Breaking Apart (al-Infitaar) 516

Surah 83. Those Who Cheat (al-Mutaffifeen) 516

Surah 84. Splitting Apart (al-Inshiqaaq) 518

Surah 85. Constellations (al-Burooj) 519

Surah 86. Night-Comer (at-Taariq) 520

Surah 87. Most High (al-A'laa) 521

Surah 88. Overwhelming Event (al-Ghaashiyah) 521

Surah 89. Dawn (al-Fajr) 522

Surah 90. City (al-Balad) 523

Surah 91. Sun (ash-Shams) 524

Surah 92. Night (al-Layl) 525

Surah 93. Mid-Morning Light (ad-Duhaa) 526

Surah 94. Opening the Heart (al-Inshiraah) 526

Surah 95. Fig (at-Teen) 527

Surah 96. That Which Clings (al-'Alaq) 527

Surah 97. Great Value (al-Qadr) 528

Surah 98. Clear Proof (al-Bayyinah) 528

Surah 99. Earthquake (az-Zilzaal) 529

Surah 100. Charging Warhorses (al-'Aadiyaat) 530

Surah 101. Crashing Shudder (al-Qaari'ah) 530

Surah 102. Competing for More (at-Takaathur) 531

Surah 103. Passing of Time (al-'Asr) 531

Surah 104. False Accuser (al-Humazah) 531

Surah 105. Elephant (al-Feel) 532

Surah 106. Quraysh 532

Surah 107. Small Necessities (al-Maa'oon) 532

Surah 108. Abundance (al-Kawthar) 533

Surah 109. Disbelievers (al-Kaafiroon) 533

Surah 110. Help (an-Nasr) 533

Surah 111. Flame (al-Lahab) 534

Surah 112. Sincerity (al-Ikhlaas) 534

Surah 113. Daybreak (al-Falaq) 534

Surah 114. People (an-Naas) 535

Notes to the Reader

The Qur'an is the Final Divine Testament and the Word of Allah. It cannot be translated nor conclusively interpreted. Here, we have attempted to interpret the meanings of the Qur'an into easy, readable English.

The Qur'an has no errors or mistakes. Anything in this interpretation that is incorrect is due to our own human failings.

Allah is referred to as God in English.

Names of Prophets have been retained according to their pronunciation in the Qur'an, in Arabic, and their Biblical equivalents in English have been placed in brackets at the first instance of their mention.

Surah is a Chapter. It can be as short as 3 verses (Surah 108) to as long as 286 verses (Surah 2).

In this version, the translation of the Qur'an's main text is in bold. Non-bold text has been used to include additional words to help understand the meanings of the main text. The use of brackets has been limited and diacritics have been avoided. At the beginning of each verse is the sequential number of the chapter – prior to the decimal point, and of the verse – after the decimal point. These have been placed in superscript for ease of flow.

The Qur'an ought not be treated, handled, conceived of, read, studied, investigated, or analysed as a book authored by humans; it is Allah's Book (3.23) of Guidance (2.2) to us, free of flaws, and full of directions. May He guide us on the Straight Path, assist us in following the truth, and help us in achieving ultimate success.

Amin[TMK]

Surah 1. Opening (*al-Faatihah*)

Allah's name I begin with, the Most Compassionate, the Ever-Merciful

[1.1] All praise is for Allah – Lord of all the worlds,
[1.2] Most Compassionate, Ever-Merciful,
[1.3] Master of Judgement Day.

[1.4] Only You we worship and only You we ask for help.

[1.5] Guide us along the Straight Path,
[1.6] the path of those You do favours to,
[1.7] not of those who have Your anger upon them nor of those who go astray.

O Allah,
accept this prayer.
Aameen.

Surah 2. Cow (al-Baqarah)

[PART 1]

Allah's name I begin with, the Most Compassionate, the Ever-Merciful

2.1 *Alif Laam Meem.*
2.2 This is the Book in which there is no doubt. It is guidance for those who are mindful of Allah, 2.3 who believe in the unseen secrets, establish the ritual prayers (salaah), and donate from what We've given them; 2.4 and who believe in what is revealed to you, O Prophet Muhammad, and in what was revealed before you, and they strongly believe in the Hereafter. 2.5 It is they who are on guidance from their Lord and it is really they who will be successful.

2.6 Those who have accepted disbelief, it makes no difference to them if you warn them or not, they still won't believe; 2.7 Allah has sealed up their hearts and their hearing, and there's a blindfold over their eyes. They will suffer a terrible punishment.

2.8 Some people who claim: "We believe in Allah and the Last Day," but they aren't really believers. 2.9 They think they can trick Allah and the Believers. They aren't even aware that they end up tricking only themselves. 2.10 In their hearts is a sickness and Allah allows it to increase in them. They will suffer a painful punishment because of the lies they used to tell. 2.11 When they are told: "Don't make trouble in the world," they reply: "We are only peacemakers!" 2.12 The truth is, they aren't even aware that they themselves are the troublemakers.

²·¹³When they are told: "Believe like other people do," they say: "Shall we believe like fools do?" The truth is, they themselves are the fools but they don't realise.

²·¹⁴When they meet the Believers, they claim: "We also believe," but when they are alone with their evil ones, they declare: "We are with you. We are only mocking the Believers."

²·¹⁵Allah punishes the disbelievers because of their mockery and leaves them confused to wander blindly in their rebellion. ²·¹⁶They're the ones who buy misguidance at the cost of guidance, but their buying and selling doesn't gain any profit as they haven't been following guidance.

²·¹⁷Their example is of someone who lights a fire that when it brightens everything around him, Allah takes away their light and leaves them in the depths of darkness, unable to see. ²·¹⁸They are choosing to be deaf, dumb, blind! – and that is why they won't come back.

²·¹⁹Or another example is that of a rainstorm coming from the sky, in which there are many layers of darkness, thunder, and lightning. They thrust their fingers into their ears from the thunderbolts for fear of death. Allah completely surrounds the disbelievers! ²·²⁰The lightning almost snatches away their eyesight. Each time it flashes for them, they walk in its light, but when it goes dark on them, they stand still. If Allah had wanted, He could have easily taken away their hearing and sight. Allah is Most Capable of anything.

²·²¹People! Worship your Lord Who created you and those before you so you can become mindful of Him ²·²²– Who made the earth a resting place for you, the sky a structure, and sends down from the sky water

with which He brings out many kinds of fruit for you to eat. Therefore, don't deliberately make others equal to Allah.

2.23If you're in any doubt about what We have revealed to Our servant – Prophet Muhammad then you should yourselves make a surah (chapter) like it. You may even call your own helpers, apart from Allah, if you are telling the truth. 2.24If you cannot do that – and you never will – then beware of the Fire whose fuel will be people and stones, prepared for the disbelievers.

2.25O Prophet Muhammad, give good news to those who believe and do good, that they will have gardens – that have rivers flowing beneath them. Whenever they will be given fruit there to eat, they will say: "This is what we were given before," but they were given only something similar to it. They will have clean and pure spouses there and they will remain there forever.

2.26Allah isn't ashamed of using the example of a mosquito or even something smaller than that. As for the Believers, they already know that it is the truth from their Lord, but the disbelievers argue: "What does Allah mean by giving this example?" Allah lets many people go astray by this example and He also guides many by it, though He only lets those people go astray by it who are already disobedient, 2.27who break Allah's promise after having confirmed it, split apart the relationships which Allah has commanded to be joined, and they make trouble in the world. It is they who are the real losers.

2.28How can you disbelieve in Allah? You were lifeless and He gave you life! He will later give you death and then bring you back to life again, and then it is Him you will all be taken back to. 2.29He is the one Who created for you everything there is in the earth, then He turned to the heaven and levelled out the seven skies. He knows everything perfectly well.

²·³⁰When your Lord said to the angels: "I am going to place a representative on earth," they asked: "Are you going to put there someone who will make trouble in it and kill people, while we are enough to glorify Your praises and honour Your holiness?" He responded: "I know what you don't."

²·³¹Allah taught Adam the names of everything. After that, He displayed them in front of the angels and ordered: "Tell me the names of these if you are right." ²·³²"Glory be to You!" they replied: "We don't have any knowledge other than what You have taught us. Only You are the All-Knowing, the All-Wise." ²·³³Allah ordered: "Adam, tell them the names of these things." When Adam told them their names, Allah asked the angels: "Didn't I tell you that I know all the unseen secrets of the heavens and the earth, as well as everything you show or hide?" ²·³⁴When We ordered the angels: "Prostrate in front of Adam," and so they did prostrate – but not Iblees (Lucifer). He refused and showed arrogance, and became a disbeliever.

²·³⁵We said: "Adam, you and your wife may live comfortably in Paradise, and eat with pleasure from it however you like, but don't go near this tree or you will be wrongdoers." ²·³⁶However, Shaytan (Satan) tricked them by the tree, and caused them to leave the place where they were staying. We ordered: "Go down from here as enemies of each other. Your place of stay and livelihood, for a while, will be on earth." ²·³⁷Then Adam learnt some words of humility and prayer from his Lord, Who then forgave him. Only Allah accepts repentance much, the Ever-Merciful.

²·³⁸We ordered: "Get down from Paradise all of you, all together. Whenever any guidance comes to you from Me, those who follow My guidance won't have anything to fear and will never be sad, ²·³⁹but those who disbelieve and call Our revelations a lie, it is they who will be the people of the Fire. They will remain in it forever."

²·⁴⁰Descendants of Ya'qub (Isra'il)! Remember My favour which I did to you, fulfil your promise to Me and I will fulfil My promise to you, and fear only Me. ²·⁴¹Believe in what I have revealed – confirming the revelations you already have, and don't be the first to disbelieve in it. Never sell My revelations for a low price, but be mindful only of Me. ²·⁴²Don't mix the truth with falsehood nor deliberately hide the truth. ²·⁴³You must establish the ritual prayers, pay zakah (obligatory poor-due), and bow down in prayer with those who bow down.

²·⁴⁴Are you telling people to be pious but forget about yourselves even though you study the Book? Don't you even think? ²·⁴⁵You should find help in patience and ritual prayers, even though they are difficult, but not for those who are humble – ²·⁴⁶who are sure they will meet their Lord and will go back only to Him.

²·⁴⁷Descendants of Ya'qub! Remember My favour which I did to you and made you superior to all the people of your time. ²·⁴⁸Be mindful of the Day when no one will be able to help anyone in any way at all; intercession won't be accepted from them, ransom won't be taken from them, and they simply won't be helped.

²·⁴⁹Remember when We saved you from Fir'awn's people: they used to oppress you with terrible suffering by slaughtering your boys but keeping your women alive. In that was a severe test from your Lord.

²·⁵⁰When We made a gap in the sea for you, We saved you but drowned Fir'awn's people while you were there watching.

²·⁵¹When We promised forty nights to Musa (Moses), in his absence, you, being wrongdoers, began to worship the calf. ²·⁵²Then, even after all that, We still forgave you, so that you might become thankful.

²·⁵³Remember when We gave Musa the Book and also the ability to distinguish between right and wrong, so that you might follow guidance.

²·⁵⁴When Musa said to his people: "My people! You have harmed yourselves by worshipping the calf. Now repent to Allah – your Maker, and kill the calf-worshippers among yourselves. This is best for you in the sight of your Maker," so Allah forgave you. Only He accepts repentance much, the Ever-Merciful.

²·⁵⁵When you all said: "Musa! We will never believe merely because you say so, unless we can see Allah clearly," and then, while you were looking, the thunderbolt took your lives. ²·⁵⁶Then, after you had died, We brought you all back to life so that you might become thankful.

²·⁵⁷We shaded you with clouds and sent down manna and quails for you: We said: "Eat from the wholesome things We've given you." However, they didn't harm Us by rebelling but were only harming themselves.

²·⁵⁸Remember when We said: "Enter this town and eat with pleasure from it however you like, but you must enter the gate with humility and praying, 'We beg forgiveness!' and We will forgive you your sins. We will soon give more to those who do good." ²·⁵⁹However, the wrongdoers changed the words to something else – something other

than what they were told. So, We sent down on them a punishment from heaven because they continued to disobey.

2.60Remember when Musa prayed for water for his people, We said: "Hit the rock with your staff," and out of it gushed twelve springs. Each group knew its own place to drink from. We said: "Eat and drink from what Allah has given, and don't go around making trouble in the world."

2.61Remember when you all said: "Musa! We cannot accept only one kind of food. Pray for us to your Lord to bring out for us something the earth grows – of its green herbs, cucumbers, garlic, lentils, and onions." Musa replied: "Do you want to swap good for bad? You might as well go down into any town and you will have whatever you want!" They were made to suffer humiliation and misery, and brought down Allah's anger upon themselves. This all happened because they used to disbelieve in Allah's signs and unlawfully kill the prophets. This was also because they disobeyed and continued to break the law.

2.62Those who believe as Muslims, as well as those who are Jews, Christians or Sabians – whoever believed in Allah and the Last Day and did good, their reward will come from their Lord. They won't have anything to fear and will never be sad.

2.63Remember when We took a promise from you and raised Mount Tur over your heads saying: "You must hold strongly on to what law We've given you and always remember what is in it so you can become mindful of Me." 2.64But then, after making that promise, you people turned back. If it wasn't for Allah's grace and mercy upon you, you would have certainly been among the losers. 2.65You very well knew those among you who broke the Sabbath, so We said to them: "Be apes! Disgraced!" 2.66We made that punishment a lesson of warning to the people of that time and of the future, as well as a source of advice for those who are mindful of Allah.

[2.67]Remember when Musa said to his people: "Allah is ordering you to slaughter a cow." They replied: "Are you making fun of us?" He replied: "I ask for Allah's protection from being one of those who are ignorant." [2.68]They demanded: "Pray for us to your Lord to make it clear to us as to what that cow should be." Musa replied: "Allah says, 'It is a cow that is neither too old nor too young but of an age between that.' Now do what you are told." [2.69]They asked: "Pray for us to your Lord to make it clear to us as to what its colour should be." He replied: "Allah says, 'It is a cow that is yellow. Its colour is bright – pleasing to those who look at it.'." [2.70]They asked: "Pray for us to your Lord to make it clear to us as to what she actually is, because all cows look the same to us. Surely we will find it, if Allah chooses." [2.71]Musa replied: "Allah says, 'It is a cow that hasn't been tamed to be used neither to plough the land nor to water the fields; it is perfect with no mark on it.'." They said: "Now you have come with the right description." So they eventually slaughtered it, even though they almost didn't.

[2.72]Remember when you killed a person and began blaming each other, Allah was going to expose what you were hiding. [2.73]We said: "Hit the dead body with a piece of the slaughtered cow." In this way Allah brings the dead back to life and shows you His signs so that you might think.

[2.74]Then, even after that, your hearts became hard like rocks or even harder: there are some rocks from which rivers gush out, some from which water only pours out when they split apart, and some others fall because they fear Allah. Allah isn't unaware of anything you do.

²·⁷⁵Do you Muslims **expect the Jews to believe merely because you say so, especially when some of them used to hear Allah's words and then deliberately change them after they had understood them?** ²·⁷⁶**When they meet the Believers, they claim: "We also believe," but when they are alone with each other, they ask: "Are you telling the Muslims what Allah has revealed to you** about Prophet Muhammad, **so that they will be able to use it as evidence against you in the presence of your Lord? Don't you even think?"** ²·⁷⁷**Don't they realise that Allah knows everything they hide or show?** ²·⁷⁸**Some of them are illiterate, whose only knowledge of the Book is based on** false **hopes, and so they're making guesses.** ²·⁷⁹**Damned are those who write the book with their own hands and then claim: "This is from Allah," only so they can sell it for a low price! They are damned for what their own hands have written! They are damned for what they're earning** with it!

²·⁸⁰**They claim: "We won't suffer the Fire for more than a few days."** O Prophet Muhammad, **say: "Allah will never break His promise, so have you taken a promise from Him? Or are you saying things about Allah what you don't even know?"** ²·⁸¹**Of course, anyone who does something bad and his sins surround him, it is they who will be the people of the Fire. They will remain in it forever.** ²·⁸²**Those who believe and do good, it is they who will be the people of Paradise. They will remain in it forever.**

²·⁸³Remember **when We took a promise from the Descendants of Ya'qub** with the command: **"You must worship only Allah; treat parents with kindness, as well as relatives, orphans, and the needy; and speak to people in a polite manner; you must establish the ritual prayers and pay zakah,"** but then you all turned away, except for a few of you, because you were neglectful.

²·⁸⁴**When We took a promise from you** with the command: "Don't kill each other nor expel each other from their homes," you agreed, and you yourselves were the witnesses. ²·⁸⁵Yet here you are: killing each other, expelling some of your own people from their homes, helping their enemies in sin and aggression against them, and ransoming them if they come to you as prisoners – even though it was unlawful for you to expel them in the first place. Do you believe in some parts of the Book and reject the rest? So, what can be the punishment for those of you who do this other than humiliation in this life and being pushed down into the harshest punishment on Judgement Day? Allah isn't unaware of anything you do. ²·⁸⁶They're the ones who are buying this life at the cost of the Hereafter. Therefore, their punishment won't be reduced and they won't be helped.

²·⁸⁷**We certainly gave Musa the Book and sent** many **messengers in** succession after him. We gave clear signs to Isa ibn Maryam (Jesus, Son of Mary) and helped him with the Holy Spirit (- Angel Jibra'il). Isn't it true that each time a messenger brought you something you yourselves didn't like, you became bigheaded? You accused some of being liars and others you murdered! ²·⁸⁸They reply: "Our hearts are wrapped up well and safe." Actually, Allah has cursed them because of their disbelief and so they have very little faith.

²·⁸⁹When a Book (- this Qur'an) came to them from Allah, confirming what they already had with them – although they used to pray for **victory against the disbelievers** through the intermediation of Prophet Muhammad – **but when that Prophet** Muhammad **they** identified came to them, they disbelieved in him. Therefore, Allah's curse is on the disbelievers. ²·⁹⁰How terrible is that for which they have sold their own souls! They disbelieve in what Allah has revealed, out of jealousy that He reveals from His grace to any of His servants

He chooses. So, they brought down on themselves anger upon anger. The disbelievers will suffer a humiliating punishment.

2.91 When they are told: "You must believe in what Allah has revealed," they reply: "We believe in only what has already been sent down to us," and they disbelieve in anything apart from that, even though it is the truth that confirms what they already have. O Prophet Muhammad, ask: "Then why have you been murdering Allah's prophets before this if you really were Believers?!"

2.92 Musa did come to you with clear signs, but in his absence, you, being wrongdoers, began to worship the calf. 2.93 Remember when We took a promise from you and raised Mount Tur over your heads saying: "You must hold strongly on to what law We've given you and listen carefully," they responded: "We hear but disobey," as their hearts had been filled with love for the calf because of their continued disbelief. O Prophet Muhammad, say: "How terrible are the things your faith tells you to do if you really are Believers!"

2.94 O Prophet Muhammad, say: "If the Home of the Hereafter, that is with Allah, is specially for you and not for other people, then you should wish for death, if you are telling the truth." 2.95 They will never ever wish for death because of the bad things they've done. Allah knows the wrongdoers perfectly well. 2.96 You will certainly find them to be most greedy for life than other people are, even more than polytheists. Each one of them wishes he was given a life of a thousand years, but it still won't save him from punishment even if his life was lengthened. Allah is Ever-Watchful of everything they do.

2.97 O Prophet Muhammad, say: "Whoever is an enemy to Jibreel should know that he has, by Allah's command, gradually brought down to your noble heart this Qur'an which confirms what came before it, a guidance, and a joy for the Believers. **2.98Whoever is an enemy to Allah, His angels, His messengers, Jibreel and Mika'eel (Michael),** should know that **Allah is an enemy to** these **disbelievers.**

2.99O Prophet Muhammad, We have certainly sent down to you clear signs, but only the disobedient people will reject them. 2.100**Isn't it true that each time they make a promise, a group of them throws it away? The truth is, most of them don't really believe.** 2.101**Now that a Messenger has come to them from Allah, confirming what they already have, a group of the People of the Book abandoned Allah's Book behind their backs pretending they didn't even know!**

2.102Instead, **they followed what the devils used to recite during the reign of Sulayman (Solomon). Sulayman didn't lose faith but the devils did; they used to teach witchcraft to people as well as what had been sent down in Babylon to the two angels: Harut and Marut. These two angels wouldn't teach anyone unless they had told** them: "We are only a test, so don't lose faith." **However, people continued to learn magic spells from them by which they would split a husband and his wife apart, though they were unable to harm anyone by witchcraft without Allah's permission. They would learn what could harm them but not help them. They certainly knew that whoever bought this magic wouldn't have any share in the Hereafter. How terrible is that for which they've sold their own souls! If they only knew!** 2.103**If only they had believed and were mindful** of Allah **then even a little reward from their Lord would have been far better. If they only knew!**

2.104**Believers! Don't say: "Raa'inaa (Pay attention to us),"** when speaking to My Beloved Prophet Muhammad, **but say: "Unzurnaa (Honour us with your vision),"** and always listen carefully. **The disbelievers will suffer a painful punishment.** 2.105**Neither the disbelievers from among the People of the Book nor the polytheists** want anything good coming down to you from your Lord, but it is Allah Who specifies anyone He chooses for His special mercy. Allah gives tremendous grace.

[2.106]If We remove a verse or make it forgotten, We replace it with something better than it or at least something similar to it. Don't you know that Allah is Most Capable of anything? [2.107]Don't you know that control of the heavens and the earth belongs to Him? You people don't have any protector or helper besides Him.

[2.108]Do you Muslims want to ask from your Messenger Muhammad questions like Musa was asked before? Anyone who swaps belief for disbelief has certainly strayed away from the Straight Way.

[2.109]Many among the People of the Book would love to turn you back into disbelievers after you having believed, because of the jealousy they have inside them even after the truth has become clear to them. You should continue to forgive and ignore until Allah brings His decision. Allah is Most Capable of anything.

[2.110]You must establish the ritual prayers and pay zakah. Whatever good you do for yourselves, you will find it with Allah. Allah is Ever-Watchful of everything you do.

[2.111]The Jews and Christians each claim: "No one can enter Paradise unless he is a Jew,' or, '... a Christian." These are their false hopes. O Prophet Muhammad, say: "Bring me your proof, if you are telling the truth." [2.112]The truth is, anyone who surrenders himself to Allah as Muslim and does good, his reward will come from his Lord. They won't have anything to fear and will never be sad. [2.113]The Jews claim: "The Christians aren't on the Right Path," and the Christians claim: "The Jews aren't on the Right Path," yet they all think they follow the

Book and laws from Allah. In the same way, those who don't have any heavenly knowledge say the same as they do. However, Allah will judge between them on Judgement Day about the disagreements they used to have.

2.114"Who could be more unjust than someone who stops Allah's name being mentioned in His places of worship and tries to ruin them! They should only enter them in fear. They will suffer disgrace in this world and a terrible punishment in the Hereafter. 2.115East and West belong to Allah. Wherever you turn, Allah's presence will be there. Allah is All-Surrounding, All-Knowing.

2.116"They claim: "Allah has a child." Glory be to Him! Never! Everything in the heavens and the earth is His! Everything is devoted to Him! 2.117He is the Originator of the heavens and the earth. Whenever He decides something to happen, He only says to it: "Be!" and it becomes.

2.118Those who are ignorant ask: "Why doesn't Allah speak to us directly?" or, "Why doesn't a sign come to us directly?" In the same way, those before them said similar things. Their thinking is the same. We've made the signs clear to any people who strongly believe.

2.119O Prophet Muhammad, **We have sent you with the truth – to give good news** of blessings **and warnings** of punishment, **and you won't be held responsible for the people of Hell-Fire.** 2.120The Jews and Christians will never be satisfied with you unless you follow their religion. Say: "Only Allah's guidance is the real guidance." If you had followed their desires after all the knowledge that has come to you then you wouldn't have had any friend or helper to protect you from the decision of **Allah.** 2.121Those We've given the Book are following it as it should be followed. It is they who truly believe in it. Anyone who disbelieves in it, it is they who are the real losers.

2.122Descendants of Ya'qub! Remember My favour which I did to you and made you superior to all the people of your time. 2.123Be mindful of the Day when no one will be able to help anyone else in any way at all; ransom won't be accepted from them, intercession will be useless to them, and they simply won't be helped.

2.124When Ibrahim's Lord tested him with some commands, and he fulfilled them, Allah said: "I am going to make you a leader of people." Ibrahim (Abraham) asked: "And from my descendants too?" Allah replied: "Yes, but My promise doesn't apply to wrongdoers." 2.125When We made the Sacred House of the Ka'bah a centre for people and a place of peace, We said: "Now make the place where Ibrahim stood into a place of ritual prayer." We urged Ibrahim and Isma'il (Ishmael) to keep My House clean and pure for those who walk around it, those who stay there for worship, and those who bow and prostrate.

2.126When Ibrahim prayed: "My Lord, make this a city of peace and give resources to its people – those of them who believe in Allah and the Last Day," Allah replied: "Yes, but anyone who disbelieves, I will let him enjoy himself for a little while but then I will drag him to the punishment of the Fire. What a dreadful final destination!"

2.127When Ibrahim was building up the foundations for the Sacred House of the Ka'bah with Isma'il, they prayed: "Our Lord! Accept this service from us. Only You are the All-Hearing, the All-Knowing. 2.128Our Lord! Keep us both surrendered to You as Muslims and make from our descendants a nation of Muslims that is obedient to You; teach us our ways of worship, and be merciful to us. Only You accept repentance much, the Ever-Merciful. ²·¹²⁹Our Lord! Send them a Messenger from among them who will recite Your verses to them, teach them the Book and wisdom, and clean and purify them. Only You are the Almighty, the All-Wise.

²·¹³⁰Other than someone who makes a fool of himself, who could turn away from Ibrahim's religion? We certainly chose him in this world, and he will definitely be among righteous people in the Hereafter. ²·¹³¹When his Lord ordered him: "Surrender as Muslim," he replied: "I surrender as Muslim to Allah – the Lord of all the worlds." ²·¹³²Ibrahim also told his children to do the same, and so did Ya'qub (Jacob), by saying: "My dear children, Allah has chosen this religion for you, so be true Muslims – surrendering to Him, when you die."

²·¹³³Were you people there when death came to Ya'qub? He asked his children: "What will you worship after I have gone?" They replied: "We will continue to worship your God and the God of your forefathers – Ibrahim, Isma'il, and Is'haq (Isaac) – the one and only God, and we will remain surrendered to Him as Muslims." ²·¹³⁴That was a nation that has been and gone. They will be rewarded or punished for what they did and you for what you did. You won't be held responsible for what they used to do.

²·¹³⁵The People of the Book each say: "Become Jews or Christians and you will follow guidance." O Prophet Muhammad, reply: "Actually, we follow the religion of Ibrahim the True, and he wasn't a polytheist." ²·¹³⁶Muslims, declare: "We believe in Allah, in what has been sent down to us, and what was revealed to Ibrahim, Isma'il, Is'haq, Ya'qub, and the Tribes, what Musa and Isa were given, and what all the prophets were given by their Lord. We make no distinction between any one of them, and we will remain surrendered to Allah as Muslims." ²·¹³⁷So, if they believe in it like you have then

they will certainly be following guidance, and if they turn away then it will be clear that **only they will be in hostility.** O Prophet Muhammad, **Allah will be enough to defend you against them. He is the All-Hearing, the All-Knowing.**

2.138We are blessed in **Allah's colour** of guidance, **and whose colour of guidance could be better than Allah's? We will continue to worship only Him.** 2.139O Prophet Muhammad, ask: "Are you disputing with us about Allah when He is our Lord and yours too? We are responsible for our actions and you for yours, and We will remain sincerely devoted to Him. 2.140Are you making claims that Ibrahim, Isma'il, Is'haq, Ya'qub, and the Tribes were Jews or Christians?" Ask: "Who knows better: you or Allah?" Who could be more unjust than someone who hides the evidence he has from Allah! Allah isn't unaware of anything you do. 2.141That was a nation that has been and gone. They will be rewarded or punished for what they did and you for what you did. You won't be held responsible for what they used to do.

[PART 2]

2.142**Foolish people will soon ask:** "What made these Muslims **turn away from their prayer-direction** (*qiblah*) **they used to face?"** O Prophet Muhammad, say: "East and West belong to Allah. He guides anyone He chooses to a path that is straight." 2.143So, in this way We've made you Muslims a moderate nation so you could be witnesses over all people and the Messenger a witness over you. The prayer-direction which you used to face before, We only made it a prayer-direction to expose those who would follow the Messenger from those who would lose faith. Of course, it was certainly difficult, but not for the people Allah had guided. Allah would never let your faith go to waste. He is Kind, Ever-Merciful to people.

²·¹⁴⁴O Prophet Muhammad, **We have been watching your** noble **face turning to the heavens again and again, and so We will certainly turn you to a prayer-direction you will be well-pleased with. Now turn your** noble **face to the direction of the Sacred Masjid in Makkah, and, O Muslims, wherever you are, you too must turn your faces to its direction. The People of the Book know very well that this is the truth from their Lord. Allah isn't unaware of anything they do.**

²·¹⁴⁵**If you brought every single proof to the People of the Book, they still wouldn't face your prayer-direction. You won't face their prayer-direction; they won't even follow each other's prayer-direction. If you had followed their desires after all the knowledge that has come to you then you would've been among the wrongdoers.**

²·¹⁴⁶**The People of the Book recognise the Messenger Muhammad as they recognise their own children, but some of them are deliberately hiding the truth.** ²·¹⁴⁷O Prophet Muhammad, **the truth comes from your Lord, so you'll never be one of those who doubt.**

²·¹⁴⁸**Each** community **has a direction to which it faces, but you** Muslims **must compete with each other in doing good. Allah will unite all of you together wherever you are. Allah is Most Capable of anything.**

²·¹⁴⁹**Wherever you go, you must turn your face to the direction of the Sacred Masjid during ritual prayers, because it certainly is the truth from your Lord. Allah isn't unaware of anything you do.** ²·¹⁵⁰**Wherever you go,** O Prophet Muhammad, **you must turn your** noble **face to the direction of the Sacred Masjid during ritual prayers, and wherever you are,** O Muslims, **you must all turn your faces to its direction during ritual prayers so that there won't be any objection** of disunity **for people against you, apart from the wrongdoers among them. Don't be afraid of them but fear** only **Me, so I will complete My**

favours to you and that you might continue to follow guidance, ²·¹⁵¹just like Our favour that **We've sent you a Messenger from among you who recites Our verses to you, cleans and purifies you, teaches you the Book and wisdom, and teaches you what you never knew.**

²·¹⁵²**So remember Me, and I will have you remembered** and honour you; continue to thank Me, and never be unthankful to Me. ²·¹⁵³Believers! You should find help in patience and ritual prayers. Allah is with those who have patience. ²·¹⁵⁴About those killed in Allah's cause, never say: "They are dead." In fact, they are alive, though you aren't aware. ²·¹⁵⁵We will certainly test you all with: a bit of fear, hunger; some loss of wealth, lives, or fruits of hard work. Give good news to those who have patience, ²·¹⁵⁶who, when they suffer a disaster, they say: "We belong to Allah and will go back to Him." ²·¹⁵⁷It is they who enjoy upon them blessings from their Lord as well as mercy, and it is really they who follow guidance.

²·¹⁵⁸Mounts Safa and Marwah are among Allah's sacred symbols. It won't be wrong if anyone walks back and forth between them when he performs Hajj or Umrah. Anyone who volunteers to do good should know that **Allah is Appreciative, All-Knowing.**

²·¹⁵⁹Those who hide the clear proofs and guidance We've sent down, after We have made them clear in the Book for people, it is those people Allah curses and so do those who are qualified to curse. ²·¹⁶⁰As for those who repent, correct themselves, and make clear the truth they have been hiding, it is those I will forgive. I am the one Who accepts repentance much, the Ever-Merciful. ²·¹⁶¹Those who disbelieve and die as disbelievers, it is they who will suffer the curse of Allah, of the angels, and of all the people. ²·¹⁶²They will remain under the curse forever. Their punishment won't be reduced, and they won't be given any chances.

2.163Your God is One God. There is no god except Him – the Most Compassionate, the Ever-Merciful. 2.164In the creation of the heavens and earth; in the rotation of the night and day; in the ships that sail the ocean for the benefit of people; in the water that Allah sends down from the sky with which He gives life to the earth after it had become dead and scatters through it all kinds of animals; in the changing of the winds; and in the clouds that are made to drift between the sky and the earth – there are certainly signs for any people who think.

2.165Some people make others equal to Allah – they love them as they should be loving Allah, but it is the Believers who love Allah the most. If only the wrongdoers could realise now when they will see the punishment later that all power belongs to Allah and that He is severe in punishing.

2.166When those leaders who were being followed will want nothing to do with their followers, when they see the punishment, when all their links will be cut off, 2.167and when the followers will cry: "If only we had a chance to go back to the world, we would also avoid them just like they are avoiding us Today," that is how Allah will show them their actions as their guilty feelings. They will never come out of the Fire.

2.168People! Eat from anything that is lawful, wholesome on earth, and never follow Shaytan's footsteps; he is your open enemy. 2.169He only tells you to do bad and shameful things, and wants you to say things about Allah what you don't even know.

2.170When the disbelievers are told: "Follow what Allah has revealed," they reply: "Never! We will only follow the way on which we found our forefathers." What? Even if their forefathers hadn't understood anything and weren't following guidance? ^{2.171}The example of preaching to these disbelievers is like someone shouting at things that cannot hear anything, and so it is nothing other than calling or yelling. They are choosing to be deaf, dumb, blind! – and that is why they won't understand.

^{2.172}Believers! Eat from the wholesome things We give you, and thank Allah if you worship Him only. ^{2.173}He has made unlawful for you only: dead meat, blood, pork, and an animal that has been slaughtered in the name of anything other than Allah's. However, if someone is forced by need – not being disobedient nor breaking the law – there won't be any sin on him. Allah is Most Forgiving, Ever-Merciful.

^{2.174}Those who hide any part of the Book that Allah has revealed, and sell it for a low price, they are only filling their bellies with the Fire. Allah won't speak to them on Judgement Day nor purify them with forgiveness, and they will suffer a painful punishment. ^{2.175}They're the ones buying misguidance at the cost of guidance and punishment at the cost of forgiveness. Oh what confidence they have for the Fire! ^{2.176}This will be their punishment because Allah has revealed the Book with the truth, yet those who disagree with it are in extreme hostility.

^{2.177}Piety doesn't mean merely to turn your faces to the East or West in ritual prayer. In fact, piety is for someone to believe in Allah, the Last Day, the angels, the Book, and the prophets; for someone to donate wealth for the love of Allah to close relatives, orphans, the needy, travellers, beggars, and for freeing slaves; for someone to establish ritual prayers; pay zakah; fulfilling the promises they make; and having patience when in poverty, weakness, and in times of

struggle. It is they who are honest, and it is really they who are mindful of Allah.

²·¹⁷⁸Believers! The Law of Retaliation is prescribed for you with regards to those killed unlawfully: a free man for a free man; a slave for a slave; and a female for a female. However, if the killer is forgiven by the victim's heir, then it must be applied accordingly, and compensation paid to the heirs in a good way. This is a concession from your Lord as well as a mercy. Anyone who breaks the law after this will suffer a painful punishment. ²·¹⁷⁹There is life for you in the Law of Retaliation, O people of understanding, so you can save yourselves from destruction.

²·¹⁸⁰When death comes to any of you, and he leaves behind any wealth, it is prescribed for you to make a will for parents and close relatives, with fairness. This is a duty for those who are mindful of Allah. ²·¹⁸¹If anyone changes the will after he has listened to it, its sin will be on those who change it. Allah is All-Hearing, All-Knowing. ²·¹⁸²However, if someone fears unfairness or wrongdoing from the testator, and he puts things right between them, there won't be any sin on him. Allah is Most Forgiving, Ever-Merciful.

²·¹⁸³Believers! Fasting is prescribed for you just like it was prescribed for those before you, so that you become mindful of Allah. ²·¹⁸⁴Fasting is for a fixed number of days. If any of you is ill or travelling, the actual number of missed fasts must be made up from later days. Those who cannot fast must pay compensation by giving food to a needy person. It will be better for someone to volunteer in giving more, though it is best for you to fast, if you only knew.

²·¹⁸⁵It was the month of Ramadan when the Qur'an was revealed – as a guidance for people, together with clear proofs for guidance and a

criterion between right and wrong. **So, anyone from among you** who is **present in this month must fast in it, but if someone is ill or travelling, the actual number** of missed fasts must be made up **from later days.** Allah wants ease for you and not difficulty so that you can complete the actual number, and glorify Him because He guided you, and so that you might become thankful.

²·¹⁸⁶O Prophet Muhammad, **when My servants ask you about Me,** tell them that **I am near:** whenever anyone prays to Me, I answer his prayer. So, they should respond to Me and have faith in Me so that they can follow true guidance.

²·¹⁸⁷It is permissible for you to have sexual relations with your wives on the night of fasting. They are a protective covering for you as you are for them. Allah knows that you used to keep secrets from yourselves but still He forgave you and excused you. So, now you may have sexual relations with your wives and try to gain what Allah has written for you. You may eat and drink until the white thread of dawn becomes clear to you from the black thread, and then complete fasting until nightfall. However, you mustn't have sexual relations with your wives when you are in spiritual retreat in masjids. These are the limits set by Allah, so don't even go near them. This is how Allah makes His verses clear to people so they can become mindful of Him.

²·¹⁸⁸You mustn't take over each other's wealth wrongfully, nor give it as a bribe **to the authorities in order to deliberately and unlawfully take over a share of** other **people's wealth.**

²·¹⁸⁹O Prophet Muhammad, **they ask you about the new moons. Reply: "They mark the time for people and the Hajj** season **too. Piety doesn't mean that you should enter homes from their rear, because piety is**

when someone is mindful of Allah. Therefore, you may enter houses through their main doors. You must continue to be mindful of Allah so that you might succeed.

2.190Fight in Allah's cause against those who attack you, but don't overstep the limits. Allah doesn't like those who overstep the limits. 2.191During battle, kill them wherever you find them, and expel them legally from where they expelled you illegally. Oppression is far worse than killing. Don't fight them at the Sacred Masjid unless they attack you there, in which case, if they attack you first, then kill them in defence. This is the punishment for the disbelievers. 2.192However, if they stop then they will find Allah is Most Forgiving, Ever-Merciful. 2.193You must continue to fight them until there's no more oppression, and obedience remains only for Allah's sake. If they stop then there mustn't be any hostility except against wrongdoers. 2.194You may retaliate in one sacred month for the offence in another sacred month, and there can be retaliation for all violations. So, if someone attacks you then you may fight him back equal to how he attacked you, but you must continue to be mindful of Allah and know that He is with those who are mindful of Him. 2.195You should donate in Allah's cause but never contribute to destruction with your own hands. You must do good. Allah loves those who do good.

2.196You must complete Hajj and Umrah for Allah to be pleased with you. If you are stopped, then send any sacrificial animal you can afford, but don't shave your heads until the sacrificial animal reaches its place of sacrifice. If any of you is ill or has an infection on his head that makes earlier shaving necessary then he must pay a compensation by either fasting, giving charity, or giving sacrifice. When you are in peaceful conditions, if anyone wants to take advantage of the Umrah with Hajj, he must sacrifice whatever sacrificial animal he can afford. Anyone who cannot afford a sacrificial animal **must fast for three days during Hajj and seven** more **when you go back** home; **that is a complete ten.** This option is only for someone whose family is not living around the Sacred Masjid. You must continue to be mindful of Allah and know that He is severe in punishing.

2.197Hajj takes place in certain months that are well known. If anyone wants to perform Hajj in these months, there mustn't be any sexual intercourse, sin, or quarrelling during Hajj. Allah knows all the good things you do. You should prepare for the journey, and the best preparation is to be mindful of Allah. So, you must continue to be mindful of Me, O people of understanding. 2.198There's nothing wrong if you **people try to gain grace from your Lord** during Hajj. **When you set off from Arafat, continue to remember Allah at the Sacred Monument** in Muzdalifah. **You must continue to remember Him as He has guided you, because you were, before this, among those who were unaware.** 2.199Then **you too, O Quraysh, must set off from where the people set off, and beg Allah to forgive you. Allah is Most Forgiving, Ever-Merciful.**

2.200So, once you've completed your rituals, you must continue to remember Allah like you remember your ancestors, or more intensely. Some people pray: "Our Lord! Give us all our share in this world," but they won't have any share in the Hereafter. 2.201Some others pray: "Our Lord! Give us good things in this world and also in the Hereafter, and protect us from the suffering of the Fire." 2.202These are the people who will have a full share of what they worked for. Allah is quick in settling accounts.

2.203You should keep remembering Allah during these **few days. There won't be any sin on someone who leaves earlier – after two days** from Mina, **nor on someone who stays on for another day – as long as he is** mindful of Allah. You must continue to be mindful of Allah and know that it is in front of Him you will all be assembled.

2.204Someone's speech about worldly affairs might fascinate you, and he might also make Allah a witness to everything inside his heart, yet he is a most quarrelsome enemy of the truth. 2.205When he goes away (or is made leader), he tries his best to make trouble in the world, and to destroy crops and life. Allah doesn't like trouble. 2.206When he is told: "Be mindful of Allah," arrogance encourages him do more bad things. So, Hell will be enough for him. What a dreadful place! 2.207Opposite to him, someone else might devote his life to gain Allah's good pleasure. Allah is Kind to His servants.

2.208Believers! You must come into Islam completely and never follow Shaytan's footsteps; he is your open enemy. 2.209If you make mistakes after the clear signs have come to you, just bear in mind that Allah is Almighty, All-Wise.

2.210Are they waiting for Allah to come to them with the punishment in coverings of clouds, together with the angels, and for the matter to be settled? It is to Allah that all matters will be returned.

2.211Ask the Descendants of Ya'qub how many clear signs We gave them. Anyone who changes Allah's favour after it has come to him should know that Allah is severe in punishing.

2.212This life has been made to seem attractive to the disbelievers so they make fun of the Believers. However, those who are mindful of Allah will be higher than them on Judgement Day. Allah gives without limits to anyone He chooses.

$^{2.213}$**All people used to be a single community** before their disagreements, **so Allah sent prophets who gave good news and warnings. He sent with them the Book with the truth to judge between the people where they disagreed. However, only the People of the Book disagreed in it and that too after the clear signs had come to them, only because they were jealous of each other. Then Allah, by His command, guided the Believers to the truth where those** people had disagreed. Allah guides anyone He chooses to a path that is straight.

$^{2.214}$**Do you people think you will enter Paradise** without facing any tests whilst you have not experienced anything like what those have who have been and gone before you? Struggle and physical suffering hit them, and they were badly shaken, until even the messenger of that time **and those who believed with him cried out: "When will Allah's help come?!" Surely, Allah's help is near.**

$^{2.215}$**O Prophet Muhammad, they ask you what they should spend. Reply: "Anything good you spend should be for: parents, close relatives, orphans, the needy, and travellers. Anything good you do, Allah knows it perfectly well."**

$^{2.216}$**Fighting** for peace **is prescribed for you** people **but disliked by you. You might not like something when it is good for you and like something when it is bad for you. Allah knows** the good and bad but you don't.

$^{2.217}$**O Prophet Muhammad, they ask you about fighting in the Sacred Month. Reply: "It is a big crime to fight in it, but it is a bigger crime in the sight of Allah: to block people from Allah's cause and disbelieve in Him, to block them from the Sacred Masjid, and to expel its people from there. Oppression is a much bigger crime than killing." They won't stop fighting you until they turn you away from your religion if they can. If any of you turns away from his religion and dies as a disbeliever, it is they whose actions will be wasted in this world and the next. It is they who will be the people of the Fire, where they will remain forever.

2.218 **Those** who believe and those who migrate and strive hard in Allah's cause, it is they who can hope for Allah's special mercy. Allah is Most Forgiving, Ever-Merciful.

2.219 O Prophet Muhammad, they ask you about intoxicants and gambling. Reply: "There is a great sin in them both, though some benefits as well for people, but their sin is greater than their benefit." They ask you what they should donate to charity. Reply: "Whatever you can spare." In this way Allah makes all commands clear to you so that you might think deeply 2.220 about this world and the next. O Prophet Muhammad, they ask you about orphans. Reply: "Working for their welfare is best, but if you let them mix in with you, it will be better because they are, after all, your siblings-in-faith. Allah knows the troublemaker from the peacemaker. If He had wanted, He could have put you in difficulties. Allah is Almighty, All-Wise."

2.221 **Don't** marry idolatresses until they become Believers; a Believing slave-woman is far better than an idolatress even if the idolatress seems attractive to you. Don't marry off your women to idolaters unless they become Believers; a Believing slave is better than an idolater even if the idolater seems attractive to you. It is they who call to the Fire, when Allah, by His command, calls to Paradise and forgiveness. He makes His commands clear to people so that they might remind themselves.

²·²²²O Prophet Muhammad, **they ask you about menstruation. Reply: "It is harmful, so stay away from women during menstruation and don't go near them** for sexual relations **until they become clean and pure. After they have become clean and pure, you may go to them in any manner Allah has allowed you. Allah loves those who repent a lot and those who keep themselves clean and pure."** ²·²²³**Your wives are your pastures, so go to your pastures however you want. Prepare something good for yourselves. You must continue to be mindful of Allah and know that you are going to meet Him.** O Prophet Muhammad, **give** this **good news to the Believers.**

²·²²⁴**Don't let Allah's name in your oaths become an excuse for not doing good, not being mindful of Allah, or not making peace between people. Allah is All-Hearing, All-Knowing.** ²·²²⁵**Allah won't punish you for being careless in your oaths but He will punish you for the cheating your hearts intend. However, Allah is Most Forgiving, Most Tolerant.**

²·²²⁶**For those who take an oath to stay away from** sexual relations with **their wives, the** maximum **period to rethink is four months. If they go back** on their oath, they should know that **Allah is Most Forgiving, Ever-Merciful.** ²·²²⁷**However, if they've made a strong intention to divorce then** they must know that **Allah is All-Hearing, All-Knowing.**

²·²²⁸**Divorced women must themselves wait for three menstrual periods** before they can marry again. **It's unlawful for them to hide what Allah has created in their wombs, if they truly believe in Allah and the Last Day. Their husbands, if they want to put things straight, have the greater right to take them back during that time. Women also have rights similar to those against them, according to what is fair, although men have a degree of responsibility over them. Allah is Almighty, All-Wise.**

²·²²⁹Revocable divorce is only allowed twice. Then he must either keep her with respect or let her go with kindness. It isn't lawful for you men to take back anything you've given them as dowry unless both fear they won't be able to respect the limits set by Allah. If you judges fear they won't be able to obey the limits set by Allah, then there won't be any sin on either of them if she gives something as ransom to free herself with. These are the limits set by Allah, so don't overstep them. Whoever oversteps the limits set by Allah, it is really they who will be the wrongdoers. ²·²³⁰If he divorces her a third time, she won't be lawful for him after that until she has consummated marriage with another husband. Then if the second husband also divorces her, it won't be wrong for her or her first husband if they go back married to each other – if they think they will be able to obey the limits set by Allah. These are the limits set by Allah which He makes clear to any people who have knowledge.

²·²³¹When you divorce women and they reach the end of their waiting period, you must either keep them with respect or let them go with honour. Don't keep them back in hardship – to overstep the limits. Anyone who does that will be doing wrong only to himself. Don't make fun of Allah's commands but remember His favours to you, as well as the Book and wisdom He has sent down to you through which He advises you. You must continue to be mindful of Allah and bear in mind that He knows everything perfectly well.

²·²³²When you divorce women and they reach the end of their waiting period, don't stop them from marrying their former husbands if they come to a fair agreement with them. This is commanded to those of you who believe in Allah and the Last Day. This is more virtuous for you, cleaner and purer. Allah knows what is best but you don't.

²·²³³Those mothers who want to complete the period of breastfeeding should breastfeed their babies for two whole years. It is the father's duty to bring suitable food and clothing for the mothers. No one should be forced to do more than what they can. No parent should be made to suffer because of their child. The heirs have similar duties. It won't be wrong for either of them if, after discussing and agreeing, they decide on weaning the child. There's nothing wrong if you fathers choose to have your babies breastfed by another woman, as long as you pay with fairness what you are supposed to give. You must continue to be mindful of Allah and know that He is Ever-Watchful of everything you do.

²·²³⁴Those of you who die and leave behind widows, those widows should themselves wait for four months and ten days before they can marry again. Once they reach the end of their waiting period, you won't be held responsible for what they suitably decide about themselves. Allah is Fully-Aware of everything you do.

²·²³⁵It won't be wrong either way if, to widows or divorced women in their waiting periods, you make a hint of a marriage proposal or if you keep it in your minds. Allah knows that you will soon mention them with the intention of marrying them, but don't make them any secret promises unless you speak honest words according to the law. Don't make a strong intention of marriage to them until the prescribed waiting period reaches its end. You must remember that Allah knows what is in your hearts. You must continue to be afraid of Him, but bear in mind that He is Most Forgiving, Most Tolerant.

²·²³⁶It won't be wrong if you divorce your wives before you've consummated marriage with them or fixed a dowry for them. However, you must give them a gift, a suitable one – to be paid by the rich and the poor according to what they can afford. It is a duty on

those who do good. [2.237]If you divorce them before you've consummated marriage with them but after you have fixed a dowry for them, then you must pay them a half of what you have fixed, unless they agree not to take it or the husband who holds the marriage contract pays it in full – though it is closer to being mindful of Allah if you pay in full. You mustn't forget to be generous to each other. Allah is Ever-Watchful of everything you do.

[2.238]Look after the ritual prayers, especially the middle prayer, and stand devotedly praying in front of Allah. [2.239]If you sense danger then pray on foot or while riding, but if you feel safe, then continue to remember Allah in the way He has taught you that you never knew.

[2.240]Those of you who die and leave widows behind should make wills for them – giving them expenses for a year without forcing them out of their husbands' homes. If they themselves leave the residence, you won't be held responsible for what they suitably decide about themselves. Allah is Almighty, All-Wise.

[2.241]There is also a fair allowance for divorced women. It's a duty on those men who are mindful of Allah. [2.242]In this way Allah makes His commands clear to you so that you might think.

[2.243]O Prophet Muhammad, don't you see those people who left their homes in their thousands for fear of death? Allah said to them: "Die!" then He brought them back to life. Allah certainly gives grace to people yet most of them don't even give thanks. [2.244]You people should continue to fight in Allah's cause and know that He is All-Hearing, All-Knowing.

2.245Who is it that will give Allah a generous loan which Allah will multiply many times for him? It is Allah Who decreases and increases wealth and it is Him you will all be taken back to.

2.246O Prophet Muhammad, don't you see those leaders among the Descendants of Ya'qub after the time of Musa? When they said to a prophet sent to them: "Give us a king and we will fight in Allah's cause," he asked: "What if you don't fight if it is prescribed for you?" They replied: "Why wouldn't we fight in Allah's cause when we've been driven away from our homes and our children?" Then, when fighting was prescribed for them, they turned away, apart from a few of them. Allah knows the wrongdoers perfectly well.

2.247Their prophet told them: "Allah has made Talut (Saul) your king." They protested: "How can he have authority over us when we are more worthy of kingship than he is? He isn't even blessed with much wealth!" He replied: "Allah has chosen him over you, and given him lots of knowledge and physical strength." Allah gives His authority to anyone He chooses. Allah is All-Surrounding, All-Knowing. 2.248He also told them: "A sign of his authority is that the Ark of the Covenant, carried by angels, will come to you – inside it is tranquillity from your Lord, as well as some relics that the families of Musa and Haroon (Aaron) have left behind. There is certainly a sign in this for you if you are true Believers."

2.249So, when Talut marched out with the troops, he warned: "Allah will test you with a river: whoever drinks from it isn't with me, and whoever doesn't drink from it – taking no more than one scoop with his hand – will be with me." So, apart from a small number of them, they all drank from it. Then, when he and those who believed with him had crossed the river, they complained: "We don't have any strength to fight Jalut (Goliath) and his troops today." Those who were sure they will meet Allah, declared: "By Allah's command, how often a small army has defeated a large army! Allah is with those who have patience."

2.250 When they went to face Jalut and his troops, they prayed: "Our Lord! Fill us with patience, keep our footing strong, and help us against these disbelieving people." 2.251 So, by Allah's command, they defeated them, and Dawud (David) killed Jalut. Allah gave Dawud kingship and wisdom, and taught him whatever He wanted to teach him. If Allah didn't remove some bad people by others who are good, this world would have been totally ruined, but Allah gives grace to everyone. 2.252 O Prophet Muhammad, these are Allah's verses. We recite them to you with the truth. You certainly are one of the messengers.

[PART 3]

2.253 These are the messengers; We made some of them superior to others. Allah spoke directly to some and He raised others in ranks. We gave many clear signs to Isa ibn Maryam and supported him with the Holy Spirit (- Angel Jibra'il). If Allah had wanted, those people who lived after these messengers wouldn't have fought among themselves after the clear signs had come to them, but they had disagreements – some of them believed while others disbelieved. If Allah had decided, they wouldn't have fought among themselves, but Allah does whatever He wants.

2.254 Believers! Donate from what We've given you before comes a Day when there will be no trading, friendship for the disbelievers, or intercession for them. The disbelievers are really the wrongdoers.

2.255 He is Allah. There is no god except Him – the Ever-Living, the Everlasting. Neither drowsiness nor sleep can affect Him. Everything in the heavens and the earth is His. Who can dare intercede with Him without His permission? He knows everything that happened before them and what will happen after them. They cannot understand anything from His knowledge other than what He chooses. His Seat of knowledge and power surrounds the heavens and the earth, and preserving them cannot make Him tired. He is the Most High, the Most Great.

2.256"There's no forcing in religion; true guidance is already clear from misguidance. So, whoever rejects fake gods and believes in Allah has actually grabbed on to the most trusty, lasting handhold. Allah is All-Hearing, All-Knowing.

2.257Allah is the Protector of Believers. He brings them out of the depths of the darkness of disbelief and into the light of belief. As for the disbelievers, their protectors are the evil ones who push them out of the light and into the depths of darkness. It is they who will be the people of the Fire, where they will remain forever.

2.258O Prophet Muhammad, haven't you seen the one Allah had given kingship to and who argued with Ibrahim about his Lord? When Ibrahim said: "My Lord is the one Who gives life and death," he replied: "I too give life and death." Ibrahim said: "It is Allah Who brings up the sun from the East. Now, why don't you bring it up from the West!" The disbeliever was baffled. Allah doesn't let unjust people succeed.

2.259What about the man who passed by a village that was in ruins? He thought: "How will Allah ever bring it back to life after its death?" So, Allah gave him death for a hundred years and then brought him back to life. Allah asked: "How long have you been here?" He replied: "I must have been here for a day or a part of a day." Allah said:

"Actually, you have been here for a hundred years. Just take a look at your food and drink; they haven't gone off – now take a look at your donkey: this is to make you a sign for all people. Just look at the donkey's bones; how We bring them together and cover them with flesh." When the reality became clear to him, he exclaimed: "I know for sure that Allah is Most Capable of anything."

2.260Remember when Ibrahim said: "My Lord! Show me how You bring the dead back to life," Allah asked: "Don't you believe?" He replied: "Of course I do! But I'm asking only to satisfy my heart." Allah said: "Get yourself four birds; tame them to yourself; then after slaughtering them, scatter them in pieces on each hill; then call out to them – they will come hurrying back to you! You should know that Allah is Almighty, All-Wise."

2.261The example of those who donate their wealth in Allah's cause is that of a grain which grows seven ears with a hundred grains in each one. Allah multiplies even more for anyone He chooses. Allah is All-Surrounding, All-Knowing.

2.262Those who donate their wealth in Allah's cause, and then don't chase up what they've donated neither with reminders of favour nor with abuse, their reward will come from their Lord. They won't have anything to fear and will never be sad. 2.263A kind word and forgiveness are far better than charity that is followed by abuse. Allah is Free of all Needs, Most Tolerant. 2.264Believers! Don't ruin your charities neither with reminders of favour nor with abuse, like someone who spends his wealth to show off to people and doesn't really believe in Allah or the Last Day. His example is that of a smooth hard rock with dust on it: then heavy rain hits it and leaves it bare. These showoffs won't be able to do anything with what they achieved. Allah doesn't let disbelieving people succeed.

²·²⁶⁵The example of those who donate their wealth trying to gain Allah's good pleasure and to make their souls strong is that of a garden on high ground: heavy rain falls on it and doubles its produce, but if heavy rain doesn't fall on it then even dew is enough. Allah is Ever-Watchful of everything you do.

²·²⁶⁶Would any of you like to have a garden of date-palms and grapevines – that has rivers flowing beneath it? He would have all kinds of fruit in it. Then, what if he reached old age while he had helpless children, and a fiery whirlwind would hit the garden and it would go up in flames! This is how Allah makes the signs clear to you so that you might think deeply.

²·²⁶⁷Believers! Donate from the good things you've achieved and of what We've brought out for you from the earth. You mustn't plan to donate anything useless from it which you yourselves wouldn't accept unless you had your eyes closed to it. You must remember that Allah is Free of all Needs, Most Praiseworthy.

²·²⁶⁸Shaytan threatens you with poverty and tells you to do shameful things, but Allah promises you His forgiveness and grace. Allah is All-Surrounding, All-Knowing. ²·²⁶⁹He gives wisdom to anyone He chooses. Whoever is given wisdom has certainly been given a lot of goodness, but only the people of understanding will learn lessons.

²·²⁷⁰Anything you donate in charity or promise to give, Allah knows about it. The wrongdoers won't have any helpers. ²·²⁷¹It is wonderful to show your acts of charity, but better for you if you hide them when you give them to the poor. Allah will remove some of your sins from you. He is Fully-Aware of everything you do.

²·²⁷²O Prophet Muhammad, **you aren't responsible for them to accept guidance but it is Allah Who guides anyone He chooses. Anything good you** people **donate will benefit you,** especially **when you're donating only to gain Allah's good pleasure. Anything good you donate will be repaid to you in full and you won't be treated unfairly.**

²·²⁷³Charity is given **to the poor, who are restricted** due to being busy in Allah's cause – they're unable to move about in the land for livelihood. It's because of the modesty they show that someone who doesn't know might think they don't need anything. You can recognise them by their appearances. They don't carry on begging from people. Anything good you donate, Allah knows it perfectly well. ²·²⁷⁴**Those who spend their wealth** in Allah's cause **night and day, secretly and openly, their reward will come from their Lord. They won't have anything to fear and will never be sad.**

²·²⁷⁵**Those who take usury will be standing** on Judgement Day **like** someone Shaytan has made crazy with his touch. That is because they claimed: "Trading is just like usury," but Allah has made trading lawful and usury unlawful. So, whoever stops taking usury **after receiving a command from his Lord, gets** to keep what he took in **the past – his case will be for Allah** to decide. **However, those who go back to usury, it is they who will be the people of the Fire, where they will remain forever.** ²·²⁷⁶**Allah destroys** the benefits of **usury but increases** the value of **charitable acts. He doesn't like anyone who is very unthankful, disobedient.**

²·²⁷⁷**Those who believe, do good, establish the ritual prayers, and pay zakah, their reward will come from their Lord. They won't have anything to fear and will never be sad.**

2.278Believers! You must continue to be mindful of Allah and give up whatever usury still remains, if you are true Believers. 2.279If you don't do that, then be warned of a war from Allah and His Messenger. If you repent then you will still get to keep the capital of your wealth, so you will neither do wrong nor will you be treated unfairly.

2.280If the debtor is in difficulty then you should give him some time until it's easy for him to pay, but if you give up the debt out of charity, it would be better for you, if you only knew. 2.281Be mindful of the Day when you will all be returned to Allah. Then, everyone will be paid in full what they had done and they won't be treated unfairly.

2.282Believers! When you give each other a loan for a fixed period, you should write it down. Someone should write it down between you accurately. He shouldn't refuse to write, as Allah has taught him. He should write, and the debtor should dictate it to him, and he must remain mindful of Allah – his Lord, and not reduce anything from it. If the debtor is mentally ill, or weak, or unable to dictate it himself, then his guardian should dictate it accurately. Make two witnesses from your men, and if there aren't two men, then a man and two women, from those you approve to be witnesses – so that if one of the female witnesses makes a mistake, the other can remind her. The witnesses shouldn't refuse when they're called for evidence. Don't disregard to write it down with its due date, whether it's a small or a large amount: it is more fair in the sight of Allah, more suitable as evidence, and more likely to stop you from having doubts about each other – unless the merchandise is present which you trade between yourselves hand-to-hand then it won't be wrong for you not to write it down. However, you should make witnesses whenever you trade with each other. The one who is writing mustn't be harmed, and nor the witness, because it would be sinful of you if you allow that to happen. You must continue to be mindful of Allah because He gives you knowledge of how to deal with each other. **Allah knows everything perfectly well.**

2.283**If you're travelling and cannot find anyone who will write then you should make a pledge with possession. If you make trusts with each other then the trustee must fulfil his trust and continue to be mindful of Allah – his Lord. You mustn't hide evidence because anyone who does that will be sinful in his heart. Allah knows perfectly well everything you do.**

2.284**Everything in the heavens and the earth belongs to Allah. Whether you show or hide what's in your minds, Allah will hold you accountable for it. He can forgive or punish anyone He chooses. He is Most Capable of anything.**

2.285**The Messenger believes in what has been revealed to him from his Lord, as do the Believers. All of them believe in Allah, His angels, His Books, and His messengers.** They say: "We make no distinction between any of His messengers," and they also declare: "We hear and obey. Our Lord! We beg Your forgiveness, and the final return will be to You."

2.286**Allah doesn't force anyone to do more than what they can. They will have** rewards for **whatever good they did and suffer** for **every bad thing they did.** Believers pray: "Our Lord! Don't punish us if we forget or make mistakes. Our Lord! Don't place on us a burden like that which you placed on the people before us. Our Lord! Don't give us duties we cannot do, but ignore our sins, forgive us, and have mercy on us. You are our Protector, so help us against the disbelieving people."

Surah 3. Family Of Imran (Aal 'Imraan)

Allah's name I begin with, the Most Compassionate, the Ever-Merciful

³·¹*Alif Laam Meem.*

³·²He is **Allah. There is no god except Him** – the Ever-Living, the Everlasting. ³·³O Prophet Muhammad, He revealed this Book to you with the truth, confirming what came before it, and He also revealed the Tawrah (Torah) and the Injeel (Gospel) ³·⁴before, as a guidance for people, and He has now revealed this Criterion to teach between right and wrong. Those who disbelieve in Allah's revelations will suffer a severe punishment. Allah is Almighty, Capable of Retaliation.

³·⁵**Allah is such that nothing is hidden from Him, be it in the earth or sky.** ³·⁶He is the one Who shapes you in the wombs as He chooses. There is no god except Him – the Almighty, the All-Wise.

³·⁷He is the one Who has revealed to you this Book; some of its verses are specific – they're the foundation of the Book, while others are unspecific. Those with corruption in their hearts are following the unspecific parts of the Book, trying to cause trouble and applying their own false meanings to it. Only Allah knows its exact meaning. Those who are firm in knowledge say: "We believe in it. All of it has come from our Lord." However, only the people of understanding will learn lessons. ³·⁸They pray: "Our Lord! Don't let our hearts go astray now after You have guided us, but give us special mercy from You. Only You are the Ever-Giving. ³·⁹Our Lord! You will gather all the people together on a Day in which there is no doubt." Allah never breaks promises.

³·¹⁰All the wealth and the children of the disbelievers won't be able to save them from the punishment of Allah in any way at all. It is really

those disbelievers who will be the fuel for the Fire. ³·¹¹Like what Fir'awn's people did, as well as those before them; they called Our revelations a lie, so Allah punished them for their sins. Allah is severe in punishing. ³·¹²Tell the disbelievers: "Soon, you will be defeated and pushed towards Hell. What a dreadful place!

³·¹³There has already been a sign for you in the two armies that clashed with each other in this Battle of Badr; one army was fighting defensively in Allah's cause but the other disbelieved. The first army saw with their own eyes the other army as twice their number. Allah gives strength with His help to anyone He chooses. There is a definite lesson of warning in this for those who can see.

³·¹⁴What has been made to seem attractive to men is the love of desired things, such as women and children, piled up treasures of gold and silver, branded horses, livestock, and fertile land. These are the enjoyments of this life, but the best destination is only with Allah.

³·¹⁵O Prophet Muhammad, say: "Shall I tell you about something better than these? Those who are mindful of Allah will have gardens with their Lord – that have rivers flowing beneath them, where they will remain forever, with clean and purified spouses, and Allah's good pleasure." Allah is Ever-Watchful of His servants, ³·¹⁶who pray: "Our Lord! We believe, so forgive us our sins and protect us from the suffering of the Fire." ³·¹⁷They have patience and are honest, devoted, making donations, and begging forgiveness at the time before dawn.

³·¹⁸Allah witnesses, 'there is no god except Him' – and so do the angels, and the people of knowledge. Allah upholds fairness. There is no god except Him – the Almighty, the All-Wise.

³·¹⁹The only way of life acceptable with Allah is Islam. It was only after knowledge had come to the People of the Book that they disagreed with each other because they were jealous of each other. Anyone who disbelieves in Allah's revelations should know that Allah is quick in settling accounts. ³·²⁰So, O Prophet Muhammad, if they argue with you, say: "I have given up my identity to Allah as Muslim, and so have those who follow me." Tell the People of the Book and also those who follow no Book: "Will you surrender to Allah as Muslims?" If they do surrender to Allah as Muslims then they will follow guidance, but if they turn away then your duty is only to deliver the message. Allah is Ever-Watchful of His servants.

³·²¹Those who disbelieve in Allah's revelations, unjustly kill prophets, and kill those who tell people to be fair, you should warn them of a painful punishment. ³·²²They're the ones whose actions will be wasted in this world and the next. They won't have any helpers.

³·²³O Prophet Muhammad, don't you see those who were given a share of the Book? They are invited to Allah's Book so it can judge between them, but then some of them turn away because they are neglectful. ³·²⁴This is because they claim: "We won't suffer the Fire for more than a few days." However, the lies they used to make up have tricked them about their own religion. ³·²⁵So, what will it be like when We gather them all together on a Day in which there is no doubt? Everyone will be paid in full for what they did and they won't be treated unfairly.

³·²⁶O Prophet Muhammad, pray: "O Allah! Lord of Authority! You give authority to anyone You choose and take it away from anyone You choose, and You give honour to anyone You choose and disgrace anyone You choose. All goodness is in Your control. You are Most Capable of anything. ³·²⁷You make the night enter into the day and the

day enter into the night, You bring the living out of the dead and the dead out of the living, and You give without limits to anyone You choose."

3.28Believers mustn't, instead of Believers, take disbelievers as their protectors. Anyone who does that won't be given anything from Allah – unless you want to protect yourselves from them out of precaution. Allah is warning you about Himself. The final return will be to Him.

3.29O Prophet Muhammad, say: "Whether you people hide or show what is in your hearts, Allah knows it. He knows everything in the heavens and in the earth. Allah is Most Capable of anything."

3.30On the Day when every person will find in front of him everything good and bad he has ever done, he will wish for there to be a great distance between him and that Day. Allah is warning you about Himself. He is Kind to His servants.

3.31O Prophet Muhammad, say: "If you people love Allah then you have to follow me, and Allah will love you and forgive you your sins. He is Most Forgiving, Ever-Merciful." 3.32Say: "You have to follow Allah and the Messenger." If they turn away, they should know that Allah doesn't like disbelievers.

3.33For prophethood, Allah chose Adam, Nuh (Noah), the family of Ibrahim, and the family of Imran over all the people. 3.34They're all one race – descendants of each other. Allah is All-Hearing, All-Knowing.

3.35Remember when Imran's wife prayed: "My Lord! Whatever baby is in my womb, I dedicate it to you totally free of any other service.

Accept it from me because only You are the All-Hearing, the All-Knowing." ³·³⁶However, when she gave birth to a female, she said: "My Lord! I've given birth to a baby girl!" Allah knows best what she had given birth to because the boy she wanted could never be like this girl. "I've named her Maryam (Mary) and I ask You to protect her and her children from Shaytan, the Rejected." ³·³⁷Allah accepted Maryam graciously and brought her up in the best way. He placed her in the care of Zakariyya (Zechariah). Each time Zakariyya entered the prayer-room, he saw there was food next to her. One day, He asked: "Maryam, where does this come to you from?" She replied: "It is from Allah. He gives without limits to anyone He chooses."

³·³⁸It was there and then that Zakariyya prayed to his Lord, saying: "My Lord! Give me noble children from Your grace. You listen to all prayers." ³·³⁹While he was still standing inside the prayer-room performing ritual prayer, the angels called out to him: "Allah is giving you the good news of Yahya (John) - who will confirm a Word (-Prophet Isa) from Allah – a leader, chaste, and a prophet from among righteous people." ³·⁴⁰He asked: "My Lord! How can I have a son now that I've reached old age and my wife cannot give birth to children?" Allah replied: "This is how it will be. Allah can do whatever He wants." ³·⁴¹Zakariyya asked: "My Lord, give me a sign!" Allah replied: "Your sign is that you won't be able to speak to people for three days except by gestures. So, remember your Lord a lot and glorify Him evening and morning."

³·⁴²Remember when the angels said: "Maryam, Allah has chosen you and made you clean and pure. He has chosen you over all the women of the world. ³·⁴³Maryam, You must continue to devote yourself to your Lord, and prostrate and bow down in prayer with those who bow down." ³·⁴⁴O Prophet Muhammad, this is from the details of the unseen secrets We reveal to you. You weren't with them when they

were casting lots with their pens to decide which of them should take care of Maryam, nor were you with them when they were arguing with each other.

3.45 Remember when the angels said: "Maryam, Allah is giving you the good news of a Word from Him whose name will be Maseeh Isa ibn Maryam (Jesus the Messiah, Son of Mary), who will be honoured in this world and the next, and will be from among those nearest to Allah. 3.46 He will speak to people as a baby from the cradle and also in maturity, and will be from among the righteous people." 3.47 She asked: "My Lord! How can I have a child when no man has ever touched me?" Allah replied: "This is how it will be." Allah can create whatever He wants. Whenever He decides something to happen, He only says to it: "Be!" and it becomes.

3.48 Allah will teach him the Book and wisdom, the Tawrah, and the Injeel. 3.49 He will be a messenger to the Descendants of Ya'qub, saying: "I have brought you a sign from your Lord: I make the figure of a bird out of clay for you, then I breathe into it, and then it becomes a flying bird – with Allah's permission; I cure those who are born blind, and lepers too; and I bring the dead back to life – with Allah's permission; I can tell you what you have eaten and also the things you have stored away in your homes. There is certainly a sign of my truth in this for you if you are true Believers. 3.50 I have come to you confirming what came before me in the Tawrah, and to make lawful for you some of what was made unlawful for you. I have come to you with a sign from your Lord, so be mindful of Allah and obey me. 3.51 Allah is my Lord and yours too, so worship Him. This is a path that is straight."

3.52 When Isa sensed rejection from them, he asked: "Who will be my helpers in guiding others to Allah?" "We will be the helpers in the religion of Allah," the disciples replied: "We believe in Allah, and you can be witness that we have surrendered to Him as Muslims." ³·⁵³They prayed: "Our Lord! We believe in what You have revealed, and we are following the messenger too, so count us alongside those who witness the truth."

³·⁵⁴**The disbelievers plotted** to kill Isa **but Allah planned** to save him. Allah is the Best of Planners. ³·⁵⁵Remember when Allah said: "Isa, I will let you reach full age and raise you up to Myself, and clean and purify you of the disbelievers' accusations. I will make your followers superior to the disbelievers until Judgement Day. Then, you will all come back to Me and I will judge between you about the disagreements you used to have.

³·⁵⁶Those who disbelieve, I will severely punish them in this world and the next. They won't have any helpers." ³·⁵⁷Those who believe and do good, Allah will pay them their rewards in full. Allah doesn't like wrongdoers.

³·⁵⁸O Prophet Muhammad, **all this that We recite to you are signs and the wise Reminder.** ³·⁵⁹According to Allah, the example of Isa is that of Adam. Allah created Adam from dust, then said to him: "Be," and he became. ³·⁶⁰O human! **This is the truth from your Lord, so don't ever be one of those who doubt.**

³·⁶¹If someone argues this matter with you, now that the knowledge about Isa has come to you, say: "Come. We will call together our children and your children, our women and your women, ourselves and yourselves, and then we will pray intensely and invoke Allah's curse on the liars!" ³·⁶²This is certainly the true account. There is no god except Allah. Allah is certainly the Almighty, the All-Wise. ³·⁶³If **they turn away,** they should know that **Allah knows the troublemakers perfectly well.**

³·⁶⁴O Prophet Muhammad, say: "People of the Book! Come to a belief that we both share: that we will worship only Allah; we won't make anything a partner-god with Him; we won't make each other lords instead of Allah." If then they turn away, say: "Be witnesses that at least we surrender to Allah as Muslims."

³·⁶⁵People of the Book! Why are you arguing about Ibrahim when the Tawrah and the Injeel weren't revealed until after him? Don't you even think? ³·⁶⁶Listen! You are the people who have been arguing in matters about which you had some knowledge, but why are you arguing in matters you don't know anything about? Allah knows but you don't. ³·⁶⁷Ibrahim was neither a Jew nor a Christian, but a true Muslim, and definitely not a polytheist. ³·⁶⁸The people closest to Ibrahim are those who have been following him since then, as well as this Prophet Muhammad and the Believers. Allah is the Protector of the Believers.

³·⁶⁹Some of the People of the Book would love to lead you astray, but they don't realise they're leading only themselves astray. ³·⁷⁰People of the Book! Why do you disbelieve in Allah's revelations when you witness them yourselves? ³·⁷¹People of the Book! Why are you mixing the truth with falsehood and deliberately hiding the truth?

³·⁷²Some of the People of the Book say: "At the beginning of the day, You can believe in the Qur'an that has been sent down to the Believers, but you should disbelieve in it at the end of the day, so that the Believers might also come back to disbelief. ³·⁷³You mustn't trust anyone unless they follow your religion." O Prophet Muhammad, say: "Only Allah's guidance is the real guidance." They say: "You mustn't believe a Book like that which was sent to you Muslims could be sent to anyone, or that anyone could argue against you with your Lord."

O Prophet Muhammad, **say: "Grace is in Allah's control; He gives it to anyone He chooses. Allah is All-Surrounding, All-Knowing.** ³·⁷⁴**He specifies anyone He chooses for His** special **mercy. Allah gives tremendous grace."**

³·⁷⁵O Prophet Muhammad, **some People of the Book are those that if you gave them a heap of gold for safekeeping, they will give it back to you. However, some of them are those that if you gave them a single gold coin for safekeeping, they will never give it back to you unless you constantly stood demanding it from them. That is because they say: "We owe nothing to these ignorant people." They also deliberately tell lies about Allah.** ³·⁷⁶**Of course! Anyone who fulfils his promise and is mindful** of Allah, will know that **Allah loves those who are mindful** of Him.

³·⁷⁷**Those who sell Allah's promise and their own oaths for a low price, it is they who won't have any share in the Hereafter. Allah will neither speak to them nor look at them on Judgement Day, and nor purify them. They will suffer a painful punishment.**

³·⁷⁸**There are some of them who, when reciting the Book, twist their tongues in such a way that you would think those twisted words are a part of the Book, but they aren't. They claim: "It's from Allah," but it isn't. They are deliberately telling lies about Allah.**

³·⁷⁹**No person that Allah gives the Book, authority, and prophethood to, would then tell people: "Be my servants and not Allah's," but rather: "Be people of the Lord because you've been teaching the Book to others and studying it yourselves."** ³·⁸⁰**That person would never tell you to make angels and prophets into lords. Would he tell you to disbelieve after you've surrendered yourselves to Allah as Muslims?**

3.81When Allah took a promise from the prophets, saying: "When I give you some Books and wisdom, and then a Messenger (- Muhammad) comes to you confirming what you already have, you must all believe in him and help him," He asked: "Do all of you agree to make My promise binding on yourselves?" They replied: "We agree." He ordered: "Then be witnesses, and I am also with you among the witnesses." 3.82Then, those who turn away after this, it is really they who will be the disobedient people.

3.83Are they looking for something other than Allah's religion when everything in the heavens and the earth have, whether they like it or not, bowed to His command? It is Him they will all be taken back to.

3.84O Prophet Muhammad, **declare:** "We believe in Allah, in what has been sent down to us, and what was revealed to Ibrahim, Isma'il, Is'haq, Ya'qub, and the Tribes, and what Musa, Isa, and all the prophets were given by their Lord. We make no distinction between any one of His prophets, and we will remain surrendered to Allah as Muslims."

3.85Whoever looks for a religion other than Islam, it will never be accepted from him, and he will be among the losers in the Hereafter.

3.86Why should Allah let those people succeed who disbelieve after having believed, after they witnessed that the Messenger Muhammad is true, and after clear signs have come to them? Allah doesn't let unjust people succeed. 3.87It is they whose punishment is to suffer the curse of Allah, of the angels, and of all the people. 3.88They will remain under the curse forever. Their punishment won't be reduced and they won't be given any chances, 3.89except those who repent after that and correct themselves, because Allah is Most Forgiving, Ever-Merciful.

3.90Those who disbelieve after having believed, and then go on increasing in their disbelief, their repentance will never be accepted and it is they who go astray. 3.91Those who disbelieve and die as disbelievers, even if any of them offered an earthful of gold as ransom to free himself with, it would never be accepted from him. It is they who will suffer a painful punishment, and they won't have any helpers.

[PART 4]
3.92**You will never achieve** true **piety unless you donate** in Allah's cause from the things you love. Allah knows perfectly well anything you donate.

3.93All food used to be lawful for the Descendants of Ya'qub, except what Ya'qub had made unlawful for himself before the Tawrah was revealed. O Prophet Muhammad, **say: "Bring the Tawrah and study it, if you are telling the truth."** 3.94Even after this, those who make lies about Allah, it is really they who are the wrongdoers. 3.95O Prophet Muhammad, **say: "Allah has spoken the truth. Now, follow the religion of Ibrahim the True, and he wasn't a polytheist."**

3.96**The first House of Allah built for people was the one in Makkah** – blessed and a guidance for everyone. 3.97There are clear signs in it, such as **the place where Ibrahim stood (- Maqaam Ibrahim).** Anyone who enters it will be safe. Hajj to this House, for those who can perform it, is a duty upon people to Allah. Anyone who disbelieves in it should know that **Allah is Free of all Needs from everyone.**

3.98O Prophet Muhammad, **ask: "People of the Book, why are you disbelieving in Allah's revelations when He Himself is a witness to everything you do?"** 3.99Ask: **"People of the Book, Why are you** blocking Believers from Allah's cause? You are looking for some crookedness in it while you yourselves are witnesses that it is straight. Allah isn't unaware of anything you do."

3.100Believers! If you obey a group of the People of the Book, they will turn you into disbelievers after you having believed. 3.101How can you disbelieve when Allah's revelations are recited to you and His Messenger Muhammad is present among you? Anyone who holds on strongly to belief in Allah will be guided to a path that is straight.

3.102Believers! Be mindful of Allah how He deserves, and be true Muslims when you die. 3.103You must hold on tightly together to Allah's rope and not break up with each other. Remember Allah's favour to you when you were enemies with each other and He joined your hearts together in love so that, with His blessing, you became brothers; and remember when you were on the edge of Hell's firepit and He saved you from falling into it. In this way Allah makes His signs clear to you so that you might follow guidance. 3.104There should be a group of you who invite to doing good, command what is right, and forbid what is wrong. It is really they who will be successful.

3.105Don't be like those people who broke up and disagreed with each other after the clear proofs had come to them. It is they who will suffer a terrible punishment 3.106on the Day when some faces will be bright and others gloomy. Those whose faces will be gloomy will be asked: "Did you disbelieve after having believed? Now taste the punishment because you were disbelievers." 3.107Those whose faces will be bright, they will be in Allah's special mercy, where they will remain forever. 3.108O Prophet Muhammad, these are Allah's revelations that We recite to you with the truth. Allah doesn't want any unfairness to anyone. 3.109Everything in the heavens and the earth belongs to Allah, and all matters are returned to Him for decision.

³·¹¹⁰You are the best community brought out for the guidance of people. You command what is right, forbid what is wrong, and believe in Allah. It would certainly have been best for the People of the Book if they had believed. Some of them are believers but most of them are disobedient.

³·¹¹¹Apart from a little abuse, they cannot harm you, because if they fight you, they will turn their backs on you and run away. They won't receive any support. ³·¹¹²Wherever they are found, they will be made to suffer humiliation, except when under a promise of protection with Allah or with the people. They've brought Allah's anger down upon themselves. They will be made to suffer misery as well. This is because they used to reject Allah's revelations and unjustly kill His prophets. This is also because they were disobedient and were breaking the law.

³·¹¹³They aren't all the same: some People of the Book are a group that stands for fairness. They recite Allah's revelations during the night and they also prostrate to Him. ³·¹¹⁴They believe in Allah and the Last Day, command what is right, forbid what is wrong, and race each other to do good. It is they who are from among righteous people. ³·¹¹⁵Whatever good they do, it won't be rejected from them. Allah knows perfectly well those who are mindful of Him.

³·¹¹⁶All the wealth and the children of the disbelievers won't be able to save them from the punishment of Allah in any way at all. It is they who will be the people of the Fire. They will remain in it forever. ³·¹¹⁷The example of anything they spend in this life is that of a frosty wind that hits and destroys the harvest of a people who have harmed themselves. Allah didn't harm them but rather they harm themselves.

³·¹¹⁸**Believers! Don't make close friends with those who aren't from among you because they won't hesitate to ruin you.** They love anything that makes you suffer. Hatred is clear in what they say, but far worse is what their hearts are hiding. We have made the signs clear to you if only you would think. ³·¹¹⁹Yet here you are, loving them when they don't even like you, even though you believe in the same whole **Book**. When they meet you, they claim: "We also believe," but when they're alone, they bite their fingertips at you in rage. O Prophet Muhammad, **say: "Die in your rage."** Allah knows the secrets of the hearts perfectly well. ³·¹²⁰It makes them sad if something good happens to you, but if you suffer something bad, they rejoice in it. However, their slyness cannot harm you in any way at all if you have patience and protect yourselves. Allah completely surrounds anything they do.

³·¹²¹Remember, O Prophet Muhammad, **when you left your family early in the morning to position the Believers at their posts for the Battle** at Uhud. Allah is All-Hearing, All-Knowing. ³·¹²²Remember when two of your groups gave up as cowards even though Allah was their Protector. True Believers must put their trust only in Allah.

³·¹²³Allah had helped you at Badr when you were weak. So, you must continue to be mindful of Allah so you can give thanks. ³·¹²⁴Remember, O Prophet Muhammad, when you told the Believers: "Isn't it enough for you that Allah will help you with three thousand angels that are especially **sent down?"** ³·¹²⁵Of course! If you Believers **remain patient and mindful of Allah, then even if they rush at you with this force of theirs, your Lord will help you with five thousand angels that will be hitting their targets.** ³·¹²⁶Allah only did this for it to be joy for you and to satisfy your hearts by it. Help comes only from Allah, the Almighty,

the All-Wise, [3.127] – and to destroy some of the disbelievers, or at least humiliate them, so that they go back defeated.

[3.128] This matter isn't any of your concern if Allah forgives them or punishes them, because they are wrongdoers. [3.129] Everything in the heavens and the earth belongs to Allah. He can forgive or punish anyone He chooses, though He is Most Forgiving, Ever-Merciful.

[3.130] Believers! Don't take usury – doubled, multiplied, but be mindful of Allah so you can be successful. [3.131] Protect yourselves from the Fire that has been prepared for the disbelievers. [3.132] You have to obey Allah and the Messenger Muhammad so you may be shown mercy.

[3.133] Race each other to get forgiveness from your Lord, and for a garden as vast as the heavens and the earth put together, prepared for those who are mindful of Allah, [3.134] those who donate to good causes in good times and bad, who control their anger, and forgive people. Allah loves those who do good, [3.135] those who immediately remember Allah if they do something shameful or harm themselves, and beg forgiveness for their sins – because who can forgive sins other than Allah – and they don't deliberately continue doing the wrong things they've done before. [3.136] It is they whose reward is forgiveness from their Lord, as well as gardens – that have rivers flowing beneath them, where they will remain forever. What an excellent reward for those who work hard!

[3.137] Many systems have been and gone before you, so travel through the earth and take a look at what was the end result of those who called the truth a lie. [3.138] This Qur'an is a plain statement for people, a guidance, and a source of advice for those who are mindful of Allah.

3.139So, you Believers must never give up nor worry because you will be the winners if you are true Believers. 3.140If you have suffered an injury then you should know that the enemy people have suffered similar injuries too. Days like these, We keep swapping them among the people so Allah can prove those who truly believe and to select some of you as martyrs – Allah doesn't like wrongdoers 3.141– and for Him to refine the Believers and destroy the disbelievers.

3.142Do you people think you will enter Paradise when Allah hasn't yet proven those of you who strive hard in His cause and those who have patience? 3.143You used to wish for death before you had faced it, but now you have seen it with your own eyes.

3.144Muhammad is only a Messenger. Many messengers have been and gone before him. If he died or was killed, would you lose faith? Anyone who loses faith won't be harming Allah in any way at all. Allah will reward those who are thankful. 3.145No one can die without Allah's command at a time that is already fixed. Whoever wants reward in this world, We give it to him here; and anyone who wants reward in the Hereafter, We give it to him there. We will reward those who are thankful.

3.146There are so many prophets who fought with many holy men alongside them, and they never gave up, never weakened, nor surrendered when they faced difficulties in Allah's cause. Allah loves those who have patience. 3.147They had nothing to say but pray: "Our Lord! Forgive us our sins and the excesses we went to in our duty, keep our footing strong, and help us against disbelieving people." 3.148So, Allah gave them the reward of this world and also an excellent reward of the Hereafter. Allah loves those who do good.

3.149Believers! If you obey the disbelievers, they will make you lose your faith and you will end up going back from the truth as losers. 3.150Rather, Allah is your Protector and He is the Best of Helpers.

3.151O Prophet Muhammad, We will plant your awe into the disbelievers' hearts because they make partner-gods with Allah – for which He hasn't sent down any permission. Their home will be the Fire. What a dreadful place for the wrongdoers to be in!

3.152Allah certainly did fulfil His promise to you Believers when you were about to crush the enemy with His help, until you lost courage and started quarrelling among yourselves about the command of Prophet Muhammad, and you disobeyed it after Allah showed you the victory you wanted. Some of you wanted this world while others preferred the Hereafter. Then, to test you, Allah made you turn back from them without defeating them. Later, He forgave you, because He gives grace to the Believers.

3.153When you were scrambling away without even glancing at anyone, and the Messenger was calling out to you from the group standing strong behind you, that is when Allah made you suffer one sorrow in place of another so that you wouldn't worry about what you had lost and suffered. Allah is Fully-Aware of everything you do. 3.154Then, after the setback, He sent down calmness in the form of sleep that overcame some of you. There was another group who were worried only about themselves, having wrongful doubts about Allah which was the doubt of ignorance, saying: "Do we have a say in this matter?" O Prophet Muhammad, you should reply: "This matter is entirely with Allah." They aren't telling you what they're hiding in their minds. They say to themselves: "If we had a say in this matter, we wouldn't have come here to be killed." O Prophet Muhammad, say: "Even if you were in your homes, those for whom being killed has been fixed would have certainly gone to the places where they will die." All this is for Allah to test what is in your hearts and to refine what is in your minds. Allah knows the secrets of the hearts perfectly well.

3.155 Those of you who turned back on the day the two armies clashed with each other, it was Shaytan who made them fail because of something they did. However, Allah has already forgiven them. He is Most Forgiving, Most Tolerant.

3.156 Believers! Don't be like those who disbelieve and say about their brothers who go travelling in the land or to fight: "If they had stayed with us, they wouldn't have died nor been killed," so that Allah might make that doubt a regret in their hearts. It is Allah Who gives life and death. Allah is Ever-Watchful of everything you do. 3.157 If you were killed in Allah's cause, or died, forgiveness from Allah and mercy would have certainly been far better than what wealth they gather together. 3.158 If you die or are killed, it is still in front of Allah you will all be assembled.

3.159 O Prophet Muhammad, it is a part of Allah's mercy that you are gentle with them. If you had been strict or hard-hearted, they would have scattered away from around you. So, you should pardon them and ask forgiveness for them, and ask their opinions in important matters. Then, once you've made a decision, you should put your trust in Allah. Allah loves those who put their trust in Him.

3.160 No one can defeat you if Allah helps you, but if He abandons you then who is there to help you apart from Him? True Believers must put their trust only in Allah.

3.161No prophet would ever hide anything. If someone does that, he will have to bring it out on Judgement Day. Then, everyone will be repaid in full for what they did, and they won't be treated unfairly.

3.162Can they be the same: someone who tries to gain Allah's good pleasure and someone who brings down on himself displeasure from Allah and whose home will be in Hell? What a horrible final destination! 3.163They have different ranks in the sight of Allah. Allah is Ever-Watchful of everything they do.

3.164Allah has certainly done the Believers a great favour that He sent them a Messenger from among them, who recites His revelations to them, cleans and purifies them, and teaches them the Book and wisdom, while before that they had been clearly astray.

3.165Isn't it true that when you suffered a disaster at Uhud, although you had struck twice as much on your enemies at Badr, you complained: "How did this happen?" O Prophet Muhammad, say: "It is from your own selves." Allah is Most Capable of anything. 3.166On the day of Uhud when the two armies clashed with each other, what you suffered was with Allah's command, so He could prove the true Believers 3.167and expose the hypocrites. They were told: "Come and fight in Allah's cause, or at least defend yourselves." They replied: "If we had known there would be a fight, we would have definitely come with you." On that day, they were closer to disbelief than to faith. They say with their mouths what isn't in their hearts. Allah knows best everything they hide. 3.168Those who said about their brothers while they themselves stayed behind: "If only they had listened to us they wouldn't have been killed." O Prophet Muhammad, say: "If what you say is true then save yourselves from death."

3.169You must never think those killed in Allah's cause are dead. In fact, they are alive with their Lord, given food, 3.170rejoicing in everything Allah has given them from His grace, and feeling happy with those who, having left them behind, haven't joined them yet, that they too won't have anything to fear and will never be sad. 3.171They're happy with Allah's favour and grace, and that He would never let the Believers' reward go to waste, 3.172who, even after they suffered injuries, responded to Allah and the Messenger Muhammad. Those of them who do good and remain mindful of Allah will have a huge reward, 3.173who, when people said to them: "People have allied against you, so fear them," but it only increased their faith, and they replied: "Allah is enough for us, and He is such an excellent Guardian!" 3.174They came back with Allah's favour and grace. They didn't suffer any harm because they were trying to gain Allah's good pleasure. Allah gives tremendous grace. 3.175It is only Shaytan who tries to threaten you through his friends. Don't be afraid of him but fear only Me if you are true Believers.

3.176O Prophet Muhammad, those who rush into disbelief shouldn't make you sad. They cannot harm Allah in any way at all. Allah doesn't want to give them any share in the Hereafter. They will suffer a terrible punishment. 3.177Those who are buying disbelief at the cost of belief, they cannot harm Allah in any way at all. They will suffer a painful punishment. 3.178The disbelievers mustn't think that Our giving them more time is any good for them. We are only giving them more time so they can increase in wrongdoing. They will suffer a humiliating punishment.

3.179Allah won't leave the Believers in the situation you are in until He has separated bad from good. Allah wouldn't give all of you the unseen secrets, but He does select from His messengers anyone He chooses for that purpose. Therefore, you must continue to believe in

Allah and His messengers. If you believe and remain mindful of Allah, you will have a huge reward.

3.180 Those who are stingy with what Allah has given them from His grace mustn't think that stinginess is any good for them. In fact, it's bad for them. The things they were stingy with will be tied to their necks on Judgement Day. The heritage of the heavens and the earth belongs only to Allah. Allah is Fully-Aware of everything you do.

3.181 Allah has certainly heard the words of those who claim: "Allah is poor and we are rich!" We will record what they say – as well as their unjust killing the prophets, and We will say: "Now taste the punishment of the Scorching Fire! 3.182 This is only because of the bad things you did. Allah doesn't treat His servants unfairly."

3.183 Those who also claim: "Allah took from us a promise that we mustn't believe merely because a messenger says so unless he brings us an offering that fire from the sky will burn." O Prophet Muhammad, reply: "Many messengers have already come to you before me with clear signs, and even with that very sign which you are asking for. So why did you kill them, if you are telling the truth?" 3.184 If they accuse you of being a liar then it is no surprise because messengers before you were also accused – even though they came with clear signs, scriptures, and the enlightening Book.

3.185 Everyone is going to taste death. You will certainly be paid your rewards in full only on Judgement Day. Therefore, anyone who is saved from the Fire and entered into Paradise will have succeeded, as this life is only fake enjoyment.

3.186 You will certainly be tested in your wealth and in your own selves, and you will certainly hear many abuses from the people who were given the Book before you, and from polytheists too. However, if you have patience and continue to be mindful of Allah, then surely this is a sign of strong will.

3.187When Allah took a strong promise from the People of the Book that: "You will make it clear to the people and won't hide it," they abandoned the promise behind their backs and sold it for a low price. What a horrible thing in loss they are buying! 3.188O Prophet Muhammad, don't ever think that those who rejoice in what they gave and love to be praised for what they haven't done – don't ever think of them as having escaped punishment. They will suffer a painful punishment.

3.189Control of the heavens and the earth belongs to Allah. He is Most Capable of anything. 3.190In the creation of the heavens and earth and in the rotation of the night and day, there are certainly signs for people of understanding, 3.191who remember Allah while standing, sitting, and lying down on their sides, and think deeply about the creation of the heavens and earth, and they pray: "Our Lord! You haven't created this without a purpose! Glory be to You! Protect us from the suffering of the Fire. 3.192Our Lord! Anyone You enter into the Fire, You will certainly humiliate him, and the wrongdoers won't have any helpers. 3.193Our Lord! We heard a caller calling towards faith, 'Believe in your Lord,' so we believed. Our Lord! Forgive us our sins, remove our evils from us, and allow us to die among pious people. 3.194Our Lord! Also, give us what You promised us through Your messengers, and don't humiliate us on Judgement Day. Of course, You never break promises." 3.195So their Lord responded to them: "I would never let any of your actions go to waste, whether you are male or female. You come from each other. However, those who migrated, were expelled from their homes, suffered in My cause, fought, or were killed, I will certainly remove their sins from them and enter them into gardens – that have rivers flowing beneath them, as a reward from Allah. The best reward comes from Him."

3.196"The free movement of the disbelievers in all the lands mustn't trick you. 3.197It's only a brief enjoyment, and eventually their home will be Hell. What a dreadful place! 3.198However, those who continue to be mindful of their Lord, they will have, as a place to stay, gardens from Allah – that have rivers flowing beneath them, where they will remain forever. For pious people, what comes from Allah is the best.

3.199Some People of the Book are those who believe in Allah, in what was sent down to you Muslims and to them, and they are humble to Allah. They don't sell Allah's revelations for a low price. It is they whose reward will come from their Lord. Allah is quick in settling accounts.

3.200Believers! You must continue to have patience, stay strong, be alert, and remain mindful of Allah so that you might be successful.

Surah 4. Women (*an-Nisaa'*)

Allah's name I begin with, the Most Compassionate, the Ever-Merciful

4.1People! Be mindful of your Lord Who created you from a single person, created his wife from him, and from them both He scattered many men and women throughout the world. So, be mindful of Allah for Whose sake you make demands from each other, and also be mindful of family relations. Allah is always Ever-Watchful over you.

4.2Give orphans their property, don't swap your worthless things for their good ones, and don't eat up their property by mixing it with your own. It is always a great sin.

⁴·³If you fear you won't be able to be fair with orphan women then marry other women you like: two, or three, or four; but if you fear you won't be able to be fair with them either then only one, or your slavewoman. This will make it less likely for you to be unfair. ⁴·⁴Give women their dowry as a free gift. However, if they give some of it to you happily, then you may take it with pleasure and comfort.

⁴·⁵Don't give weak-minded people your property which Allah has made a means of financial support for you, but feed them from it, clothe them, and speak to them with kind words.

⁴·⁶Keep assessing the orphans until they reach the age of marriage. Then, if you see good judgement in them, hand them their property. Don't eat it up wastefully nor hastily before they grow up. If the guardian is rich then he should stay away from taking compensation from it, but if he is poor then he may take what is fair. Then, when you hand them their property, make witnesses over them, even though Allah is enough as a Reckoner.

⁴·⁷There's a share for men as well as for women in what parents and close relatives leave behind, as a fixed share, whether it is small or large.

⁴·⁸If non-inheriting relatives, orphans, or the needy are present at the distribution of the inheritance, give them some of it, and speak to them with kind words.

⁴·⁹The guardians of the orphans should be afraid as if they would die and leave behind helpless children and be worried about them. They must continue to be mindful of Allah and speak in a straightforward manner. ⁴·¹⁰Those who wrongfully eat up orphans' property are only

filling their own bellies with fire. They will soon burn in a Blazing Fire.

$^{4.11}$**Allah commands you about** the inheritance of **your children: the son has the equivalent share of two daughters. If there are only daughters: two or more, they have two-thirds of what the deceased leaves behind; if she is only one, then she has a half. For parents: for each of them is a sixth of what the deceased leaves behind, if he has a child; but if he has no child, and only his parents are inheriting him, for his mother is a third; if he has siblings, then for his mother is a sixth.** All this is **after** the payment of **any will he has made or any debt. Your parents or your children, you don't know which of them benefits you more.** These are shares **fixed by Allah. Allah is always All-knowing, All-Wise.**

$^{4.12}$**For you** husbands **is a half of what your wives leave behind, if they don't have any child; but if do have a child, then for you is a quarter of what they leave behind –** after the payment of **any will they've made or any debt. For your wives is a quarter of what you leave behind, if you don't have any child; but if you do have a child, then for them is an eighth –** after the payment of **any will you've made or any debt. If the man or woman leaving behind something to be inherited has neither parents nor children but has one brother or one sister, for each of the two is a sixth; but if they are more than that, then they all share a third between them;** all this is **after** the payment of **any will that was made or any debt, without harm** to anyone. **This is the command from Allah. Allah is All-Knowing, Most Tolerant.** $^{4.13}$**These are the limits set by Allah. Whoever obeys Allah and His Messenger** Muhammad, **Allah will enter him into gardens – that have rivers flowing beneath them, where they will remain forever. This is the tremendous victory.** $^{4.14}$**However, anyone who disobeys Allah and His Messenger** Muhammad, **and oversteps His limits, Allah will throw** him into a fire, where he will remain forever. He will suffer a humiliating punishment.

4.15If any of your women commit adultery, you must make four of your men witnesses against them. If they testify then keep those women inside their houses until death takes them or Allah gives them another way out. 4.16Punish both of those from among you who commit fornication. Then, if they repent and correct themselves, leave them alone. Allah always accepts repentance much, is Ever-Merciful.

4.17Allah accepts the repentance of those who unknowingly do something bad and then repent quickly afterwards. It is they Allah forgives. Allah is always All-Knowing, All-Wise. 4.18Those who continue to do bad things such that death comes to any of them and he says: "I repent now," repentance isn't available for them nor for those who die as disbelievers. It is for these people We've prepared a painful punishment.

4.19Believers! It isn't lawful for you to inherit women by force. Don't treat them with strictness to take away some of anything you've given them, unless they do something clearly shameful. Treat them with respect. If you don't like them, perhaps you don't like something Allah has placed a lot of good in. 4.20If you decide to replace one wife with another, and had given any of the two wives a heap of wealth, you mustn't take back any of it. Would you want to take it back by making false accusations and acting very sinfully? 4.21How could you take back the dowry after you have had husband-wife privacy with each other, and after your wives have taken a strong promise from you?!

4.22 **Don't marry any women your fathers married** – except what has happened in the past. It was shameful, hateful, and a disgusting custom. 4.23 Also **unlawful for you** to marry are your: mothers, daughters, sisters; father's sisters, mother's sisters; brother's daughters, sister's daughters; milk-mothers, milk-sisters; wives' mothers; step-daughters in your care – from your wives you've had sexual relations with, but it won't be wrong to marry them if you haven't had sexual relations with their mothers; wives of your own sons; and two sisters at the same time – except what has happened in the past. Allah is always Most Forgiving, Ever-Merciful.

[PART 5]

4.24 **Also** unlawful for you are **married women, except your slavewomen** taken in war. This is Allah's command to you. Other than these, all women are lawful for you to marry, so you can look for them with your wealth with the intention of marriage and spending on them and not unlawful sexual relations. When you consummate marriage with them, give them their fixed dowry, but it won't be wrong if you agree with each other to change the dowry after fixing it. Allah is always All-Knowing, All-Wise.

4.25 **Whoever among you cannot afford to marry Believing free women may marry Believing slavewomen.** Allah knows best the state of your faith. You come from each other. You may marry them with their owners' permission, and give them their dowry according to tradition, as chaste women who have you as their husbands – not in unlawful sexual relations nor having secret lovers. If the slavewomen have unlawful sexual relations after they're taken in marriage, their punishment will be half that of free women. This permission to marry slavewomen is for those of you who are afraid of sinning. It is better for you to have patience. Allah is Most Forgiving, Ever-Merciful.

⁴·²⁶Allah wants to make His commands clear to you, guide you along the ways of those good people who lived before you, and forgive you. Allah is All-Knowing, All-Wise. ⁴·²⁷Allah wants to forgive you but the people who follow their own desires want you to turn far away from the truth. ⁴·²⁸Allah wants to lighten your burden because humans are created weak.

⁴·²⁹Believers! Don't take over each other's wealth wrongfully, but you may buy and sell based upon agreement between you. Don't kill yourselves because Allah is always Ever-Merciful to you. ⁴·³⁰If anyone does that in hostility and unfairness, We will very soon burn him in a fire of Hell. This is always easy for Allah.

⁴·³¹If you continue to avoid the worst sins you are forbidden, We will remove your sins from you and enter you into Paradise through an honourable entrance.

⁴·³²You mustn't wish for anything Allah has preferred for some of you to others. Men and women have a share in what each have earned. However, you must keep asking Allah for some of His grace. He always knows everything perfectly well. ⁴·³³We have made heirs for everyone in the things parents and close relatives leave behind. You must give the shares to the people your promises were made. Allah is always a Witness to everything.

⁴·³⁴Men are the protectors and guardians of women because Allah has made them higher in responsibility to women, and because they spend their own wealth on their women. Righteous women are devoted – in their husband's absence, protecting what Allah protects. Those women whose disloyalty you are concerned about, first advise them gently, if they still disobey then separate their beds, and if they still disobey then gently push them away. If they become faithful to

you then you mustn't look for any way against them. Allah is always Most High, Great.

4.35If you fear the couple will break up then bring a mediator from his family and one from hers. If both mediators want to put things right then Allah will create harmony between the couple. Allah is always All-Knowing, Fully-Aware.

4.36You must worship Allah and never make anything a partner-god with Him; be kind to parents, close relatives, orphans, the needy, neighbours who are near or far, close friends, travellers, and your slaves. Allah doesn't like anyone who is arrogant, showoff, 4.37those who are themselves stingy and tell others to be stingy, or hide what Allah has given them from His grace. We have prepared a humiliating punishment for the disbelievers, 4.38as well as for those who spend their wealth to show off to people and don't really believe in Allah or the Last Day. Whoever has Shaytan as a close friend should know what an evil close friend he is!

4.39What would they lose if they believed in Allah and the Last Day, and donated from what Allah has given them! Allah always knows them perfectly well. 4.40Allah doesn't do even an atom's weight of unfairness. If something done is good, He multiplies it and gives a great reward from Himself.

4.41O Prophet Muhammad, what will it be like when We bring a witness from each community and you as a witness over them all? 4.42On that Day, those who disbelieved and disobeyed the Messenger Muhammad will wish the earth was flattened over them. They won't be able to hide any fact from Allah.

4.43 Believers! Don't go near ritual prayers when you are: intoxicated unless you know what you are saying; nor in the state of major ritual impurity requiring a bath – except travellers – until you have bathed. If you are ill or travelling, or any of you comes to pray after relieving himself, or after having sexual relations with women married to you, and you cannot find any water, then you must clean yourselves through intention with clean earth, and wipe your faces and arms with it. Allah is always Most Pardoning, Most Forgiving.

4.44 O Prophet Muhammad, don't you see those people who've been given a share of the Book? They're buying misguidance and want you Muslims to stray away from the right path. 4.45 Allah knows best your enemies. He is enough as a Protector and a Helper.

4.46 Some Jews change the words from their places and say: "We hear but disobey," "You should listen but not be listened to," and "*Raa'inaa* (Pay attention to us)," – twisting their tongues and insulting Islam. If only they had said: "We hear and obey," "Listen," and "*Unzurnaa* (Honour us with your vision)," it would have been far better for them and more appropriate, but Allah has cursed them because of their disbelief and so they have very little faith.

4.47 People of the Book! You must believe in what We've sent down – confirming what you already have, before We disfigure some faces and turn them backwards, or before We curse them like We cursed the people who broke the Sabbath. Allah's orders have to be followed.

4.48 Allah doesn't forgive partner-gods being made with Him though He forgives anything else for anyone He chooses. Whoever makes partner-gods with Allah has made a terrible mistake.

⁴·⁴⁹O Prophet Muhammad, **don't you see those who claim to clean and purify themselves?** The truth is, it is Allah Who cleans and purifies anyone He chooses, and they won't be treated unfairly even as much as a hair on a date-seed. ⁴·⁵⁰Just look at how they make lies about Allah! That itself is enough as a clear sin.

⁴·⁵¹O Prophet Muhammad, **don't you see those who have been given a share of the Book?** They now believe in idols and fake gods, and they say about the disbelievers: "These people follow guidance on a right way better than the Believers do." ⁴·⁵²It is those people Allah has cursed. You won't be able to find any helper for someone Allah curses.

⁴·⁵³Do they have a share of Allah's kingdom? In that case, they wouldn't give people even as much as a speck on a date-seed. ⁴·⁵⁴Are they jealous of what Allah has given people from His grace? We've given Ibrahim's descendants the Book and wisdom, as well as a great kingdom. ⁴·⁵⁵Some people believe in Prophet Muhammad while others turn away from him. The Fire will be enough as a blaze to punish those who turn away!

⁴·⁵⁶Anyone who disbelieves in Our revelations, We will very soon burn them in a fire of Hell. Each time their skins have burned off, We will replace them with new skins so they will continue to taste the punishment. Allah is always the Almighty, the All-Wise.

⁴·⁵⁷Those who believe and do good, We will enter them into gardens – that have rivers flowing beneath them, where they will remain forever and ever, and where they will have clean and pure spouses. We will also enter them under cooling shades.

⁴·⁵⁸Allah tells you to give entrusted items back to their owners and to judge with fairness whenever you make judgements between people. How excellent is the advice Allah gives you! Allah is always All-Hearing, Ever-Watchful.

⁴·⁵⁹Believers! You have to obey Allah and the Messenger too, and those of authority among you. If you disagree in anything among yourselves, you have to refer it back to Allah and the Messenger if you really believe in Allah and the Last Day. That is best and good for the end result.

⁴·⁶⁰O Prophet Muhammad, **don't you see those who claim to believe in what is revealed to you and in what was revealed before you? They want their judgements to come from fake gods even though they've been told to reject them. Shaytan wants to lead them far, far astray.** ⁴·⁶¹When they are told: "Come to what Allah has revealed, and also to the Messenger Muhammad," you see the hypocrites turning away from you completely. ⁴·⁶²So how is it then, when they suffer a disaster because of what they've done, they come to you swearing by Allah: "We only wanted goodness and to make peace."? ⁴·⁶³It is those people Allah knows well what is in their hearts, so avoid them but continue to advise them, and speak to them about themselves using effective words.

⁴·⁶⁴We sent messengers so they would be obeyed by Allah's command. When the people are unjust to themselves, if only they come to you, O Beloved Prophet Muhammad, **and beg Allah to forgive them, and the Messenger also asks forgiveness for them, they would certainly find Allah accepting repentance much, Ever-Merciful.**

⁴·⁶⁵**But no!** O Prophet Muhammad, **I swear by your Lord that: they'll never be true Believers until they let you make judgements in all the**

disputes that come between them, and then they mustn't disagree among themselves against what you decide but accept it wholeheartedly. [4.66]If We had told them: "Sacrifice your lives," or "Leave your homes," only a few of them would have done that. If only they had done what they were advised, it would have been best for them and more intense in proving their faith, [4.67]in which case We would have given them a great reward from Us, [4.68]and certainly guided them on a path that is straight.

[4.69]Those who obey Allah and the Messenger Muhammad, it is they who will be with those people Allah has done favours to: the prophets, sincere people, martyrs, and righteous people. How magnificent these companions are! [4.70]That is the special grace from Allah. He is enough as being All-Knowing.

[4.71]Believers! Be careful, and then go out if needed either in separate groups or all together. [4.72]Some of you who will certainly be deliberately slow, so if you suffer a disaster, they will say: "Allah has done me a favour in that I wasn't there with them." [4.73]However, if some grace comes to you from Allah, he will certainly say – as if there had never been any friendship between you and him: "Oh! If only I had been with them then I too would have gained a tremendous victory."

[4.74]Those who want to sell this life for the Hereafter must fight in Allah's cause. If anyone is killed or is victorious while fighting in Allah's cause, We will very soon give him a huge reward. [4.75]But what is wrong with you? Why aren't you fighting in Allah's cause when oppressed men, women, and children are crying out: "Our Lord! Help us get out of this town whose people are cruel. Give us a protector from You. Give us a helper from You!"?

4.76 Believers will fight in Allah's cause, but disbelievers will fight in Shaytan's cause. So, you Believers must fight against Shaytan's supporters. His plan is always weak.

4.77 O Prophet Muhammad, don't you see those who were told: "You must hold back from fighting, but establish the ritual prayers and pay zakah."? When fighting was prescribed for them, that is when a group of them began to fear the people as much as or even more than Allah should be feared. They said: "Our Lord! Why have You prescribed fighting for us? If only You had given us a little more time." O Prophet Muhammad, say: "The enjoyment of this world is brief and little whereas the Hereafter is best for those who are mindful of Allah. You won't be treated unfairly even as much as a hair on a date-seed. 4.78 Death will track you down wherever you are, even if you are in towers that are built high and strong!" If something good comes to them, they say: "This is from Allah," but if they suffer something bad, they claim: "This is from you, O Muhammad." Say: "Everything is from Allah." But what is wrong with these people? They hardly understand a single word! 4.79 O human! Anything good that comes to you is from Allah, but whatever bad you suffer is from yourself. O Prophet Muhammad, We have sent you as a Messenger to all people, and Allah is enough as a Witness.

4.80 Anyone who obeys the Messenger has obeyed Allah, but whoever turns away should know that We haven't sent you, O Prophet Muhammad, to watch over them. 4.81 They say: "We obey," but when they go away from you, O Prophet Muhammad, some of them spend all night long plotting against what you told them. Allah is recording what they plot all night long. So, you should stay away from them and continue to put your trust in Allah, because He is enough as a Guardian.

4.82Don't they even think over the Qur'an? If it had been from other than Allah, they would have certainly found lots of inconsistencies in it.

4.83When any news of peace or fear reaches them, they spread it about. If only they had taken it to the Messenger, or to those of authority among them, those who can investigate it would have learnt the truth from them. If it wasn't for Allah's grace and mercy upon you, you would have all – except for a few – followed Shaytan.

4.84So, O Prophet Muhammad, **you must continue to fight in Allah's cause** – being responsible only for yourself, and urge the believers too. Perhaps Allah will hold back the disbelievers' force. He is stronger in might and more severe in punishing.

4.85Anyone who makes a good recommendation will have a share of its reward and whoever makes an evil recommendation will have a share of its burden. Allah always has control over everything.

4.86When you are greeted with a welcome you should respond to the greeting with something better than it or at least return the same. Allah always takes account of everything.

4.87He is **Allah. There is no god except Him.** He will certainly gather all of you together on Judgement Day in which there is no doubt. Who can be more truthful in words than Allah!

4.88**What is wrong with you** Muslims that you have split into **two** groups regarding the hypocrites? Allah has toppled them over because of the bad things they did. Do you want to guide those Allah has called misguided? You won't find any way of guidance for someone Allah calls misguided. 4.89They would love it if you disbelieved as they do, in which case you would all be the same. You mustn't take protectors from among them until they migrate into Allah's cause. However, if they break the peace treaty, then you should take hold of them during battle and kill them wherever you find them. Don't take any of them as protectors or helpers, [4.90]but don't kill those who have made peaceful contact with a group you have a peace treaty with, or those who come to you not wanting to fight you or their own people anymore. If Allah had wanted, He could have given them power over you and then they would have certainly fought you. So, if they leave you alone, don't fight you, and ask you for peace, then Allah hasn't given you any permission to harm them. [4.91]You will find some other people who wish to remain in peace from you and from their own people. Each time they're sent back to hostility, they are toppled over into it and forced to fight you. If they don't leave you alone, ask you for peace, or hold back from fighting you, then you should take hold of them during battle and kill them wherever you find them. It is they We've given you complete authority over.

[4.92]It isn't permitted for a Believer to kill a Believer, unless by mistake. If someone kills a Believer by mistake, then the killer must free a Believing slave and pay compensation to the victim's family – unless they forgive it out of charity. If the victim is from people who are your enemies and was a Believer, then free a Believing slave. If the victim is from people you have a peace treaty with, then pay compensation to the victim's family and also free a Believing slave. If the killer cannot afford to free a slave, then fast for two months consecutively – as a way of repenting to Allah. Allah is always All-Knowing, All-Wise. [4.93]If someone kills a Believer deliberately, his punishment is Hell, where he will remain forever. Allah will be angry with him and curse him, and He has prepared a terrible punishment for him.

4.94 Believers! When you make efforts in Allah's cause, make sure everything is clear, and don't say to anyone who asks you for peace: "You aren't a Believer!" You're trying to gain the temporary wealth of this life when Allah has many riches for you. That is what you were before until Allah did you a favour. So, make sure everything is clear. Allah is always Fully-Aware of everything you do.

4.95 Believers who stay behind at home – except those with real excuses – aren't the same as those Believers who strive hard in Allah's cause with their wealth and their lives. Allah has given a rank higher to those who strive hard with their wealth and their lives than to those who stay behind. Allah has promised good to all, but He has made those who strive hard superior to those who stay behind by giving them a huge reward, 4.96 high ranks from Himself, forgiveness and mercy. Allah is always Most Forgiving, Ever-Merciful.

4.97 When taking away the souls of those people who ruined themselves, the angels ask: "What were you doing?" They reply as an excuse: "We were oppressed in the world." The angels ask: "Wasn't Allah's earth spacious enough for you to migrate in it?" It is they whose home will be Hell. What a horrible final destination! 4.98 However, those men, women, and children who are really oppressed and cannot make a plan to survive, and don't know any way out won't be punished. 4.99 It is they Allah will certainly forgive. Allah is always Most Pardoning, Most Forgiving.

4.100 Anyone who migrates in Allah's cause will find many places of safety in the world and plenty of resources too. Anyone who leaves his home migrating to Allah and His Messenger Muhammad and then death tracks him down on the way, his reward from Allah has already been guaranteed. Allah is always Most Forgiving, Ever-Merciful.

4.101When you travel in the land, there is nothing wrong if you shorten the ritual prayers – if you fear the disbelievers will harass you. The hostile disbelievers are always your open enemies.

4.102O Prophet Muhammad, when you are among them and leading them in the ritual prayers during battle, a group of them should stand with you holding on to their weapons. Once they've prostrated, they should move to the back. Then the other group, that hasn't yet prayed, should come and pray with you, and they should be careful, holding on to their weapons. The disbelievers would love it if you forgot about your weapons and equipment, so they can launch a sudden attack against you. There is nothing wrong if you put down your weapons because you had difficulties due to rain or you were ill, but you must still be careful. Allah has prepared a humiliating punishment for the disbelievers. 4.103When you've finished the ritual prayers, you must continue to remember Allah while standing, sitting, and lying down on your sides. When you feel safe, you must establish the ritual prayers as normal. The ritual prayers are a duty on Believers at times that are fixed.

4.104You Believers mustn't show weakness in going after the enemy. If you are feeling pain, they're feeling pain too, just like you are, but you can hope from Allah what they cannot. Allah is always All-Knowing, All-Wise.

4.105O Prophet Muhammad, We have revealed to you the Book with the truth so that you can judge between the people according to what Allah has shown you, and not become a supporter of cheaters. 4.106You should ask for Allah's forgiveness, because He is always Most Forgiving, Ever-Merciful. 4.107You mustn't argue for those who cheat against themselves. Allah doesn't like any disobedient traitor.

4.108They might be able to hide from the people but they cannot hide their intentions from Allah because He is among them when they spend all night long saying things He disagrees with. Allah always completely surrounds anything they do. 4.109Yet here you are, arguing for them in this life, but who will argue for them with Allah on Judgement Day, or who will be their supporter!

4.110Anyone who does something bad or wrongs himself but then begs Allah to forgive him will find Allah Most Forgiving, Ever-Merciful. 4.111Anyone who deliberately does something wrong, does so to his own loss. Allah is always All-Knowing, All-wise. 4.112However, anyone who makes a mistake or deliberately does something wrong, and then blames it on an innocent person, will carry the burden of a false accusation and an obvious sin.

4.113O Prophet Muhammad, if it wasn't for Allah's grace and mercy upon you, some of them had certainly decided to try and mislead you, but they're only misleading themselves. They cannot harm you in any way at all. Allah has revealed to you the Book and wisdom, and He has taught you anything you didn't know. Allah's grace upon you is tremendous.

4.114There's nothing good in most of their private discussions, unless someone instructs to do some charity, show some kindness, or put things right between people. Whoever does this, trying to gain Allah's good pleasure, We will very soon give him a huge reward.

4.115Anyone who goes against the Messenger Muhammad even after guidance has become clear to him, and follows a path different from that of the Believers, We will let him turn away to whichever path he wants, and We will burn him in Hell. What a horrible final destination!

4.116Allah doesn't forgive partner-gods being made with Him though He forgives anything else for anyone He chooses. Whoever makes partner-gods with Allah has certainly gone far, far astray.

4.117Instead of Him, they pray only to female idols, and they pray only to Shaytan, the Rebel! 4.118Allah cursed him, and Shaytan said: "I will certainly take for myself a fixed share of Your servants. 4.119I will definitely lead them astray, give them false hopes, and make them follow my orders: they will slit the ears of cattle and change Allah's creation." Anyone who takes Shaytan instead of Allah as his protector will suffer a huge loss. 4.120Shaytan makes them promises and gives them false hopes, but he can promise them nothing but lies. 4.121It is they whose home will be Hell, and they won't find any way out of it.

4.122However, those who believe and do good, We will enter them into gardens – that have rivers flowing beneath them, where they will remain forever and ever. Allah's promise is true. Who can be more truthful in speech than Allah!

4.123People! The truth isn't based on your hopes nor on those of the People of the Book. Whoever does anything bad will be punished for it, and he won't find any protector or helper apart from Allah. 4.124Anyone who is a Believer – male or female, and does good, it is they who will enter Paradise and they won't be treated unfairly even as much as a speck on a date-seed.

4.125Who can be better in religion than someone who gives up his identity to Allah as Muslim, does good, and follows the religion of Ibrahim the True! Allah made Ibrahim a close friend. 4.126Everything in the heavens and the earth belongs to Allah. Allah always completely surrounds everything.

4.127O Prophet Muhammad, **they ask you the ruling about women. Say: "It is Allah Who gives you the ruling about them, in addition to what is recited to you from the Book about the orphan women you aren't giving their prescribed rights** of dowry and inheritance **to but want to marry them** to take their wealth, **and also about helpless children: that you must maintain fairness to orphans. Anything good you do, Allah always knows it perfectly well.**

4.128**If any wife is concerned about disloyalty or neglect from her husband, there is nothing wrong if they put things right between themselves. It's best to put things right, even though people can be selfish. If you do good and remain mindful** of Allah **then you should know that Allah is always Fully-Aware of everything you do.**

4.129**You'll never be able to be perfectly fair between your wives however much you want, so don't completely turn** towards one and away from the other **leaving her as if she were suspended** between marriage and divorce. **If you correct yourselves and remain mindful** of Allah **then** you should know that **Allah is always Most Forgiving, Ever-Merciful.** 4.130**If the couple choose to separate** by divorce, **Allah will make them free of all needs** from each other **through His plentiful resources. Allah is always All-Surrounding, All-Wise.**

4.131**Everything in the heavens and in the earth belongs to Allah. We've already told those given the Book before you, and** are telling **you Muslims too, that you must remain mindful of Allah. If you disbelieve then** you should know that **everything in the heavens and in the earth belongs to Allah, and He is always Free of all Needs, Most Praiseworthy.** 4.132**Everything in the heavens and in the earth belongs** to Allah, and He is enough as a Guardian. ⁴·¹³³People! If He wanted, He could get rid of you and replace you with others. Allah is always Most Capable of doing this. ⁴·¹³⁴Whoever wants the reward of this world should know that the reward of this world and the next comes only from Allah. Allah is always All-Hearing, Ever-Watchful.

⁴·¹³⁵Believers! You should be the upholders of fairness as witnesses for Allah's sake, even against yourselves, your parents, or your close relatives. Even if that person is rich or poor, Allah wants the best for both. So, don't follow desires so that you can be fair. If you twist the truth or neglect fairness then be warned that Allah is always Fully-Aware of everything you do.

⁴·¹³⁶Believers! You must continue to believe in Allah and His Messenger Muhammad, as well as the Book He has revealed to His Messenger, and the Book He revealed previously. Anyone who disbelieves in Allah, His angels, His Books, His messengers, and the Last Day, has gone far, far astray.

⁴·¹³⁷Those who believe, then disbelieve, then believe again, and then disbelieve again, and then go on further disbelieving, they should know that Allah doesn't need to forgive them nor guide them on any straight way. ⁴·¹³⁸O Prophet Muhammad, warn the hypocrites that they will suffer a painful punishment, ⁴·¹³⁹who take disbelievers as protectors instead of Believers. Are they looking for glory and power from them? Glory and power belong entirely to Allah.

⁴·¹⁴⁰He has gradually sent down to you in the Book that when you hear Allah's revelations being rejected and made fun of, you Muslims mustn't sit with them unless they start talking about something else, or else you will be just like them. Allah is going to gather the hypocrites and the disbelievers all together in Hell, ⁴·¹⁴¹who are

waiting to see what happens **against you: if you gain a victory from Allah, they say: "Weren't we on your side?" but if the disbelievers gain a share** of success, **they say: "Didn't we gain an advantage over you** enemy of Muslims, **and yet we protected you from the Believers?"** O hypocrites! **Allah will judge between you on Judgement Day. He won't let the disbelievers have any control over the Believers.**

4.142**The hypocrites think they can trick Allah but He is going to punish them for their trickery. When they get up to pray, they do so lazily, only showing off to people, and hardly remembering Allah at all;** 4.143**remaining doubtful between faith and disbelief – neither with the Believers nor with the disbelievers. You won't find any way of guidance for someone Allah calls misguided.**

4.144**Believers! Don't take disbelievers as protectors instead of Believers. Do you want to give Allah a clear authority against you?** 4.145**The hypocrites will be in the lowest depths of the Fire, and you won't be able to find any helper for them,** 4.146**but those who repent, correct themselves, hold tightly to** the commands of **Allah, and make their religion purely for Allah – it is they who are with the Believers, and very soon Allah will give the Believers a huge reward.** 4.147**Why should Allah punish you if you are thankful and you believe? Allah is always Appreciative, All-Knowing.**

[PART 6]

4.148**Allah doesn't like bad things spoken aloud, apart from** when someone has been treated unfairly. **Allah is always All-Hearing, All-Knowing.** 4.149**Whether you show or hide anything good** you do, **or forgive something bad,** you should know that **Allah is always Most Pardoning, All-Powerful.**

⁴·¹⁵⁰Those who disbelieve in Allah and His messengers and want to separate Allah from His messengers, and they say: "We believe in some but disbelieve in others," and they want to take a middle path between faith and disbelief, ⁴·¹⁵¹they are actually disbelievers. We have prepared a humiliating punishment for the disbelievers. ⁴·¹⁵²Those people who believe in Allah and His messengers without making distinctions between any of them, it is they He will soon give their rewards to. Allah is always Most Forgiving, Ever-Merciful.

⁴·¹⁵³The People of the Book ask you to bring down to them a book from heaven. They already did ask Musa for something even bigger than that; they said: "Show us Allah clearly," but a thunderbolt hit them for their unfair demand. Then, even after the clear signs had appeared to them, they began to worship the calf. However, We even then, forgave them for that and gave Musa clear authority over them. ⁴·¹⁵⁴We raised Mount Tur over their heads for their promise, and We told them: "Enter the gate with humility," and also: "Don't break the Sabbath," and We took a firm promise from them.

⁴·¹⁵⁵However, they were punished for breaking their firm promise, disbelieving in Allah's revelations, unjustly killing the prophets, and for saying: "Our hearts are wrapped up well and safe." The truth is, Allah has put a seal on their hearts because of their disbelief and so they have very little faith. ⁴·¹⁵⁶Their hearts are sealed because of their disbelief and their terrible accusation against Maryam, ⁴·¹⁵⁷and their claim: "We killed Maseeh Isa ibn Maryam – the Messenger of Allah – though they neither killed nor crucified him, but it was only made to appear to them. Even those who disagree about this are in doubt about it. They don't have any real knowledge about it except to follow guesswork. They definitely did not kill him! ⁴·¹⁵⁸In fact, Allah raised him up to Himself. Allah is always Almighty, All-Wise. ⁴·¹⁵⁹All the People of the Book will certainly believe in Maseeh Isa ibn Maryam

before his death after his second coming, **and he will be a witness against them on Judgement Day.**

4.160**We made wholesome things unlawful for the Jews that used to be lawful for them, all because of their wrongdoing, and because they blocked many people from Allah's cause;** 4.161**because they took usury when they had been forbidden to do so; and because they ate up other people's wealth wrongfully. We've prepared a painful punishment for the disbelievers among them.** 4.162**However: those among them who are firm in knowledge; as well as the Believers – they all believe in what is revealed to you,** O Prophet Muhammad, **and what was revealed before you; those who establish the ritual prayers; pay zakah; and believe in Allah and the Last Day – it is they We will soon give a huge reward to.**

4.163O Prophet Muhammad, **We have revealed to you as We revealed to Nuh and the prophets after him. We revealed to Ibrahim, Isma'il, Is'haq, Ya'qub, the Tribes, to Isa, Ayyub (Job), Yunus (Jonah), Haroon, and Sulayman, and We gave Dawud the Zabur.** 4.164O Prophet Muhammad, **there are messengers whose stories We have already told you about and others We haven't; Allah spoke to Musa directly.** 4.165**We sent messengers to give good news and warnings so that, after these messengers, there wouldn't be any excuse for people against Allah. Allah is always Almighty, All-Wise.**

4.166**However, Allah is witness that everything He revealed to you, He did so from His Own knowledge. The angels are witnesses too, even though only Allah being a Witness is enough.**

4.167**Those who disbelieve and block** people **from Allah's cause have gone far, far astray.** 4.168**Those who disbelieve and do wrong, they should know that Allah doesn't need to forgive them nor guide them** on any path, ^{4.169}other than their choosing the path to Hell. They will remain in Hell forever and ever. This is always easy for Allah.

^{4.170}People! The Messenger Muhammad has come to you with the truth from your Lord, so you must believe; it is best for you. If you disbelieve then you should know that everything in the heavens and the earth belongs to Allah. Allah is always All-Knowing, All-wise.

^{4.171}People of the Book! Don't be extreme in your religion, nor say anything about Allah other than the truth. Maseeh Isa ibn Maryam was only a messenger of Allah and His Word – which Allah passed to Maryam – and he was a Spirit from Him. You must believe in Allah and all His messengers. Never say "They are three gods." Stop! It is best for you. Allah is only One God. He is too glorious to have a child. Everything in the heavens and the earth belongs to Him. Allah is enough as a Guardian. ^{4.172}The Maseeh would never feel awkward in being a servant of Allah nor would the angels nearest to Him. Whoever feels awkward in worshipping Allah and shows arrogance, should remember that Allah will assemble them all together in front of Himself.

^{4.173}As for those who believe and do good, Allah will repay them their rewards in full, and even more from His grace. However, those who feel awkward and show arrogance, He will make them suffer a painful punishment. They won't find any protector or helper for themselves besides Allah.

^{4.174}People! A Proof (- Prophet Muhammad) has come to you from your Lord, and We have revealed a clear Light (- Qur'an) to you. ^{4.175}Those who believe in Allah and hold on strongly to the commands from Him, He will take them into His special mercy and grace, and He will guide them to Himself on a path that is straight.

4.176O Prophet Muhammad, they ask you for a ruling. Reply: "Allah gives you the ruling about someone who has neither ascendants nor descendants as heirs: if a man dies without a child but has a sister, for her is a half of what he leaves behind as inheritance: and he inherits her if she dies and has no child. If the sisters are two, both together will get two-thirds of what he leaves behind: if they are siblings – brothers with sisters – the brother has the equivalent share of two sisters." Allah makes His commands clear to you in case you go astray. Allah knows everything perfectly well.

Surah 5. Diningspread (al-Maa'idah)

Allah's name I begin with, the Most Compassionate, the Ever-Merciful

5.1Believers! You must fulfil all promises. Livestock animals have been made lawful for you as food, except those you will be told about – without making hunting lawful while you are in *ihram* (holy status of a pilgrim). Allah commands anything He wants.

5.2Believers! You mustn't disrespect Allah's sacred symbols, nor the sacred month, the sacrificial animal, the sacrificial animals decorated with garlands, and nor the pilgrims heading to the Sacred House trying to gain their Lord's grace and good pleasure. You are allowed to hunt once you're free from *ihram*. Some people's hatred, because they blocked you from the Sacred Masjid, mustn't make you overstep the limits. You must support each another in piety and mindfulness but never in sin and aggression. You must always be mindful of Allah. Allah is severe in punishing.

5.3Forbidden for you to eat are: dead meat, blood, pork, and the animal slaughtered in the name of anything other than Allah's; the animal killed by strangling, beating, falling, or gored; the animal which a wild animal has partly eaten – unless you slaughter it; the animal sacrificed on altars of idolatry. It is also unlawful if you take your share by drawing lots using arrows. All these are sins. Today, the disbelievers have given up all hope of defeating your religion, so don't be afraid of them but fear only Me. Today, I have made your religion perfect for you, completed My favour to you, and chosen Islam as the way of life for you. However, if someone is forced by hunger to eat anything unlawful, not intending to sin, then he should know that **Allah is Most Forgiving, Ever-Merciful.**

5.4 O Prophet Muhammad, **they ask you what is lawful for them. Reply: "All wholesome things are lawful for you,** and also what you've trained hunting animals to catch – if you've trained them according to how Allah has instructed you. You may eat from what they catch for you but first mention Allah's name over it." You must continue to be mindful of Allah. Allah is quick in settling accounts.

5.5 Today, all wholesome things have been made lawful for you. The food of the People of the Book is lawful for you and your food is lawful for them; as well as chaste women, from Believers and from those given the Book before you – who have you as their husbands – when you give them their dowries, intending marriage and spending on them and not unlawful sexual relations nor having secret lovers. Whoever rejects faith, his actions will be wasted, and in the Hereafter he will be among the losers.

5.6 Believers! When you get up to establish the ritual prayers, you must first **wash your faces, your hands and arms up to** and including **the elbows, wet-wipe your heads, and wash your feet up to** and including **the ankles. If you are in a state of major ritual impurity, then you must clean and purify yourselves** by taking a bath. However, if you are ill or travelling, or any of you comes after relieving himself, or after having sexual relations with women, and you cannot find any water, then you must clean yourselves through intention with clean earth, and wipe your faces and arms with it. Allah doesn't want to put you in any difficulty, but wants to clean and purify you and complete His favour to you so that you might become thankful. [5.7]You must continue to remember Allah's favour to you, and His firm promise that He took from you when you said: "We hear and obey." You must continue to be mindful of Allah. Allah knows the secrets of the hearts perfectly well.

[5.8]Believers! Be strong for Allah's sake, as witnesses to fairness. Even hating some people mustn't move you away from being fair. You must always be fair; it's the closest thing to being mindful of Allah. Always be mindful of Allah; He is Fully-Aware of everything you do.

[5.9]Allah has promised those people who believe and do good that they will have forgiveness and a huge reward. [5.10]However, those who disbelieve and call Our revelations a lie, it is they who will be the people of Hell-Fire.

[5.11]Believers! You must continue to remember Allah's favour to you when some people had decided to raise their hands to harm you but Allah held their hands back from you. You must continue to be mindful of Allah. True Believers must put their trust only in Him.

[5.12]Allah took a strong promise from the Descendants of Ya'qub, and We appointed twelve leaders from among them. Allah said: "I am on your side if you establish the ritual prayers, pay zakah, believe in My messengers, continuously help them, and give Allah a generous loan; I will certainly remove your sins from you, and enter you into gardens – that have rivers flowing beneath them; but if, after this, any of you disbelieves, then he has certainly strayed away from the Straight Way. ⁵·¹³Then, because they broke their promise, We cursed them and made their hearts hard. They changed the Words of Allah's revelation from their places, and neglected an important part of what they were told to do. O Prophet Muhammad, you will always find some sort of trickery coming from them, except from a few of them, but you should forgive them and ignore. Allah loves those who do good.

⁵·¹⁴We also took a strong promise from some of those who say: "We are Christians," but they too neglected an important part of what they were reminded to do. We, therefore, let enmity and hatred rage between them until Judgement Day. Allah will soon tell them everything they used to do.

⁵·¹⁵People of the Book! Our Messenger Muhammad has come to you exposing to you a lot of the Book that you've been hiding and He is forgiving a lot of your crimes. There has certainly come to you from Allah a Light (- Prophet Muhammad) and a clear Book (- Qur'an), ⁵·¹⁶by which Allah guides to the ways of peace anyone who tries to gain His good pleasure, and He brings them out of the depths of darkness into the light, by His authority, and guides them to a path that is straight.

⁵·¹⁷They have certainly disbelieved who say: "Allah is Maseeh ibn Maryam." Ask: "Then who has any power to stop Allah if He chooses to destroy Maseeh ibn Maryam, his mother, and everyone on earth, all together?" Control of the heavens and the earth and everything in between them belongs only to Allah. He can create whatever He wants, because He is Most Capable of anything.

⁵·¹⁸The Jews and Christians each claim: "We are Allah's children and most beloved to Him." Ask: "Then why does He punish you for your

sins? The truth is, you're only humans from among those He has created. He can forgive or punish anyone He chooses. Control of the heavens and the earth and everything in between them belongs only to Allah, and the final return will be to Him.

5.19People of the Book! Our Messenger has come to you after a time with no messengers, and he is making Our commands clear to you in case you say: "No one came to give us good news or warnings." Now there has come to you someone to give good news and warnings. Allah is Most Capable of anything.

5.20Remember when Musa said to his people: "My people! Remember Allah's favour to you when He sent you prophets from among you, made you kings, and gave you what He hadn't given anyone else in the whole world. 5.21My people! You may enter the Holy Land that Allah has given you, but never turn back or you will go back losers." 5.22They said: "Musa! There are people in this land who are tyrants. We're never going to enter it until they leave from it, and once they leave from it, only then will we enter." 5.23Two men from among those who were afraid of Allah and He had done favours to, they said: "Enter upon them through the gate. Once you've entered through it, you will certainly win, but you must put your trust only in Allah if you are true Believers." 5.24The people said: "Musa! We are still never ever going to enter this land as long as they're still there. So, you and your Lord may go and fight; we will sit right here."

5.25Musa prayed: "My Lord! I have control over only myself and my brother. Separate us from these disobedient people!" 5.26Allah replied: "This land is now forbidden to them for forty years. They will wander about in the earth aimlessly. You shouldn't feel sorry for these disobedient people."

5.27 O Prophet Muhammad, **tell them truthfully the story of Adam's two sons, when both offered a sacrifice and it was accepted from one (- Haabeel) and not from the other (- Qaabeel). The other said: "I'm definitely going to kill you!" The former replied: "Allah only accepts from people who are mindful of Him.** 5.28 Even if you raise your hand against me to kill me, I still won't raise my hand against you to kill you because I fear Allah – Lord of all the worlds. 5.29 I will let you bring down on yourself the sin of killing me as well as your previous sin, in which case you will be among the people of the Fire. That is the punishment of the wrongdoers." 5.30 Then, his lower self made killing his own brother easy for him; he killed him and became one of the losers. 5.31 Then Allah sent a crow that started scratching the ground to show him how to hide his brother's dead body. He cried: "I am damned! Couldn't I even be like this crow and hide my own brother's dead body?!" That is when he became regretful.

5.32 This is why We told the Descendants of Ya'qub that if someone kills a person – unless it's a legal punishment for murder or for making trouble in the world – it would be as if he had killed all the people: and if someone saves a person, it would be as if he had saved the lives of all the people. Our messengers have come to them with clear signs, yet even after all that, many of them still to go to extremes in the world.

5.33 The punishment of those who start war against Allah and His Messenger, and try their best to make trouble in the world, is that they should be killed or crucified, or their hands and feet be cut off from opposite sides, or they should be banished from the land. That will be their humiliation in this world and they will suffer a terrible punishment in the Hereafter, 5.34 but not those who repent before you arrest them. You must all know that Allah is Most Forgiving, Ever-Merciful.

5.35Believers! You must continue to: be mindful of Allah, look for ways to get close to Him, and strive hard in His cause so that you might be successful.

5.36If the disbelievers had everything in the world, and as much more with it, to offer it as ransom from the punishment of Judgement Day, it would never be accepted from them. They will suffer a painful punishment. 5.37They'll want to get out of the Fire but never will. They will suffer an everlasting punishment.

5.38You must cut off the hands of the male and female thieves as a punishment for what they did, and as a lesson of warning to others from Allah. Allah is Almighty, All-Wise. 5.39However, Allah can forgive anyone who repents after his crime and corrects himself. Allah is Most Forgiving, Ever-Merciful.

5.40Don't you know that control of the heavens and the earth belongs to Allah? He can forgive or punish anyone He chooses. Allah is Most Capable of anything.

5.41O Messenger! Those who race each other into disbelief shouldn't upset you, from among those who say with their mouths: "We believe," but their hearts don't believe; or from among the Jews who spy to make lies – they spy for others who haven't come to you, changing the words from their places, telling each other: "If you are given this order then take it, otherwise stay away." If Allah decides to test someone, you won't be able to do anything at all for him against Allah. They're the ones whose hearts Allah doesn't allow to be clean and pure. They will suffer disgrace in this world and a terrible punishment in the Hereafter.

5.42"They spy to make lies. They eat up unlawful things. O Prophet Muhammad, if they come to you then you may either judge between them or avoid them. If you avoid them, they won't be able to harm you in any way at all, but if you make judgements between them then do it with fairness. Allah loves those who are fair. 5.43But why are they making you give judgement when they have the Tawrah containing Allah's commands? Yet even after that they still turn away from the truth. They don't really believe in the Tawrah.

5.44We revealed the Tawrah with guidance and light inside it. The prophets – who really surrendered to Allah as Muslims – judged by it for the Jews, as did the holy people and the rabbis, because they were made to protect Allah's Book and be witnesses over it. So, you people mustn't be afraid of the people but fear only Me, and don't sell My revelations for a low price. Those who don't judge by what Allah has revealed, it is really they who are disbelievers.

5.45In the Tawrah, We prescribed for them: "Life for life, eye for eye, nose for nose, ear for ear, tooth for tooth, and the Law of Retaliation for wounds." However, if anyone forgives his right of retaliation by way of charity, it will be an atonement for himself. However, those who don't judge by what Allah has revealed, it is really they who are wrongdoers.

5.46In their footsteps, We sent Isa ibn Maryam, confirming the Tawrah that came before him. We gave him the Injeel with guidance and light inside it, confirming the Tawrah that came before it, and a guidance and a source of advice for those who are mindful of Allah. 5.47The People of the Injeel must give judgements by what Allah has revealed in it, because those who don't give judgements by what Allah has revealed, it is really they who are disobedient.

5.48 O Prophet Muhammad, **We revealed to you the Book (- Qur'an) with the truth, confirming and guarding some of the Book that came before it. So, you should give judgements between them by what Allah has revealed. Never follow their desires by leaving the truth that has come to you. We have made a** common law and an open path of individual lifestyle **for each one of you. If Allah had wanted, He could have made you all a single community** with the same facilities and lifestyle, **but He wants to test you with what He has given you. So, you must compete with each other in doing good. You will all go back to Allah, and He will tell you about the disagreements you used to have.**

5.49 **So, O Prophet Muhammad, you must judge between them by what Allah has revealed, and never follow their desires but beware of them** in case they **try and distract you from any of what Allah has revealed to you. If they turn away, then you should know that Allah chooses to make them suffer for some of their sins, and that many people are disobedient.** 5.50 **Are they looking for judgement from the Age of Ignorance before Islam? Who can give better judgement than Allah for any people who strongly believe!**

5.51 **Believers! Don't take** hostile **Jews or** hostile **Christians as protectors. They're only protectors of each other. Any of you who takes them as protectors will be counted as one of them. Allah doesn't let unjust people succeed.** 5.52 **O Prophet Muhammad, you will see that those** people **in whose hearts is sickness will be rushing to the Jews and Christians, saying: "We fear that a change of fortune will harm us." Perhaps Allah will bring victory or a decision** for you Muslims **from Himself, and then they will regret** the hypocrisy **they hid inside their hearts.** 5.53 **The Believers will say: "Are these the people who swore by Allah with their strongest oaths that they were on your side?" Their actions are wasted and they have become losers.**

⁵·⁵⁴Believers! If any of you turns away from his religion, Allah will very soon after bring about some people He will love and who will love Him, who are humble with the Believers, firm against the hostile disbelievers, striving hard in Allah's cause, and not fearing anyone's criticism. That is Allah's grace that He gives to anyone He chooses. Allah is All-Surrounding, All-Knowing.

⁵·⁵⁵Your only protectors are Allah, His Messenger, and those Believers – those who establish the ritual prayers, pay zakah, and bow down worshipping Allah. ⁵·⁵⁶Whoever takes Allah, His Messenger, and the Believers as protectors, should know that it is Allah's group that will win.

⁵·⁵⁷Believers! Don't take protectors from those who make a mockery and fun of your religion – from among those who were given the Book before you or from the disbelievers. You must continue to be mindful of Allah if you are true Believers. ⁵·⁵⁸When you call to ritual prayer, they make a mockery and fun of it. That is because they are a people who don't understand.

⁵·⁵⁹O Prophet Muhammad, say: "People of the Book! Do you hate us only because we believe in Allah, and what is sent down to us and what was sent down before, while most of you are disobedient?" ⁵·⁶⁰Say: "Shall I tell you who are far worse than this with regards to a punishment from Allah? They are those Allah has cursed and became angry with and changed some of them into apes and pigs, and also worse are those who worship fake gods. It is they who are in the worst position and furthest from the Straight Way."

⁵·⁶¹When they come to you Muslims, they claim: "We also believe," but in fact they entered your gathering with disbelief and left with it too.

Allah knows best what they were hiding. ⁵·⁶²You'll see many of them racing each other to sin, aggression, and their eating unlawful things. How terrible are the things they continue to do! ⁵·⁶³Why don't the holy people and the rabbis stop them from speaking sinful words and from eating unlawful things? How horrible are the things they continue to do!

⁵·⁶⁴The Jews said: "Allah is tight-fisted." May their own hands be tied up! May they be cursed for what they've said! In fact, Allah is open-handed, giving generously as He chooses. O Prophet Muhammad, that which has been revealed to you from your Lord will certainly increase rebellion and disbelief in many of them. We have placed enmity and hatred between them until Judgement Day. Each time they start the fire of war, Allah puts it out, but they still try their best to make trouble in the world. Allah doesn't like troublemakers.

⁵·⁶⁵If only the People of the Book believed and were mindful of Allah, We would certainly remove their sins from them and enter them into the Gardens of Delight. ⁵·⁶⁶If only they had applied the Tawrah, the Injeel, and anything else sent down to them from their Lord, they would have enjoyed plenty of food from above them and from below their feet. There is among them a group that is moderate, but what many of them do is terrible.

⁵·⁶⁷O Messenger, you must pass on everything revealed to you from your Lord. If you don't then you won't have delivered His Message. Allah will protect you from the people. Allah doesn't let disbelieving people succeed.

⁵·⁶⁸Say: "People of the Book! You aren't on the Right Path unless you apply the Tawrah, the Injeel, and anything else sent down to you from your Lord." O Prophet Muhammad, that which is revealed to

you from your Lord will certainly increase rebellion and disbelief in many of them, but you shouldn't feel sorry for these disbelieving people.

⁵·⁶⁹Those who believe as Muslims, as well as those who are Jews, Sabians or Christians – whoever believed in Allah and the Last Day and did good, they won't have anything to fear and will never be sad.

⁵·⁷⁰We took a promise from the Descendants of Ya'qub and sent them many messengers. Each time a messenger brought them something that they themselves didn't like, they accused some of them of being liars and others they murdered. ⁵·⁷¹They thought there would be no punishment for them, so they stopped looking or listening, yet Allah still forgave them. Then, again, many of them stopped looking or listening. Allah is Ever-Watchful of everything they do.

⁵·⁷²Those who say: "Allah is Maseeh ibn Maryam," have certainly become disbelievers, because the Maseeh himself said: "Descendants of Ya'qub! You must worship Allah – my Lord and yours too." Allah has forbidden Paradise to anyone who makes partners with Him, and his home will be the Fire. The wrongdoers won't have any helpers. ⁵·⁷³Those who say: "Allah is the third of three gods," have also become disbelievers, because there is no god except Allah – the One God. If they don't stop what they're saying, the disbelievers among them will certainly suffer a painful punishment. ⁵·⁷⁴Aren't they going to repent to Allah and beg Him to forgive them? Allah is Most Forgiving, Ever-Merciful.

⁵·⁷⁵Maseeh ibn Maryam was only a messenger. Many messengers have been and gone before him. His mother was a truthful woman and they both used to eat food. Take a look at how We make the signs clear to

the disbelievers, and then just take a look at how they are being misled!

5.76Ask them, O Prophet Muhammad: "Are you people worshipping, besides Allah, something that has no power to harm or help you? Only Allah is the All-Hearing, the All-Knowing." 5.77Say: "People of the Book! You mustn't go to extremes in your religion beyond the truth nor follow the desires of any people who: previously went astray, misguided many others, and then continued to stray further from the Straight Way.

5.78The disbelievers from among the Descendants of Ya'qub were cursed by the tongues of Dawud and of Isa ibn Maryam. That was because they disobeyed and used to break the law. 5.79They wouldn't stop each other from the bad things they were doing. How horrible were the things they used to do! 5.80You see many of them taking disbelievers as protectors. How horrible are the things they've done for themselves, such that Allah is now angry with them! They will remain in punishment forever. 5.81If only they had believed in Allah, in the Prophet Muhammad, and in what has been revealed to him, they wouldn't have taken those disbelievers as protectors, but many of them are disobedient.

5.82You will certainly find the Jews and polytheists to be the worst enemies of the Believers, and the friendliest to the Believers are those who say: "We are Christians." This is because there are priests and monks among them, and because they don't behave arrogantly.

[PART 7]

5.83When they listen to what is revealed to the Messenger Muhammad, you see their eyes overflowing with tears because of the truth they recognise. They pray: "Our Lord! We believe, so count us among those who witness the truth. 5.84Why shouldn't we believe in Allah when the truth has come to us? We hope our Lord will enter us in the company of righteous people." ⁵·⁸⁵So, because of what they said, Allah rewarded them with gardens – that have rivers flowing beneath them, where they will remain forever. That is the reward of those who do good. ⁵·⁸⁶However, those who disbelieve and call Our revelations a lie, it is they who will be the people of Hell-Fire.

⁵·⁸⁷Believers! Don't make unlawful the wholesome things Allah has made lawful for you, and don't overstep the limits either. Allah doesn't like those who overstep the limits. ⁵·⁸⁸You must eat from the lawful, wholesome things Allah has given you. Keep being mindful of Allah because you believe in Him.

⁵·⁸⁹Allah won't punish you for the oaths you make without thinking but He will punish you for breaking the oaths you make deliberately. Its penalty is to: feed ten needy people from the average of what you feed your own families; or give them clothes; or free a slave. Anyone who cannot afford these must fast for three days. This is the penalty for breaking your oaths after you've made them; so fulfil your oaths. This is how Allah makes His revelations clear to you so that you might become thankful.

⁵·⁹⁰Believers! Intoxicants, gambling, worshipping idols, and divining arrows are from Shaytan's filthy doings. Stay clear of them so you can be successful. ⁵·⁹¹With intoxicants and gambling, Shaytan wants to stir up enmity and hatred between you, and to stop you from remembering Allah and from ritual prayers. Won't you give them up? ⁵·⁹²You have to obey Allah and the Messenger too, and continue to be careful. If you turn away, you should know that Our Messenger's duty is only to deliver the message clearly. ⁵·⁹³Those who believe and do good, there won't be any sin on them for anything they may have eaten before the law came as long as they were mindful of Allah,

believed, and did good; and again, they still **remain mindful of Allah and believe**; and again, they will **continue to remain mindful of Allah and do good. Allah loves those who do good.**

5.94**Believers! Allah will certainly test you** by putting **within reach of your hands and spears something of the animals you hunt, to prove those who fear Him without seeing Him. Anyone who breaks the law after that will suffer a painful punishment.** 5.95**Believers! Don't kill any hunted animal while you're in pilgrim clothing. If any of you kills it deliberately, the punishment is: an offering to reach the Ka'bah of a domestic animal similar to the one he killed – as judged by two men among you who are completely fair; or a penalty of food to needy people, or fasting equal to it – so he gets to taste the seriousness of what he did. Allah forgives what is past, but He will punish anyone who does it again. Allah is Almighty, Capable of Revenge.**

5.96**Catching seafood and eating it is lawful for you, to benefit you and travellers too, but animals hunted on land are unlawful for you as long as you are in** *ihram*. **You must continue to be mindful of Allah in front of Whom you will all be assembled.**

5.97**Allah has made the Ka'bah – the Sacred House – a means of safety for people, as well as the Sacred Months, the sacrificial animals, and the** sacrificial animals decorated with **garlands. This so you realise that Allah knows everything in the heavens and the earth, and that He knows everything perfectly well.** 5.98**You should know that Allah is severe in punishing, but He is also Most Forgiving, Ever-Merciful.** 5.99**The Messenger's duty is only to deliver the message, and Allah knows what you show or hide.**

5.100**O Prophet Muhammad, say: "Good and bad can never be the same, even though the abundance of bad might surprise you. So, you must** continue to be mindful of Allah, O people of understanding, so that you might be successful."

[5.101] Believers! Don't ask questions about things which, if made clear to you, might put you in difficulty. However, they will be made clear to you if you ask about them when the Qur'an is being revealed. Allah has left them out. He is Most Forgiving, Most Tolerant. [5.102] Some people before you did ask questions about them, but then they ended up rejecting the answers.

[5.103] **Allah didn't make** the beliefs they made up about **any Baheerah, Saa'ibah, Waseelah or Haam** camels, but the disbelievers make up lies about Allah when most of them can't even think. [5.104] When they're told: "Come to what Allah has revealed, and also to the Messenger Muhammad," they reply: "What we saw our forefathers doing is enough for us." What? Even if their forefathers didn't know anything and weren't following guidance?

[5.105] Believers! Protect yourselves. Someone who is astray cannot harm you when you are following guidance. You will all go back to Allah and then He will tell you about everything you used to do.

[5.106] Believers! When death comes to any of you, when making a will, you should make witnesses between you of two men from among you who are completely fair, or if you're travelling in the land, and the disaster of death hits you, witnessing may be done by two men other than from those among you. If you are in doubt, keep both of them back after prayer, and they should swear: "By Allah, we would never sell our testimony for any price, even if it is about a close relative. We would never hide the testimony bound by Allah, or else we would certainly be among the sinful people." [5.107] However, if it becomes known that they are guilty of lying, then two others from among those who have the most right should replace them and swear: "By Allah, our testimony is certainly more truthful than theirs. We haven't overstepped the limits or else we would certainly be among the wrongdoers." ⁵·¹⁰⁸That will make it more likely for them to give evidence properly, and they will fear that other oaths could go against their oaths. You must continue to be mindful of Allah and listen. Allah doesn't let disobedient people succeed.

⁵·¹⁰⁹On the Day when Allah will gather the messengers together and ask: "What response were you given?" they will reply: "We have no knowledge. Only You are the Knower of the unseen secrets."

⁵·¹¹⁰Allah will say: "Isa ibn Maryam, remember My favour to you and to your mother, when I gave you strength through the Holy Spirit (- Angel Jibra'il), you spoke to the people while you were a baby in the cradle and also in maturity; when I taught you the Book and wisdom, the Tawrah and the Injeel; when you made the figure of a bird out of clay – with My permission, and breathed into it and it became a flying bird – with My permission; you healed those who were born blind, and lepers too – with My permission; and when you brought the dead back to life – with My permission; and when I held back the Descendants of Ya'qub from harming you when you brought them clear signs and the disbelievers among them said, 'This is clearly magic,' ⁵·¹¹¹how I inspired the Disciples, 'Believe in Me and in My Messenger Isa,' and they replied, 'We believe, and be witness, O Allah, that we surrender to You as Muslims.'."

⁵·¹¹²When the Disciples asked: "Isa ibn Maryam, can your Lord send down to us a diningspread with food from heaven?" He replied: "Be mindful of Allah if you are true Believers!" ⁵·¹¹³They said: "We only want to eat from it and satisfy our hearts, to be sure that you have told us the truth, and for us to be among those who witness it." ⁵·¹¹⁴Isa

ibn Maryam prayed: "O Allah – our Lord! Send us a diningspread with food from heaven, that it may be a Day of Celebration for the first of us and the last of us, and a sign from You; and give us even more food, because You are the Best Giver of all." [5.115]Allah answered: "I am going to send it down to you, but if any of you disbelieves afterwards, I will make him suffer such a punishment that I won't inflict on anyone else in the whole world."

[5.116]Allah will say: "Isa ibn Maryam, did you tell the people, 'Make me and my mother as two gods besides Allah.'?" He will reply: "Glory be to You! How could I say what I had no right to. You would certainly have known it if I ever did say such a thing. You know what is in my heart though I don't know what is in Your knowledge. Only You are the Knower of the unseen secrets. [5.117]I only told them what You had ordered me to say, that, 'You must worship Allah – my Lord and yours too.' I witnessed what they did as long as I was among them, but when You took me up, You watched over them Yourself. You are a Witness to everything. [5.118]If You punish them, You can because they are Your servants; but if You forgive them, only You are the Almighty, the All-Wise." [5.119]Allah will say: "This is the Day when the truthfulness of truthful people will benefit them. They will have gardens – that have rivers flowing beneath them, where they will remain forever and ever. Allah is well-pleased with them and they are well-pleased with Him. This is the tremendous victory." [5.120]Control of the heavens and the earth and everything within them belongs only to Allah. He is Most Capable of anything.

Surah 6. Cattle (al-An'aam)

Allah's name I begin with, the Most Compassionate, the Ever-Merciful

6.1 All praise is for Allah Who created the heavens and the earth, and the many layers of darkness and the light, yet the disbelievers still make others equal to their Lord. 6.2 He is the one Who created you people from clay, and then fixed an end date when you die, and there is another end date fixed with Him for Judgement Day, yet you continue to doubt! 6.3 He is Allah in the heavens and the earth. He knows your secrets and what you show openly, as well as everything you do.

6.4 Whenever a sign of their Lord appears to them, they turn away from it. 6.5 Whenever the truth came to them, they called it a lie. However, the details of what they used to make fun of will come to them very soon.

6.6 Don't they see how many generations We have destroyed before them? We had given them more power in this world than We've given you. We sent them plenty of rain and made rivers flow beneath them, yet We destroyed them because of their sins and raised up other generations after them.

6.7 O Prophet Muhammad, if We had revealed to you a book written on paper, which the disbelievers could have touched with their own hands, they would have still said: "This is clearly magic." 6.8 They ask: "Why wasn't an angel sent down to him?" If We did send down an angel, the matter would have been settled immediately, and they wouldn't have been given any chances. 6.9 If We had made the Messenger an angel, We would have still made him in the form of a man, leaving them in the same confusion.

^{6.10}O Prophet Muhammad, many **messengers before you were also mocked** but the punishment the mockers used to make fun of ended up punishing them. ^{6.11}Say: "Travel through the earth, and then take a look at what was the end result of those who called the truth a lie."

^{6.12}Ask: "Whose is everything in the heavens and the earth?" Reply: "Allah's." He has chosen Himself to be Merciful. He will certainly gather all of you together on Judgement Day in which there is no doubt. However, those who have ruined themselves, they still won't believe. ^{6.13}Everything belongs to Allah, whether it rests at night or day. He is the All-Hearing, the All-Knowing.

^{6.14}Ask: "Would I take a protector other than Allah – the Maker of the heavens and the earth, Who feeds others but doesn't Himself need to be fed?" Reply: "I've been ordered to be the first to surrender to Allah as Muslim, and, 'You must never be a polytheist.'." ^{6.15}Say: "I fear the punishment of a Dreadful Day if I disobey my Lord." ^{6.16}On that Day, Allah will have certainly been merciful to anyone the punishment is turned away from. That is the clear victory.

^{6.17}If Allah gives you suffering, no one can remove it except Him. If He gives you something good, then that is because He is Most Capable of anything. ^{6.18}He is the Supreme Master over His servants, and He is the All-Wise, the Fully-Aware.

^{6.19}Ask: "Who is the greatest witness?" Reply: "Allah is. He is a Witness between me and you all. This Qur'an has been revealed to me to warn by it you and anyone it reaches. Do you really testify that there are other gods together with Allah?" Say: "I won't testify to that!" Then say: "He is only One God, and I have nothing to do with the partner-gods you make with Him."

⁶·²⁰The People of the Book recognise Messenger Muhammad as the last prophet like they recognise their own children. However, those who have ruined themselves, they still won't believe. ⁶·²¹Who could be more unjust than someone who makes lies about Allah or calls His revelations a lie! The wrongdoers will never succeed.

⁶·²²One Day We will gather them all together and then ask the polytheists: "Where are those you used to claim to be your partner-gods with Allah?" ⁶·²³Then there won't be any excuse left for them but to say: "By Allah – Our Lord! We were never polytheists." ⁶·²⁴Just look at how they will lie against themselves, and how the idols they made up will abandon them!

⁶·²⁵O Prophet Muhammad, some of them only pretend they're listening to you, and so We've put covers over their hearts so they won't be able to understand it, and deafness in their ears too. Even if the disbelievers saw every sign, they still won't believe in them, such that when they come to you to argue with you, they can only say: "This Qur'an is nothing but stories made up by previous people!" ⁶·²⁶They keep other people away from it and run from it themselves. They aren't even aware that they are destroying only themselves.

⁶·²⁷If only you could see when they will be made to stand over the Fire, they will cry: "Oh! If only we could be sent back to the world then we wouldn't say our Lord's signs are lies. We would be Believers!" ⁶·²⁸Never! Everything they were hiding before will appear to them clearly. However, if they were sent back, they would certainly go back to doing what they were forbidden because they are definitely liars.

⁶·²⁹They claim: "There's nothing beyond our life in this world, and we won't be brought back to life." ⁶·³⁰If only you could see when they will

be made to stand in front of their Lord. He will ask: "Isn't this life after death real?" They will reply: "Yes, of course! We swear by our Lord!" He will say: "Now taste the punishment because you used to disbelieve." ⁶·³¹Those people have already lost who call the meeting with Allah a lie. When the Last Hour will suddenly come upon them, they will cry: "Ah! We are damned for neglecting this!" They will be carrying their burdens of sins on their backs. Beware! How terrible is the burden they will be carrying!

⁶·³²This life is just games and some kind of amusement, but the Home of the Hereafter is best for those who are mindful of Allah. Won't you people even think?

⁶·³³O Prophet Muhammad, We already know what they say upsets you, but it isn't you they're accusing of being a liar. In fact, these wrongdoers are rejecting Allah's revelations. ⁶·³⁴Messengers before you were also accused of being liars – but they had patience with the allegations they faced and the injuries they suffered – until Our help came to them. Nothing can change Allah's words, as some stories of other messengers have reached you proving this.

⁶·³⁵If their turning away from the truth is unbearable for you then bring them a stronger sign if you can find a tunnel into the ground or a ladder into the sky. If Allah had wanted, He could have gathered them together in guidance. So, O human, don't be one of those who are ignorant. ⁶·³⁶Only those who listen will respond. Allah will bring the dead back to life, then it is Him they will all be taken back to. ⁶·³⁷They ask: "Why wasn't a permanent sign sent down to him from his Lord?" Reply: "Allah has the power to send down any kind of sign but most of them don't know."

6.38All the animals in the earth and the birds that fly on their wings are communities just like you humans. We haven't left out anything from the Book. Eventually, it is in front of their Lord they will be assembled.

6.39Those who call Our revelations a lie are deaf and dumb – lost in the depths of darkness. Allah lets anyone He chooses wander astray or puts him on a path that is straight.

6.40O Prophet Muhammad, ask: "What do you think: if Allah's punishment or the Final Hour came to you people, if you were being honest, would you call out to anyone other than Allah? 6.41Never! It is only Him you would call out to, and if He chooses, He can remove the difficulties for which you called out to Him, and you will forget those you had made partner-gods with Him."

6.42We sent messengers to many communities before you, and when they disobeyed, We made them poor and weak so that they might humble themselves. 6.43If only they had humbled themselves when Our hardship came to them! Instead, their hearts became hard, and Shaytan made the bad things they were doing seem attractive to them. 6.44However, when they ignored what they had been reminded of, We opened up the gates to everything good for them. As they rejoiced in what they were given, We punished them suddenly, and that is when they lost all hope. 6.45The wrongdoers were uprooted. All praise is for Allah – Lord of all the worlds.

6.46O Prophet Muhammad, ask: "What do you think: if Allah took away your hearing and sight, and sealed up your hearts, then what god other than Allah could give them back to you?" Take a look at how We vary the signs, yet they still turn away. 6.47Ask: "What do you think: if Allah's punishment comes upon you, whether suddenly or openly, will anyone be destroyed apart from the people who are unjust?"

⁶·⁴⁸We send messengers only to give good news and warnings. So, those who believe and correct themselves, they won't have anything to fear and will never be sad. ⁶·⁴⁹However, those who call Our revelations a lie, they will suffer punishment because of their disobedience.

⁶·⁵⁰O Prophet Muhammad, say: "I'm not saying to you that I have Allah's treasures nor that I personally know the unseen secrets, and nor am I saying to you that I'm an angel. I follow only what is revealed to me." Ask: "Can the blind and the seeing person be equal? Won't you think deeply?"

⁶·⁵¹Using this Qur'an, warn those who fear they will be gathered in front of their Lord without having any protector or intercessor apart from Him, so that they might continue to be mindful of Him.

⁶·⁵²Don't push away those poor Muslims who pray to their Lord morning and evening, wishing to gain His good pleasure. O Prophet Muhammad, you aren't responsible for them in any way at all nor are they responsible for you, but you would still be among those who are unjust if you did push them away. ⁶·⁵³In this way We test some of them by others so the rich disbelievers may joke about the poor Believers: "Out of all of us, are these the people Allah has done favours to?" Doesn't Allah know best those who are thankful? ⁶·⁵⁴O Prophet Muhammad, when those who believe in Our revelations come to you, you should say: "Peace be upon you." Your Lord has chosen Himself to be Merciful. If any of you does something bad without knowing, and then repents afterwards and corrects himself, he will see that Allah is Most Forgiving, Ever-Merciful. ⁶·⁵⁵This is how We explain the

revelations in detail, and so that the way of the criminals becomes clearly separate and known.

6.56O Prophet Muhammad, say: "I'm forbidden to worship those you pray to besides Allah." Say: "I don't follow your desires or else I would be astray and not among those who follow guidance."

6.57Say: "I'm on a clear proof from my Lord, yet you call it a lie. I don't have that punishment which you want to bring sooner. The decision is only Allah's. He tells the truth. He is the Best Decider of all." 6.58Say: "If that punishment which you want to bring sooner was in my power, the matter between me and you would have already been settled. Allah knows best those who are wrongdoers."

6.59Only He has the keys to the unseen secrets; only He personally knows those keys. He also knows everything in the land and sea. A leaf doesn't fall without Him knowing it. Any seed in the depths of darkness inside the ground, and anything moist or dry, it is all written in a record that is clear.

6.60He is the one Who takes away your souls at night and knows what you've done during the day, then He wakes you up in it again for an end date of your life to be completed. Eventually, you will all go back to Him, and He will tell you about everything you used to do. 6.61He is the Supreme Master over His servants. He sends guardian-angels over you, such that when death comes to any of you, the angels We send take away his soul, never neglecting their duty. 6.62Then they will be returned to Allah, their True Master. Beware! The command is only His, and He is the quickest in settling accounts.

6.63O Prophet Muhammad, ask: "Who saves you from the many layers of darkness in the land and sea? You pray to Him with humility and in private, 'If He saves us from this, we will certainly be thankful.'." ⁶·⁶⁴Reply: "It is Allah Who saves you from it, and from every other kind of difficulty too, yet you still make partner-gods with Him!" ⁶·⁶⁵Say: "Only He has the power to send on you a punishment from above you or from right under your legs, and all around you, or split you up into groups and make you taste each other's violence." Take a look at how We vary the signs so they can understand.

⁶·⁶⁶Your people called this Qur'an a lie, though it is the truth. O Prophet Muhammad, say: "I am not responsible for you." ⁶·⁶⁷Every prophecy has a fixed time and place, and you will very soon find out.

⁶·⁶⁸When you see people mocking Our revelations, you should stay away from them unless they start talking about something else. If Shaytan ever makes you forget, then after remembering, you mustn't continue to sit with those unjust people. ⁶·⁶⁹Those who are mindful of Allah aren't responsible for the mockers in any way at all, but giving reminders is the Believers' duty so that they too might become mindful of Allah.

⁶·⁷⁰O Prophet Muhammad, you should leave those who have turned their own religion into just games and some kind of amusement, and this life has tricked them, but you should continue to give reminders by the Qur'an so no person is ruined by what he has done. He will have no protector or intercessor apart from Allah. Any kind of ransom he offers, it would still not be accepted from him. They're the ones who are ruined by what they've done. They will have to drink a boiling liquid and suffer a painful punishment because they used to disbelieve.

⁶·⁷¹O Prophet Muhammad, ask: "Besides Allah, should we pray to things that can neither help nor harm us, and lose our faith after

Allah has guided us, like someone the evil ones have led astray and he is **wandering confused in the wilderness though he has friends calling him to guidance, 'Come to us!'?"** Reply: "Only Allah's guidance is the real guidance." We have been ordered to surrender as Muslims to Allah – the Lord of all the worlds, ^{6.72}that: "you must establish the ritual prayers and be mindful of Him." It is in front of Him you will all be assembled. ^{6.73}He is the one Who created the heavens and the earth for a real purpose. One Day He will say: "Be!" and it will be! What He says is the truth. The kingdom will be only His on the Day the Trumpet will be blown. Only He knows both the unseen secrets and the visible. He is the All-Wise, the Fully-Aware.

^{6.74}Remember **when Ibrahim said to his foster father Aazar: "Are you worshipping idols as gods? I can see that you and your people are clearly astray."** ^{6.75}In this way We showed Ibrahim the kingdoms of the heavens and the earth, so that he might become one of the strong believers. ^{6.76}So, when the night covered him, he saw a star. He asked: "Do you think this is my Lord?" But when it went away, he said: "I don't like things that go away." ^{6.77}Then, when he saw the moon coming up, he asked: "Do you think this is my Lord?" But when it also went away, he said: "If my Lord hadn't guided me, I would certainly have become one of those people who go astray." ^{6.78}Then, when he saw the sun coming up, he asked: "Do you think this is my Lord? This is the biggest." But when it also went away, he said: "My people! I have nothing to do with the partner-gods you make with Allah. ^{6.79}I've turned my face sincerely to the one Who made the heavens and the earth, and I'm not a polytheist."

^{6.80}When **his people argued with him, he replied: "Are you disputing with me about Allah when He has guided me? I'm not afraid of anything you make partner-gods with Him, unless my Lord decides something** to happen to me. My Lord surrounds everything in His

knowledge. So, won't you even remind yourselves? ⁶·⁸¹How can I be afraid of the things you make partner-gods with Allah while you yourselves don't even fear that you are making partner-gods with Him when He hasn't given you any permission? So, which of the two groups has more right to be safe from punishment, if you know?" ⁶·⁸²Those who believe without mixing their faith with anything wrong, it is they who will be safe because they follow guidance. ⁶·⁸³That was Our proof We gave Ibrahim to use against his people. We raise up in ranks anyone We choose. Your Lord is All-Wise, All-Knowing.

⁶·⁸⁴We gave him Is'haq and Ya'qub. We guided them all. Previously, We had guided Nuh, and among his descendants, Dawud, Sulayman, Ayyub, Yusuf (Joseph), Musa, and Haroon. This is how We reward those who do good. ⁶·⁸⁵We also guided Zakariyya, Yahya, Isa, and Ilyas (Elijah/Elias). They are all from among righteous people. ⁶·⁸⁶Also Isma'il, al-Yasa' (Elisha), Yunus, and Lut (Lot). We made each of them superior to all the people of their time. ⁶·⁸⁷We also guided some of their forefathers, children, and siblings. We selected and guided them to a path that is straight.

⁶·⁸⁸This is Allah's guidance. He guides with it any of His servants He chooses. However, if they made partner-gods with Him, anything good they used to do would have been wasted for them. ⁶·⁸⁹They're the ones We gave the Book, authority, and prophethood. So, if these people of Makkah disbelieve in these things now then they should know that in charge of these things We have put some people who won't disbelieve in them. ⁶·⁹⁰They're the ones Allah has guided, so you must follow their guidance. Say: "I'm not asking you any payment for this Qur'an. It's a reminder for everyone."

⁶·⁹¹The Jews **didn't truly appreciate Allah when they said: "Allah didn't reveal anything to any human."** O Prophet Muhammad, ask: **"Then Who revealed the Book which Musa brought as a light and guidance for people? You have split it into** separate **sheets, showing some but hiding a lot. You have been taught what neither you nor your forefathers knew."** Reply: **"Allah** revealed it." Then leave them playing their own silly games.

⁶·⁹²**This Qur'an is a blessed Book We have revealed, confirming what had come before it, and for you,** O Prophet Muhammad, **to** firstly **warn the Mother of Cities (- Makkah) and then everyone around it. Those who believe in the Hereafter also believe in this too, and they also look after their prayers.**

⁶·⁹³**Who could be more unjust than someone who makes lies about Allah, or claims: "A revelation was given to me… ," when nothing was revealed to him, or who says: "I will send down something like what Allah has sent down."! If only you could see when the wrongdoers will be suffering the agonies of death while the angels will be stretching out their hands,** saying: **"Give up your souls! Today you will be given a punishment of humiliation because of the untrue things you used to say about Allah, and because you used to arrogantly reject His revelations."** ⁶·⁹⁴**Now that you've come to Us all alone – just like We created you the first time, and you've left behind you everything We gave you. We don't see your intercessors with you – those you claimed to be your partner-gods with Allah! The links between you all are now cut off, and the claims you used to make have also abandoned you.**

⁶·⁹⁵**It is Allah Who splits open the seeds and fruit-stones** to sprout. **He brings out the living from the dead and the dead from the living. That is Allah. So how are you being misled!** ⁶·⁹⁶**Only He breaks the morning.**

He made the night for rest, and the sun and moon for calculating time. This is the fixed plan of Allah – the Almighty, the All-Knowing. ^{6.97}He is the one Who made the stars for you to guide yourselves with through the many layers of darkness in the land and sea. We have explained the signs in detail for any people who have the right knowledge. ^{6.98}He is the one Who created you from a single person, then gave you a time and place to live and a time and place to go in death. We have explained the signs in detail for any people who understand. ^{6.99}He is the one Who sends down from the sky water with which We bring out plants of all kinds: from which We bring out green stalks, while from them We bring out close-packed grains. Out of the spathes of palm trees come bunches of low-hanging dates. We bring out gardens of grapes, olives, and pomegranates – that look the same yet they are different. As they begin to bear fruit, just watch their fruits and their ripening too. There are certainly signs in these for any people who believe.

^{6.100}Some people make the jinns partner-gods with Allah though He is the one Who created them, and out of ignorance, they attribute sons and daughters to Him. Glory be to Him! He is much higher than what they describe! ^{6.101}He is the Originator of the heavens and the earth. How can He have a child when He doesn't even have a wife? He created everything! He knows everything perfectly well. ^{6.102}That is Allah – your Lord! There is no god except Him. He is the Creator of every thing, so worship Him, and He is in charge of every thing. ^{6.103}No vision can track Him though He can track every vision. He knows all details, the Fully-Aware.

^{6.104}Now that clear proofs have come to you from your Lord, anyone who sees, it will be for his own good; anyone who remains blind to the truth, does so to his own loss. I won't be watching over you. ^{6.105}This is how We vary the signs so the disbelievers can say: "You

have studied from somewhere," and so We can make it clear for any people who have the right knowledge.

6.106O Prophet Muhammad, follow what is revealed to you from your Lord – there is no god except Him, and turn away from the polytheists. 6.107If Allah had wanted to force them, they wouldn't have made partner-gods with Him, but We haven't sent you to watch over them, nor are you responsible for them.

6.108You Muslims must never insult anything they pray to besides Allah or they will, in enmity, insult Allah out of ignorance. In this way We made the actions of every nation seem attractive to them. Eventually, they will go back to their Lord and He will tell them about everything they used to do.

6.109With their strongest oaths, they swear by Allah that if a miraculous sign appeared to them, they will definitely believe in it. O Prophet Muhammad, say: "The signs come only from Allah. What will make you Muslims realise that even if that miraculous sign did appear, they still won't believe?" 6.110We will turn their intelligence and sight upside down as they didn't believe in it the first time. We will leave them confused to wander blindly in their rebellion.

[PART 8]

6.111Even if We sent them angels, the dead spoke to them, and We gathered everything together in front of them, they still won't believe – except what Allah decided. However, most of them behave ignorantly.

6.112In this way We made for every messenger, enemies – evil ones from both humans and jinns, influencing each other with attractive words to cheat. If your Lord had wanted, they couldn't have done that. So, leave them as well as the lies they are making; 6.113and so that the hearts of those who don't believe in the Hereafter can be attracted to this trickery, so they might be pleased with it and will continue doing the bad things they are doing.

6.114O Prophet Muhammad, ask: "Would I look for a judge other than Allah when He is the one Who has sent down to you the Book explained in detail?" Those We gave the Book to know for sure that this Qur'an has been sent down from your Lord with the truth, so you'll never be one of those who doubt. 6.115Your Lord's promise will be fulfilled in truth and justice. Nothing can change His promises. He is the All-Hearing, the All-Knowing.

6.116Most people in this world, if you followed them, will lead you away from Allah's cause. They're only following suspicion; they are only guessing. 6.117It is your Lord Who knows best anyone who strays from His cause as well as those who follow guidance.

6.118So, you may eat only from those lawful slaughtered animals on which Allah's name has been mentioned, if you believe in His revelations. 6.119Not including the unlawful foods you are forced to eat, how could you not wilfully eat from those lawful slaughtered animals on which Allah's name has been mentioned when He has explained to you in detail the foods He has made unlawful for you? Many people, based on their desires and out of ignorance, are leading others astray. It is your Lord Who knows best those who break the law. 6.120You must avoid sins, both open and secret. Those who do bad things will soon be punished for everything bad they've been doing. 6.121You mustn't eat from those lawful slaughtered animals on which Allah's name hasn't been mentioned. It's a sin. The evil ones keep influencing their companions to argue with you. If you obeyed them, you would also become polytheists.

⁶·¹²²**Someone We brought back to life** in Islam **when he was dead** in disbelief, **and gave him a light** of faith **by which he can walk among people, can he be like someone who is** trapped **in the depths of darkness** of disbelief, **unable to escape from it? This is how the things the disbelievers used to do were made to seem attractive to them.** ⁶·¹²³**In the same way, We made the leaders in every town its criminals so they could do fraud in it. However, they aren't** even **aware that they're doing fraud only against themselves.**

⁶·¹²⁴**When a sign appears to them, they say: "We won't believe until we are also given something like Allah's messengers were given." Allah knows best where to place His Message. The criminals will soon suffer humiliation in front of Allah, as well as a severe punishment because of the fraud they used to do.**

⁶·¹²⁵**Anyone Allah chooses to guide, He opens up their heart to Islam; but anyone He leaves to go astray, He makes their chest tight, cramped as if they were climbing up into the sky. This is how Allah disgraces those who don't believe.** ⁶·¹²⁶**This is your Lord's Path, leading straight. We have already explained the revelations in detail for any people who learn lessons.** ⁶·¹²⁷**They will have the Home of Peace with their Lord. He is their Protector because of the good things they used to do.**

⁶·¹²⁸**On the Day He will gather them all together and say: "O assembly of jinns! You have made many human beings** go astray," **their human friends will say: "Our Lord! We benefitted from each other but now we've reached the end of our time which You fixed for us." He will reply: "The Fire will be your place to stay, where you will remain forever – unless Allah decides something else. Your Lord is All-Wise, All-Knowing."** ⁶·¹²⁹**In this way We make some wrongdoers overpower other wrongdoers because of the bad things they continue to do.**

⁶·¹³⁰"O assembly of jinns and humans! Didn't some messengers from among you come to you, reciting My revelations to you and warning you of the meeting of this Day of yours?" They will reply: "We testify against ourselves." This life had tricked them, so they will testify against themselves that they were disbelievers. ⁶·¹³¹That sending of messengers was because your Lord would never destroy the towns for wrongdoing when their people were unaware of the truth.

⁶·¹³²All people have different ranks according to what they did, and Your Lord isn't unaware of anything they do.

⁶·¹³³Your Lord, being Free of all Needs, is the Lord of Mercy. If He wanted, He could get rid of you all and make successors after you anyone He chose, just like He raised you up from the descendants of other people. ⁶·¹³⁴Everything you are being promised will certainly happen, and you won't be able to escape.

⁶·¹³⁵O Prophet Muhammad, say: "My people! Continue working as you all are; I am also working. You will very soon come to know who will have the best end in the Hereafter. The wrongdoers will never succeed."

⁶·¹³⁶The polytheists fix a share for Allah out of the crops and cattle He created, and they say, according to their claim: "This share is for Allah and this share is for our partner-gods," but their partner-gods' share doesn't reach Allah whereas Allah's share reaches their partner-gods. How terrible are the decisions they make!

⁶·¹³⁷In the same way, to destroy the polytheists and confuse them in their religion, their partner-gods made killing their own children seem attractive to a lot of them. If Allah had chosen, they couldn't have done that. So, leave them and also the lies they make.

⁶·¹³⁸They also say, according to their claim: "These livestock and crops are restricted. Only the people We allow may eat them." There are livestock whose backs are forbidden to carry things and livestock on which they don't mention Allah's name when slaughtering – by making lies about Him. He will soon punish them for the lies they used to make. ⁶·¹³⁹They also say: "The babies inside the wombs of these livestock are exclusively for our men but forbidden to our wives, but they can all share it if it is stillborn." Allah will soon punish them for their false claims. He is All-Wise, All-Knowing.

⁶·¹⁴⁰Those people are in loss who, by making lies about Allah, foolishly and out of ignorance kill their own children, and make unlawful what Allah has given them. They went astray and never followed guidance.

⁶·¹⁴¹He is the one Who creates gardens – some with frames and some without, with palm trees, plants of different flavours, olives, and pomegranates – some are similar and others are different. You may eat of the fruit when the plants give it and you must pay their dues on the day of their harvest, but don't waste. Allah doesn't like wasteful people.

⁶·¹⁴²Some livestock are for carrying burdens and some are too small. You may eat from what Allah has given you but never follow Shaytan's footsteps; he is your open enemy. ⁶·¹⁴³Allah has created eight kinds of animals in pairs: a pair of sheep, and a pair of goats. Ask: "Is it the two males He has forbidden or the two females, or what the wombs of the two females carry? Tell me with reliable knowledge, if you are telling the truth." ⁶·¹⁴⁴He has created a pair of camels, and a pair of cattle. Ask: "Is it the two males He has forbidden or the two females, or what the wombs of the two females carry? Were you witnesses when Allah told you to do this?" Who could be more unjust

than someone who, out of ignorance, makes lies about Allah to lead people astray! Allah doesn't let unjust people succeed.

[6.145] O Prophet Muhammad, say: "In what is revealed to me, I don't find anything forbidden for anyone to eat, unless it is dead meat, flowing blood, or pork – because it is filth, or a sinful slaughter on which any name other than Allah's has been mentioned. However, if someone is forced by need – not being disobedient nor breaking the law, then he should know that your Lord is Most Forgiving, Ever-Merciful."

[6.146] For those who are Jews, We made unlawful every animal that has claws, as well as the fat of cows and sheep – but not what lines their backs or intestines, or is mixed with bone. We punished them in this way because of their disobedience, and We are certainly Truthful.

[6.147] O Prophet Muhammad, if they accuse you of being a liar, say: "Your Lord is the Master of all-surrounding mercy, but His punishment won't be turned away from criminal people."

[6.148] The polytheists will say: "If Allah had wanted, neither we nor our forefathers would have made partner-gods with Allah, and nor made anything unlawful." In the same way people before them also called the truth a lie, until they tasted Our punishment. O Prophet Muhammad, ask: "Do you have any knowledge you can give us? You're only following suspicion; you are only guessing." [6.149] O Prophet Muhammad, say: "Definite proof is only Allah's. If He had chosen, He could have easily guided all of you." [6.150] Say: "Bring forward your witnesses who can testify that Allah made this unlawful." If they do testify, you mustn't testify with them. Don't follow the desires of those who call Our revelations a lie, who don't believe in the Hereafter, and who make others equal to their Lord.

⁶·¹⁵¹O Prophet Muhammad, say: "Come! I will recite what your Lord has made unlawful for you: Don't make a partner with Him of anything at all; be kind to your parents; don't kill your children because of poverty – We give to you and to them; don't go near anything shameful, whether open or secret; don't kill a person Allah has made sacred, except by lawful right. This is what He has told you to do so that you might think. ⁶·¹⁵²And don't go anywhere near an orphan's property – unless it is with the best intentions, until he reaches his full strength; give full measure and weight with fairness. We don't force anyone to do more than what they can. Be fair whenever you speak, even if it is about a close relative; and fulfil the promise to Allah. This is what He has told you to do so that you might remind yourselves. ⁶·¹⁵³This is My Path, leading straight. Follow it. Don't follow other ways because they will break you all off from His way. This is what He has told you to do so that you become mindful of Him."

⁶·¹⁵⁴Then, We gave Musa the Book, to complete Our favour to anyone who does good, explaining everything in detail, a guidance, and a mercy, so that they might believe in the meeting with their Lord.

⁶·¹⁵⁵This Qur'an is a blessed Book We have revealed. Now, follow it and be mindful of Allah so you may be shown mercy, ⁶·¹⁵⁶in case you say: "The Book was only sent down to two sections of people – Jews and Christians before us and we remained unaware of their learning and teaching," ⁶·¹⁵⁷or in case you say: "If a Book had been sent down to us, we would have definitely followed its guidance better than they do." A clear sign has appeared to you from your Lord, a guidance, and a mercy. Now, who could be more unjust than someone who calls Allah's revelations a lie and turns away from them! Those who turn away from Our revelations, We will punish them with terrible suffering because they used to turn away from the truth.

⁶·¹⁵⁸Are they waiting to see if the angels, your Lord Himself, or some signs from your Lord will appear to them? On the Day some signs from your Lord will appear, the faith of any person won't benefit him or her who had no faith before, nor worked for something good with true faith in it. Say: "Wait; we are also waiting."

⁶·¹⁵⁹O Prophet Muhammad, you have nothing to do with those who divided their religion and split up into sects. Their case is for Allah to decide. Eventually, He will tell them about everything they used to do.

⁶·¹⁶⁰Anyone who comes with something good will have ten like it as a reward but whoever comes with something bad will be punished only one equal to it. They won't be treated unfairly.

⁶·¹⁶¹O Prophet Muhammad, say: "My Lord has guided me to a path that is straight, as a way of life that is correct, which is the religion of Ibrahim the True, and he wasn't a polytheist." ⁶·¹⁶²Say: "My ritual prayers, sacrifice, living, and dying are all for Allah – Lord of all the worlds. ⁶·¹⁶³He has no partner. This is what I've been ordered and I am the first to surrender to Allah as Muslim." ⁶·¹⁶⁴Say: "Would I look for a lord other than Allah when He is the Lord of everything? A person is responsible for whatever he does. No one will carry someone else's burden of sins. In the end, you will all go back to your Lord, and He will tell you about the disagreements you used to have."

⁶·¹⁶⁵He is the one Who made you successors in this world. He raised some of you above others in ranks to test you with what He has given you. Your Lord is quick in punishing yet He is certainly Most Forgiving, Ever-Merciful.

Surah 7. Heights (al-A'raaf)

Allah's name I begin with, the Most Compassionate, the Ever-Merciful

⁷·¹*Alif Laam Meem Saad.*

⁷·²O Prophet Muhammad, this is the Book revealed to you, so there wouldn't be any tightness in your noble heart from it – so you can give warnings by it, and it is a reminder for the Believers.

⁷·³You people must follow what has been sent down to you from your Lord, and never follow any protectors apart from Him. How little you remind yourselves! ⁷·⁴How many towns have We destroyed! Our punishment came to them at night or while they were having their afternoon nap. ⁷·⁵When Our punishment came to them, all they could say was to cry out: "We have been wrongdoers!"

⁷·⁶We will definitely question those the messengers were sent to, as well as the messengers themselves. ⁷·⁷We will certainly tell them their full story with certain knowledge as We were never absent.

⁷·⁸The weighing on that Day is true. Those whose scales of the good they did will be heavy, it is really they who will be successful, ⁷·⁹but as for those whose scales will be light, it is they who will have ruined themselves because they used to treat Our revelations unfairly.

⁷·¹⁰We have settled you people in the world, and also showed you ways of making a living in it. How little thanks you give!

⁷·¹¹We created you, then shaped you, then We ordered the angels: "Prostrate in front of Adam," and so they did prostrate – but not Iblees. He wasn't one of those who prostrated. ⁷·¹²Allah asked: "What stopped you from prostrating when I told you to?" He replied: "I'm

better than he is. You created me from fire but him from clay." ⁷·¹³Allah ordered: "Then get down from Paradise! You don't have any right to be arrogant here. Now get out! You are certainly among the disgraced." ⁷·¹⁴He pleaded: "Give me a chance until the Day people will be brought back to life." ⁷·¹⁵Allah replied: "You are one of those given chances." ⁷·¹⁶He said: "Because you have let me go astray, I will certainly lie in wait for them on Your Straight Path. ⁷·¹⁷Then, I will attack them from in front of them, from behind them, from their right and their left sides – from everywhere, and You won't find most of them thankful." ⁷·¹⁸Allah ordered: "Get out of here! You are shamed! rejected! Those of them who follow you, I will fill up Hell with the lot of you, all together!"

⁷·¹⁹Allah said: "Adam, you and your wife may live comfortably in Paradise, and eat from it however you like, but don't go near this tree or you will be wrongdoers." ⁷·²⁰However, Shaytan tempted them so he could expose their private parts to them that had been hidden from them. He said: "Your Lord has forbidden you from eating the fruit of this tree only so that you don't become angels or immortals." ⁷·²¹He swore to them both: "I am your well-wisher."

⁷·²²So, he made them fall from their high position by trickery. When they had tasted the fruit of the tree, their private parts became exposed to them, and they began to cover themselves with some leaves of the Garden. Their Lord called out to them: "Didn't I forbid you that tree, and didn't I tell you, 'Shaytan is your open enemy.'?" ⁷·²³They replied: "Our Lord! We have harmed ourselves. If You don't forgive us and have mercy on us, we will certainly be losers." ⁷·²⁴Allah ordered: "Go down, as enemies of each other. Your place of stay and livelihood, for a while, will be on earth." ⁷·²⁵He said: "That is where you will live, die, and be taken out from."

7.26Descendants of Adam! We've sent down to you knowledge of clothing that covers your private parts and as an adornment. However, the clothing of being mindful of Allah – that is the best! This is all from among Allah's signs so that they might learn some lessons.

7.27Descendants of Adam! Don't let Shaytan trick you as he made your first parents leave Paradise, and had their clothing removed from them so as to expose their private parts to them. He and his community watch you in a way that you cannot see them. We have made the evil ones friends of the disbelievers. 7.28When they do something shameful, they say: "We saw our forefathers doing it and Allah has also told us to do it." Say to them: "Allah doesn't command anything shameful. Are you saying things about Allah what you don't even know?"

7.29O Prophet Muhammad, say: "My Lord has ordered fairness, so straighten your directions towards the Ka'bah at each time and place of prayer, and pray to Him in sincere devotion to Him. You will all go back just like He created you." 7.30He guided one group, but error proved true against the other group; because they took the evil ones as protectors instead of Allah, and think they themselves are following guidance.

7.31Descendants of Adam! Dress yourselves well at each time and place of prayer. You may eat and drink, but don't be excessive nor waste. Allah doesn't like wasteful people. 7.32O Prophet Muhammad, ask: "Who has forbidden the adornment from Allah that He has brought out for His servants, and also the wholesome things among food?" Say: "In this life, these are for the Believers too, but only for the Believers on Judgement Day." This is how We explain the revelations in detail for any people who have the right knowledge.

7.33 O Prophet Muhammad, say: "My Lord has made unlawful anything shameful – whether they are open or secret, and all sins, unjust aggression, or that you to make partner-gods with Allah – for which He hasn't sent down any permission, and that you say things about Allah what you don't even know." 7.34 Every nation has an end date. When the end of their time comes, they can neither delay it a moment longer nor bring it any sooner.

7.35 Descendants of Adam! Whenever some messengers from among you come to you teaching you My revelations, then those who become mindful and correct themselves, they won't have anything to fear and will never be sad. 7.36 However, those who call Our revelations a lie and turn arrogantly away from them, it is they who will be the people of the Fire, where they will remain forever.

7.37 Who could be more unjust than someone who makes lies about Allah or calls His revelations a lie! It is they whose share of what is written will reach them, until when Our angels come to them to take their souls away and ask: "Where are those you used to pray to besides Allah?" they will reply: "They've abandoned us," and they will testify against themselves that they were disbelievers. 7.38 Allah will say: "Enter the Fire along with the groups of jinns and humans who have been and gone before you." Each time one group enters, it will curse the other, until they will all be gathered in it, all together. The latter group will say about the former groups: "Our Lord! These people misled us. Give them double the punishment in the Fire." Allah will say: "Each will have a double even though you people don't realise." 7.39 Then the former group will say to the latter: "You don't have any superiority over us, so taste the punishment because of the bad things you used to do."

7.40Those who call Our revelations a lie and turn arrogantly away from them, Heaven's gates won't be opened for them nor will they ever enter Paradise – not until a camel can pass through the eye of a needle! This is how we punish criminals. 7.41They will suffer Hell as a bed with coverings of fire over them. This is how We punish wrongdoers.

7.42Those who believe and do good – We don't force anyone to do more than what they can – it is they who will be the people of Paradise, where they will remain forever. 7.43We will remove all grudges from their hearts. Rivers will flow beneath them. They will say: "All praise is for Allah Who guided us to this because We would never have found guidance if Allah hadn't guided us. Our Lord's messengers certainly did bring us the truth." It will be called out to them: "This is Paradise! You are made its inheritors because of the good things you used to do."

7.44The people of Paradise will call out to the people of the Fire: "Everything our Lord promised us, we've found it to be true. Everything your Lord promised you, did you also find it to be true?" They will reply: "Yes, it is." However, an announcer will call out between them: "Allah's curse be on the wrongdoers, 7.45who used to block people from Allah's cause, look for some crookedness in it, and disbelieve in the Hereafter."

7.46There will be a screen between the two, with some men on high places who will recognise everyone by their appearances. They will call out to the people of Paradise: "Peace be upon you!" These men won't have entered Paradise but will be hoping to. 7.47When their eyes will be turned towards the people of the Fire, they will pray: "Our Lord! Don't put us among these wrongdoing people." 7.48The people on those high places will call out to certain men they will recognise by their appearances, saying: "Neither your large group nor the arrogance you used to show could benefit you. [7.49]What? Are these the people you swore Allah would never bless with mercy? They are being told: 'Enter Paradise. You won't have anything to fear and will never be sad.'."

[7.50]The people of the Fire will cry out to the people of Paradise: "Pour down some water to us or give us some of the food Allah has given you." They will reply: "Allah has forbidden both to the disbelievers [7.51]who had turned their own religion into some kind of amusement and just games, and the worldly life had tricked them." We will ignore them Today as they forgot the meeting of this Day of theirs, and because they used to reject Our revelations.

[7.52]We have already brought them a Book which We've explained in detail with certain knowledge, a guidance, and a mercy to any people who believe. [7.53]Are they only waiting for its final result? On the Day its final result will take place, those people who ignored it before will say: "Our Lord's messengers really did bring us the truth. Do we have anyone to intercede for us or can we be sent back so that we can do good things and not those bad things we used to do?" They'll have already ruined themselves and those idols and lies they made up will have abandoned them.

[7.54]Your Lord is Allah, Who created the heavens and the earth in six stages, and then established His authority on the Throne. He covers the night as a veil over the day, chasing each other quickly. He created the sun, moon, and stars, made to obey His command. Beware! Creating and giving orders belong to Him. Blessed is Allah – Lord of all the worlds. [7.55]Pray to your Lord with humility and in private. Allah doesn't like those who break the law. [7.56]You mustn't make trouble in the land after it has been set right, but pray to Him with fear and hope. Allah's special mercy is near to those who do good.

7.57He is the one Who sends the winds like good news before His mercy, until when they've picked up the heavy clouds, We blow them to a land that is dead, send down upon it water – with which We bring out all kinds of fruit. This is how We will bring out the dead, so that you might remind yourselves. 7.58Good soil, its growth comes out by its Lord's permission, but hardly any from soil that is bad. This is how We vary the signs for any people who are thankful.

7.59We sent Nuh to his people, and he said: "My people! You must worship Allah. You don't have any god besides Him. I fear for you the punishment of a Dreadful Day!" 7.60The leaders among his community said: "We can see that you are clearly astray." 7.61He replied: "My people! I'm not misguided. In fact, I am a messenger from Allah – the Lord of all the worlds. 7.62I'm delivering my Lord's messages to you, I am giving you good advice, and I know from Allah things that you don't. 7.63Are you surprised that a reminder has come to you from your Lord through a man from among you so he can give you warnings, so that you become mindful of Allah and be shown mercy?" 7.64However, they accused him of being a liar, so We saved him and those with him in the Ark, and drowned those who called Our revelations a lie. They were a people who were blind to the truth.

7.65To the people of 'Ad, We sent their brother Hud. He said: "My people! You must worship Allah. You don't have any god besides Him. So, won't you be mindful of Him?" 7.66The disbelieving leaders among his community said: "We see that you certainly are a fool and we think you are a liar." 7.67He replied: "My people! I'm not a fool. In fact, I am a messenger from Allah – the Lord of all the worlds. 7.68I'm delivering my Lord's messages to you. I am your trustworthy adviser.

7.69 Are you surprised that a reminder has come to you from your Lord through a man from among you so he can give you warnings? So, you should remember when He made you successors after the people of Nuh, and increased you in physical height. Also, you should remember Allah's blessings so that you might be successful." 7.70 They said: "Have you come to us so we worship Allah on His own and leave what our forefathers used to worship? So, bring down on us the punishment you keep threatening us with, if you are telling the truth." 7.71 He replied: "Punishment and anger from your Lord have already been guaranteed against you. Are you arguing with me about the names you and your forefathers have given those idols for which Allah hasn't sent down any permission? Then wait for your punishment. I'm with you among those who are waiting." 7.72 So, with special mercy from Us, We saved him and those with him, and We uprooted those who called Our revelations a lie. They were never going to believe.

7.73 To the people of Thamud, We sent their brother Salih. He said: "My people! You must worship Allah. You don't have any god besides Him. A clear proof has appeared to you from your Lord: this Allah's she-camel is a sign for you. So, leave her to graze on Allah's earth and don't harm her in any way, or a painful punishment will destroy you. 7.74 Remember when He made you successors after the 'Ad, and let you live in the land where you now build palaces on its plains and carve out homes in the mountains. So, you must remember Allah's blessings and don't go around making trouble in the land." 7.75 The arrogant leaders among his community asked those Believers who were considered weak: "Are you sure that Salih has been sent as a messenger from his Lord?" They replied: "We certainly believe in what he has been sent with." 7.76 Those arrogant people said: "We reject what you believe in." 7.77 Then they hamstrung the she-camel, arrogantly disobeyed their Lord's command, and said: "Salih! Bring down on us the punishment you keep threatening us with, if you really are one of the messengers." 7.78So the earthquake shook them, and in the morning they lay dead in their homes facing down! 7.79Salih turned away from them and said: "My people! I have delivered my Lord's message to you and given you good advice, but you don't like well-wishers."

7.80We also sent Lut. Remember when he said to his people: "Do you do something so shameful that no one in the world has ever done before you? 7.81You lustfully approach men instead of women. In fact, you are a people who are going to extremes." 7.82However, the only response from his people was for them to say: "Expel them from your town. They are people who want to remain clean and pure!" 7.83We saved him and his family, but not his wife: she was one of those who stayed behind. 7.84We rained down on them a shower of stones. Now take a look at what was the end result of those criminals!

7.85To the people of Madyan (Midian), We sent their brother Shu'ayb (Jethro). He said: "My people! You must worship Allah. You don't have any god besides Him. A clear proof has already appeared to you from your Lord! Give full measure and weight, don't cheat people out of their things, nor make trouble in the land after it has been set right. This is best for you if you are true Believers. 7.86Don't sit on every pathway making threats and blocking Allah's Believers from His cause, or looking for some crookedness in it. Instead, you should remember how He increased you when you were few. Just take a look at what was the end result of the troublemakers. 7.87If some of you believe in what I've been sent with and some don't believe, then have patience until Allah decides between us. He is the Best to decide."

[PART 9]

7.88The arrogant leaders among his community threatened: "Shu'ayb! We will definitely expel you from our town, as well as those who believe with you, unless you all come back to our religion." He said: "What? Even if we don't want to? ⁷·⁸⁹We would be making lies about Allah if we ever went back to your religion after Allah has saved us from it. We aren't allowed to go back to it unless Allah – our Lord, wants us to. Our Lord surrounds everything in His knowledge. We put our trust only in Allah and we pray: 'Our Lord! Judge between us and our people with the truth because You are the Best Judge of all.'." ⁷·⁹⁰The disbelieving leaders among his community said: "You will certainly be losers if you follow Shu'ayb!" ⁷·⁹¹So the earthquake shook them, and in the morning they lay dead in their homes facing down! ⁷·⁹²Those who accused Shu'ayb of being a liar, it was as if they had never lived there. Those who accused him of being a liar, they were the real losers. ⁷·⁹³So Shu'ayb turned away from them and said: "My people! I have delivered my Lord's messages to you and given you good advice. Now why should I be sad over some people who choose to disbelieve!"

⁷·⁹⁴Whenever we sent a prophet to any place, We made its disbelieving people suffer poverty and weakness so that they might humble themselves. ⁷·⁹⁵Then We would change their bad state into good, until they progressed, but they would say: "Our forefathers also experienced bad times and good times." However, they weren't even aware when We suddenly punished them for being unthankful.

⁷·⁹⁶If only the people of those places had believed and become mindful of Allah, We would have opened up for them blessings from the sky and the earth, but they called the truth a lie, so We punished them for the bad things they used to do. ⁷·⁹⁷Do the people of these places feel safe that Our punishment won't come to them at night as they sleep? ⁷·⁹⁸Do they feel safe that it won't come to them during the day as they play games? ⁷·⁹⁹Do they feel safe from Allah's plan? Only losers think they're safe from Allah's plan! ⁷·¹⁰⁰Isn't it clear to those people

who inherit the earth after the destruction of the people who used to live there that, if We wanted, We can punish them too because of their sins, and seal up their hearts so they won't be able to hear the truth?

7.101We are telling you some of the stories of those places. Their messengers brought them clear proofs, but they weren't going to believe what they had previously called a lie. In this way Allah seals up the hearts of disbelievers. 7.102We found most of them were disobedient and not true to their promise.

7.103After them, We sent Musa with Our miracles to Fir'awn (Pharaoh) and his ministers, but they rejected them. Now take a look at what was the end result of the troublemakers. 7.104Musa said: "Fir'awn! I am a messenger from Allah – the Lord of all the worlds, 7.105and I am only allowed to say the truth about Allah. I've brought you people a clear proof from your Lord. Now, you must let the Descendants of Ya'qub go with me." 7.106Fir'awn demanded: "If you have brought a sign then show it, if you are telling the truth." 7.107So Musa threw down his staff, and it immediately turned into an actual large snake! 7.108Then he pulled out his hand from under his collar opening, and it immediately became shining white to everyone who was watching! 7.109The ministers among Fir'awn's people said: "He is certainly an expert magician. 7.110He wants to expel you from your land." Fir'awn asked: "So, what do you advise?" 7.111They replied: "Delay him and his brother while you send out marshals to the cities 7.112to bring you every skilful magician."

7.113The magicians came to Fir'awn. They said: "There should be some reward for us if we win." 7.114He replied: "Yes, and you will certainly be among those nearest to me in high positions."

⁷·¹¹⁵They asked: "Musa! Are you going to throw, or should we throw first?" ⁷·¹¹⁶Musa replied: "You throw first." So, when they threw down their tools of magic, they put a magic spell on the people's eyes and frightened them. They had brought powerful magic! ⁷·¹¹⁷Then We told Musa: "Throw down your staff," and it immediately began swallowing up what they had made through illusion. ⁷·¹¹⁸So, the truth was established, and everything they had been doing proved to be false. ⁷·¹¹⁹They were defeated there and then, and they backed away humiliated. ⁷·¹²⁰The magicians were made to fall down in prostration. ⁷·¹²¹They declared: "We believe in Allah – the Lord all of the Worlds, ⁷·¹²²the Lord of Musa and Haroon."

⁷·¹²³Fir'awn said: "How dare you believe in Him before I give you permission! This is certainly a plot you have made in this city to expel its people from it, but you will very soon come to know my power. ⁷·¹²⁴I will definitely cut off your hands and feet from opposite sides, and then I will crucify the lot of you!" ⁷·¹²⁵They said: "We will go back to our Lord ⁷·¹²⁶but you are only punishing us because we believed in our Lord's signs when they appeared to us." They prayed: "Our Lord! Fill us with patience, and let us die as those who surrender to You as Muslims."

⁷·¹²⁷The ministers among Fir'awn's people argued: "Are you going to leave Musa and his people to spread corruption in the land, and to abandon you and your gods?" He replied: "We will kill their boys but keep their women alive because we are completely dominant over them."

⁷·¹²⁸Musa told his people: "You should look for help from Allah and have patience. This world belongs to Him. He makes heirs to it whichever of His servants He chooses. The best end in the Hereafter will be for those who are mindful of Allah. ⁷·¹²⁹They complained: "We

suffered both before as well as after you came to us." He replied: "Your Lord will soon destroy your enemy and make you successors in the land, and then He will observe how you behave."

7.130We punished Fir'awn's people with years of famine and a shortage of resources so they would learn a lesson. 7.131When good times came to them, they said: "This is what we deserve," but when they suffered a disaster, they would blame it as bad luck on Musa and those with him. Beware! The bad result of their actions is up to Allah, but most of them don't know.

7.132Fir'awn's people said to Musa: "We won't believe merely because you say so, no matter what sign you bring us to cast a spell on us." 7.133So We sent on them: storms, locusts, lice, frogs, and blood – all clear signs, but they still showed arrogance and were a criminal people. 7.134Whenever a plague would hit them, they pleaded: "Musa! Pray for us to your Lord about the promise He made to you. If you remove the plague from us, we will certainly believe for your sake and we will let the Descendants of Ya'qub go with you." 7.135But whenever We removed the plague from them until the end date they had to complete as a deadline, they would immediately break their promise. 7.136So, eventually, We punished them: We drowned them in the sea because they called Our revelations a lie and never paid any attention to them.

7.137We made people who were oppressed inheritors of the eastern and western parts of the land where We had placed blessings. The good promise of your Lord was fulfilled for the Descendants of Ya'qub because of what they had suffered, and We destroyed what Fir'awn and his people used to make and what they used to build high.

⁷·¹³⁸We brought the Descendants of Ya'qub across the sea, until they came upon some people devoting themselves to their idols. They demanded: "Musa! Make for us a god like their gods." He replied: "You are a group of people behaving ignorantly. ⁷·¹³⁹What these people are devoted to will be ruined, and what they're doing is false." ⁷·¹⁴⁰He continued: "Would I look for you a god other than Allah when He has made you superior to all the people of your time? ⁷·¹⁴¹Remember when We saved you from Fir'awn's people! They used to oppress you with terrible suffering and by killing your boys but keeping your women alive. There was a severe test in that from your Lord.

⁷·¹⁴²We promised Musa thirty nights, to which We added ten more – so the term fixed by his Lord was completed in forty nights. Before he went to Mount Tur, Musa told his brother Haroon: "Take my place among my people. Keep things right and don't follow the way of the troublemakers." ⁷·¹⁴³When Musa arrived at Our promised time and place and his Lord spoke to him, he asked: "My Lord! Show me Yourself so I can look at You." Allah replied: "You can never see Me. However, look at the mountain; if it remains firm in its place then you will be able to see Me." When his Lord displayed His glory on the mountain, He crushed it flat! Musa fell down unconscious! When he recovered, he declared: "Glory be to You! I repent to You, and I am the first to believe."

⁷·¹⁴⁴Allah said: "Musa, I have raised you above all the people by giving you My messages and My speaking to you. So keep hold of what I have given you and be among those who are thankful." ⁷·¹⁴⁵We wrote about everything for him in the Tablets – as a source of advice and explaining everything in detail – and told him: "Now hold strongly on to them and tell your people to hold on to their beautiful teachings. Very soon, I will show you the future home of those who

are disobedient." ⁷·¹⁴⁶I will turn away from My signs those who behave arrogantly in this world without them having any right to do so. Even though they can see every sign, they still aren't believing in them; and even though they can see the way of true guidance, they still aren't accepting it as a way of life. However, if they see the way of misguidance, they accept it as a way of life. This is because they called Our revelations a lie and never paid any attention to them. ⁷·¹⁴⁷The actions of those people will be wasted who think Our revelations and meeting in the Hereafter are lies. Should they be rewarded for anything other than what they used to do?!

⁷·¹⁴⁸In Musa's absence, his people made, out of their ornaments, an image of a calf that made a mooing sound. Couldn't they see that it could neither speak to them nor guide them in any way? Being wrongdoers, they started worshipping it. ⁷·¹⁴⁹When they felt ashamed of what they had done and realised they really had gone astray, they cried: "If our Lord doesn't have mercy on us and forgive us, we will certainly be among the losers!"

⁷·¹⁵⁰When Musa came back to his people, angry and sad, he said: "What terrible things have you people done after I had gone! Did you try and bring your Lord's commandments sooner?" He put the Tablets down, grabbed hold of his brother's head pulling him towards himself. Haroon said: "Son of my mother! The people overpowered me and almost killed me! Don't give the enemies an opportunity to laugh at me, and don't count me among these wrongdoing people." ⁷·¹⁵¹Musa prayed: "My Lord! Forgive me and my brother! Take us into Your mercy because You are the Most Merciful of all."

⁷·¹⁵²Those who worshipped the calf will suffer anger from their Lord as well as humiliation in this life. This is how We punish those who make things that are false. ⁷·¹⁵³Those who do bad things but repent

afterwards and believe, your Lord will then most certainly be Most Forgiving, Ever-Merciful. ^{7.154}When anger left Musa, he picked up the Tablets, and in their writing was guidance and mercy for those who fear their Lord.

^{7.155}Musa chose seventy men from his people for Our promised time and place, but when the earthquake killed them, he prayed: "My Lord! If You had wanted, You could have destroyed them long ago, and me too. Are You going to destroy us all for what some fools among us have done? I know this is only a test from You, through which You let anyone You choose go astray and guide whoever You want. You are our Protector, so forgive us and have mercy on us, because You are the Best Forgiver of all. ^{7.156}Give us goodness in this world and in the Hereafter too. We have turned in humility to You." Allah replied: "I will punish anyone I choose, but My mercy surrounds everything, and I will give it to those who are mindful of Me, and who pay zakah, and who believe in Our revelations. ^{7.157}They are those who follow the Messenger – the Prophet who wasn't taught by any created being – whom they find mentioned with them in the Tawrah and the Injeel. He commands them what is right and forbids them what is wrong, makes wholesome things lawful for them and bad things unlawful for them, removes from them their heavy burdens and the iron collars that are on them. Those who believe in him, continuously assist him, help him, and follow the Light (- Qur'an) that is sent down with him, it is really they who will be successful."

^{7.158}O Prophet Muhammad, say: "People! I have been sent to you all as a Messenger from Allah – Who has control of the heavens and the earth. There is no god except Him. He gives life and death. So, believe in Allah and His Messenger – the Prophet who wasn't taught by any created being – who believes in Allah and His words. Follow him so that you might find the right way."

⁷·¹⁵⁹Among Musa's people, there is a community who guide with the truth and do justice with it. ⁷·¹⁶⁰We divided the Descendants of Ya'qub into twelve tribes, as communities. When his people asked him for water, We told Musa: "Hit the rock with your staff," and out of the rock gushed twelve springs. Each tribe knew its own drinking-place. We shaded them with clouds and sent down manna and quails for them. We said: "Eat from the wholesome things We've given you." However, they didn't harm Us by rebelling but were only harming themselves. ⁷·¹⁶¹Remember when they were told: "Live comfortably in this town and eat from it however you like, but pray, 'We beg forgiveness!' and enter the gate with humility, then We will forgive you your sins. Soon We will give more to those who do good." ⁷·¹⁶²However, the wrongdoers among them changed the words to something else – to something other than what they were told. So, We sent on them a punishment from heaven because they continued to do wrong.

⁷·¹⁶³O Prophet Muhammad, ask them about the town that stood by the sea – they broke the Sabbath, since their fish would come to them at the surface on the day of their Sabbath but not on the day they had no Sabbath. This is how we were testing them because they continued to be disobedient. ⁷·¹⁶⁴When a different group of them asked: "Why are you advising some Sabbath-breaking people when Allah will destroy them or severely punish them?" They replied: "To free ourselves of blame from your Lord, and so they might become mindful of Him." ⁷·¹⁶⁵When they ignored what they were being reminded of, We saved those who forbade evil, but seized with a grievous punishment those who did wrong because they continued to disobey. ⁷·¹⁶⁶When they arrogantly disobeyed what they had been forbidden, We ordered them: "Be apes! Disgraced!"

^{7.167}Remember, O Prophet Muhammad, **when your Lord announced that, until Judgement Day, He will continue to send against them those who will oppress them with terrible suffering. Your Lord is certainly quick in punishing yet He is certainly Most Forgiving, Ever-Merciful.** ^{7.168}**We divided them into separate communities on earth. Some of them are righteous but some aren't. We tested them with both blessings and tragedies so that they might turn back** to Us.

^{7.169}**After them came other generations who inherited the Book while taking the temporary wealth of this world and claiming: "We will be forgiven." If more temporary wealth like that came to them, they would take that too. Wasn't a strong promise taken from them in the Book that they would speak only the truth about Allah? They had already studied what was in it. Anyway, the Home of the Hereafter is best for those who are mindful** of Allah. **Won't you even think?** ^{7.170}**Those who stick firmly to** the teachings of **the Book and establish the ritual prayers** should know that **We would never let the reward go to waste of those who put things right.**

^{7.171}**When We raised the mountain over their heads, as if it were a dark cloud, and they thought it was going to fall on top of them,** We said: **"You must hold strongly on to what We've given you and remember what is inside it so that you become mindful."**

^{7.172}**When your Lord brought out the humans from the loins of the descendants of Adam, and We made them witness against themselves,** asking: **"Aren't I your Lord?"** they replied: **"Yes, of course! We testify!"** This was done **in case you say on Judgement Day: "We didn't know anything about this,"** ^{7.173}**or in case you say: "It was our forefathers who were polytheists long ago and we were descendants long after them. Are You going to destroy us because of**

what the supporters of falsehood did?" ⁷·¹⁷⁴In this way We explain the revelations in detail, and so that they might turn back to Us.

⁷·¹⁷⁵O Prophet Muhammad, tell them the story of the man We gave Our signs to but he avoided them, so Shaytan made him follow him which is why he went astray. ⁷·¹⁷⁶If We had wanted, We could have raised his status high with Our signs but he clung to the earth and followed his own desires. His example is that of a dog: if you attack it or leave it alone, in both cases it will merely loll out its tongue. This is the example of those people who call Our revelations a lie. So, tell people these stories and they might think deeply. ⁷·¹⁷⁷Those who called Our revelations a lie, what a bad example they are! It is themselves they continued to harm.

⁷·¹⁷⁸Anyone Allah guides will really follow guidance, but whoever He calls misguided, they are the real losers. ⁷·¹⁷⁹Many of the jinns and humans We have created are heading for Hell; who have minds they don't think with, eyes they don't look with, and ears they don't listen with. It is they who are like cattle. In fact, they are further astray. It is really they who are neglectful.

⁷·¹⁸⁰Allah has the most beautiful names, so call Him by them. You people must stay away from those who abuse His names. They will be punished for the bad things they used to do.

⁷·¹⁸¹Among the people We have created is a community who guide with the truth and do justice with it. ⁷·¹⁸²As for those who call Our revelations a lie, We will let them gradually fall into ruin in ways they won't even realise. ⁷·¹⁸³I am giving them more time, but My plan is strong.

7.184Don't they think deeply that he (- Prophet Muhammad) who makes them his companions hasn't gone mad? He is giving clear warnings. 7.185Don't they look into the kingdoms of the heavens and the earth, and everything Allah has created, and realise perhaps the end of their time is near? Then what message after this Qur'an will they believe in? 7.186There can be no guide for someone Allah calls misguided. Allah leaves them confused to wander blindly in their rebellion.

7.187O Prophet Muhammad, they ask you about the Final Hour: "When will it be?" Reply: "Only my Lord knows about it. Only He can reveal its due time. It hangs heavy in the heavens and the earth. Only, it will come upon you all of a sudden." They ask you as if you were eager to find out about it. Say: "Only Allah knows about it," but most people don't realise. 7.188Say: "I don't own any profit or loss for myself apart from what Allah chooses. If I had personally known the unseen secrets, I would have increased all good, and harm would never have come to me. However, I'm only giving warnings and bringing good news to any people who believe."

7.189He is the one Who created all of you from a single person and made his wife from him to have a comfortable living with her. Then, when he covers her, she becomes pregnant and, carrying a light burden, moves around with it. Then, when she grows heavy, they both pray to Allah – their Lord: "If You give us a good child, we will certainly be among those who are thankful." 7.190However, when He does give them a good child, they begin making partner-gods with Him with regards to what He gave them. Allah is much higher than the partner-gods they make with Him.

7.191Do people make with Allah partner-gods of things that cannot create anything but are themselves created? 7.192Those things can neither help them nor even help themselves. ⁷·¹⁹³If you Muslims **invite them to guidance, they won't follow you. It makes no difference to them if you invite them or remain silent.** ⁷·¹⁹⁴Disbelievers! **Those** idols you pray to besides Allah are His servants just like you. So, if you **pray to them, they should respond to you if you are telling the truth** that they are gods. ⁷·¹⁹⁵Do they have feet to walk with, hands to hold with, eyes to see with, or ears to hear with? Say: "Pray to those you make partner-gods with Allah, then make your plots against me, and don't spare me! ⁷·¹⁹⁶My Protector is Allah – Who revealed this Book (-Qur'an), and He takes care of righteous people. ⁷·¹⁹⁷Those idols you pray to besides Him, they can neither help you nor even help themselves." ⁷·¹⁹⁸If you invite them to guidance, they cannot even hear. You think they're looking at you, but they cannot even see. ⁷·¹⁹⁹O Prophet Muhammad, **you should keep on forgiving, command what is right, and turn away from those who are ignorant.**

⁷·²⁰⁰O human! **If a suggestion from Shaytan tempts you, you should ask Allah to protect you. He is All-Hearing, All-Knowing.** ⁷·²⁰¹When some **temptation from Shaytan comes to those who are mindful** of Allah, they only **think** of Allah, **and they can immediately see clearly!** ⁷·²⁰²However, **the brothers of these evil ones pull them into misguidance, and they don't stop even after that.**

⁷·²⁰³O Prophet Muhammad, **if you don't bring them any sign, they ask: "Can't you just choose one yourself?" Reply: "I only follow what is revealed to me from my Lord. These are clear proofs from your Lord, as well as guidance and mercy for any people who believe."**

⁷·²⁰⁴**When the Qur'an is recited, you must all listen to it carefully and remain silent so you may be shown mercy.** ⁷·²⁰⁵**You must remember your Lord morning and evening – in your noble heart, with humility, and in fear, and not necessarily with a loud voice; and don't be among**

those who are neglectful. ⁷·²⁰⁶Those angels who are in the presence of your Lord, they don't turn arrogantly away from worshipping Him, but glorify Him and prostrate only to Him. *<Prostration Point 1>*

Surah 8. Spoils of War (al-Anfaal)

Allah's name I begin with, the Most Compassionate, the Ever-Merciful

⁸·¹O Prophet Muhammad, they ask you about the spoils of war. Reply: "The spoils of war are for Allah and the Messenger. So, you must continue to be mindful of Allah and keep things right between yourselves. You have to obey Allah and His Messenger if you are true Believers."

⁸·²True Believers are those whose hearts tremble with awe when Allah is mentioned, His revelations increase them in faith when they are recited to them, and they put their trust only in their Lord, ⁸·³who establish the ritual prayers, and donate from what We've given them. ⁸·⁴In truth, they are the real Believers. They have different ranks in the sight of their Lord, as well as forgiveness and some honourable wealth.

⁸·⁵Similarly, as your Lord brought you out of your home with the truth and a group from among the Believers didn't want to, ⁸·⁶they were still arguing with you about the truth even after it had become clear, as if they were being driven to their death while they looked on!

⁸·⁷When Allah promised you Muslims that one of the two groups would to be defeated by you, you wanted the unarmed one to be yours to defeat, but Allah wanted to prove the truth through His words and to uproot the disbelievers, ⁸·⁸to prove the truth and disprove falsehood, even if the criminals hate it.

⁸·⁹When you asked your Lord for help, He responded to you: "I will help you with a thousand angels coming in rows behind each other." ⁸·¹⁰Allah only did this sending of angels for it to be joy, and for your hearts to be satisfied by it. Help comes only from Allah. Allah is Almighty, All-Wise.

⁸·¹¹Remember when He covered you with drowsiness to give you calmness from Himself, and He sent down on you water from the sky to clean and purify you with, to remove Shaytan's stain of doubts from you, to strengthen your hearts, and to keep your footing strong with it.

⁸·¹²Remember when your Lord told the angels: "I am with you, so give strength to those who believe. I will put awe into the disbelievers' hearts, so strike above their necks and strike all of their joints." ⁸·¹³This is because they went against Allah and His Messenger. Anyone who goes against Allah and His Messenger should know that Allah is severe in punishing. ⁸·¹⁴This is your punishment, so taste it! The disbelievers will also suffer the punishment of the Fire.

⁸·¹⁵Believers! When you meet the disbelievers in battle, even as a large army, never turn your backs on them to run away. ⁸·¹⁶Anyone who turns his back on them that day – unless he is making a strategic move for the fight or retreating to join another group – he will bring down on himself anger from Allah and his home will be Hell. What a dreadful final destination! ⁸·¹⁷It wasn't you Muslims who killed them but it is Allah Who killed them. O Prophet Muhammad, it wasn't you who threw the handful of dust but it is Allah Who threw it, and also to do from Himself an excellent favour to the Believers. Allah is All-Hearing, All-Knowing. ⁸·¹⁸This is your reward, and also because Allah weakens the disbelievers' plots.

8.19Disbelievers! **If you were looking for judgement, then that judgement has come to you. It will be better for you if you stop. If you go back to aggression, We will repeat Our punishing you, and your troops, even if they are many, won't be able to save you in any way at all. Allah is with the Believers.**

8.20Believers! You have to obey Allah and His Messenger, and never turn away from him when you can hear. 8.21You mustn't be like those who claim: "We are listening," when they don't. 8.22The worst of beasts in the sight of Allah are the deaf, the dumb! – those who don't think. 8.23If Allah had known any good in them, He would certainly have made them listen. However, even if He did make them listen, they would still have turned away because they don't pay any attention to the truth.

8.24Believers! You must respond to Allah and the Messenger when He calls you to anything that gives you life. You must bear in mind that Allah comes between a man and his heart, and it is in front of Him you will all be assembled. 8.25You must fear a test which will affect not only the wrongdoers among you but everyone, and you should know that Allah is severe in punishing.

8.26Remember when you were few in number, oppressed in the land, afraid that people might snatch you away, but then Allah gave you refuge, supported you with His help, and gave you wholesome things, all so that you might become thankful.

8.27Believers! Don't break the trust of Allah and the Messenger, nor deliberately abuse the things you are keeping as trusts between you. 8.28You must realise that your wealth and children are only a test, and that from Allah will come a huge reward.

⁸·²⁹**Believers! If you are mindful of Allah, He will give you a criterion to know between right and wrong, remove your sins from you, and forgive you. Allah gives tremendous grace.**

⁸·³⁰Remember, O Prophet Muhammad, **when the disbelievers plotted against you to take you captive, kill you, or expel you. They plot and Allah plans** to stop them. **Allah is the Best of Planners.**

⁸·³¹**When Our revelations are recited to them, they say: "We have heard this before. If we wanted, we could say something like this too. This Qur'an is nothing but stories made up by previous people."**

⁸·³²**Remember when they said: "O Allah, if this Qur'an is the real truth from You, then make stones from the sky rain down on top of us, or give us some painful punishment."** ⁸·³³**However, Allah would never punish them while you are among them**, O Beloved Prophet Muhammad, **nor would He ever punish them when they beg forgiveness.** ⁸·³⁴**But why shouldn't Allah punish them when they are blocking** people **from the Sacred Masjid, and they aren't even its real guardians? Only those who are mindful of Allah can be its real guardians, but most of them don't know** this reality. ⁸·³⁵**Their praying at the House** of Allah **is nothing more than whistling and clapping hands: "Disbelievers! Now taste the punishment because you used to disbelieve."**

⁸·³⁶**The disbelievers spend their wealth to block** people **from Allah's cause. They will continue to spend** more of it **but it will become a matter of regret for them afterwards. They will eventually be defeated. The disbelievers will be pushed towards Hell,** ⁸·³⁷**for Allah to separate the bad people from the good; He will put the bad ones on**

top of each other, pile it up all together into a heap, and throw it into Hell. It is they who are the real losers.

8.38Tell the disbelievers that if they stop disobeying then they will be forgiven for what is past, but if they repeat their disobedience then the example of previous people has already passed as a warning. 8.39You must continue to fight these troublemakers until there's no more oppression, and until all of obedience remains only for Allah's sake. If they stop oppressing then they should remember that Allah is Ever-Watchful of everything they do. 8.40If they refuse then you people should know that Allah is your Protector. He is such an excellent Protector and such and an excellent Helper.

[PART 10]

8.41You should know that anything you gain in battle: a fifth of it is for Allah and the Messenger, and for close relatives, orphans, the needy, and travellers – if you believe in Allah and what We revealed to Our servant the Messenger Muhammad on the Deciding Day – the day the two armies clashed with each other in the Battle of Badr. Allah is Most Capable of anything. 8.42When you were on the near side of the valley, the enemy were on the far side of the valley, and the trade caravan was below you; if you had fixed a time to fight them, you would certainly have missed the fixed time. However, the fight took place because it was for Allah to decide a matter that was already bound to happen, so that those who died or lived would do so because of some clear evidence of the truth. Allah is certainly All-Hearing, All-Knowing.

8.43Remember, O Prophet Muhammad, when, in your dream, Allah showed them to you as being only a few in number. If He had shown them to you to be many, you Muslims would have been discouraged and would have argued with each other about the matter, but Allah saved you. He knows the secrets of the hearts perfectly well. ⁸·⁴⁴When you met them in battle, He showed them to you as only a few in your eyes and made you appear as few in their eyes, because it was for Allah to decide a matter that was already bound to happen. All matters are returned to Allah.

⁸·⁴⁵Believers! When you clash with an army in battle, you must stand strong and remember Allah a lot so that you might be successful. ⁸·⁴⁶You have to obey Allah and His Messenger, and never quarrel among yourselves or you will lose courage and become weak. You should have patience because Allah is with those who have patience. ⁸·⁴⁷You mustn't be like those who came out of their homes in arrogance and showing off to people, and blocking people from Allah's cause. Allah completely surrounds anything they do.

⁸·⁴⁸When Shaytan made their actions seem attractive to them and boasted: "None of the people can defeat you today because I am protecting you," when the two forces came in sight of each other, Shaytan turned on his heels and ran away, and he said: "I have nothing to do with you! I can see what you cannot. I fear Allah, and He is severe in punishing."

⁸·⁴⁹When the hypocrites and those with sickness in their hearts claim: "These Muslims, their religion has tricked them!" when actually, anyone who puts his trust in Allah knows that Allah is Almighty, All-Wise.

⁸·⁵⁰O human, if only you could see when the angels take away the disbelievers' souls, smashing their faces and backs with hammers and saying: "Taste the punishment of the Scorching Fire! ⁸·⁵¹This is only because of the bad things you have done, as Allah would never treat His servants unfairly."

8.52Like what Fir'awn's people did, as well as those before them; they disbelieved in Allah's revelations, so Allah punished them because of their sins. Allah is Strong, severe in punishing. 8.53This is because Allah never changes the favour He does to any people unless they change what is within themselves. Allah is All-Hearing, All-Knowing. 8.54Like what Fir'awn's people did, as well as those before them; they called their Lord's signs a lie, so We destroyed them because of their sins, and We drowned Fir'awn's people. They were all wrongdoers.

8.55The worst of creatures in the sight of Allah are the disbelievers. They just won't believe. 8.56They are those of them you made a treaty with many times, who then continue to break their treaty each time, not being mindful of Allah. 8.57O Prophet Muhammad, if you come across them in war, you must scare them away as an example to those who come after them, who might learn lessons of warning!

8.58If you fear cheating in the treaty from any people, throw the treaty back at them in rejection in the same way. Allah doesn't like cheaters. 8.59The disbelievers mustn't think they've got away. They cannot escape Allah. 8.60Prepare whatever power you can against them, including warhorses, with which to frighten off Allah's enemies, yours, and others besides them – those you might not know but Allah does. Anything you donate in Allah's cause will be repaid to you in full and you won't be treated unfairly.

8.61However, if the enemy show they want peace then you have to move towards it too, and put your trust in Allah. Only He is the All-Hearing, the All-Knowing. 8.62O Prophet Muhammad, if they try to trick you then Allah is enough for you. He is the one Who supported you with His help and with the Believers, 8.63and joined their hearts together in love. Even if you spent everything in this world, you wouldn't have been able to join their hearts together in love, but Allah has done it. He is Almighty, All-Wise. ⁸·⁶⁴O Prophet, Allah is enough for you, and so are the Believers who follow you.

⁸·⁶⁵O Prophet, you should urge the Believers to fight in Allah's cause. If there are twenty of you who have patience, they can defeat two hundred; if there are a hundred of you, they can defeat a thousand disbelievers – because the disbelievers are a people who don't understand Allah's secrets. ⁸·⁶⁶For now, Allah has made things light for you, because He knows there is some weakness in you. So, if there are a hundred of you who have patience, they can defeat two hundred; if there are a thousand of you, they can defeat two thousand – with Allah's permission, because Allah is with those who have patience.

⁸·⁶⁷It is not the status of a prophet to take prisoners of war until he has become dominant in the land. You people want the temporary wealth of this world but Allah wants you to have the Hereafter. Allah is Almighty, All-Wise. ⁸·⁶⁸If it wasn't for something already fixed by Allah to forgive bad decisions, you would have suffered a terrible punishment because of what you took as ransom. ⁸·⁶⁹So, you may enjoy the lawful, wholesome things you gained in battle, but continue to be mindful of Allah. Allah is Most Forgiving, Ever-Merciful.

⁸·⁷⁰O Prophet, tell those you are holding as prisoners: "If Allah knows any good in your hearts, He will give you something better than what was taken from you, and He will forgive you. Allah is Most Forgiving, Ever-Merciful." ⁸·⁷¹O Prophet Muhammad, if they want to break your trust then it is no surprise because they have already broken Allah's trust before, but He gave you power over them. Allah is All-Knowing, All-Wise.

8.72Those who believed, migrated and strove hard with their wealth and their lives in Allah's cause, as well as those who gave refuge and helped, it is they who are the real friends of each other. Those who believed but didn't migrate, you Muslims don't have any responsibility to protect them until they migrate. However, if they ask you for help for the sake of the religion then you must help them, but not against any people you have a peace treaty with. Allah is Ever-Watchful of everything you Muslims do.

8.73The disbelievers are each other's protectors. Unless you Muslims do the same, there will continue to be oppression in the world and severe trouble.

8.74Those who believed, migrated, and strove hard in Allah's cause, as well as those who gave refuge and helped, in truth, they are the real Believers. They will have forgiveness and some honourable wealth. 8.75Those who believed later on, migrated, and strove hard alongside you, they are also from among you. However, for inheritance some blood relatives are closer than others in Allah's Book. Allah knows everything perfectly well.

Surah 9. Repentance (*at-Tawbah*)

9.1Freedom from punishment is declared from Allah and His Messenger for those polytheists you Muslims had made a peace treaty with. 9.2You polytheists can travel about in the land for four months, but you should know you cannot escape Allah, and that He will humiliate the disbelievers. 9.3An announcement from Allah and His Messenger to the people on the Day of the Great Pilgrimage is that Allah and His Messenger have nothing to do with the polytheists who broke the peace treaty. So, it is best for you polytheists to repent, but if you turn away then you should realise you cannot escape Allah. O Prophet Muhammad, **warn the disbelievers of a painful punishment.**

⁹·⁴**As for those polytheists you** Muslims **have a treaty with and who haven't caused you any loss nor helped anyone against you, you must fulfil their treaty to the end of their term. Allah loves those who are mindful** of Him.

⁹·⁵**Once the sacred months are over, you may kill** in battle **the polytheists** who broke the peace treaty and restarted the war **wherever you find them; capture them, put them in prison, and lie in ambush for them at every place of ambush. If they repent, establish the ritual prayers, and pay zakah, then you must let them go on their way. Allah is Most Forgiving, Ever-Merciful.** ⁹·⁶**If a polytheist asks you for protection, you must give it to him, so that he may hear Allah's Word, and then you must escort him to a place where he is safe. This is because they are a people who don't know** the truth.

⁹·⁷**How can there be any treaty with Allah and with His Messenger for the polytheists except those you made a promise with near the Sacred Masjid? As long as they remain true to you** in the treaty, **you** Muslims **must remain true to them. Allah loves those who are mindful** of Him. ⁹·⁸**How can there be** a treaty! **If they become stronger than you, they would respect neither family ties nor treaties. They might please you with their words but their hearts disagree, and most of them will break agreements.**

⁹·⁹**They sell Allah's revelations for a low price, and they block** people **from His cause. How terrible are the things they keep doing!** ⁹·¹⁰**Where a Believer is concerned, they respect neither family ties nor treaties. It is really they who are the lawbreakers.** ⁹·¹¹**However, if they repent, establish the ritual prayers, and pay zakah, they are, after all, your**

brothers-in-faith. We explain the revelations in detail for any people who have the right knowledge.

⁹·¹²If they break their oaths after making their treaty, and make fun of you because of your religion, then fight the leaders of disbelief who broke the peace treaty so they stop, because their oaths and treaties mean nothing to them. ⁹·¹³Won't you fight any people who broke their oaths and peace treaty and planned to expel the Messenger Muhammad? They're the ones who attacked you first. Are you afraid of them? Allah has more right that you should fear Him if you are true Believers! ⁹·¹⁴You should fight them, and Allah will: punish them at your hands, humiliate them, help you against them, and heal the hearts of Believing people. ⁹·¹⁵He will also remove any anger from their hearts. Allah will forgive anyone He chooses. Allah is All-Knowing, All-Wise.

⁹·¹⁶Did you think you will be left alone without being tested, and that Allah won't prove those of you who strive hard and don't make any intimate friend other than Him, His Messenger, and the Believers? Allah is Fully-Aware of everything you do.

⁹·¹⁷It isn't right for polytheists to look after Allah's masjids while testifying against themselves of disbelief. It is they whose actions will be wasted and they will remain in the Fire forever. ⁹·¹⁸Only those people will look after Allah's masjids who believe in Allah and the Last Day, establish the ritual prayers, pay zakah, and fear no one except Allah. Perhaps it would be they who will be among those who follow guidance.

⁹·¹⁹Do you consider giving water to pilgrims and looking after the Sacred Masjid to be equal to the good things of those who believe in Allah and the Last Day, and strive hard in Allah's cause? They are not

equal in the sight of Allah. Allah doesn't let unjust people succeed. ⁹·²⁰Those who believed, migrated, and strove hard with their wealth and their lives in Allah's cause, they have the highest rank in the sight of Allah. It is they who will be the winners. ⁹·²¹Their Lord gives them good news of a mercy from Himself, of His good pleasure, and of gardens where they will have everlasting delights. ⁹·²²They will remain there forever and ever. With Allah there is a huge reward.

⁹·²³Believers! Don't take protectors from your fathers or your brothers if they prefer disbelief to faith. If any of you does that then it is really they who will be the wrongdoers. ⁹·²⁴Say: "If your fathers, sons, brothers, wives, relatives; the wealth you've earned; the business you fear might suffer a loss; or the houses you are so fond of are dearer to you than Allah and His Messenger and striving hard in His cause, then wait and see when Allah brings His decision to punish. Allah doesn't let disobedient people succeed."

⁹·²⁵Allah has already helped you on many occasions, including the Day of Hunayn – when your great numbers made you feel proud but couldn't benefit you in any way at all; when the land, despite its being vast, seemed to close in on you; and you eventually turned your backs in retreat. ⁹·²⁶Then Allah sent down His special tranquillity on His Messenger and on the Believers, and He sent down troops you couldn't see, and He made the disbelievers suffer. That is their punishment. ⁹·²⁷Then again, even after that, Allah forgives anyone He chooses. Allah is Most Forgiving, Ever-Merciful.

⁹·²⁸Believers! The polytheists are spiritually unclean. They aren't allowed to come near the Sacred Masjid after this year of theirs. If you are afraid of poverty, Allah will very soon make you rich from His grace, if He chooses. Allah is All-Knowing, All-Wise.

⁹·²⁹**From among the People of the Book, those** who broke the peace treaty who don't believe in Allah and the Last Day, nor consider unlawful what Allah and His Messenger have made unlawful, nor follow the True Religion, you should fight them until they willingly pay tax while surrendering.

⁹·³⁰The Jews claimed: "Uzayr (Ezra) is the son of Allah," and the Christians claimed: "The Maseeh is the son of Allah." These are their sayings from their own mouths, copying the sayings of those who had previously disbelieved. May Allah ruin them! How are they being misled!

⁹·³¹**Instead of Allah, they make lords** to worship of: their rabbis, monks, and Maseeh ibn Maryam too, yet they were ordered to worship only One God: there is no god except Him. Glory be to Him above the partner-gods they make with Him.

⁹·³²They want to blow out Allah's light with their mouths, but Allah rejects this and He will only make His light full even if the disbelievers hate it. ⁹·³³He is the one Who sent His Messenger with guidance and the True Religion, to make him dominant over every other religion, even if the polytheists hate it.

⁹·³⁴Believers! Many rabbis and monks wrongfully eat up other people's wealth and block them from Allah's cause. Those who hoard gold and silver and don't spend it in Allah's cause, you should give them warnings of a painful punishment ⁹·³⁵on the Day when it will be heated up in the fire of Hell, and their foreheads, sides, and backs will be branded with it. They will be told: "This is what you hoarded for yourselves. Now taste what you used to hoard."

⁹·³⁶According to Allah, the number of months is twelve in His Book since the day He created the heavens and the earth. Four of them are sacred. That is the correct religion. So, don't wrong yourselves in them, but you may fight totally against the polytheists in retaliation just as they're fighting totally against you. You should know that Allah is with those who are mindful of Him. ⁹·³⁷Postponing the sacred months is only an increase in disbelief, by which the disbelievers are misguided: they make it lawful one year and unlawful another year, to match up to the number that Allah has made sacred, but they end up making lawful what Allah has made unlawful. The terrible nature of their actions is made to seem attractive to them. Allah doesn't let disbelieving people succeed.

⁹·³⁸Believers! When you were told: "Go out and fight in Allah's cause," how could you remain heavily attached to the ground and not move? Do you prefer this life to the Hereafter? The enjoyment of this life is very brief compared to the Hereafter. ⁹·³⁹If you don't go out and fight, He will make you suffer a painful punishment and replace you with other people, and you won't be able to harm Him in any way at all. He is Most Capable of anything.

⁹·⁴⁰Even if you don't help Prophet Muhammad, you should know that Allah has already helped him – when the disbelievers expelled him from Makkah, and he was the second of the two when both were in the Cave of Thawr, and he said to his companion Abu Bakr: "Don't worry. Allah is with us." Then, Allah sent down His special tranquillity on him, supported him with troops you couldn't see, and made the disbelievers' plan fail because Allah's plan is the one that wins. Allah is Almighty, All-Wise.

⁹·⁴¹Go out and fight, armed lightly or heavily, and strive hard with your wealth and your lives in Allah's cause. This is best for you if you

only knew. ⁹·⁴²If it had been easy to gain and a short journey, they would certainly have followed you, but the distance was too long for them. They will swear: "By Allah, if we could, we would certainly have gone out with you." They're destroying themselves, and Allah knows that they are certainly telling lies.

⁹·⁴³O Prophet Muhammad, **may Allah protect you. Why did you give them permission** to stay behind? Those who spoke the truth would have become clear to you and you would have recognised the liars. ⁹·⁴⁴**Those who believe in Allah and the Last Day will never ask your permission** to stay behind **so they could strive hard with their wealth and their lives. Allah knows perfectly well those who are mindful** of Him. ⁹·⁴⁵**Only they will ask your permission** to stay away from striving hard **who don't believe in Allah and the Last Day, and their hearts are in doubt, which is why they're hesitating in their doubts.**

⁹·⁴⁶**If they had really wanted to go out** and fight, they would certainly have made some serious preparation for it, but Allah didn't even like their rising up for it so He let them stay behind, and they were told: "Continue sitting with those who stay behind." ⁹·⁴⁷**If they had gone out with you** in your army, they would have only increased trouble for you, and they would have run about between you trying to cause conflict among you, and they even now **have spies among you. Allah knows the wrongdoers perfectly well.** ⁹·⁴⁸O Prophet Muhammad, **they have already tried to cause conflict before, and turn matters against you, until the truth appeared and Allah's command became clear, even though they hated it.**

⁹·⁴⁹**Some of them ask: "Allow me** to stay home **and don't put me into a test." Beware! They have already fallen into the test! Of course, Hell will completely surround the disbelievers.** ⁹·⁵⁰**If something good comes to you, it upsets them; but if you suffer a disaster, they say:**

"We have already prepared for ourselves in advance," and they go away rejoicing.

⁹·⁵¹O Prophet Muhammad, say: "Nothing can happen to us except what Allah has written for us. He is our Protector. True Believers must put their trust only in Allah." ⁹·⁵²Say: "Are you waiting for one of the two best things martyrdom or victory to happen to us? Well, we are waiting for Allah to make you suffer with a punishment from Himself or at our hands. So, keep waiting. We will wait with you to see what happens."

⁹·⁵³O Prophet Muhammad, say: "Whether you donate willingly or unwillingly, it will never be accepted from you because you have been a disobedient people." ⁹·⁵⁴The only reasons that stop their donations from being accepted are: they disbelieve in Allah and His Messenger, they come to prayer lazily, and they donate unwillingly. ⁹·⁵⁵Their lots of wealth and children shouldn't impress you. Allah wants to make them suffer through these things in this life, and to allow them to die as disbelievers.

⁹·⁵⁶They swear by Allah that they're certainly from among you, though they are not. Actually, they are a people who are scared. ⁹·⁵⁷If they could find a place of refuge, caves, or a burrow, they would turn and run quickly towards it.

⁹·⁵⁸O Prophet Muhammad, some of them are those who criticise you regarding the distribution of charities: they are pleased if they're given some from them, but feel annoyed if they aren't given any. ⁹·⁵⁹If only they were pleased with what Allah and His Messenger had given them, and had said: "Allah is enough for us. Allah will give us from His grace and so will His Messenger. We turn in hope to Allah."

⁹·⁶⁰Charities – prescribed by Allah – are only for the poor, the needy, those in charge of them, those whose hearts need winning over, those in slavery, those in debt, in Allah's cause, and needy travellers. Allah is All-Knowing, All-Wise.

⁹·⁶¹Some of them are those who annoy the Prophet and say: "He listens to anything!" O Prophet Muhammad, say: "He listens to what is best for you: believing in Allah, having faith in the Believers, and a mercy to those of you who believe." Those who annoy Allah's Messenger will suffer a painful punishment.

⁹·⁶²The hypocrites swear by Allah to you Muslims just to please you, but Allah and His Messenger have more right that these people should please them, if they are really Believers. ⁹·⁶³Don't they know that anyone who goes against Allah and His Messenger will suffer the fire of Hell, where he will remain forever? That is the ultimate humiliation.

⁹·⁶⁴The hypocrites are afraid that a surah will be sent down to the Believers clearly telling them what is inside the hypocrites' hearts. Say: "Continue mocking! Allah will expose everything you are afraid of." ⁹·⁶⁵If you asked them, they will certainly say: "We were only joking and playing." Ask: "Was it Allah, His revelations, and His Messenger that you were making fun of?" ⁹·⁶⁶Don't make excuses! You have disbelieved after apparently being Believers. Even if We forgive some of you, We will punish the others for being criminals.

⁹·⁶⁷The male and female hypocrites are just the same. They command what is wrong, forbid what is good, and they are stingy. They have forgotten Allah so He will ignore them. The hypocrites are really the disobedient ones. ⁹·⁶⁸Allah has threatened the male and female hypocrites, and the disbelievers too, with the fire of Hell, where they

will remain forever. It will be enough for them. Allah curses them, and they will suffer an everlasting punishment.

⁹·⁶⁹You hypocrites are just like those before you, though they were stronger than you with more wealth and children. They enjoyed their share of this world, now you've enjoyed your share just like those before you enjoyed theirs, and you've done useless things just like they did. It is they whose actions are wasted in this world and the next, and it is they who are the real losers. ⁹·⁷⁰Haven't stories reached them of those before them: the people of Nuh, the 'Ad, and the Thamud; the people of Ibrahim, the citizens of Madyan, and of the overturned cities (- where Lut lived)? Their messengers brought them clear proofs. Allah wouldn't harm them but rather they used to harm themselves.

⁹·⁷¹Believing men and women are each other's protectors. They command what is right, forbid what is wrong, establish the ritual prayers, pay zakah, and obey Allah and His Messenger. It is they Allah will have special mercy on. Allah is Almighty, All-Wise. ⁹·⁷²Allah promised the Believing men and women; gardens – that have rivers flowing beneath them, where they will remain forever; and beautiful mansions in the Gardens of Eden; and the greatest happiness will be Allah's good pleasure. That is the tremendous victory.

⁹·⁷³O Prophet, you should continue to strive hard against the disbelievers and the hypocrites, and be firm with them. Their home will be Hell. What a horrible final destination! ⁹·⁷⁴They swear by Allah that they didn't say words of disbelief, but they certainly did. They disbelieved after being Muslims and decided to do something they couldn't achieve. They paid back in hate only because Allah and His Messenger had made them rich from His grace. It is best for them to repent; if they turn away, Allah will make them suffer a painful

punishment in this world and the next, and they won't have any protector or helper on earth.

[9.75] Some of them are those who made a treaty with Allah, that 'if He gives us from His grace, we will definitely give charity and be among the righteous people.'. [9.76] However, when He gave them from His grace, they became stingy with it, and turned away ignoring their promise. [9.77] So, because they broke the promise they made with Him and because of the lies they used to tell, He let hypocrisy enter their hearts until the Day they will meet Him. [9.78] Don't they realise Allah knows their secrets and their private discussions, and that He is the Knower of the unseen secrets?

[9.79] Those who look for mistakes in the Believers who give generously in acts of charity, and who make fun of those who cannot afford to give anything other than their own hard work, Allah will humiliate them and they will suffer a painful punishment. [9.80] O Prophet Muhammad, whether you ask forgiveness for them or not, Allah will never forgive them, even if you ask forgiveness for them seventy times. This is because they disbelieve in Allah and His Messenger Muhammad. Allah doesn't let disobedient people succeed.

[9.81] Those who were left behind were delighted in their staying back and going against the orders of Allah's Messenger. They didn't want to strive hard in Allah's cause with their wealth and their lives. They told each other: "Don't go out in the heat." O Prophet Muhammad, say to them: "The fire of Hell will be far hotter." If only they would understand. [9.82] They should laugh less and cry a lot because they will suffer a punishment for the bad things they've been doing.

[9.83] If Allah brings you back to a group of them, and they ask your permission to go out with you to fight, you should say: "You can never go out with me nor fight an enemy alongside me. You preferred to stay behind the first time, so continue sitting with those who will stay behind."

9.84O Prophet Muhammad, you must never offer funeral prayers for any of these hypocrites who dies, nor even stand at his grave. They disbelieved in Allah and His Messenger, and they died as disobedient people. 9.85Their lots of wealth and children shouldn't impress you. Allah wants to make them suffer through these things in this world, and to allow them to die as disbelievers. 9.86When a surah is revealed that: "You must believe in Allah and strive hard alongside His Messenger," the rich among them ask your permission, and they plead: "Leave us to be with those who stay behind." 9.87They prefer to be with those who stay behind. Their hearts are sealed up, so now they won't understand true success.

9.88However, the Messenger, and the Believers with him, strove hard with their wealth and their lives. It is they who will have the best things, and it is really they who will be successful. 9.89Allah has prepared for them gardens – that have rivers flowing beneath them, where they will remain forever. That is the tremendous victory.

9.90Some desert Arabs offering excuses also came along asking to be allowed not to fight. Those who lied to Allah and His Messenger, they stayed behind. The disbelievers among them will soon suffer a painful punishment.

9.91There is no blame on the weak, the ill, or those who cannot find anything to spend, if they are sincere to Allah and His Messenger. There is no way to blame those who do good. Allah is Most Forgiving, Ever-Merciful. 9.92There is no blame on those who came to you, O Prophet Muhammad, so you could mount them on transport, but you had to say: "I cannot find any transport for you." They turned away with their eyes overflowing with tears out of sadness that they couldn't find anything to donate.

⁹·⁹³The way of blame is on those who ask your permission not to donate even though they are rich. They prefer to be with those who stay behind. Allah has sealed up their hearts, so now they won't know true success.

[PART 11]

⁹·⁹⁴They offer you excuses when you go back to them. You should reply: "Don't make excuses! We won't believe merely because you say so. Allah has already told us the true things about you. Allah and His Messenger will soon see your work, and then you will be taken back to Allah – the Knower of the unseen secrets and the visible, and He will tell you about everything you used to do." ⁹·⁹⁵When you go back to them, they will swear oaths to you by Allah so that you might leave them alone. So, stay away from them because they are spiritually unclean. Their home will be Hell, as a punishment for the bad things they've been doing. ⁹·⁹⁶They swear to you that you might be pleased with them, but even if you are pleased with them, Allah won't be pleased with these disobedient people.

⁹·⁹⁷The desert Arabs are the most stubborn in disbelief and hypocrisy, and least likely to know the limits and commandments Allah has revealed to His Messenger. However, Allah is All-Knowing, All-wise. ⁹·⁹⁸Some desert Arabs think that what they donate is a punishing fine, and they're waiting for disasters to hit you Muslims. May the disasters of devastation be upon them! Allah is All-Hearing, All-Knowing. ⁹·⁹⁹Some other desert Arabs believe in Allah and the Last Day, and they believe what they donate is a way of getting close to Allah and of receiving prayers from the Messenger. Of course, it is a

way for them to get close to Allah. Allah will take them into His special mercy. Allah is Most Forgiving, Ever-Merciful.

9.100 Allah is well-pleased with those who were the very first among the Migrants and the Helpers, and those who followed them in goodness. They are also well-pleased with Him. He has prepared for them gardens – that have rivers flowing beneath them, where they will remain forever and ever. That is the tremendous victory.

9.101 Around you Muslims are some desert Arabs who are hypocrites, and so are some people of Madinah. They are stubborn in hypocrisy. O Prophet Muhammad, you don't know them but We know them well. We will punish them twice in this world, and eventually they will be pushed down into a painful punishment in the Hereafter. 9.102 There are others who have confessed their sins; they had unintentionally mixed a good action with a bad one. Allah will certainly forgive them because He is Most Forgiving, Ever-Merciful.

9.103 O Prophet Muhammad, take some charity from their wealth, to clean and purify them with it; and pray for them. Your prayers are a comfort for them. Allah is All-Hearing, All-Knowing. 9.104 Don't they know that it is Allah Who accepts repentance from His servants, and receives their charity? It is Allah Who accepts repentance much, the Ever-Merciful.

9.105 O Prophet Muhammad, say: "Do good. Allah will see what you do, and so will His Messenger, and the Believers too. Then you will all be taken back to Allah – the Knower of the unseen secrets and the visible, and He will tell you about everything you used to do."

9.106 There are others, made to hope for Allah's decision; He will either punish them or forgive them. Allah is All-Knowing, All-Wise.

⁹·¹⁰⁷There are also **those** hypocrites **who used a masjid to cause harm and promote disbelief, to split the Believers apart, and as a base for whoever is already at war against Allah and His Messenger.** They will definitely swear: "We only intended good." Allah is a Witness that they are certainly liars. ⁹·¹⁰⁸O Prophet Muhammad, **don't ever stand inside it.** A masjid founded on the fear of Allah from the very first day has more right for you to stand inside it, in which there are men who keep themselves clean and pure. Allah loves those who keep themselves clean and pure. ⁹·¹⁰⁹Who is better: someone who founded his building on mindfulness of Allah and His good pleasure or someone who founded his building on a crumbling cliff edge that tumbled down with him into the fire of Hell? Allah doesn't let unjust people succeed. ⁹·¹¹⁰What they built will continue to be a source of doubt in their hearts, until their hearts will be torn apart. Allah is All-Knowing, All-Wise.

⁹·¹¹¹Allah has bought from the Believers their lives and their wealth because they will have Paradise – they fight in Allah's cause, killing or being killed – as a promise binding upon Him that is true in the Tawrah, Injeel, and Qur'an. Who could be more faithful to his promise than Allah! So, you should be happy with the bargain you have made. It is this which is the tremendous victory.

⁹·¹¹²True Believers are those: **who repent, worship** Allah, **praise** Him, fast, bow down, prostrate, command what is right, forbid what is wrong, and look after the limits set by Allah. So, give good news to the Believers.

⁹·¹¹³The Prophet and the Believers wouldn't ask forgiveness for the polytheists, even if they are close relatives, after it has become clear to them that they will be the people of Hell-Fire. ⁹·¹¹⁴Ibrahim asked

forgiveness for his foster father only because of a promise he had made to him, but when it became clear to him that he is an enemy of Allah, Ibrahim didn't want anything to do with him. Ibrahim was certainly tender-hearted, forbearing.

9.115 Allah wouldn't let any people go astray after He has guided them, until He has made clear to them what they should be mindful of. Allah knows everything perfectly well. 9.116 Control of the heavens and the earth belongs to Allah. He gives life and death. You don't have any protector or helper besides Him.

9.117 Allah has turned in mercy towards the Prophet, the Migrants, and the Helpers – who followed him at a time of difficulty after the hearts of some of them nearly strayed, but then He turned towards them in mercy. He is Kind, Ever-Merciful to them. 9.118 He also turned in mercy towards the three who were left behind, until the land, despite its being vast, seemed to close in on them, and their own lives became depressing for them, and they realised that there is no place of refuge from Allah except in Him. Then He turned towards them in mercy so they could repent. It is Allah Who accepts repentance much, the Ever-Merciful. 9.119 Believers! You must continue to be mindful of Allah and be with those who stick to the truth.

9.120 It isn't right for the people of Madinah and the desert Arabs around them to stay away from helping Allah's Messenger or to prefer their own lives to his. This is because a good action will be recorded for them: because of any thirst, tiredness, or hunger they suffer in Allah's cause; or if they go down a path that angers the disbelievers; or if they win anything from an enemy. Allah would never let the reward go to waste of those who do good. 9.121 Anything they donate, a little or a lot, or even if they cross a valley, it will be recorded for them so Allah may give them the best reward for the good they used to do.

⁹·¹²²It isn't possible for the Believers to all go out together. So, why shouldn't a section from within each community among them not go out so they can gain a deeper understanding of the religion of Islam, and then warn their people when they come back to them so they too can guard themselves against doing anything wrong?

⁹·¹²³Believers! Fight those disbelievers in battle who are near you. They should find toughness in you. You should bear in mind that Allah is with those who are mindful of Him.

⁹·¹²⁴Whenever a surah is revealed, some of the hypocrites ask just to make fun of it: "Which of you has this surah increased in faith?" As for the Believers, it has increased them in faith and they're happy. ⁹·¹²⁵As for those in whose heart is a sickness, it has added more filth to their own filth, and they will die as disbelievers. ⁹·¹²⁶Don't they see they're being tested once or twice every year? Even then they don't repent nor learn any lessons. ⁹·¹²⁷Whenever a surah is sent down, they look at each other, asking: "Is anyone watching you?" Then they slip away. Allah has turned their hearts around because they are a people who won't understand.

⁹·¹²⁸A Messenger has come to you from among yourselves. It is painful to him when you suffer because he is deeply concerned for you, as he is kind, merciful to the Believers. ⁹·¹²⁹However, if they turn away, O Prophet Muhammad, say: "Allah is enough for me. There is no god except Him. I put my trust only in Him. He is the Lord of the Mighty Throne."

Surah 10. Yunus (Jonah)

Allah's name I begin with, the Most Compassionate, the Ever-Merciful

10.1 *Alif Laam Raa.* These are the verses of the Book Full of Wisdom. 10.2 Is it a surprise to people that We've made revelations to a man from among them, telling him to: "Give warnings to people, and good news to the Believers that they have a high status of truth in the sight of their Lord."? Yet the disbelievers say: "This man is clearly a magician!"

10.3 Your Lord is Allah, Who created the heavens and the earth in six stages, and then established His authority on the Throne, governing every affair. No one can intercede without His permission. That is Allah – your Lord, so worship Him. Won't you even remind yourselves? 10.4 You will all go back to Him. Allah's promise is true. He starts creating, then He will repeat it, to reward with fairness those who believed and did good. The disbelievers will suffer a boiling liquid to drink and a painful punishment because they used to disbelieve.

10.5 He is the one Who made the sun a shining radiance and the moon a light – and fixed for it some phases for you to know the number of years and the calculation of time. Allah created this only for a real purpose. He explains the signs in detail for any who have the right knowledge. 10.6 In the rotation of the night and day, and everything Allah has created in the heavens and the earth, there are certainly signs for people who are mindful of Allah.

10.7 Those people who don't expect to have a meeting with Us and are pleased and satisfied with this life, as well as those who don't pay any attention to Our signs, ¹⁰·⁸it is they whose home will be the Fire because of the bad things they used to do.

¹⁰·⁹Those people who believe and do good, their Lord will guide them because of their faith. Rivers will flow beneath them in Gardens of Delight. ¹⁰·¹⁰There, their prayer will be: "Glory be to You, O Allah!" their greeting will be: "Peace," and their prayer will end: "All praise is for Allah – Lord of all the worlds!"

¹⁰·¹¹If Allah brought bad things any sooner to people like they want good things to come early, the end of their time would have been settled immediately. However, those who don't expect to have a meeting with Us, We will leave them confused to wander blindly in their rebellion.

¹⁰·¹²When harm comes to anyone, He cries out to Us – whether lying down on his side, sitting, or standing, but when We remove his suffering from him, he goes on his way as if he had never called out to Us in the harm that he suffered. In this way the wrongs of those who go to extremes are made to seem attractive to them.

¹⁰·¹³We destroyed generations before you when they did wrong. Their messengers brought them clear proofs but they still wouldn't believe. This is how We punish criminal people. ¹⁰·¹⁴Then, after them, We made you successors in this world to see how you would behave.

¹⁰·¹⁵When Our clear verses are recited to them, those who don't expect to have a meeting with Us, they demand: "Bring us a different Qur'an or change this one." O Prophet Muhammad, reply: "It isn't for me to change of my own choice. I only follow what is revealed to me. I fear the punishment of a Dreadful Day if I disobey my Lord." ¹⁰·¹⁶Say: "If Allah had wanted, I wouldn't have recited it to you nor would He have

made it known to you. I have lived a whole life-time among you before this Qur'an. Don't you even think? [10.17]Who could be more unjust than someone who makes lies about Allah or calls His revelations a lie! The criminals will never succeed.

[10.18]They worship, besides Allah, things that can neither harm nor help them, and they claim: "These will intercede for us with Allah." O Prophet Muhammad, ask: "Are you telling Allah of things He doesn't already know about in the heavens and the earth? Glory be to Him! He is much higher than the partner-gods they make with Him."

[10.19]All the people used to be a single community, but then they began to have disagreements. If it wasn't for something already fixed by your Lord, their disagreements would have been settled immediately between them.

[10.20]They ask: "Why wasn't a permanent sign sent down to him from his Lord?" Reply: "The unseen secrets are Allah's. So, wait for that sign all of you. I'm with you among those who are waiting." [10.21]When We give people a taste of some special mercy after they had suffered some hard times, they immediately begin to plot against Our signs! Say: "Allah is quicker in punishing you for your planning." Our angels are recording everything you plot.

[10.22]He is the one Who lets you travel on land and sea, so that when you're aboard ships that sail with the people in a favourable wind, and they rejoice in it, a stormy wind suddenly hits those ships, and waves crash over them from all sides, and they realise they're completely surrounded by disaster, they pray to Allah in sincere devotion to Him, crying: "If you save us from this, we will certainly be among those who are thankful." [10.23]However, when He saves them, they immediately begin rebelling in the land without having any right to do so. People! You are only rebelling against yourselves. You may have some enjoyment of this life, but in the end, you will all come back to Us, and We will tell you about everything you used to do.

10.24"The example of this life is that of water: We send it down from the sky with which the plants of the land grow thick – from which humans and animals can eat. Then, when the earth takes on its blossoms and turns beautiful, and its people begin to think they have power over it, Our order of destruction comes upon it at night or day, and We turn it into mown down harvest as if it wasn't even there yesterday! In this way We explain the signs of Our power in detail for any people who think deeply.

10.25Allah calls to Paradise – the Home of Peace, and He guides anyone He chooses to a path that is straight. 10.26Those who do good will have the most beautiful reward, and more! Neither gloom nor humiliation will cover their faces. It is they who will be the people of Paradise, where they will remain forever.

10.27Those who did bad things should know that the punishment for doing something bad will be equal to it and humiliation will cover them as if their faces have been covered with dark patches of night, and they won't have anyone to defend them from the punishment of Allah. It is they who will be the people of the Fire, where they will remain forever.

10.28On the Day We will gather them all together, We will say to the polytheists: "Stay where you are! You and your partner-gods!" We will separate them from each other, and their partner-gods will say: "It wasn't really us you used to worship. 10.29Allah is enough as a

Witness between us and you lot. We weren't even unaware of your worship!"

^{10.30}Every person will realise there and then the bad things they had done in the past. They will be brought back to Allah – their Real Master, and those idols and lies they made up will abandon them.

^{10.31}O Prophet Muhammad, ask: "Who is it that gives you from the sky and the earth, or Who is it that controls hearing and seeing? Who is it that brings out the living from the dead and the dead from the living? Who is it that governs every affair?" They will say: "Allah!" Reply: "Then won't you be mindful of Him?" ^{10.32}That is Allah – your true Lord! So, apart from being astray, what is there beyond the truth? So, how are you being turned away? ^{10.33}This is how something already fixed by your Lord proved true against those who disobeyed – that they won't believe.

^{10.34}O Prophet Muhammad, ask: "Can any of those you make partner-gods with Allah start creating and then repeat it?" Reply: "It is Allah Who starts creating and then repeats it. So how are you being misled!" ^{10.35}Ask: "Can any of those you make partner-gods with Allah guide to the truth?" Reply: "It is Allah Who guides to the truth. So, who has more right to be followed: someone who guides to the truth or someone who himself cannot find guidance unless he is guided? Then what is wrong with you? How are you making bad decisions?" ^{10.36}Most of them follow only guesswork. Guesswork cannot replace the truth in any way at all. Allah knows perfectly well everything they do.

^{10.37}This Qur'an isn't something that could have been made up by anyone other than Allah. In fact, it is a confirmation of what came before it, and a detailed explanation of the Book in which there is no

doubt that it is from Allah – the Lord of all the worlds. [10.38]Are they claiming: "He made it up."? O Prophet Muhammad, say: "Then you make a surah like it. You may even call anyone you can to help you, apart from Allah, if you are telling the truth." [10.39]The fact is, anything whose knowledge they couldn't fully understand and whose final fulfilment hadn't appeared to them yet, they called it a lie. In the same way those before them also called the truth a lie. Just take a look at what was the end result of the wrongdoers.

[10.40]Some of them believe in it while others won't. However, O Prophet Muhammad, your Lord knows best those who make trouble. [10.41]If they accuse you of being a liar, say: "My work is for me, and yours is for you. You aren't responsible for what I do nor I for what you do." [10.42]Some of them only pretend to listen to you, but will you make the deaf people listen even if they won't think? [10.43]Some of them look towards you, but will you show guidance to the blind people even if they won't want to see? [10.44]Allah doesn't harm people in any way at all, but rather they harm themselves.

[10.45]On the Day He will assemble them together, it will be as if they had lived in the world for hardly a single hour of a day, trying to get to know each other. Those who think the meeting with Allah is a lie, they will already have lost because they haven't been following guidance.

[10.46]O Prophet Muhammad, it doesn't matter if We show you some of the punishment We are warning them of or if We take away your soul before that, they will still come back to Us. Then again, Allah is a Witness over anything they do.

[10.47]Every community was sent a messenger. So, when their messenger came to them, judgement was made between them with fairness, and they weren't treated unfairly. ¹⁰·⁴⁸They ask: "When will this warning be fulfilled, if you are telling the truth?" ¹⁰·⁴⁹Reply: "I don't own any profit or loss for myself apart from what Allah chooses. Every nation has an end date. When the end of their time comes, they can neither delay it a moment longer nor bring it any sooner."

¹⁰·⁵⁰Ask: "If His punishment was to come to you disbelievers at night or day, have you ever thought what part of it the criminals are wanting to bring sooner?" ¹⁰·⁵¹In the end when it does take place, they will be asked: "Do you believe in it? Now? And you wanted to bring it sooner!" ¹⁰·⁵²Then the wrongdoers will be told: "Now taste the everlasting punishment! Aren't you being punished only for the bad things you used to do?"

¹⁰·⁵³O Prophet Muhammad, they ask you: "Is it true?" Reply: "Yes! I swear by my Lord that: it is very true, and you won't be able to escape!" ¹⁰·⁵⁴If every wrongdoer owned everything in the world, he would certainly give it up as ransom. They would hide their regret when they see the punishment, but judgement will be made between them with fairness. They won't be treated unfairly. ¹⁰·⁵⁵Beware! Everything in the heavens and the earth belongs to Allah. Of course, Allah's promise is true but most of them don't know. ¹⁰·⁵⁶He gives life and death, and it is Him you will all be taken back to.

¹⁰·⁵⁷People! What has come to you from your Lord is a source of advice, a cure for what is in the hearts, a guidance, and a mercy to the Believers. ¹⁰·⁵⁸O Prophet Muhammad, say: "All this is due to Allah's grace and mercy, so it is in this they should rejoice, as it is far better than what they're gathering together."

¹⁰·⁵⁹O Prophet Muhammad, ask: "Have you people ever thought about the food Allah sends down for you? You yourselves declare some of it

to be unlawful and lawful." Ask: "Did Allah give you permission to do this or are you making lies against Him?" ¹⁰·⁶⁰Those who make lies about Allah, what are their thoughts about Judgement Day? Allah gives grace to people yet most of them don't even give thanks.

¹⁰·⁶¹In whatever condition you people may be, whatever portion of the Qur'an you recite in that condition, and anything you do, We witness you when you are busy doing it. Not even an atom's weight is hidden from your Lord, neither in the earth nor sky, and there isn't anything smaller or bigger than that but is written in a record that is clear (- the Well-Preserved Tablet).

¹⁰·⁶²Beware! The Friends of Allah – they won't have anything to fear and will never be sad, ¹⁰·⁶³who believe and continue to be mindful of Allah. ¹⁰·⁶⁴There is good news for them in this life and the next. There is no changing Allah's words of promise. It is that which is the tremendous victory.

¹⁰·⁶⁵O Prophet Muhammad, don't let their words upset you, because glory and power belong entirely to Allah. He is the All-Hearing, the All-Knowing. ¹⁰·⁶⁶Beware! Everyone in the heavens and on earth belongs to Allah. Those who pray to anything besides Allah don't really follow any of their partner-gods. They're only following suspicion; they are only guessing. ¹⁰·⁶⁷He is the one Who made the night for you to rest in and the day clear to see. There are certainly signs in this for any people who listen carefully.

¹⁰·⁶⁸They say: "Allah has a child." Glory be to Him! He is free of all needs. Everything in the heavens and the earth belongs to Him. You don't have any proof for this lie. Are you saying things about Allah what you don't even know?! ¹⁰·⁶⁹O Prophet Muhammad, say: "Those who make lies about Allah will never succeed." ¹⁰·⁷⁰Then after a little

enjoyment in this world, they will come back to Us. Then We will make them taste severe punishment because they used to disbelieve.

[10.71]O Prophet Muhammad, tell them the story of Nuh, when he said to his people: "My people, if my position and my reminders through Allah's revelations are unbearable for you, then you should know that I put my trust only in Allah. With your partner-gods, you can make an agreement about your plan – and your plan shouldn't remain secret to you – then do what you want with me, and don't spare me! [10.72]If you turn away from my advice, then you should know that I haven't asked you for any payment. My reward will come only from Allah. I've been ordered to be among those who surrender to Allah as Muslims." [10.73]However, they accused him of being a liar, but We saved him and those with him in the Ark, and made them successors in this world, while We drowned those who called Our revelations a lie. Now take a look at what was the end result of those who were given warnings.

[10.74]Then, after him, We sent many messengers to their people. The messengers brought them clear proofs, but those people wouldn't believe what they had previously called lies. In this way We seal up the hearts of lawbreakers.

[10.75]Then, after them, We sent Musa and Haroon with Our signs to Fir'awn and his ministers – but they showed arrogance and were a criminal people. [10.76]So, when the truth from Us appeared to them, they said: "This is clearly magic." [10.77]Musa replied: "Are you saying this about the truth now that it has appeared to you? Is this magic? Because magicians don't succeed." [10.78]They asked: "Have you two come to turn us away from what we saw our forefathers doing, so that both of you can have greatness in this land of Egypt? We won't believe for your sake." [10.79]Fir'awn ordered: "Bring me every skilful magician!" ¹⁰·⁸⁰When the magicians came, Musa said to them: "Throw down whatever you want to throw down!" ¹⁰·⁸¹When they had thrown, Musa said: "What you have brought is magic. Allah will prove it false. Allah doesn't let the work of troublemakers be put right. ¹⁰·⁸²Allah proves the truth with His words even if the criminals hate it."

¹⁰·⁸³Other than some youths from his people, no one believed in Musa because of their fear of Fir'awn and his ministers – in case they might punish them. Fir'awn was certainly a tyrant in the land and definitely among those who go to extremes in oppressing. ¹⁰·⁸⁴Musa said: "My people! If you believe in Allah and really surrender to Him as Muslims then you must put your trust only in Him." ¹⁰·⁸⁵They replied: "We put our trust only in Allah," and prayed: "Our Lord! Don't make us victims of these oppressive people, ¹⁰·⁸⁶but save us by Your special mercy from these disbelieving people."

¹⁰·⁸⁷We revealed to Musa and his brother: "Make homes for your people in Egypt. Make your homes facing the prayer-direction, establish the ritual prayers, and give good news to the Believers." ¹⁰·⁸⁸Musa prayed: "Our Lord! You have given Fir'awn and his ministers luxury and wealth in this life, and so, our Lord, they are leading others away from Your cause. Our Lord! Destroy their wealth, and make their hearts hard so they cannot believe until they see the painful punishment." ¹⁰·⁸⁹Allah replied: "Your prayer has been accepted, O Musa and Haroon. You must stay strong and never follow the path of those who have no knowledge."

¹⁰·⁹⁰We brought the Descendants of Ya'qub across the sea but Fir'awn and his armies chased after them in aggression and enmity. Then, as he was drowning, Fir'awn cried out: "I believe there is no god except Him in the one the Descendants of Ya'qub believe! I am among those who surrender to Allah as Muslims!" ¹⁰·⁹¹Allah said: "Now? But only a

little while ago you rebelled! and you were one of the troublemakers! ¹⁰·⁹²From today, We will preserve your dead body so you can be a sign of warning for those who will come after you. Many people don't pay any attention to Our signs."

¹⁰·⁹³We let the Descendants of Ya'qub stay in a place of honour and gave them wholesome things. It was only after knowledge came to them that they had disagreements with each other. Your Lord will judge between them on Judgement Day about the disagreements they used to have.

¹⁰·⁹⁴O human! If you are in any doubt about what We've sent down on Our Messenger Muhammad to you then ask those who have been reading the Book from before you. The truth has certainly come to you from your Lord, so you'll never be one of those who doubt ¹⁰·⁹⁵nor of those who call Allah's revelations a lie, or you will end up among the losers.

¹⁰·⁹⁶"Those against whom something already fixed by your Lord proved true, they will never believe, ¹⁰·⁹⁷even if all the signs did appear to them, until they see the painful punishment.

¹⁰·⁹⁸Why hasn't there been a single town that believed, so that its faith could have helped it, other than the people of Yunus? When they believed, We removed from them the suffering of humiliation in this life, and We let them enjoy themselves for a while.

¹⁰·⁹⁹O Prophet Muhammad, if your Lord had wanted to force them, all those in the world would certainly have believed – every one of them. So, would you force people to become Believers? ¹⁰·¹⁰⁰No one would believe without Allah's permission, and He humiliates with disbelief those who don't think.

¹⁰·¹⁰¹O Prophet Muhammad, say: "Take a look at everything in the heavens and the earth." However, neither signs nor warners can benefit any people who don't want to believe. ¹⁰·¹⁰²What are they waiting for: similar days of punishment as those who passed away before them? O Prophet Muhammad, say: "Then keep waiting. I'm with you among those who are waiting." ¹⁰·¹⁰³In the end, We will save Our messengers and the Believers. This is how it is: it is Our duty to save the Believers.

¹⁰·¹⁰⁴O Prophet Muhammad, say: "People! If you are in any doubt about my religion then you should know that I don't worship what you worship besides Allah, but I worship Allah Who will let you die. I've been ordered to be among the Believers, ¹⁰·¹⁰⁵and, 'Put your identity truly in the religion of Islam and never be a polytheist. ¹⁰·¹⁰⁶Never pray to anything besides Allah that can neither help nor harm you. If you do, then you will certainly be a wrongdoer.'." ¹⁰·¹⁰⁷If Allah lets some harm come to you, no one can remove it except Him. If He wants any good for you, no one can turn His grace away; He makes it reach any of His servants He chooses. He is the Most Forgiving, the Ever-Merciful.

¹⁰·¹⁰⁸O Prophet Muhammad, say: "People! The truth has come to you from your Lord. Anyone who accepts guidance, accepts it for his own good; anyone who goes astray, does so to his own loss. I won't be responsible for you."

¹⁰·¹⁰⁹O Prophet Muhammad, you should follow what is revealed to you, and have patience until Allah gives His decision. He is the Best to decide.

Surah 11. Hud

Allah's name I begin with, the Most Compassionate, the Ever-Merciful

11.1*Alif Laam Raa.* This is a Book, whose verses are made specific, then further explained in detail, from an All-Wise, Fully-Aware Lord: 11.2that you mustn't worship anyone besides Allah. I've been sent to you from Him to give warnings and good news, 11.3and to tell you that you must beg your Lord to forgive you and then continue to repent to Him; He will let you have good enjoyment for a fixed term, and He will give His grace to everyone who deserves it. However, if you continue to turn away, then I fear for you the punishment of a Difficult Day. 11.4You will all go back to Allah, and He is Most Capable of anything.

11.5Look! How they fold up their hearts to try and hide their intentions from Him! Beware! Even when they cover themselves with their clothing, He knows everything they hide or show. He knows the secrets of the hearts perfectly well.

[PART 12]

11.6There is no creature on earth whose food is not guaranteed by Allah. Allah knows the time and place where it lives and the time and place it will go in death. Everything is written in a record that is clear. 11.7He is the one Who created the heavens and the earth in six stages – and His Throne of authority was over the waters – so He can test which of you does the best. O Prophet Muhammad, if you told them: "You will be brought back to life after death," the disbelievers will definitely say: "This is clearly magic."

11.8If We delay the punishment for them for a fixed term, they will certainly joke: "What is holding it back?" Beware! On the Day it will come upon them, it won't be turned away from them, and the punishment they used to make fun of will end up punishing them. ¹¹·⁹If We give anyone a taste of some special mercy from Us and then take it away from him, he will certainly be disappointed, unthankful. ¹¹·¹⁰However, if We give him a taste of some favours after he had suffered some hard times, he will certainly say: "All my troubles have gone." He becomes excited, boastful, ¹¹·¹¹except those who have patience and do good; it is they who will have forgiveness and a large reward.

¹¹·¹²O Prophet Muhammad, how can it be possible for you to leave out a part of what is revealed to you, with your noble heart feeling tight by it because the disbelievers would ask: "Why wasn't a treasure sent down to him or an angel come with him?" You are a warner, and it is Allah Who is in charge of everything.

¹¹·¹³They might claim: "He made it up." Say: "Then you should make up ten surahs just like it. You may even call anyone you can to help you, apart from Allah, if you are telling the truth." ¹¹·¹⁴However, if your helpers don't respond to you, then you should be certain that this has been sent down by Allah's knowledge, and that there is no god except Him. Now, will you surrender to Him as Muslims?

¹¹·¹⁵Those who want only this life and its luxuries, We will repay them in full for what they did in this life and they won't be underpaid in it. ¹¹·¹⁶It is they who will have nothing but Fire in the Hereafter. What they made in this life will be wasted, and anything good they used to do will become useless.

¹¹·¹⁷Can they be compared to those who have a clear proof from their Lord, as well as a witness from Him supporting them, and the Book of Musa had come before him as a guide and a mercy? It is those

Believers who believe in it. Those groups that disbelieve in it, their destination will be the Fire they've been warned about. Be in no doubt about it. It is the truth from your Lord yet most people don't believe.

11.18Who could be more unjust than someone who makes lies about Allah! It is they who will be brought in front of their Lord and the witnesses will say: "These are the ones who lied about their Lord." Beware! Allah's curse is on the wrongdoers 11.19who block people from Allah's cause and look for some crookedness in it, and they disbelieve in the Hereafter. 11.20It is they who cannot escape Allah in this world nor do they have any protectors besides Allah. The punishment will be doubled for them! They could neither hear nor did they look for the truth. 11.21It is they who have ruined themselves, and everything they made up will abandon them. 11.22There is no doubt they will be the worst losers in the Hereafter.

11.23Those who believe, do good, and humble themselves in front of their Lord, it is they who will be the people of Paradise, where they will remain forever.

11.24The example of these two groups is that of the blind and deaf, and the seeing and hearing. Can they be equal in comparison? So, won't you even remind yourselves?

11.25We sent Nuh to his people saying: "I'm giving you clear warnings, 11.26that you mustn't worship anyone other than Allah. I fear for you the punishment of a Painful Day." 11.27The disbelieving leaders among his community said: "We only see you as a human being just like us, and we only see the lowliest among us who follow you – those who cannot think deeply enough. We don't see anything in you people better than us. In fact, we think you are liars." 11.28He replied: "My people! If I was following a clear proof from my Lord, and had He given me special mercy from Himself that is hidden from your sight, what do you think: would we force it upon you if you didn't like it? ^{11.29}My people! I'm not asking you any wealth for it. My reward will come only from Allah. I'm not going to push the Believers away. They are going to meet their Lord. However, I find you to be a group of people behaving ignorantly. ^{11.30}My people! Who could save me from the decision of Allah if I pushed the Believers away? So, won't you even remind yourselves? ^{11.31}I'm not saying to you that I have Allah's treasures nor that I know the unseen secrets, nor am I saying to you that I'm an angel, and nor do I say about those people your eyes look down upon that Allah won't give them anything good – Allah knows best what is in their hearts. If I did say that then in that case I would certainly be among the wrongdoers."

^{11.32}They protested: "Nuh! You argued with us and have been disputing with us for a long time now. Just bring down on us the punishment you keep threatening us with, if you are telling the truth!" ^{11.33}He replied: "Only Allah will bring it down on you if He wants, and you won't be able to escape. ^{11.34}My advice won't benefit you even if I tried to advise you if it is Allah Who allows you to go astray. He is your Lord and it is Him you will all be taken back to."

^{11.35}They also claim: "He made it up." O Prophet Muhammad, say: "If I had made it up, then I am responsible for my own sin and I have nothing to do with the crimes you're involved in."

^{11.36}It was revealed to Nuh that: "None of your people will believe apart from those who already have. So, don't be upset over what they are doing. ^{11.37}Build the Ark under Our watchful eyes and with Our guidance, and don't pray to Me for the wrongdoers because they will be drowned." ^{11.38}Nuh began building the Ark. The leaders among his

community made fun of him each time they passed him by. He replied: "If you make fun of us now, we will make fun of you later in the same way. ¹¹·³⁹You will very soon come to know who will suffer a punishment that will humiliate him in this world, and an everlasting punishment will come down on him in the next world."

¹¹·⁴⁰When Our command of punishment came, and the oven overflowed with water, We ordered Nuh: "Take aboard the Ark a pair – male and female – from each species, as well as your family – apart from those against whom the decision has already been made that they will drown – and Believers too. Only a few believed with him. ¹¹·⁴¹So Nuh said: "Board the Ark: in Allah's Name, may it sail and stop. My Lord is certainly Most Forgiving, Ever-Merciful."

¹¹·⁴²So the Ark sailed with them on huge waves like mountains, and Nuh called out to his son, who had separated himself: "My dear son! Come aboard with us, and don't stay with the disbelievers!" ¹¹·⁴³The son replied: "I will take shelter on a mountain that will save me from the water!" Nuh replied: "Today, there won't be any protection from Allah's command of punishment except for those He has mercy on!" Then a wave came between them, and the son ended up among those who drowned. ¹¹·⁴⁴Eventually, it was ordered: "Earth! Swallow up your water!" and: "Sky! Hold back your rain!" The water sank away and the matter was settled. The Ark came to rest on Mount Judi. It was said: "Gone are those unjust people!"

¹¹·⁴⁵Nuh called out to his Lord and said: "My Lord! My son was a member of my family! and Your promise is true! You are the Greatest of Judges!" ¹¹·⁴⁶Allah replied: "Nuh! He wasn't a member of your family; he was someone whose behaviour wasn't good. So, don't ask Me for something you don't know anything about. I am advising you in case you end up being unwise." ¹¹·⁴⁷Nuh asked: "My Lord! I beg You

to protect me in case I ask You for something I don't know anything about. If You don't forgive me and have mercy on me, I will be among the losers." [11.48]It was said: "Nuh! Get down from the Ark with peace from Us, and blessings on you and on some of the nations who will come from those who are with you. However, We will let some bad people among some nations enjoy themselves for a while, but then they will suffer from Us a painful punishment."

[11.49]O Prophet Muhammad, these are some of the stories of the unseen secrets We reveal to you. Neither you nor your people knew them before this. So, you must continue to have patience. The best end in the Hereafter will be for those who are mindful of Allah.

[11.50]To the people of 'Ad, We sent their brother Hud. He said to them: "My people! You must worship Allah. You don't have any god besides Him. You are only making things up. [11.51]My people! I'm not asking you any payment for it. My reward will come only from Him Who made me. Won't you even think? [11.52]My people! You must beg your Lord to forgive you and then continue to repent to Him. He will send you plenty of rain from the sky, and add more strength to your strength, so don't turn away as criminals."

[11.53]They said: "Hud! You haven't brought us any clear proof, and we won't leave our gods for what you say. We won't believe merely because you say so! [11.54]We can only say that some of our gods have made you suffer a mental illness." He replied: "I make Allah a witness, and you must also be witness that I have nothing to do with the partner-gods you make [11.55]besides Him! So make your plots against me, all together, and then don't even spare me! [11.56]I put my trust in Allah – my Lord and yours too. There is no creature that isn't in His control. My Lord can only be reached on a path that is straight. [11.57]However, if you turn away, then you should know that I have already delivered to you what I was sent to you with. My Lord will replace you with other people, and you cannot harm Him in any way at all. My Lord is the Protector of everything."

$^{11.58}$So, when Our command of punishment came, We saved Hud and those who believed with him, by a special mercy from Us. We saved them from a severe punishment. $^{11.59}$Those were the people of 'Ad. They rejected their Lord's revelations, disobeyed His messengers, and followed the orders of every stubborn tyrant. $^{11.60}$They were followed around by a curse in this world, as they shall be on Judgement Day. Beware! The 'Ad disbelieved in their Lord. Beware! Gone are the 'Ad – the people of Hud!

$^{11.61}$To the people of Thamud, We sent their brother Salih. He said to them: "My people! You must worship Allah. You don't have any god besides Him. He created you from the earth and settled you in it. So, beg Him to forgive you and then continue to repent to Him. My Lord is Near, Answering Prayers."

$^{11.62}$They said: "Salih! Before this, you used to be the centre of hopes for us. Are you now forbidding us from worshipping what our forefathers used to worship? We are really in serious doubt about what you are inviting us to."

$^{11.63}$He replied: "My people! If I was following a clear proof from my Lord, and had He given me special mercy from Him, who do you think could save me from the punishment of my Lord if I disobeyed Him? You only want to increase me in loss. $^{11.64}$My people! This is Allah's she-camel, a sign for you. So leave her to graze on Allah's earth and don't let any harm come to her otherwise a swift punishment will seize you." $^{11.65}$But they hamstrung her, so he said: "Enjoy yourselves in your homes for only three more days. This is a warning that cannot be proven false." ¹¹·⁶⁶So, when Our command of punishment came, We saved Salih and those who believed with him, by a special mercy from Us, and also from the humiliation of that day. Only your Lord is the Strong, the Almighty. ¹¹·⁶⁷The Mighty Blast seized the wrongdoers, and in the morning they lay dead in their homes facing down ¹¹·⁶⁸as if they had never even lived there. Beware! The Thamud rejected their Lord. Beware! Gone are the Thamud!

¹¹·⁶⁹Our messenger-angels brought good news to Ibrahim. They greeted with words of peace and he replied: "Peace," and without delay he brought them a roasted calf. ¹¹·⁷⁰However, when he saw their hands not reaching for it, he felt something strange about them and became afraid of them. They said: "Don't be afraid. We have been sent to Lut's people."

¹¹·⁷¹His wife Sara was standing there, and she giggled. So We gave her the good news of Is'haq, and after him, of Ya'qub. ¹¹·⁷²She said: "Wow! How can I give birth to a child now that I'm an old woman and my husband here is an old man? This is something very strange!" ¹¹·⁷³They replied: "Are you surprised at Allah's command? People of this house! Allah's mercy and blessings are upon you. He is Most Praiseworthy, Glorious."

¹¹·⁷⁴Then, when fear had left Ibrahim and the good news had reached him and sunk in, he began pleading with Us for Lut's people. ¹¹·⁷⁵Ibrahim was certainly forbearing, tender-hearted, turning to Us. ¹¹·⁷⁶The angels said: "Ibrahim! Stay out of this. Your Lord's command has already arrived. A punishment is coming to them that won't be turned back."

¹¹·⁷⁷When Our messenger-angels came to Lut, he felt sorry and powerless for them. He said: "This is a distressful day." ¹¹·⁷⁸The men

from his people came rushing to him, and they were already used to doing bad things. He said: "My people! Here are my tribe's daughters. They are pure for you to marry. Now be mindful of Allah, and don't humiliate me with my guests. Isn't there a single man among you who is sensible?" ¹¹·⁷⁹They replied: "You know very well that we don't have any interest in your tribe's daughters. You certainly know what we want." ¹¹·⁸⁰He said: "If only I had the power to stop you or if I could find help in some strong support!"

¹¹·⁸¹The angels said: "Lut, we are angels sent by your Lord. These people will never get to you. You should set out with your family in a dark part of the night, and none of you should look back. However, you must leave your wife behind because she will suffer what they will suffer. Their promised time is the morning. Isn't the morning near?"

¹¹·⁸²Then, when Our command came, We turned the town upside down, and rained down on them stones of hard-baked clay, layer upon layer, ¹¹·⁸³marked by your Lord. These stones are never far from the wrongdoers.

¹¹·⁸⁴To the people of **Madyan**, We sent their brother Shu'ayb. He said to them: "My people! You must worship Allah. You don't have any god besides Him. Don't give short in measure or weight. I see you are wealthy now, but I fear for you the punishment of a Day which will surround everything. ¹¹·⁸⁵My people! Give full measure and weight with fairness, don't cheat people out of their things nor go around making trouble in the world. ¹¹·⁸⁶What remains with Allah is best for you if you are true Believers. I won't be watching over you."

¹¹·⁸⁷They asked: "Shu'ayb! Do your ritual prayers tell you that we must abandon what our forefathers used to worship or that we must stop

doing what we want with our wealth? Only you must be the forbearing, the rightly-guided!"

[11.88]He replied: "My people! If I was following a clear proof from my Lord, and He had given me plenty of wealth from Him, what do you think? I don't want to go against you in personally doing what I'm forbidding you to do. I only want to correct what I can. My ability comes only from Allah. I put my trust only in Him, and I turn only to Him. [11.89]My people! Disagreeing with me mustn't make you suffer what hit the people of Nuh, Hud, and Salih, and nor are Lut's people far off from you in time. [11.90]You must beg your Lord to forgive you and then continue to repent to Him. My Lord is Ever-Merciful, Most Loving.

[11.91]They threatened: "Shu'ayb! We don't understand much of what you are saying. In fact, we see you as someone weak among us. If it wasn't for your family, we would have certainly stoned you to death and you couldn't have done anything to us."

[11.92]He replied: "My people! Is my family more respectable to you than Allah that you have abandoned Him? My Lord completely surrounds anything you do. [11.93]My people! Continue working as you all are; I am also working. You will very soon come to know who will suffer a punishment that will humiliate him and who is telling lies. Keep watching. I will be watching with you."

[11.94]So, when Our command came, We saved Shu'ayb and those who believed with him, by a special mercy from Us, but the Mighty Blast seized the wrongdoers, and in the morning they lay dead in their homes facing down [11.95]as if they had never lived there. Beware! Gone are the Madyan just like the Thamud!

¹¹·⁹⁶We sent Musa with Our signs and clear authority ¹¹·⁹⁷to Fir'awn and his ministers, but they followed Fir'awn's orders, though his orders were not right. ¹¹·⁹⁸On Judgement Day, he will be ahead of his people, leading them into the Fire. What a dreadful place to be led into! ¹¹·⁹⁹They were followed around by a curse in this world as they shall be on Judgement Day. What a dreadful gift to be given!

¹¹·¹⁰⁰These are some of the stories of those destroyed towns that We are telling you. Some of them still exist today while some have been mown down. ¹¹·¹⁰¹We didn't wrong them but they wronged themselves. O Prophet Muhammad, when your Lord's command came, their gods they prayed to besides Allah couldn't help them in any way at all. They only increased them in ruin. ¹¹·¹⁰²This is what your Lord's grip is like when He punishes towns doing wrong. His grip is painful, severe!

¹¹·¹⁰³There is certainly a sign in this for anyone who fears the punishment of the Hereafter. That is a Day when the people will be gathered together. That is a Day which will be witnessed by everyone. ¹¹·¹⁰⁴We are only delaying it for an end date already fixed. ¹¹·¹⁰⁵When that Day comes, no one will speak without Allah's permission. Some people will be sad while others will be happy.

¹¹·¹⁰⁶Those who will be sad will be in the Fire, where they will suffer screaming and wailing, ¹¹·¹⁰⁷where they will remain for the time the heavens and the earth exist – unless your Lord decides otherwise. O Prophet Muhammad, your Lord does absolutely whatever He wants.

¹¹·¹⁰⁸As for those who will be happy, they will be in Paradise, where they will remain for the time the heavens and the earth exist – unless your Lord decides otherwise. It is a gift that will never end.

[11.109] So, O human, you mustn't be in any doubt about what these people worship. They worship just like their forefathers did previously. We will certainly repay them their share of punishment in full without taking anything away.

[11.110] We already gave Musa the Book but disagreements arose about it. If it wasn't for something already fixed by your Lord, the matter would have been settled immediately between them. They are in serious doubt about the Qur'an. [11.111] And, of course, your Lord will repay them in full for what they're doing. He is Fully-Aware of everything they do.

[11.112] So, O Prophet Muhammad, you should stay strong as you've been ordered, and those too who have turned to Allah with you should do the same without breaking the limits. He is Ever-Watchful of everything you do.

[11.113] Believers! Don't rely on the wrongdoers, or else the Fire will punish you – because you don't have any protectors other than Allah – and then you won't be helped.

[11.114] O Prophet Muhammad, you must establish the ritual prayers at both ends of the day and some parts of the night too. Good actions remove sins. This is a reminder for those who accept advice. [11.115] You should have patience because Allah would never let the reward go to waste of those who do good.

[11.116] Among the generations before you, why weren't there any people of wisdom to stop troublemaking in the land, other than a few of those We saved? Anyway, the wrongdoers followed a life of luxury they were addicted to, and they were criminals. [11.117] Your Lord would never destroy communities wrongfully if its people were doing things right.

11.118If your Lord had wanted, He could have made all the people a single community. However, they will keep on having disagreements with each other, 11.119except those your Lord has mercy on, and that is why He has created them. O Prophet Muhammad, the good promise of your Lord will be fulfilled, that is: "I will certainly fill up Hell with jinns and humans, all together!".

11.120O Prophet Muhammad, the stories of the messengers We tell you, with each one We make your noble heart strong. There has come to you in this surah: the truth, a source of advice, and a reminder for the Believers. 11.121So, tell those who don't believe: "Continue working as you are; we are also working, 11.122and continue to wait; we are also waiting."

11.123The unseen secrets of the heavens and the earth belong only to Allah, and every matter is completely returned to Him. So, O Prophet Muhammad, continue to worship Him, and put your trust in Him. Your Lord isn't unaware of anything you people do.

Surah 12. Yusuf (Joseph)

Allah's name I begin with, the Most Compassionate, the Ever-Merciful

12.1*Alif Laam Raa.* These are the verses of the Clear Book. 12.2We have revealed it as a Qur'an in Arabic so that you people might think and understand it. 12.3O Prophet Muhammad, We will tell you one of the most beautiful stories through this Qur'an We've revealed to you, because before this you were also unaware of this story.

¹²·⁴When Yusuf told his father: "Dear Father! I saw eleven stars, the sun, and the moon in a dream. I saw them prostrating to me!" ¹²·⁵Ya'qub replied: "My dear son! Don't tell your brothers about your dream in case they make a plot against you out of jealousy. Of course, Shaytan is every human's open enemy. ¹²·⁶In this way your Lord will select you and teach you how to explain dreams, and fulfil His favour to you and to the Family of Ya'qub, just like He fulfilled it before to your forefathers – Ibrahim and Is'haq. Your Lord is All-Knowing, All-Wise."

¹²·⁷There are signs in Yusuf and his brothers for those who investigate. ¹²·⁸Remember when they said: "Yusuf and his brother Binyameen are definitely more beloved to our father than we are, even though we are a strong group. Our father is clearly confused. ¹²·⁹Kill Yusuf or expel him to some distant land so that your father's attention will be only on you, and after that you can become righteous people by repenting." ¹²·¹⁰One of them – Sham'un, said: "Don't kill Yusuf, but if you want to do something, throw him down into the hidden darkness of a well. A caravan of travellers might pick him up."

¹²·¹¹They said: "Father! Why don't you trust us with Yusuf when we are certainly his well-wishers? ¹²·¹²Send him with us tomorrow so that he can eat well and play, and we will definitely look after him." ¹²·¹³He replied: "I will be worried if you take him away. I fear a wolf might kill him and eat him when you aren't paying attention to him." ¹²·¹⁴They said: "If a wolf could eat him when we are a strong group, then we will certainly be losers."

¹²·¹⁵So when they took him away, and they all agreed on throwing him down into the hidden darkness of the well, We revealed to Yusuf: "One day, you will certainly remind them of this act of theirs when they won't even be aware of your high status."

12.16At night, they came to their father, weeping. 12.17They cried: "Father! We went racing with each another and left Yusuf with our belongings, and a wolf killed him and ate him. You aren't going to believe us even though we are telling the truth!" 12.18Then they brought out Yusuf's shirt with false blood on it. Ya'qub cried: "Never! Your own selves tempted you into doing something! However, I will have amazing patience! It is Allah Whose help is asked for against what you are describing."

12.19Then, a caravan of travellers arrived, who sent out their water-drawer, who lowered his bucket down into the well. He cried out: "Wow! Some good news! There's a boy over here!" So they hid him away like a valuable trade item. Allah knows perfectly well what they were doing. 12.20They sold him for a low price – a few silver coins – because they weren't interested in him.

12.21The man who bought him in Egypt told his wife Zulaykha: "Look after him well because he could be useful to us or we might adopt him as a son." In this way We created possibilities for Yusuf in the land, and so that We could teach him how to explain dreams. Allah has Full Power over His affairs but most people don't realise. 12.22When Yusuf reached his full strength, We gave him wisdom of prophethood and knowledge. In this way We reward those who do good.

12.23However, the woman in whose house he was staying tried to seduce him. She locked the doors and said: "Come to me." He replied: "I ask for Allah's protection! Your husband is my master. He has looked after me in a good way, and wrongdoers never succeed." 12.24She had already decided to have him, and he could have decided to push her away with force if he didn't see his Lord's sign. This happened so We would turn bad and shameful things away from him.

He was one of Our specially chosen servants. ¹²·²⁵They raced for the door and she tore his shirt from the back, and that was where they found her husband standing. She asked: "What is the punishment for someone who tries to abuse your wife other than be given prison or a painful punishment?"

¹²·²⁶Yusuf said: "It was she who tried to seduce me!" A witness from her own family testified: "If his shirt is torn from the front then she is telling the truth and he is a liar. ¹²·²⁷If his shirt is torn from the back then is she is lying and he is telling the truth." ¹²·²⁸So when her husband saw Yusuf's shirt torn from the back, he said: "This is from the trickery of you women, and it is highly dangerous! ¹²·²⁹Yusuf! Ignore all this. My wife! You must ask forgiveness for your sin because it is you who is sinful!"

¹²·³⁰Some ladies in the city talked: "The governor's wife is trying to seduce her young slaveboy. He has really made her a prisoner of his love. We can see she is clearly lost in love." ¹²·³¹When she heard of their gossip, she called them over, prepared a feast for them, and gave them each a knife. She said to Yusuf: "Come out for them." As soon as they saw him, they began praising him, and they cut their own hands in astonishment, and exclaimed: "Allah save us! This is no human being! He must be some noble angel!" ¹²·³²She said: "This is the man you blamed me for! I did try to seduce him but he remained safe from sin. Now, if he doesn't do what I tell him, he will certainly be put into prison and be disgraced!"

¹²·³³Yusuf prayed: "My Lord! The prison is more preferable to me than what these women are calling me to. If You don't turn their trickery away from me, I might feel like giving myself up to the commands given by them and will end up being unwise." ¹²·³⁴So his Lord responded to him and turned their trickery away from him. Only He

is the All-Hearing, the All-Knowing. ¹²·³⁵Then, even after they had seen the signs of Yusuf's innocence, it seemed appropriate to them that they should still put him in prison for a while.

¹²·³⁶Two young men had gone to prison with Yusuf. One of them said: "I dreamt I was pressing wine from grapes." The other said: "I dreamt I was carrying bread on my head and birds were eating from it." They pleaded to Yusuf: "Tell us its explanation. We see you as someone who does good." ¹²·³⁷Yusuf replied: "Any food that usually comes to you, I will tell you the explanation of these dreams before that food even comes to you. This is some of what my Lord has taught me. I have kept myself away from the religion of any people who don't believe in Allah, who disbelieve even in the Hereafter too. ¹²·³⁸I follow the religion of my forefathers – Ibrahim, Is'haq, and Ya'qub. We have no right to make anything a partner-god with Allah. This is from Allah's grace upon us and upon all the people, yet most people don't give thanks. ¹²·³⁹My two fellow prisoners! Who is better: many separate gods who disagree with each other, or Allah, the One, the Dominant over them all? ¹²·⁴⁰What you worship besides Him are only names that you and your forefathers have made up for which Allah hasn't sent down any permission. Judgement is only Allah's. He has ordered that you mustn't worship anyone except Him. This is the correct religion, yet most people don't know. ¹²·⁴¹My two fellow prisoners! One of you will serve wine to his king and the other will be crucified and birds will eat from his head. The matter you are asking about has already been settled."

¹²·⁴²Of the two, Yusuf said to the one he was sure would be released: "Tell your master about me." But Shaytan made him forget mentioning him to his master, and so Yusuf remained in prison for many years.

12.43One day, the King said: "I dreamt of seven thin cows eating seven fat ones, and of seven green ears of corn and seven others dry. Ministers! Tell me the meaning of my dream if you know how to explain dreams." 12.44They replied: "This is a confused mixture of dreams, and we don't know how to explain them." 12.45Then, of the two prisoners, the one who had been released and now remembered his promise to Yusuf after a long period of time, said: "I will tell you how to explain it, so send me out to the prison."

12.46He said to Yusuf: "Yusuf! O man of truth! Tell us the meaning of seven thin cows eating seven fat ones, and of seven green ears of corn and seven others dry, so that I can go back to the people with your explanation, and they might realise your value." 12.47Yusuf replied: "You will grow crops for seven years as usual, and you will leave the seeds in the ears of whatever you harvest, except for a little amount from which you will eat. 12.48Then after that there will come seven difficult years, which will make you eat up what you will have invested for them, except for a little amount which you will save. 12.49Then after that there will come a year in which the people will have lots of rain and in which they will press juice from fruits."

12.50The King ordered: "Bring him to me." But when the messenger came to him, Yusuf said: "Go back to your master and ask him, 'What happened to the ladies who cut their hands?' My Lord knows their trickery perfectly well." 12.51The King asked the ladies: "What happened when you tried to seduce Yusuf?" They replied: "Allah save us! We don't know anything bad about him." The Governor's wife said: "Now that the truth is out, it was I who tried to seduce him. He was certainly telling the truth."

¹²·⁵²Yusuf said: "I did this so the Governor would realise that I didn't break his trust in his absence, and that Allah doesn't let the trickery of cheaters succeed.

[PART 13]

¹²·⁵³I'm not freeing myself from blame, because the soul certainly does command to do bad things, except someone my Lord has special mercy on. My Lord is Most Forgiving, Ever-Merciful."

¹²·⁵⁴So the King ordered: "Bring him to me. I will make him my personal advisor." Then, when he had spoken to Yusuf, he said: "From this day on, you are a man of authority with us, fully trusted." ¹²·⁵⁵Yusuf said: "Put me in charge of the country's storehouses. I'm a good manager, knowing things perfectly well." ¹²·⁵⁶This is how We created possibilities for Yusuf in the land. He could live in it anywhere he wanted. We give parts of Our special mercy to anyone We choose, and We would never let the reward go to waste of those who do good. ¹²·⁵⁷But certainly the reward of the Hereafter is best for those who believe and continue to be mindful of Allah.

¹²·⁵⁸Then, during the famine, Yusuf's brothers came. They came to him and he recognised them, but they couldn't recognise him. ¹²·⁵⁹When he had given them their supplies, he said: "Bring me a brother you have on your father's side. Don't you see I'm giving out measure of grain in full and I'm the best host too? ¹²·⁶⁰If you don't bring him to me then you cannot have any measure of grain from me in the future nor will you be able to come near me." ¹²·⁶¹They replied: "We will ask his father for him. We definitely will."

¹²·⁶²Yusuf told his servants: "Put their money into their saddle-bags so they can recognise it when they go back to their family, so they might come back."

¹²·⁶³When they had gone back to their father, they said: "Father! We've been refused any more measure of grain. Let our brother Binyameen go with us so we can get more measure of grain. We will certainly look after him." ¹²·⁶⁴He said: "Shall I trust you with him as I trusted you with his brother Yusuf long ago? Allah is the Best Protector, and He is the Most Merciful of all."

¹²·⁶⁵Then, when they opened their baggage, they found their money had been given back to them. They exclaimed: "Father! What more could we ask for! This is our money given back to us! Now we can get more food for our family, keep our brother safe, and get a further camel-load of grain as well! That would be such an easy load." ¹²·⁶⁶Ya'qub said: "I will never let him go with you unless you make a firm promise to me, in Allah's name, that you will definitely bring him back to me unless you are made powerless." When they had made their firm promise, he said: "Allah is a Witness to what we are saying." ¹²·⁶⁷He said: "My dear sons! You mustn't all enter the city from the same gate, but from different gates. I cannot save you from the decision of Allah in any way at all. Judgement is only Allah's. I put my trust only in Him, and those who trust must also put their trust only in Him."

¹²·⁶⁸When they entered as their father had told them to, it wasn't to save them from the decision of Allah at all, but a desire in Ya'qub's heart that he carried out. He was full of knowledge because of what We had taught him, but most people don't know.

¹²·⁶⁹Now, when they came into Yusuf's presence, he gave his brother Binyameen a place close to him. He said to him: "Me, I am your brother, so don't be upset about what they've been doing."

¹²·⁷⁰Then, when he had given them their supplies, he placed a drinking cup into his brother's saddle-bag. Later, an announcer called out: "People of the caravan! You are thieves!" ¹²·⁷¹The brothers asked, turning around towards them: "What have you lost?" ¹²·⁷²The guards said: "We are missing the King's goblet. Anyone who brings it will be given a camel-load of grain. I guarantee that." ¹²·⁷³The brothers replied: "By Allah! You already know that we haven't come to make trouble in the land nor are we thieves." ¹²·⁷⁴The servants asked: "Then what should be the punishment of someone who did it, if you are telling lies?" ¹²·⁷⁵They replied: "The punishment of someone in whose saddle-bag the cup is found is that person himself should be kept a slave. This is how we punish wrongdoers."

¹²·⁷⁶So Yusuf began by searching their baggage before searching the baggage of his brother Binyameen. Eventually, he brought out the cup from his brother's baggage. That is how We had planned it for Yusuf. He couldn't have taken his brother according to the King's law unless Allah had decided. We raise up in ranks anyone We choose. Above every person of knowledge is the One Who knows more than all.

¹²·⁷⁷Yusuf's brothers said: "No wonder he steals! He had a brother who stole previously." But Yusuf kept these things secret inside his heart and didn't let his brothers know. He said to himself: "You are in such a bad situation, and Allah knows best what you are describing."

¹²·⁷⁸They said: "Your honour! He has a father who is very old. So, arrest one of us instead of him. We see you as someone who does good." ¹²·⁷⁹Yusuf replied: "I ask Allah to save us from arresting someone other than the person we found our property with, in which case we would be unjust."

¹²·⁸⁰Now, when they lost hope in him, they discussed separately. Rubil, the eldest of them said: "Don't you remember that your father had made you swear a firm promise in Allah's name because you had previously failed in your duty with Yusuf? Therefore, I will never leave this land unless either my father allows me or Allah decides for me. He is the Best to decide. ¹²·⁸¹Go back to your father and say, 'Dear Father! Your son stole! We've only testified to what we know and couldn't have protected against what we didn't know. ¹²·⁸²You can even ask the people of the town where we've been, and the caravan which we came in. We are definitely telling the truth.'."

¹²·⁸³Ya'qub cried: "Never! Your own selves tempted you into doing something! However, I will have amazing patience! Perhaps Allah will bring them all to me. Only He is the All-Knowing, the All-Wise." ¹²·⁸⁴Then he turned away from them and cried: "How sad it is for poor Yusuf!" His eyes had gone white with grief as he was trying to hide his sadness. ¹²·⁸⁵They said: "By Allah! You never stop remembering Yusuf, such that you will become extremely ill or will die." ¹²·⁸⁶He replied: "I complain of my sorrow and grief only to Allah, and I have learnt from Allah what you don't know. ¹²·⁸⁷My dear sons! Go and find out about Yusuf and his brother, and don't lose hope in Allah's mercy. Only disbelieving people lose hope in Allah's mercy."

¹²·⁸⁸Then, when they came to Yusuf, they said: "Your honour! We are suffering from hardship, and so is our family. We've brought very little money with us, so give us a full measure of supplies and some charity too. Allah rewards those who give charity." ¹²·⁸⁹He replied: "Do you realise what you did to Yusuf and his brother when you were unwise?" ¹²·⁹⁰They asked in surprise: "What? You? Are you Yusuf?" He replied: "Yes, I am Yusuf, and this is my brother. Allah has done us a favour. Whoever is mindful of Allah and has patience knows that Allah doesn't let the reward go to waste of those who do good."

¹²·⁹¹The brothers said: "By Allah! Allah really has preferred you over us, and we have certainly been sinful." ¹²·⁹²He said: "There is no blame on you today. May Allah forgive you. He is the Most Merciful of all. ¹²·⁹³Take this shirt of mine and place it over my father's face; he will be able to see again. Then bring your whole family to me."

¹²·⁹⁴As the caravan left Egypt, their father in Kan'aan (Canaan) said: "You might think I am physically weak and mentally slow because of my old age but I can definitely smell Yusuf's scent." ¹²·⁹⁵The people said: "By Allah! You are still lost in your old love." ¹²·⁹⁶Then, when the giver of good news arrived, he placed the shirt over Ya'qub's face, and he was able to see again. He said: "Didn't I tell you, 'I have learnt from Allah what you don't know.'?" ¹²·⁹⁷They said: "Father! Ask forgiveness for our sins because we have made mistakes." ¹²·⁹⁸He replied: "I will soon ask my Lord to forgive you. Only He is the Most Forgiving, the Ever-Merciful."

¹²·⁹⁹Then, when they all came into Yusuf's presence, he gave his parents a place close to him and said: "Enter Egypt and you will be safe – if Allah chooses." ¹²·¹⁰⁰As he raised his parents up onto the throne, they fell down prostrating in front of him. He said: "Dear Father! This is the meaning of my dream I saw long ago! My Lord has made it come true! He has been kind to me when He took me out of prison and brought you all out of the desert, especially after Shaytan had ruined the relationship between me and my brothers. My Lord is Perfect in doing anything He chooses. Only He is the All-Knowing, the All-Wise." ¹²·¹⁰¹He prayed: "My Lord! You have given me power in this land and taught me how to explain dreams. O Maker of the heavens and the earth! You are my Protector in this world and the next. Let me die surrendering to You as Muslim and join me with righteous people."

[12.102] O Prophet Muhammad, this is one of the stories of the unseen secrets We reveal to you. You weren't with Yusuf's brothers when they agreed upon their plan when making the plot. [12.103] Most people, no matter how hard you try, won't believe. [12.104] You aren't asking them any payment for it. This Qur'an is a reminder for everyone.

[12.105] There are many signs in the heavens and the earth these people pass by, but they don't pay any attention to them. [12.106] Most of them don't believe in Allah without making partner-gods with Him. [12.107] So, do they feel safe from the coming of the overwhelming event of Allah's punishment against them, or of the coming of the Final Hour suddenly upon them when they least expect it?

[12.108] O Prophet Muhammad, say: "This is my way. I'm inviting to Allah. I am based on clear evidence and so is anyone who follows me. Glory be to Allah! I'm not a polytheist."

[12.109] From among the people of the towns, We sent before you as messengers only men We gave revelations to. Don't the people travel through the earth and take a look at what was the end result of those before them? The Home of the Hereafter is best for those who are mindful of Allah. Don't you even think? [12.110] There came a time when the messengers gave up hope and the disbelievers thought they had been lied to, that is when Our help came to the messengers and We saved anyone We chose. Our punishment won't be turned away from criminal people.

[12.111] In their stories is a definite lesson of warning for people of understanding. This Qur'an isn't a message that can just be made up, but: a confirmation of what came before it, a detailed explanation of everything, a guidance, and a mercy for any people who believe.

Surah 13. Thunder (ar-Ra'd)

Allah's name I begin with, the Most Compassionate, the Ever-Merciful

13.1 Alif Laam Meem Raa. These are the verses of the Book. O Prophet Muhammad, that which is revealed to you from your Lord is the truth, yet most people don't believe.

13.2 Allah is the one Who raised the heavens up without any pillars that you can see, and then established His authority on the Throne. He has made the sun and the moon obey a system – each one running its course for a fixed term. He governs every affair. He explains the signs in detail so that you people might strongly believe in the meeting with your Lord. 13.3 He is the one Who stretched out the earth and placed in it firm mountains and rivers. He placed two types of every kind of fruit in it. He covers up the day with night. There are certainly signs in this for any people who think deeply. 13.4 In the earth there are plots next to each other, as well as gardens of grapevines, crops, and palm trees – growing in bunches or alone. They're all given the same water, yet We make some of them better to eat than others. There are certainly signs in this for any people who think.

13.5 If you are surprised at their disbelieving, then what is stranger is their question: "What? Once we have died and become dust, will we be created into something new?" They're the ones who disbelieve in their Lord. It is they who will have iron collars on their necks, and it is they who will be the people of the Fire. They will remain there forever. 13.6 They want you to bring the punishment before rewards, even though many punishments have taken place before them. O Prophet Muhammad, your Lord certainly has forgiveness for people despite their wrongdoing, but He is severe in punishing too.

¹³·⁷The disbelievers ask: "Why wasn't a permanent sign sent down to him from his Lord?" You are only a warner, as well as a guide to every community.

¹³·⁸Allah knows what every female carries in its womb, and by how much the wombs shrink and expand. With Him, everything has a fixed plan. ¹³·⁹He is the Knower of the unseen secrets and the visible, and He is the Great, the Highest. ¹³·¹⁰If any of you speaks secretly or openly, or hides at night or moves about during the day, it is all the same to Him.

¹³·¹¹There is a succession of angels for each person, in front of him and behind him, guarding him by Allah's command. Allah won't change the condition of any people until they change what is within themselves. When He wants harm to come to any people, nothing can turn it away, as only He can protect them.

¹³·¹²He is the one Who shows you the lightning – striking fear and giving hope, and raises up the heavy clouds. ¹³·¹³The thunder glorifies His praises, and so do the angels, in fear of Him. He sends thunderbolts and strikes with them anyone He chooses, yet they still argue about Allah. He is mighty in power.

¹³·¹⁴Praying to Him is the truth. Those they pray to besides Him can never respond to them in any way at all, like someone who stretches out his hands towards water for it to reach his mouth but it won't. The disbelievers' prayer is useless.

¹³·¹⁵To Allah prostrates everything in the heavens and the earth, whether they want to or not, and so do their shadows – morning and evening. *<Prostration Point 2>* ¹³·¹⁶O Prophet Muhammad, ask: "Who is the Lord of the heavens and the earth?" Reply: "Allah!" Ask: "Then

have you taken protectors other than Him who can neither help nor harm even themselves?" Ask: "Can they be equal: the blind and the seeing person, or the depths of darkness and light?" Have they made with Allah partner-gods who have created like He has? Creating has confused them. Say: "Allah is the Creator of everything. He is the One, the Dominant." [13.17]He sends down from the sky water, and the valleys flow according their capacity, but the current carries scum that rises up to the surface. There is similar slag in the things people heat up in fire to make ornaments or other things. This is how Allah compares truth to falsehood. The scum passes away useless but what benefits people stays behind in the world. This is how Allah uses examples.

[13.18]Those who respond to the commands of their Lord will have the most beautiful reward. However, those who don't respond to Him – even if they owned everything in the world and just as much more with it, they would want to give it up as ransom to save themselves – it is they who will suffer a harsh judgement and their home will be Hell. What a dreadful place!

[13.19]O Prophet Muhammad, someone who knows that what has been revealed to you from your Lord is the truth, can he be like someone who is blind? Only the people of understanding will remind themselves: [13.20]who fulfil their promise with Allah and don't break the treaty; [13.21]who join the relationships Allah has ordered to be joined, are afraid of their Lord, and fear the harsh judgement; [13.22]and who have patience when trying to gain their Lord's good pleasure, establish the ritual prayers, donate secretly and openly from what We've given them, and continue to turn bad things away with good. It is they who will have the ultimate home: [13.23]Gardens of Eden, which they will enter along with the righteous among their forefathers, spouses, and descendants. Angels will come to them from every gate, saying: ¹³·²⁴"Peace be upon you for your patience. Now see, how excellent is this ultimate home!"

¹³·²⁵However, those who break their promise with Allah after making a treaty with Him, who break the relationships Allah has ordered to be joined, and who make trouble in the world, it is they who are cursed and will have the dreadful home.

¹³·²⁶It is Allah Who can increase or restrict wealth for anyone He chooses. The disbelievers are rejoicing in this life, but it is only a little enjoyment compared to the Hereafter.

¹³·²⁷The disbelievers ask: "Why wasn't a permanent sign sent down to him from his Lord?" Reply: "There are many signs but Allah lets anyone He chooses go astray and also guides to Himself whoever turns to Him: ¹³·²⁸who believe and whose hearts find satisfaction in remembering Allah. Of course! It's only by remembering Allah that hearts can find satisfaction. ¹³·²⁹Those who believe and do good will enjoy bliss as well as the best destination."

¹³·³⁰O Prophet Muhammad, in this way We have sent you to a community – when many communities have been and gone before it – to recite to them what We have revealed to you, yet they still disbelieve in Allah – the Most Compassionate. Say: "He is my Lord. There is no god except Him. I put my trust only in Him, and I turn only to Him." ¹³·³¹They would still disbelieve even if there was a Qur'an with which mountains could be moved, the earth split open, or the dead made to speak. But no! All matters are in Allah's control. Haven't the Believers realised that if Allah decided, He could have easily guided all the people? The disbelievers will continue to suffer disaster because of what they did, or it will fall close to their homes until Allah's promise is fulfilled. Allah never breaks promises.

¹³·³²Many messengers before you were also mocked, so I gave more time to the disbelievers before I punished them. How terrible was My punishment!

¹³·³³Is there anything like Allah, Who is watching and knowing everyone what they've done? They still make partner-gods with Him! O Prophet Muhammad, say: "Name them! Are you telling Him about something in this world He doesn't already know, or are they just meaningless words?" But no! The plotting of the disbelievers is made to seem attractive to them and they're blocked from the path to Allah. There can be no guide for someone Allah calls misguided. ¹³·³⁴They will suffer a punishment in this life, but the punishment of the Hereafter will be much harder. They won't have anyone to save them from the punishment of Allah.

¹³·³⁵The Paradise promised to those who are mindful of Allah, its description is that: there are rivers flowing beneath it, and its food and shade will last forever. This will be the ultimate end of those who are mindful of Allah whereas the ultimate end of the disbelievers will be the Fire.

¹³·³⁶O Prophet Muhammad, those We gave the Book to are rejoicing at what has been revealed to you, but some of their groups reject parts of it. Say: "I've been ordered to worship Allah and not to make partner-gods with Him. I'm inviting only to Him, and to Him is my destination." ¹³·³⁷This is how We revealed it as a judgement in Arabic. If you had followed their desires after the knowledge that has come to you, then you wouldn't have had anyone to protect you or save you from the decision of Allah.

¹³·³⁸O Prophet Muhammad, we sent messengers before you, and gave them wives and children. It was never the duty of any messenger to show a sign without Allah's permission. There's a fixed time for each event to take place. ¹³·³⁹Allah deletes or confirms whatever He wants. Only He has the Master Record.

¹³·⁴⁰O Prophet Muhammad, it doesn't matter if We show you some of the punishment that We are warning them of or We take away your soul before that, because your duty is only to deliver the message, and the judgement is up to Us.

¹³·⁴¹Don't they see how We come to the land reducing it from its borders? Allah decides, and no one can change His decision. He is quick in settling accounts. ¹³·⁴²People before them also made plots, but Allah has the master plan of everything. He knows what everyone is doing. The disbelievers will soon find out who will have the ultimate home.

¹³·⁴³Those disbelievers claim: "You haven't been sent as a messenger." O Prophet Muhammad, reply: "Allah is enough as a Witness between me and you all, and so is anyone who has some knowledge of the Book."

Surah 14. Ibrahim (Abraham)

Allah's name I begin with, the Most Compassionate, the Ever-Merciful

¹⁴·¹*Alif Laam Raa.* This Qur'an is a Book We have revealed to you, O Prophet Muhammad, for you to bring people out of the depths of darkness into the light – with their Lord's permission – to the path of the Almighty, the Most Praiseworthy, ¹⁴·²Allah, Who owns everything in the heavens and the earth. The disbelievers are damned because

of a severe punishment, ^{14.3}who prefer this life to the next, they block people from Allah's cause, and they look for some crookedness in it. It is they who have gone far, far astray.

^{14.4}We haven't sent any messenger except in the language of his people so he can make things clear to them. However, Allah lets anyone He chooses go astray and also guides anyone He wants. He is the Almighty, the All-Wise.

^{14.5}We sent Musa with Our signs telling him: "Bring your people out from the depths of darkness into the light, and remind them of the Days of Allah." There are certainly signs in this for anyone who is very patient, very thankful. ^{14.6}Remember when Musa told his people: "You must remember Allah's favour to you when He saved you from Fir'awn's people! They used to oppress you with terrible suffering and by slaughtering your boys but keeping your women alive. There was a severe test in that from your Lord. ^{14.7}Remember when your Lord announced, 'If you are thankful, I will certainly give you more, but if you are unthankful, then be warned that My punishment is certainly severe!'." ^{14.8}Musa also said: "If you are unthankful, you along with everyone in the world, then bear in mind that Allah is Free of all Needs, Most Praiseworthy."

^{14.9}Hasn't the story reached you of those before them: the people of Nuh, the 'Ad, and the Thamud; as well as those who came after them? No one knows them except Allah. Their messengers came to them with clear proofs, but they put their hands into their mouths out of mockery and said: "We reject what you've been sent with, and we are in serious doubt about what you're inviting us to."

^{14.10}Their messengers asked: "Is there any doubt about Allah – the Maker of the heavens and the earth? He is inviting you to forgive you

your sins and give you more time until an end date." They replied: "You're only humans, just like us! You want to stop us from what our forefathers used to worship. So, show us some clear proof." ^{14.11}Their messengers told them: "Though we're only humans in appearance just like you, but Allah does favours to any of His servants He chooses. We don't have any right to show you any proof without Allah's permission. So, true Believers must put their trust only in Allah. ^{14.12}Why shouldn't we put our trust in Allah when He has guided us on our ways to success? We will certainly have patience in any harm you do to us. Those who trust must put their trust only in Allah."

^{14.13}The disbelievers said to their messengers: "We will definitely expel you from our land unless you come back to our religion." So, their Lord revealed to the messengers: "We will certainly destroy the wrongdoers, ^{14.14}and definitely settle you in the land after them. This promise is for anyone who fears standing in front of Me and is afraid of My warning."

^{14.15}The messengers prayed for victory, and every stubborn tyrant failed. ^{14.16}There is only Hell after this failure, and he will be given some oozing pus to drink. ^{14.17}He will gulp at it but won't be able to swallow it. Death will come to him from all sides, but he won't be able to die. After this, there will be more severe punishment.

^{14.18}The example of those who disbelieve in their Lord is that the things they do are like ashes the wind blows furiously away on a stormy day. They won't be able to do anything at all with what they achieved. That is the farthest anyone can stray. ^{14.19}Don't you see that it is Allah Who created the heavens and the earth for a real purpose? If He wants, He can remove the lot of you and bring about a new creation. ^{14.20}This isn't difficult for Allah.

[14.21] They will all come together in front of Allah, and the weak followers will say to those leaders who showed arrogance: "We used to be your followers, so will you save us from Allah's punishment in any way at all?" They will reply: "If Allah had guided us, we would certainly have guided you. It makes no difference to us if we have patience or not, because there is no way out for us."

[14.22] Once the matter will have been settled, Shaytan will say: "Allah made you a true promise, but I made you a promise which I broke. I had no power over you except to call you and you responded to me. Now, don't blame me but yourselves. I cannot help you nor can you help me. I am now rejecting what you previously ascribed to me." The wrongdoers, they will suffer a painful punishment!

[14.23] Those who believe and do good will be entered into gardens – that have rivers flowing beneath them, where they will remain forever, with their Lord's permission. Their greeting there will be: "Peace."

[14.24] Don't you see how Allah gives the example of a good word as that of a healthy tree? Its roots are firm in the ground, and its branches are high in the sky. [14.25] It gives fruit all the time, with its Lord's command. Allah uses examples for people so that they might remind themselves.

[14.26] The example of a bad word is that of a rotten tree. It is pulled up from the ground, having no firmness. [14.27] Allah makes the Believers firm with the Firm Word, in this life and the next, but lets the wrongdoers go astray. Allah does whatever He wants.

[14.28] Don't you see those who responded to Allah's favour with unthankfulness, and because of that they lowered their people down into the House of Ruin? [14.29] into Hell? They will burn in it. What a dreadful place to be in! ¹⁴·³⁰They make others equal to Allah to lead people away from His cause. O Prophet Muhammad, say: "You can enjoy yourselves for a while, but your final destination will be the Fire!"

¹⁴·³¹Tell My Believing servants that they must establish the ritual prayers and donate secretly and openly from what We've given them, before comes a Day when there will be no trading or friendship to help them.

¹⁴·³²Allah is the one Who created the heavens and the earth, and sent down from the sky water with which He brought out fruits as food for you, made the ships obey you to sail through the sea by His command, and also made the rivers obey a system for you. ¹⁴·³³He has made the sun and the moon obey a system for you – both continuing on their courses, and also made the night and the day obey a system for you. ¹⁴·³⁴He gave you everything you asked Him for. You will never be able to add up Allah's favour even if you tried. Humans are certainly unfair, very unthankful.

¹⁴·³⁵Remember when Ibrahim prayed: "My Lord, make this a land of peace, and keep me and my children away from worshipping idols. ¹⁴·³⁶My Lord! These idols have led many people astray. So, whoever follows me will be with me, and anyone who disobeys me then You are Most Forgiving, Ever-Merciful. ¹⁴·³⁷Our Lord! I have settled some of my descendants in a valley where there are no plants, close to Your Sacred House so that, our Lord, they can establish the ritual prayers. Therefore, make the hearts of people have affection for them, and give them fruits so they will remain thankful. ¹⁴·³⁸Our Lord! You know everything we hide or show. Nothing at all is hidden from Allah, on earth or in heaven. ¹⁴·³⁹All praise is for Allah, Who gave me Isma'il and Is'haq in my old age. My Lord is certainly the Hearer of Prayers. ¹⁴·⁴⁰My

Lord! Make me someone who establishes the ritual prayers, and my descendants too. Our Lord! Accept my prayer. ¹⁴·⁴¹Our Lord! Forgive me, my parents, and the Believers, on the Day when the judgement will take place."

¹⁴·⁴²Don't ever think Allah is unaware of anything the wrongdoers are doing. He is only giving them more time until a Day when all eyes will stare in horror. ¹⁴·⁴³They will be running forwards with their heads raised up, eyelids not blinking, and hearts empty!

¹⁴·⁴⁴O Prophet Muhammad, **warn the people of the Day when** punishment will come to them and the wrongdoers will pray: "Our Lord! Give us a little more time. We will accept Your invitation and follow the messengers." They will be asked: "Didn't you people used to swear previously that you will never have an end? ¹⁴·⁴⁵You lived in the abandoned homes of people who had wronged themselves, so it was clear to you how We had dealt with them. We had even made them examples for you."

¹⁴·⁴⁶They made their plots, but Allah had the answer to their plots despite their plots being powerful enough by which mountains could disappear.

¹⁴·⁴⁷Don't ever think Allah will break His promise to His messengers. Allah is Almighty, Capable of Retaliation. ¹⁴·⁴⁸One Day the earth will be changed into something else, and the heavens too, and the people will all come together in front of Allah, the One, the Dominant, ¹⁴·⁴⁹and you will see, on that Day, the criminals tied up in chains, ¹⁴·⁵⁰their clothes of tar, and the Fire covering up their faces, ¹⁴·⁵¹so Allah can reward or punish each person for the things they had done. Allah is quick in settling accounts.

¹⁴·⁵²This Qur'an is a message to all people. They must be warned by it and know that He is only One God. The people of understanding must learn lessons from it.

Surah 15. Valley of Rocks (al-Hijr)

Allah's name I begin with, the Most Compassionate, the Ever-Merciful

¹⁵·¹*Alif Laam Raa.* These are the verses of the Book and of a clear Qur'an. [PART 14]

¹⁵·²On Judgement Day, the disbelievers will wish they had surrendered to Allah as Muslims. ¹⁵·³You might as well leave them to eat and enjoy themselves, and for their false hopes to distract them. They will very soon come to know the end result. ¹⁵·⁴We have never destroyed any town unless there was an end time fixed for it. ¹⁵·⁵No community can go before or after the end of its time.

¹⁵·⁶The disbelievers say: "You – given the Reminder, you must be mad! ¹⁵·⁷Why don't you bring us some angels, if you are telling the truth?" ¹⁵·⁸We don't send down angels unless there was a real purpose of death or destruction, after which the people aren't given any more chances. ¹⁵·⁹It is We Who revealed the Reminder, and certainly We will preserve it.

¹⁵·¹⁰O Prophet Muhammad, before you, We sent messengers to the previous communities, ¹⁵·¹¹but they would make fun of any messenger who came to them. ¹⁵·¹²In this way We let that misguidance soak into the hearts of the criminals. ¹⁵·¹³They won't believe in this Qur'an, just like the doing and disbelieving of previous people has passed before them. ¹⁵·¹⁴If We opened up a gate to heaven for them through which they could keep going up all day, ¹⁵·¹⁵they would still say: "Our eyes

have been hypnotised. Actually, we are a people who have been put under a magic spell."

15.16We have placed constellations in the sky and made it beautiful for those who look. 15.17We have protected it from every rejected devil, 15.18but if any tries to eavesdrop, a bright shooting star chases after it. 15.19As for the earth, We have stretched it out, fixed firm mountains in it, and made all kinds of things grow there in proportion. 15.20We showed ways of making a living in it both to you as well as to those creatures you don't provide for. 15.21There is nothing whose resources We don't have, and We send it down only in specific amounts. 15.22We send winds to pollinate, then send down from the sky water which We give you to drink. You people are unable to preserve this water. 15.23It is We Who give life and death, and We are the real inheritors. 15.24We certainly know both those of you who have already lived and those who will come later. 15.25It is your Lord Who will gather them all together. He is All-Wise, All-Knowing.

15.26We created the first human out of sounding clay from dark stinky mud; 15.27and jinns, We created previously, out of smokeless scorching fire. 15.28O Prophet Muhammad, remember when your Lord told the angels: "I am going to create a human being out of sounding clay from dark stinky mud. 15.29When I have given him proportion and breathed from My spirit into him, you must all fall down in prostration in front of him," 15.30and the angels did prostrate, every one of them, all together 15.31– but not Iblees. He refused to be with those who prostrated. 15.32Allah asked: "Iblees! What is wrong with you that you weren't with those who prostrated?" 15.33He replied: "I won't prostrate to a human. You created him out of sounding clay from dark stinky mud." 15.34Allah ordered: "Then get out of here. You are rejected! 15.35You will be cursed until Judgement Day!"

15.36Iblees pleaded: "My Lord! Give me a chance until the Day people will be brought back to life." 15.37Allah replied: "You are one of those who will be given chances 15.38until the Day of the time that is fixed."

15.39Iblees said: "My Lord, because you have let me go astray, I will certainly make things seem attractive to people in the world, and I will mislead them all, 15.40but not Your specially chosen servants among them." 15.41Allah said: "This is a path that leads straight to Me. 15.42You won't have any power over My servants apart from those who go astray and follow you. 15.43Hell is the destination they've been warned about. 15.44It has seven gates; each gate will have its fixed share of them."

15.45Those who are mindful of Allah will be among gardens and fountains. 15.46They will be told: "Enter them in peace, in safety." 15.47We will remove all grudges from their hearts, to be brothers facing each other on sofas. 15.48They will neither feel tired there nor will they be expelled from it.

15.49O Prophet Muhammad, tell My servants that I am certainly the Most Forgiving, the Ever-Merciful, 15.50yet My punishment is the most painful.

15.51O Prophet Muhammad, tell them about Ibrahim's guests, 15.52when they came to him and greeted with words of peace, he replied: "We are afraid of you." 15.53They said: "Don't be afraid. We're giving you good news of a son full of knowledge." 15.54He asked: "Are you giving me good news now that old age has taken over me? What are you giving me good news of?" 15.55They replied: "We've given you good news with the truth. Now don't be of those who lose hope." 15.56He said: "Who could lose hope in his Lord's mercy apart from those who go astray!" 15.57He asked: "Then what is your mission, O Messenger-

Angels?" ¹⁵·⁵⁸They replied: "We have been sent to a criminal people." ¹⁵·⁵⁹Apart from Lut's family – as We will certainly save them all, ¹⁵·⁶⁰but not his wife, who, We've decided, should be among those who will stay behind.

¹⁵·⁶¹So, when the messenger-angels came to Lut's family, ¹⁵·⁶²he said: "You are a group of strangers." ¹⁵·⁶³They replied: "Actually, we've come to you with something these people had doubts about. ¹⁵·⁶⁴We've brought you the punishment with the truth and we are certainly truthful. ¹⁵·⁶⁵So, you should set out with your family in a dark part of the night, and you should follow closely behind them. None of you should look back but keep going where you've been told." ¹⁵·⁶⁶We gave him that decision, that those people would be uprooted in the morning.

¹⁵·⁶⁷The town's men came along, feeling happy. ¹⁵·⁶⁸Lut pleaded: "These are my guests, so don't embarrass me. ¹⁵·⁶⁹Be mindful of Allah and don't humiliate me." ¹⁵·⁷⁰They asked: "Didn't we forbid you from protecting anyone?" ¹⁵·⁷¹He replied: "Here are my tribe's daughters to marry, if you want to do anything."

¹⁵·⁷²O Prophet Muhammad, I swear by your life! They were confused and distracted in their drunken state of power, ¹⁵·⁷³but the Mighty Blast seized them at sunrise. ¹⁵·⁷⁴We turned their town upside down and rained down on them stones of hard-baked clay. ¹⁵·⁷⁵There are certainly signs in this for those who try to understand. ¹⁵·⁷⁶That ruined town lies along a road visited often. ¹⁵·⁷⁷There is certainly a sign in this for the Believers.

¹⁵·⁷⁸The People of the Forest (As'haab al-Aykah) were also wrongdoers, ¹⁵·⁷⁹so We punished them. The ruins of both are along an open road.

¹⁵·⁸⁰The People of the Rock (*al-Hijr*) also accused the messengers of being liars, ¹⁵·⁸¹so We sent them Our signs, but they kept turning away from them. ¹⁵·⁸²They used to carve homes out of mountains, feeling safe in them, ¹⁵·⁸³but the Mighty Blast seized them as they entered the morning, ¹⁵·⁸⁴and nothing they achieved could save them.

¹⁵·⁸⁵We created the heavens and the earth and everything in between them for a real purpose. The Final Hour will certainly come, so, O Prophet Muhammad, you should keep forgiving graciously. ¹⁵·⁸⁶Only your Lord is the Supreme Creator, the All-Knowing.

¹⁵·⁸⁷We've given you the Seven Verses that are recited again and again, and the Tremendous Qur'an too. ¹⁵·⁸⁸Don't let your eyes desire what We've let some of their groups enjoy. Don't worry about them. Continue to be merciful to the Believers, ¹⁵·⁸⁹and say: "I only give clear warnings," ¹⁵·⁹⁰like the ones We sent down to those people who split up the Holy Books, ¹⁵·⁹¹those who accept and reject parts of the Qur'an.

¹⁵·⁹²O Prophet Muhammad, I swear by your Lord: We will certainly ask them all ¹⁵·⁹³about everything they used to do. ¹⁵·⁹⁴So, you should openly announce what you are ordered, and turn away from those who make partners with Allah. ¹⁵·⁹⁵We are enough for you against the mockers, ¹⁵·⁹⁶who make another god with Allah. They will very soon come to know the end result.

¹⁵·⁹⁷We certainly know that your noble heart is upset by what they are saying. ¹⁵·⁹⁸However, you should still continue to glorify the praises of your Lord, be among those who prostrate, ¹⁵·⁹⁹and worship your Lord until that rank of certainty which is certain comes to you.

Surah 16. Bee (*an-Nahl*)

Allah's name I begin with, the Most Compassionate, the Ever-Merciful

16.1 Allah's command is nearly here, so you mustn't wish to bring it any sooner. Glory be to Him! He is much higher than the partner-gods they make with Him.

16.2 By His command, He sends down angels with revelations to any of His servants He chooses, saying: "Give this warning that there is no god apart from Me, so be mindful of Me."

16.3 He created the heavens and the earth for a real purpose. He is much higher than the partner-gods they make with Him. 16.4 He created humans from a drop of semen, yet they challenge Him openly! 16.5 Livestock, He created them too, in which there is a source of warmth and many other benefits for you, and you can eat from them too. 16.6 They look beautiful to you when you bring them home to rest in the evening and when you take them out to graze in the morning. 16.7 They also carry your loads to distant lands you couldn't have reached without a lot of physical difficulty. Your Lord is certainly Kind, Ever-Merciful. 16.8 He also created horses, mules, and donkeys for you to ride and use for show. He also creates other things you know nothing about.

16.9 It is Allah's responsibility to show the right way because there are paths that turn away from the truth. If He had wanted, He could have certainly guided all of you, all together.

16.10 He is the one Who sends down from the sky water, some of which is a drink for you and some from which come shrubs you feed to your animals. 16.11 With this water, Allah grows crops for you, as well as olives, date-palms, grapes, and all kinds of fruit. There is certainly a sign in this for any people who think deeply.

[16.12] He has made the night and day obey a system for you, as well as the sun and the moon. The stars are made to obey His command. There are certainly signs in this for any people who think. [16.13] Everything He has created for you in this world is of various colours. There is certainly a sign in this for any people who learn lessons.

[16.14] He is the one Who has made the sea obey a system so you can eat fresh meat from it and bring out jewellery from it to wear. You can see ships cutting through it as you gain some of Allah's grace, and so that you might become thankful.

[16.15] He has fixed firm mountains in the earth in case it shakes under you, and rivers and paths so you can find your way, [16.16] and also landmarks. People can find their way by the stars too. [16.17] So, can the Creator be compared to someone who cannot create? Won't you even think?

[16.18] You will never be able to count Allah's favours even if you tried. Allah is certainly Most Forgiving, Ever-Merciful. [16.19] Allah knows everything you hide or show.

[16.20] Those idols they pray to besides Allah, they cannot create anything but are themselves created. [16.21] They are non-living, lifeless. They don't have any sense of when people will be brought back to life.

[16.22] Your God is One God. However, those who don't believe in the Hereafter, their hearts are in rejection and they themselves are arrogant. ^{16.23}There is no doubt that Allah knows everything they hide or show. He doesn't like arrogant people.

^{16.24}When they are asked: "What is it that your Lord has revealed?" they reply: "Stories made up by previous people." ^{16.25}So, on Judgement Day, they will be carrying their own burdens of sins in full, as well as some burdens of those they mislead out of ignorance. Beware! How terrible is the burden they will be carrying!

^{16.26}People before them also made plots but Allah attacked their building of trickery at the foundations. The roof fell down on top of them and the punishment came at them in a way they least expected. ^{16.27}Then, on Judgement Day, He will humiliate them and ask: "Where are the partner-gods you made with Me for whose sake you used to have arguments?" Those given knowledge will say: "Today, humiliation and misery is on the disbelievers, ^{16.28}whose souls the angels take away while they're doing wrong to themselves." Then they will fall into surrender and say: "We weren't doing anything bad." Of course you were! Allah knows perfectly well the bad things you used to do. ^{16.29}Now enter the gates of Hell, to remain in it forever. What a dreadful place for arrogant people to be in!

^{16.30}Those who are mindful of Allah are asked: "What is it that your Lord has revealed?" they reply: "The best!" Those who do good will have goodness in this world but the Home of the Hereafter will be even better. What an excellent home for those who remain mindful of Allah! ^{16.31}They will enter the Gardens of Eden – that have rivers flowing beneath them, where they will have anything they wish. This is how Allah rewards those who are mindful of Him, ^{16.32}whose souls the angels take away while they're doing good things, with the angels saying to them: "Peace be upon you. Enter Paradise because of the good things you used to do."

¹⁶·³³Are the disbelievers waiting for the angels of punishment to come to them or your Lord's judgement? Those before them did the same. It wasn't Allah who harmed them but rather they used to harm themselves. ¹⁶·³⁴They finally suffered because of the bad things they did, and what they used to make fun of ended up punishing them.

¹⁶·³⁵The polytheists argue: "If Allah had wanted, neither we nor our forefathers would have worshipped anything besides Him nor forbidden anything without His order." Those before them argued the same. What more could the messengers do besides deliver the message clearly!

¹⁶·³⁶We certainly sent a messenger within every community saying: "You must worship Allah and stay clear of fake gods." Allah guided some of those people while misguidance proved true against others. So, travel through the earth and take a look at what was the end result of those who called the truth a lie. ¹⁶·³⁷O Prophet Muhammad, you might be concerned for their guidance, but Allah doesn't let the people He calls misguided succeed, nor do they have any helpers.

¹⁶·³⁸They swear by Allah with their strongest oaths that Allah won't bring back to life anyone who dies. Why not! It's a true promise binding on Him, but most people don't know. ¹⁶·³⁹He will do that to make it clear to them about the disagreements they used to have, and for the disbelievers to realise that they were liars. ¹⁶·⁴⁰Our command for anything when We want it to exist is that We only say to it: "Be!" and it becomes.

¹⁶·⁴¹Those who migrated for Allah's sake after suffering oppression, We will certainly give them a good place to live in this world, but the reward of the Hereafter will certainly be far greater. If they only

knew! ¹⁶·⁴²They are those who have patience and put their trust only in their Lord.

¹⁶·⁴³We sent before you as messengers only men We gave revelations to. So, if you yourselves don't know then ask the people of knowledge. ¹⁶·⁴⁴We sent them with clear signs and Holy Books. O Prophet Muhammad, We have revealed to you the Reminder, so you can make it clear to the people what has been sent down for them, and so that they might think deeply.

¹⁶·⁴⁵Do those who make evil plots feel safe that Allah won't make the earth swallow them up or that the punishment won't come at them in a way they least expect? ¹⁶·⁴⁶Or that He won't destroy them as they go about their work? They cannot escape. ¹⁶·⁴⁷Or that He won't destroy them when they are suffering in fear? However, O Prophet Muhammad, your Lord is certainly Kind, Ever-Merciful.

¹⁶·⁴⁸Don't they look into anything Allah has created: how their shadows move from the right and left, prostrating to Allah, in complete humility? ¹⁶·⁴⁹Without showing any arrogance, everything in the heavens and the earth prostrates to Allah, even if they're earthly creatures or heavenly angels. ¹⁶·⁵⁰They continue to fear their Lord above them and they do as they are told. <Prostration Point 3>

¹⁶·⁵¹Allah said: "Don't make two gods; there is only One God. So fear only Me!" ¹⁶·⁵²Everything in the heavens and the earth belongs only to Him, and obedience is only to Him, forever. So, do you fear anyone other than Allah?

¹⁶·⁵³All your blessings come from Allah, but you only cry out to Him when you suffer harm, ¹⁶·⁵⁴yet when He removes the harm from you, some of you start making partner-gods with Him, ¹⁶·⁵⁵being

unthankful for what We've given them. You may enjoy yourselves for now because you will very soon come to know the end result.

^{16.56}They even give a share of what We've given them to things like idols they themselves don't know anything about. By Allah! You will certainly be asked about the lies you used to make.

^{16.57}They attribute daughters to Allah – glory be to Him! They attribute to themselves anything they desire. ^{16.58}When good news of the birth of a baby daughter is given to any of them, his face turns gloomy as he tries to hide his anger. ^{16.59}He hides himself from the people because of the good news, which he thinks is bad news, he has been given. Should he keep her with shame or bury her in the ground? Beware! How terrible are the decisions they make! ^{16.60}Those who don't believe in the Hereafter, they have a bad character whereas Allah has the best qualities. He is the Almighty, the All-Wise.

^{16.61}If Allah punished people immediately because of their wrongdoing, He wouldn't have left any living creature alive in this world. However, He gives them more time until an end date. When the end of their time in death comes, they can neither delay it a moment longer nor bring it any sooner.

^{16.62}They attribute to Allah what they themselves hate, and their tongues utter the lie that they themselves will have the good things. There is no doubt that they will suffer the Fire, and they will be the first to be sent into it.

^{16.63}By Allah! We have certainly sent many messengers to communities before you, but Shaytan made the bad actions of those communities seem attractive to them, which is why he is their friend even Today. They will suffer a painful punishment. ^{16.64}O Prophet

Muhammad, We only revealed the Book to you so you can make clear to them the things they disagree about, and as guidance and mercy for any people who believe.

16.65It is Allah Who sends down from the sky water with which He gives life to the earth after it had become dead. There is certainly a sign in this for any people who listen to the truth.

16.66There is a definite lesson to think about for you in cattle too. From somewhere between the waste and the blood, We give you a pure drink from within their bodies that is pleasant to those who drink it. 16.67From the fruit of the date-palm and the grapevine, you take sweet juice and healthy food. There is certainly a sign in this as well for any people who think.

16.68O Prophet Muhammad, your Lord inspired the bee: "Build hives in mountains, on trees, and in what people build. 16.69Then suck out nectar from every kind of fruit and follow your Lord's simple paths." What comes from its body is a liquid of different colours in which there is a cure for people. There is certainly a sign in this as well for any people who think deeply.

16.70It is Allah Who creates you and then lets you die. Some of you are left to reach the most weak old age so that, after having lots of knowledge, they know nothing at all. Allah is All-Knowing, All-Powerful.

16.71It is Allah Who gives some of you more wealth than others. So, will those given more pass their wealth to their dependents so they can become equal? Or will they reject Allah's favours?

¹⁶·⁷²It is Allah Who has created for you spouses from among yourselves, and created from them children and grandchildren for you, and given you wholesome things. Then, are they still believing in falsehood, and are they still unthankful for Allah's favours? ¹⁶·⁷³Besides Allah, they worship those that don't have the power to give them anything at all, neither from the heavens nor the earth. They cannot do anything. ¹⁶·⁷⁴So, don't try to give Allah any examples. He has full knowledge but you don't.

¹⁶·⁷⁵Allah gives the example of a slave who is owned – unable to do anything at all, and someone free whom We have given plenty of wealth – who secretly and openly donates some of it. Can they be the same? All praise is for Allah. The truth is, most of them don't know.

¹⁶·⁷⁶Allah gives the example of two men: one of them is dumb – unable to do anything at all, and a burden to his carer; anywhere his carer sends him, he brings no good. Can he be the same as someone who commands others to do justice and himself follows a straight path?

¹⁶·⁷⁷The unseen secrets of the heavens and the earth belong only to Allah. Making the Final Hour happen only takes the blink of an eye, or even quicker. Allah is Most Capable of anything.

¹⁶·⁷⁸It is Allah Who brought you out of your mothers' wombs when you didn't know anything at all, and He gave you hearing, sight, and intelligence so that you might give thanks.

¹⁶·⁷⁹Don't they see the birds allowed to fly in the air in the sky? Only Allah is holding them up. There are certainly signs in this for any people who believe.

¹⁶·⁸⁰It is Allah Who has given you a place of rest in your homes, and made you tents out of animal skins which you find to be so light on days when you travel and stop to rest, and also household goods and useful things that last for a while, made from their wool, fur, and hair.

¹⁶·⁸¹It is Allah Who has given you shades from the things He has created, made for you: shelters in mountains; clothes that protect you from the heat and cold, and armour that protects you in your battles. In this way He completes His favours to you so that you might surrender to Him as Muslims.

¹⁶·⁸²O Prophet Muhammad, if they turn away, your duty is only to deliver the message clearly. ¹⁶·⁸³They recognise Allah's favour, yet they still reject it. Most of them are disbelievers.

¹⁶·⁸⁴One Day We will bring forward a witness from each community, then the disbelievers won't be excused or allowed to repent. ¹⁶·⁸⁵Once the wrongdoers see the punishment, it won't be reduced, and they won't be given any more chances. ¹⁶·⁸⁶When the polytheists see those they made partner-gods with Allah, they will say: "Our Lord! These are the partner-gods we made with You – those we used to pray to besides You." However, the partner-gods will throw the words back at them saying: "You are certainly telling lies!" ¹⁶·⁸⁷They will fall into surrender to Allah on that Day, and those idols and lies they made up will abandon them. ¹⁶·⁸⁸Because of the trouble they used to make, We will add punishment upon punishment for those who disbelieved and blocked people from Allah's cause.

¹⁶·⁸⁹O Prophet Muhammad, one Day We will bring forward a witness against each community from among them, and We will bring you as a witness over them all. We have revealed to you the Book explaining everything, as well as a guidance, mercy, and joy for the Muslims.

16.90Allah orders: justice, doing good, and giving to close relatives; and He forbids shamefulness, doing bad things, and disobedience. He advises you so that you might remind yourselves.

16.91You must fulfil your promise to Allah when you make it, and don't break your oaths after confirming them, because you have certainly made Allah a surety over you. Allah knows everything you do. 16.92Don't be like the woman who breaks her yarn into pieces after spinning it strong, by making your oaths a way to cheat each other so that one group can make more profit than the other. Allah is testing you by this, and on Judgement Day, He will certainly make clear to you the disagreements you used to have.

16.93If Allah had wanted, He could have made you all a single community, but He lets anyone He chooses go astray and also guides anyone He wants. You will certainly be asked about everything you used to do.

16.94You must never make your oaths a way to cheat each other in case any foot might slip after being firmly placed in guidance. You will then taste hardship because you blocked people from Allah's cause, and you will suffer a terrible punishment too. 16.95Don't sell Allah's promise for a low price. Anything coming from Allah is best for you if you only knew. 16.96What you have will end but what Allah has will last forever. We will certainly give those who have patience the best reward for the good they used to do.

16.97Whoever does good, whether they're male or female, and being a Believer, We will certainly give them a decent life and the best reward for the good they used to do.

¹⁶·⁹⁸Whenever you recite the Qur'an, you should ask Allah to protect you from Shaytan, the Rejected. ¹⁶·⁹⁹Shaytan doesn't have any power over those who believe and put their trust only in their Lord. ¹⁶·¹⁰⁰His power is only over those who make friends with him and who make partner-gods with Allah.

¹⁶·¹⁰¹When We replace one verse with another – and Allah knows best what He reveals – they claim: "You are making this up!" In fact, most of them don't know why We replaced it. ¹⁶·¹⁰²O Prophet Muhammad, say: "The Holy Spirit has brought this down from your Lord with the truth, to make the Believers strong in belief, as well as a guidance and as a joy for the Muslims." ¹⁶·¹⁰³We certainly know they are saying: "Someone is teaching him," but the language of the person they're referring to isn't Arabic whereas this is a language which is clearly Arabic.

¹⁶·¹⁰⁴Those who don't believe in Allah's revelations, He won't let them succeed, and they will suffer a painful punishment. ¹⁶·¹⁰⁵Only they make lies who don't believe in Allah's revelations. It is really they who are the liars.

¹⁶·¹⁰⁶After having believed, anyone who disbelieves in Allah – not someone who was forced while his heart remained satisfied with belief – he won't be punished, but those who open their hearts to disbelief will have Allah's anger upon them, and they will suffer a terrible punishment.

¹⁶·¹⁰⁷This is because they prefer this life to the next, and because Allah doesn't let disbelieving people succeed. ¹⁶·¹⁰⁸It is they whose hearts, ears, and eyes Allah has sealed up, and it is really they who are neglectful. ¹⁶·¹⁰⁹There's no doubt that, in the Hereafter, they will be the real losers. ¹⁶·¹¹⁰However, your Lord, to those who migrated after

being oppressed, and then strove hard and had patience, your Lord, after all that, is certainly Most Forgiving, Ever-Merciful.

16.111 One Day, every person will come up pleading for himself, and everyone will be paid in full for what they had done, and they won't be treated unfairly.

16.112 Allah gives the example of a city that was safe and peaceful, whose wealth came plentifully from everywhere, but its people were unthankful to Allah's favours, so He made them suffer extreme famine and fear because of the bad things they used to do. 16.113 A messenger from among themselves had come to them but they accused him of being a liar, so the punishment seized them as they were wrongdoers.

16.114 So, you may enjoy the lawful, wholesome things Allah has given you, and you must continue to be thankful for Allah's favour if it is only Him you worship. 16.115 He has made unlawful for you only: dead meat, blood, pork, and an animal that has been slaughtered in the name of anything other than Allah's. However, if someone is forced by need – not being disobedient nor a lawbreaker – then he will find Allah is Most Forgiving, Ever-Merciful.

16.116 Don't tell lies: "This is lawful, and this is unlawful," merely because your tongues utter it, so as to make lies about Allah. Those who make lies about Allah will never be successful. 16.117 It is only a tiny benefit, but then they will suffer a painful punishment.

16.118 O Prophet Muhammad, We made unlawful for the Jews only the things We previously mentioned to you. It wasn't Us who harmed them but rather they used to harm themselves.

¹⁶·¹¹⁹However, your Lord, to those who did wrong out of ignorance but repented after that and corrected themselves, your Lord, after all that, is certainly Most Forgiving, Ever-Merciful.

¹⁶·¹²⁰Ibrahim was a true model of perfection, devoted to Allah, and true in faith. He wasn't a polytheist. ¹⁶·¹²¹He was thankful for Allah's favours, Who selected him and guided him to a path that is straight. ¹⁶·¹²²We gave him good in this world and he will definitely be among righteous people in the Hereafter. ¹⁶·¹²³Then, O Prophet Muhammad, We revealed to you: "Follow the religion of Ibrahim the True. He wasn't a polytheist."

¹⁶·¹²⁴The Sabbath was only prescribed for those who had differences about it. Your Lord will certainly judge between them on Judgement Day about the disagreements they used to have.

¹⁶·¹²⁵You should continue to invite to your Lord's cause with wisdom and good advice, and argue with them in the finest manner. Your Lord knows best anyone who strays from His cause and also those who follow guidance.

¹⁶·¹²⁶If you want to retaliate, then do it according to what you suffered; if you have patience, then patience is certainly best for those who have it. ¹⁶·¹²⁷So, O Prophet Muhammad, have patience, because your patience comes only with Allah's help. Don't worry about the disbelievers nor distress yourself because of the plots they make.

¹⁶·¹²⁸Allah is with those who are mindful of Him and those who do good.

Surah 17. Night Journey (al-Israa')

[PART 15]

Allah's name I begin with, the Most Compassionate, the Ever-Merciful

^{17.1}Glory be to Him Who took His Servant Muhammad on a journey in a small part of the night from the Sacred Masjid in Makkah to the Furthest Masjid in Jerusalem – whose surroundings We have blessed – to show him some of Our signs. Only He is the All-Hearing, the Ever-Watchful.

^{17.2}We gave Musa the Book, and made it a guidance for the Descendants of Ya'qub, telling them: "Don't take a guardian besides Me." ^{17.3}O descendants of those We carried in the Ark with Nuh! He was a very thankful servant.

^{17.4}In the Book, We warned the Descendants of Ya'qub: "You will certainly make trouble twice in the land, and become highly arrogant."

^{17.5}When the first of these two warnings took place, We sent against you Our servants who were mighty warriors, who invaded right into the places where you lived. It was a warning that was bound to happen. ^{17.6}Afterwards, we gave you another chance to defeat them, and We helped you with more resources and children, and made you the group with the greater number. ^{17.7}If you do good, you do it for yourselves; if you do something bad, it will be to your own loss. So, when the second of the warnings took place, they came to disfigure your faces, and to enter the place of worship as they had entered it the first time, so that they could completely destroy what they had conquered. ^{17.8}Perhaps your Lord will have mercy on you, but if you

go back to disobedience, **We too will go back** to punishing you. **We have made Hell a prison for the disbelievers.**

17.9 This Qur'an guides to the way that is most right, and gives good news to the Believers who do good that they will have a large reward. 17.10 As for those who don't believe in the Hereafter, We've prepared a painful punishment for them.

17.11 However, humans hastily **pray** for harm as they do for good, because they're always hasty.

17.12 We made the night and day as two signs: We made the sign of the night dim, while We made the sign of the day bright; so that you can look for some grace from your Lord, and to know the number of years and the calculation of time. We have explained everything in fine detail.

17.13 We have tied every person's data of actions to himself. On Judgement Day, We will bring out for him a record which he will find spread wide open. 17.14 We will say: "Read your own record. You should be enough to judge yourself today." 17.15 Anyone who accepts guidance, accepts it for his own good; anyone who goes astray, does so to his own loss. No one will carry someone else's burden of sins. We would never punish people until We have sent a messenger.

17.16 When We decide to destroy any town, We first tell its elite to do good, but they disobey in it, and that is when something already fixed by your Lord proves true against them, and then We completely destroy that town. 17.17 Just think how many generations have We destroyed after Nuh! Your Lord is enough to be Fully-Aware, Ever-Watchful of the sins of His servants.

¹⁷·¹⁸If anyone wants this available world, We make available for him anything We decide in this life and for anyone We choose. After that, We prepare for him Hell, in which he will burn – disgraced! rejected! ¹⁷·¹⁹Anyone who is a Believer, who wants the Hereafter, and tries for it the best that it deserves, it is they whose hard work will be appreciated. ¹⁷·²⁰We give out to everyone, these as well as those, through your Lord's generous giving. His generous giving is never restricted to anyone. ¹⁷·²¹Take a look at how We made some people superior to others, but the Hereafter is certainly superior to this world in rank and in grace.

¹⁷·²²Don't make another god with Allah or you will fall back disgraced, helpless. ¹⁷·²³Your Lord has ordered that: "You must never worship anyone except Him, and be kind to parents – if one or both of them reach old age with you, don't even say 'Ugh!' to them nor be strict with them, but speak to them politely. ¹⁷·²⁴You must be merciful to them and pray: "My Lord! Have mercy on them as they looked after me when I was little." ¹⁷·²⁵Your Lord knows best what is in your hearts. If you are righteous, then you should know that He is Most Forgiving to those who always turn to Him.

¹⁷·²⁶You must give close relatives their rights, as well as to the needy, and to travellers; and don't waste things. ¹⁷·²⁷Wasteful people are brothers of the evil ones, whereas Shaytan himself is always unthankful to his Lord. ¹⁷·²⁸Even if you have to turn away from these needy people, wanting to give them the mercy you hope for from your Lord, then you should at least say kind words to them.

¹⁷·²⁹Don't let your hand be tied to your neck out of stinginess and nor stretch it out completely to give away everything, or you will end up falling back blameworthy or impoverished. ¹⁷·³⁰It is your Lord Who

can increase or restrict wealth for anyone He chooses. He is always Fully-Aware, Ever-Watchful of His servants.

17.31Don't kill your children for fear of poverty - We give to you and to them. Killing them is a terrible crime.

17.32Don't go anywhere near unlawful sexual relations because it is something shameful and a terrible way.

17.33Don't kill a person Allah has made sacred, except by lawful right. We have given authority to demand justice to the heirs of anyone who is killed wrongfully, but they mustn't overstep the limits when taking life as retaliation. They are being helped by Allah.

17.34Don't go anywhere near an orphan's property – unless it is with the best intentions, until he reaches his full strength; and you must fulfil promises because they will be asked about.

17.35Whenever you measure, you must give it in full, and weigh with an even balance. That is best, and good for the end result.

17.36Don't go following after what you don't know anything about. Hearing, seeing, and intellect will all be asked about.

17.37Don't walk on the ground arrogantly because you can never split it apart and nor can you ever reach the mountains in height.

17.38The terrible nature of all such actions is disliked by your Lord. 17.39This is some of the wisdom your Lord has inspired you. Don't make another god with Allah or you will be thrown into Hell – blameworthy! rejected!

17.40Has your Lord chosen sons for you polytheists, and made the angels His own daughters? You are definitely making a terrible claim! 17.41In this Qur'an, We have explained things in various ways so they might learn lessons, but it only increases their hatred of the truth.

17.42O Prophet Muhammad, say: "If there had been other gods with Him, as they claim, then in that case they would certainly have looked for a way to defeat Allah – the Lord of the Throne." 17.43Glory be to Him! He is far higher and greater than what they say. 17.44The seven heavens and the earth glorify Him, and so does everyone in them. There isn't a single thing that doesn't glorify His praises, but you people don't understand the way they do this. He is always Most Tolerant, Most Forgiving.

17.45Whenever you recite the Qur'an, We place an invisible veil between you and those who don't believe in the Hereafter. 17.46We've put covers over their hearts so they won't be able to understand it, and deafness in their ears too. When you mention your Lord alone in the Qur'an, they turn their backs in hatred of the truth. 17.47We know best why they listen to it carefully when they listen to you because when they have their private discussions, that is when the wrongdoers say: "You are only following a man who is under a magic spell." 17.48Just look at how they're making comparisons of you, which is why they've gone astray and cannot find a way.

17.49They ask: "What? When after we have died and become bones and dust, will we then be brought back to life as a new creation?" 17.50Reply: "Yes, even if you become stones or iron, 17.51or anything which, in your minds, is harder to create." They will then ask: "Who will bring us back?" Reply: "He Who made you the first time." Then they will shake their heads at you and ask: "When will that be?" Reply: "It could be very soon." 17.52It is a Day when He will call you, and you will all respond by praising Him, and you will think you lived in this world **for only a short time.**

17.53**Tell My servants that they should say only what is best, because Shaytan tries to cause trouble among them. Shaytan is always every human's open enemy.**

17.54**Your Lord knows you best. He can have mercy on you if He wants, or He can punish you if He wants.** O Prophet Muhammad, **We haven't sent you to be responsible for them.** 17.55**Your Lord knows best everyone in the heavens and the earth. We have made some prophets superior to others. We gave Dawud the Zabur.**

17.56**Say: "Pray for help to those you made claims for** that they are gods besides Allah; they don't have any power to remove suffering from you nor to make any change to it." 17.57**Those they pray to are themselves looking for ways to their Lord** to see **who is the closest, and they're hoping for His special mercy and fearing His punishment. Your Lord's punishment is something to be afraid of.**

17.58**There is no town** of wrongdoers **We won't destroy or severely punish before Judgement Day. This has been written in the Master Record.** 17.59**Nothing has stopped Us from sending signs, even though previous people rejected them. We sent the she-camel to the Thamud as a clear sign, but they were cruel to her. We send signs only to warn people of punishment.**

17.60Remember **when We told you that your Lord surrounds the people in knowledge and power. The sights We showed you, as well as the tree that has been cursed in the Qur'an, We have made them only as tests for people. We warn them** of punishment, **but it only increases their excessive rebellion.**

¹⁷·⁶¹When We ordered the angels: "Prostrate in front of Adam," and so they did prostrate – but not Iblees. He protested: "Why should I prostrate in front of someone You have created from clay?" ¹⁷·⁶²He added: "Tell me why You have given more honour to this Adam than to me. If You give me enough time until Judgement Day, I will certainly bring destruction to all but a few of his descendants." ¹⁷·⁶³Allah replied: "Go away. If any of them follow you, then Hell will be the punishment for the lot of you – a full punishment! ¹⁷·⁶⁴You can try and lead to destruction those of them that you can with your voice, attack them with your cavalry and your infantry, share with them wealth and children, and make promises to them." However, Shaytan promises them nothing but lies. ¹⁷·⁶⁵Allah continued: "As for My servants, you won't have any influence over them. Your Lord is enough for them as a Guardian."

¹⁷·⁶⁶People! Your Lord is the one Who makes the ships go smoothly for you through the sea so you can look for some of His grace. He is always Ever-Merciful to you. ¹⁷·⁶⁷When you suffer harm at sea, those you pray to will abandon you except Him. Then, when He brings you safely to land, you turn away from thanking Him. Humans are unthankful.

¹⁷·⁶⁸Do you then feel safe that He won't make the shore swallow you up, or that He won't send a violent hurricane of stones upon you? In these cases, you won't find any guardian for yourselves. ¹⁷·⁶⁹Do you feel safe that He won't put you back into the sea once again and send upon you a ship-wrecking storm to drown you because of your disbelief? In this case, you won't find anyone there to defend you against Us.

¹⁷·⁷⁰We have certainly given honour to the descendants of Adam, carried them across land and sea, gave them wholesome things, and made them far superior to many things We have created. ¹⁷·⁷¹On the Day We call together all the groups of people with their leaders: those who will be given their record in their right hands, it is they who will happily read it, and they won't be treated unfairly even as much as a hair on a date-seed. ¹⁷·⁷²However, anyone who was blind to the truth in this world, will be blind to the blessings in the Hereafter, and even further from the way to Paradise. ¹⁷·⁷³They had tried to lead you away from what We revealed to you because they wanted you to make up other things as lies about Us, in which case they would certainly have made you a close friend. ¹⁷·⁷⁴If We hadn't made you strong, you would have certainly ended up trusting them a little bit. ¹⁷·⁷⁵If that was the case, We would have made you taste double punishment in this life and double punishment in death, and then you wouldn't have found anyone to help you against Us. ¹⁷·⁷⁶They had tried to scare you off the land to expel you from it, but in that case they themselves would have only lived there for a short time after you. ¹⁷·⁷⁷This was Our way with Our messengers We sent before you. You won't find any change in Our ways.

¹⁷·⁷⁸You must establish the ritual prayers after the sun's decline at noon until the darkness of the night, and the Qur'an recitation at Fajr Prayer; the Qur'an recitation at Fajr Prayer is witnessed by the angels. ¹⁷·⁷⁹O Prophet Muhammad, as for some part of the night, you should wake up to pray the Tahajjud prayer – with Qur'an recitation – as an extra prayer specifically for you. Your Lord will certainly raise you up to a highly-praised status. ¹⁷·⁸⁰You should pray: "My Lord! Let me enter truthfully, and let me exit truthfully; and give me from Yourself some special power that gives support." ¹⁷·⁸¹Say: "The truth is here and falsehood has vanished. Falsehood was bound to vanish."

17.82We reveal in the Qur'an that which is a healing and a mercy for the Believers, and it increases the wrongdoers only in loss.

17.83However, when We do favours to people, they turn away and move to the side, and when they suffer harm they begin to lose hope. 17.84Say: "Everyone does things in their own way, but your Lord knows best who it is that follows guidance the best on a right way."

17.85O Prophet Muhammad, they ask you about the soul. Say: "The soul is from my Lord's command, but you've only been given very little knowledge."

17.86If We had wanted, We could take away everything We have revealed to you, and then you wouldn't find any agent for yourself to take it back from Us, 17.87except for some special mercy from your Lord. His grace to you is always immense.

17.88Say: "If humans and jinns joined together to make something like this Qur'an, they wouldn't be able to make anything like it however much they supported each other."

17.89In this Qur'an, We have explained all kinds of examples in various ways for people, yet most of them reject everything but choose to be unthankful. 17.90They say: "We will never believe merely because you say so unless: you make a fountain gush out of the ground for us; 17.91or you have a garden of date-palms and grapevines, and make rivers flow through them with lots of water; 17.92or you make the sky, as you claim, fall in pieces upon us; or you bring Allah and the angels face to face with us; 17.93or you have a house of gold; or you climb up into the sky. Even then we will never believe merely because you climb up into the sky unless you bring down for us a Holy Book to read." Say:

"Glory be to my Lord! Am I anything other than a human messenger?"

17.94The only thing that prevented people from believing when guidance came to them is that they argued: "Has Allah sent a human as a messenger?" 17.95Say: "If there had been angels on the earth, walking about, settled here, We would have certainly sent down an angel from heaven as a messenger for them." 17.96Say: "Allah is enough as a Witness between me and you all. He is always Fully-Aware, Ever-Watchful of His servants."

17.97Anyone Allah guides will really follow guidance, and whoever He calls misguided, you won't find any protectors for them other than Him. On Judgement Day, We will assemble them all together dragging them on their faces – blind, dumb, and deaf. Their home will be Hell. Each time it cools down, We will flare it up for them into a roaring blaze. 17.98That is their punishment because they disbelieved in Our revelations and said: "What? When after we have died and become bones and dust, will we then be brought back to life as a new creation?" 17.99Don't they see that Allah, Who created the heavens and the earth, has the power to create anything just like them? He has fixed for them a term in which there is no doubt, yet the wrongdoers reject everything but choose to be unthankful. 17.100O Prophet Muhammad, say: "If you had any control over the treasures of my Lord's mercy, even then you would hold on to them fearing they might run out. Humans are stingy."

17.101We gave Musa nine clear signs. Ask the Descendants of Ya'qub that when he came to them, Fir'awn said to him: "Musa, I'm sure you are under a magic spell." 17.102Musa replied: "You know that only the Lord of the heavens and the earth has sent these signs as clear proofs of warning and understanding, **and I am sure you will be totally destroyed, O Firʻawn!"**

17.103Firʻawn wanted to scare them off the land, so We drowned him and all those who were with him. 17.104After him, We said to the Descendants of Yaʻqub: "You may live comfortably in the land, but when the promise of the Hereafter comes, We will bring you all together in a mixed crowd."

17.105O Prophet Muhammad, **it is with the truth that We revealed the Qur'an, and with the truth it came. We have sent you only to give good news and warnings.** 17.106We divided the Qur'an into parts so you can recite it to people slowly with pauses; and We sent it down in stages. 17.107Say: "Whether you believe in it or not, those who were previously given knowledge of it, they fall down on their faces in prostration whenever it is recited to them, 17.108and they say, 'Glory be to our Lord! The promise of our Lord is always bound to happen!'." 17.109They fall down on their faces crying, and it increases them even more **in humility.** *<Prostration Point 4>*

17.110Say: "You may call on Allah or on ar-Rahman. It doesn't matter **by which name you call on Him because He has the most beautiful names."** Neither be too loud in your prayer and nor too quiet, but find a middle way somewhere between the two.

17.111Say: "All praise is for Allah Who has never had any child nor any partner in running His **kingdom, nor does He need anyone to protect Him from weakness. So, proclaim His greatness a lot!"**

Surah 18. Cave (al-Kahf)

Allah's name I begin with, the Most Compassionate, the Ever-Merciful

^{18.1}All praise is for Allah Who revealed to His Servant the Book – and did not allow any crookedness in it, ^{18.2}but made it correct to give warnings of a severe punishment coming from Him, and to give good news to the Believers who do good that they will have an excellent reward of Paradise, ^{18.3}where they will stay forever; ^{18.4}and to give warnings to those who claim that Allah has a child! ^{18.5}They don't know anything about it and nor did their forefathers. The utterance that comes from their mouths is outrageous! They are only telling lies!

^{18.6}O Prophet Muhammad, **you might end up destroying yourself with worry for them if they don't believe in this Message.** ^{18.7}We have made everything on earth to be its beauty so We can test which of the people does the best. ^{18.8}One Day We will turn everything on earth into a lifeless wasteland.

^{18.9}O Prophet Muhammad, **do you think the Companions of the Cave (As'haab al-Kahf) and of the Inscription were the only wonders from among Our signs?** ^{18.10}When the youths took refuge in the cave and prayed: "Our Lord! Give us some special mercy from You, and give us true guidance in our situation," ^{18.11}We patted their ears in the cave for a number of years. ^{18.12}We eventually woke them up to prove which of the two groups would best calculate the length of time they had been there.

^{18.13}We are telling you their story with the truth: They were some youths who believed in their Lord, and We increased them in guidance. ^{18.14}We made their hearts strong when they stood up in

front of their king and said: "Our Lord is the Lord of the heavens and the earth. We will never pray to any god besides Him, otherwise we would have certainly uttered something outrageous. ¹⁸·¹⁵These people of ours have made gods besides Him. Why don't they bring forward some clear proof of them being gods? Who, then, could be more unjust than someone who makes lies about Allah!" ¹⁸·¹⁶Now that you youths have moved away from them and from anything they worship instead of Allah, you should take refuge in the cave; your Lord will spread out His special mercy for you and give you an easy way out of your situation.

¹⁸·¹⁷You can see the sun: when it rose – turning away from their cave to the right, and when it set – cutting them off to the left, while they lay in the open space inside the cave. This is one of Allah's signs. Anyone Allah guides will really follow guidance, and whoever He calls misguided, you won't find any protector to show them true guidance. ¹⁸·¹⁸You would think they were awake though they were asleep, because We were turning them over to the right and to the left, with their dog stretching out its forelegs at the entrance. If you had only glanced at them, you would have certainly turned away from them and run away, terrified of them!

¹⁸·¹⁹In this way We woke them up so they could ask each other some questions. One of them asked: "How long have you been here?" Some replied: "We've been here for a day or part of a day." Others said: "Your Lord knows best how long you've been here. Now send one of you to the city with this money of yours so he can find out which of its food is the purest and bring some of it back for you to eat. He should be polite and careful and not let anyone become aware of you. ¹⁸·²⁰If they find out about you, they will stone you to death or force you to go back to their religion, and then you will never ever be successful."

18.21That is how We let them be found, so the people could know that Allah's promise is true, and about the Final Hour in which there is no doubt. After they had died, when the people started quarrelling among themselves about what they should do with them, some said: "Make a building as a monument over them. Their Lord knows best about them." Those who were influential in their matter said: "We will certainly build a place of worship over them."

18.22Some will say: "They were three, the fourth was their dog," while others will say: "They were five, the sixth was their dog," – guessing without seeing; yet others will say: "They were seven, and the eighth was their dog." You should say: "My Lord knows best how many they were; only a few really know about them." So, you shouldn't dispute about them other than what is clearly known, and don't ask any of these people about them.

18.23You should never say about anything: "I will do that tomorrow," 18.24without adding: "If Allah chooses." If you forget, you should remember your Lord and say: "Perhaps my Lord will guide me to something even closer to true guidance than this."

18.25They were in their cave for three hundred years, and some added nine more. 18.26Say: "Allah knows best how long they were there." The unseen secrets of the heavens and the earth belong only to Him: how well He sees, how well He hears! They don't have any protector besides Him, and He doesn't share His rule with anyone.

18.27Recite what has been revealed to you from your Lord's Book. Nothing can change Allah's words, and you will never find any place of refuge away from Him. 18.28Keep yourself patiently with those who pray to their Lord morning and evening, wanting His good pleasure.

Don't let your eyes move away from them, by wrongfully wanting only the luxuries of this life. Don't obey anyone: whose heart We have let go to be neglectful in remembering Us; and who follows his own desires; and whose way of life has gone beyond all limits.

18.29Say: "This truth is from your Lord. Anyone who wants to believe or disbelieve is free to do so." For the wrongdoers, We've prepared a fire whose walls will completely surround them. If they ask for any help, they will be given water like molten brass that will fry their faces. What a horrible thing to drink! What a terrible place to rest!

18.30Those who believe and do good – anyone who does something good, We won't let their reward go to waste. 18.31It is they who will have Gardens of Eden – with rivers flowing beneath them, where they will be adorned with gold bracelets, and dressed in green clothing of fine silk and heavy brocade, where they will be relaxing on raised thrones. What an excellent reward! What a fine place to rest!

18.32Give them the example of two men: We gave one of them two gardens of grapevines and surrounded them with palm trees. We put cultivated land between them both. 18.33Each of those gardens brought out its fruit in full and didn't fall short in any way at all. We even made a river flow through the middle of them. 18.34He had plenty of other resources too. So, he said to his companion, whilst discussing with him: "I have more wealth and a larger following than you do." 18.35He entered his own garden doing harm only to himself when he said: "I don't think this will ever end, 18.36and I don't think the Final Hour will ever come. Even if I was taken back to my Lord, I will definitely get a place far better than this."

18.37His companion said to him, whilst discussing with him: "Do you disbelieve in Him Who originally created you from dust, then from a drop of semen, and then gave you proportion as a man? ¹⁸·³⁸But me? I believe He is Allah – my Lord! I will never make anyone a partner-god with my Lord. ¹⁸·³⁹When you entered your garden, why didn't you say, 'As Allah chooses. There is no strength except through Allah.'? Even if you do see me with less wealth and children than you, ¹⁸·⁴⁰perhaps my Lord will give me something better than your garden, and send down on your garden some destruction from the sky, so it will become a lifeless, slippery piece of land, ¹⁸·⁴¹or the garden's water will sink so deep underground that you will never be able to reach it."

¹⁸·⁴²His resources were completely destroyed, and he began to wring his hands in grief over what he had invested in his property, which was now in ruins. All he could say was: "Oh! If only I hadn't made any partner-god with my Lord!" ¹⁸·⁴³There was no group of people to help him besides Allah nor could he even defend himself. ¹⁸·⁴⁴It was proven there and then that protection comes only from Allah, Who is the Truth. He is the Best to reward, and the Best to give the final results.

¹⁸·⁴⁵Give them the example of this worldly life. It is like some water We send down from the sky. The plants of the land absorb it, but soon they become dry stubble that the winds blow about. Allah always has perfect control over everything. ¹⁸·⁴⁶Wealth and children are the beauty of this worldly life, but everlasting good actions are the best in the sight of your Lord, both as reward and as basis for hope.

¹⁸·⁴⁷One Day We will move the mountains away, and you will see the earth without any cover, and We will gather all the people together without leaving out any one of them. ¹⁸·⁴⁸They will be brought lined up in front of your Lord and We will say: "Now you have come to Us just like We created you the first time, yet you claimed We would never set up any time or place promised for you." ¹⁸·⁴⁹The record will be placed in front of them and you will see the criminals terrified of

what is written inside it. They will cry: "Oh! What kind of record is this! It doesn't leave out anything small or big! It includes everything!" They will find right there everything they had done, and your Lord won't treat anyone unfairly.

$^{18.50}$When We ordered the angels: "Prostrate in front of Adam," and so they did prostrate – but not Iblees. He was one of the jinns and he disobeyed his Lord's command. Are you making him and his descendants your guardians instead of Me when they are your enemy? What a terrible replacement the wrongdoers are making! $^{18.51}$I didn't make them witness the creation of the heavens and the earth, nor even their own creation, and I don't take supporters from those who mislead. $^{18.52}$On that Day, Allah will say: "Pray to those you claimed to be My partner-gods," and they will pray to them, but the partner-gods won't respond to them. We will separate them by a place of destruction. $^{18.53}$The criminals will see the Fire and realise they're going to fall into it, and will find no way to escape from it.

$^{18.54}$In this Qur'an, We've explained all kinds of examples in various ways for people, yet humans more than anything else like to argue. $^{18.55}$The only thing that prevents people from believing when guidance has come to them, and from begging their Lord to forgive them, is that they want anything that happened to previous people should happen to them too or the punishment should come to them face to face. $^{18.56}$We send messengers only to give good news and warnings, yet the disbelievers use false arguments to try and wipe out the truth. They make fun of My revelations and of everything they've been warned about. $^{18.57}$Who could be more unjust than someone who is reminded of his Lord's revelations but turns away from them forgetting all the bad things he has done! We've put covers over their hearts so they won't be able to understand it, and deafness in their ears too. If you invite them to guidance, they will still never ever follow it.

$^{18.58}$However, your Lord, being the Most Forgiving, is the Lord of Mercy. If He punished them for what they've done then He would have certainly brought their punishment sooner, but they have a time and place they've been warned about, and they won't find any shelter away from Allah. $^{18.59}$We destroyed those towns whenever they did wrong; and We fixed a time for their destruction.

$^{18.60}$Remember when Musa said to his youthful servant: "I won't give up until I reach the place where the two seas come together, even if I have to spend ages travelling." $^{18.61}$When they reached the place where the two seas come together, they forgot about their fish, and it slipped away into the sea like a tunnel. $^{18.62}$Then, when they had journeyed on, Musa said to his youthful servant: "Bring us our morning meal. We have certainly experienced a lot of tiredness in this journey of ours." $^{18.63}$He replied: "Do you remember when we took a rest next to the rock? Well, I forgot the fish there – it was only Shaytan who made me forget mentioning it to you – and it made its way into the sea. How strange!" $^{18.64}$Musa said: "That is what we were looking for." So, they went back along the tracks they had come, $^{18.65}$and they met there one of Our servants – someone We had given a special mercy from Us and had taught special and secret knowledge from Us.

$^{18.66}$Musa asked him: "May I come with you so you can teach me some of the true guidance you have been taught?" $^{18.67}$The man replied: "You won't be able to have patience with me. $^{18.68}$How can you have patience with what your information doesn't fully cover?" $^{18.69}$Musa replied: "If Allah chooses, you will find me having patience, and I won't break any of your rules." ¹⁸·⁷⁰The man said: "If you do come with me then don't ask me about anything until I tell you about it myself."

¹⁸·⁷¹So they both moved on until they boarded a boat. The man made a hole in it. Musa protested: "Have you made a hole in it to drown its passengers? What a terrible thing you've done!" ¹⁸·⁷²He answered: "Didn't I say that you won't be able to have patience with me?" ¹⁸·⁷³Musa said: "Excuse me for forgetting. Don't make my mission too difficult for me."

¹⁸·⁷⁴So they both moved on until they met a young boy. The man killed him. Musa protested: "Have you killed an innocent person who hasn't killed anyone? What a horrible thing you've done!"

[PART 16]

¹⁸·⁷⁵He answered: "Didn't I tell you that you won't be able to have patience with me?" ¹⁸·⁷⁶Musa said: "If I ask you about anything from now on then don't keep me with you. You've received all excuses from me now."

¹⁸·⁷⁷So they both moved on until they came to some village people. They asked them for some food, but those people refused to have them as guests. Anyway, the two found a wall in that village about to fall, so the man fixed it. Musa protested: "If you wanted you could have taken some payment for doing that." ¹⁸·⁷⁸The man answered: "This is where we break up, me and you. Now I will tell you the reason behind the things I did and you weren't able to have patience about:

¹⁸·⁷⁹As for the boat, it belonged to some needy people who worked on the sea. I wanted to damage it because there was a cruel king further ahead who was taking every good boat by force. ¹⁸·⁸⁰As for the young boy, his parents were Believers, and we feared he would force them into crime and disbelief. ¹⁸·⁸¹We hoped their Lord will give them a

purer and more loving child in his place. ¹⁸·⁸²As for the wall, it belonged to two young orphan boys in the town. There was some treasure beneath it that was theirs. Their father had been a righteous man, and so your Lord wanted them to reach their full strength and dig out their treasure themselves, as a special mercy from your Lord. I didn't do any of it of my own choice. This is the reason behind the things I did and you weren't able to have patience about."

¹⁸·⁸³O Prophet Muhammad, they ask you about Dhu'l-Qarnayn. Reply: "I will tell you something about him." ¹⁸·⁸⁴We gave him control in the land, as well as the means to achieve anything.

¹⁸·⁸⁵He followed a certain route, ¹⁸·⁸⁶until, when he reached a place where the sun sets, he saw it as if it was setting in a pool of dark stinky muddy water, where he met some people. We said: "Dhu'l-Qarnayn, you may either punish them or treat them kindly." ¹⁸·⁸⁷He responded: "We will punish anyone who does wrong. Eventually he will be taken back to his Lord Who will make him suffer a dreadful punishment, ¹⁸·⁸⁸but whoever believes and does good, he will have the most beautiful reward, and we will give him orders to do that are easy."

¹⁸·⁸⁹Then he followed another route, ¹⁸·⁹⁰until, when he reached a place where the sun rises, he saw it rising over some people for whom We hadn't provided any shelter from the sun. ¹⁸·⁹¹That is how it was. Our information fully covers everything about him.

¹⁸·⁹²Then he followed another route, ¹⁸·⁹³until, when he reached a place between two barriers, he met behind them some people who could barely understand a word. ¹⁸·⁹⁴They said: "Dhu'l-Qarnayn! The Ya'juj (Gog) and Ma'juj (Magog) are making trouble in this region. Can we pay you a fee to build a barrier between us and them?" ¹⁸·⁹⁵He replied: "The possibilities my Lord has created for me in this regard are far

better. You should help me with resources, and I will put up a strong wall between you and them. ¹⁸·⁹⁶Bring me large blocks of iron." Eventually, when he had filled up the space between the two mountainsides, he said: "Blow!" Then, when he had turned that iron into fire, he said: "Bring me molten copper to pour over it." ¹⁸·⁹⁷Thus, the Ya'juj and Ma'juj could neither climb over it nor dig through it. ¹⁸·⁹⁸He said: "This is a special mercy from my Lord. However, when my Lord's promise is fulfilled, He will crush this wall flat. My Lord's promise is always true."

¹⁸·⁹⁹On that Day, We will leave them to rush into each another like waves. The Trumpet will be blown and then We will gather them all together. ¹⁸·¹⁰⁰On that Day, We will fully expose Hell in front of the disbelievers ¹⁸·¹⁰¹whose eyes had been under a veil of neglect for not remembering Me, and who couldn't even listen to the truth. ¹⁸·¹⁰²Do the disbelievers think that, instead of Me, they can take My servants as protectors? We have prepared Hell as a place for the disbelievers to come and stay.

¹⁸·¹⁰³Say: "Shall we tell you who are the biggest losers in the things they do? ¹⁸·¹⁰⁴They are those whose hard work in this life is wasted while they believe they're doing something good." ¹⁸·¹⁰⁵They are the ones who disbelieve in their Lord's signs and the meeting with Him. Their actions are wasted, and We won't give them any weight of reward on Judgement Day. ¹⁸·¹⁰⁶That is their punishment: Hell, because they disbelieved and made fun of My signs and messengers.

¹⁸·¹⁰⁷However, those who believe and do good, they will have, as a special place to come and stay, the Highest Gardens of Paradise, ¹⁸·¹⁰⁸where they will remain forever, not looking to move away from there.

18.109O Prophet Muhammad, say: "If the ocean was ink for my Lord's words, it would certainly finish before my Lord's words would come to an end, even if We brought another similar ocean to add to it."

18.110Say: "I'm only human in appearance just like you, but it is revealed to me that your God is One God. So, anyone who expects to have a meeting with his Lord should do good and not make anyone a partner-god in the worship of his Lord."

Surah 19. Maryam (Mary)

Allah's name I begin with, the Most Compassionate, the Ever-Merciful

19.1*Kaaf Haa Yaa 'Ayn Saad.*
19.2This is a reminder of your Lord's mercy to His servant Zakariyya. 19.3Remember when he called out to his Lord in a low voice. 19.4He prayed: "My Lord! My bones have become weak, and my head is shining with white hair because of old age, but I've never been disappointed when praying to You, my Lord! 19.5I now fear for my relatives losing their religion after me whereas my wife cannot give birth to children, so give me from Yourself someone to inherit me, 19.6who will represent me as well as some of the household of Ya'qub in prophethood; and make him pleasing to You, my Lord!"

19.7Allah responded: "Zakariyya, We give you the good news of a son whose name will be Yahya – a name We haven't given to anyone before him." 19.8He asked: "My Lord! How can I have a son when my wife cannot give birth to children and I've reached extreme old age?" 19.9Allah replied: "This is how it will be!" Your Lord said: "It is easy for Me. Look at how I created you before when you were nothing." 19.10Zakariyya said: "My Lord! Give me a sign." Allah replied: "Your sign is that you won't be able to speak to people for three nights and days even though you will be fit and healthy." ¹⁹·¹¹So, Zakariyya came out to his people from his prayer-room and signalled to them that they must glorify Allah morning and evening.

¹⁹·¹²We said: "Yahya, you must hold strongly on to the Book." Even as a child, We gave him wisdom, ¹⁹·¹³special tenderness from Us, and purity. He was Godfearing ¹⁹·¹⁴and kind to his parents, and not bossy or rebellious. ¹⁹·¹⁵So, peace be upon him the day he was born, the day he dies, and the day he will be brought back to life.

¹⁹·¹⁶O Prophet Muhammad, **mention in the Book** the story of **Maryam**: how she separated herself from her family and went to a place in the east. ¹⁹·¹⁷She veiled herself from them. Then We sent Our Holy Spirit (- Angel Jibra'il) to her, and he appeared to her as a complete human being. ¹⁹·¹⁸She said: "I ask Allah – the Most Compassionate to protect me from you! Stay away if you are Godfearing!" ¹⁹·¹⁹He said: "I am a messenger-angel from your Lord, come to give you a holy son." ¹⁹·²⁰She asked in surprise: "How can I have a son when no man has touched me and I'm not immoral?" ¹⁹·²¹He replied: "This is how it will be! Your Lord said, 'It is easy for Me. It will be so that We make him a sign for people and a special mercy from Us.' It is a matter that has already been decided."

¹⁹·²²So she became pregnant with the baby and moved away with him to a remote place. ¹⁹·²³When the time for childbirth forced her to go to the trunk of a palm tree, she cried: "Oh! If only I had died before this and become totally forgotten!" ¹⁹·²⁴But a voice from below her called out to her: "Don't worry. Your Lord has made a small stream flow beneath you. ¹⁹·²⁵Shake the trunk of the palm tree towards you and it will drop fresh ripe dates over you. ¹⁹·²⁶Now eat and drink, and cool your eyes in happiness. If you see anyone, say by gestures, 'I have

promised a fast of silence for Allah – the Most Compassionate, and that is why I'm not talking to anyone today.'."

19.27Then, she came back to her people carrying the baby. They said: "Maryam! What a terrible thing you have done! 19.28O Sister of Haroon! Neither was your father an indecent man nor was your mother an immoral woman!" 19.29But she simply pointed to the baby. They asked: "How can we talk to someone who is an infant still in the cradle?"

19.30The baby Isa spoke: "I am a servant of Allah. He has given me the Book and made me a prophet. 19.31He has made me blessed wherever I go, and has ordered me to establish the ritual prayers and pay zakah as long as I live. 19.32He has made me kind to my mother, and not made me bossy or unblessed. 19.33So, peace be upon me the day I was born, the day I die, and the day I will be brought back to life."

19.34That is Isa ibn Maryam. This is the word of truth which they have doubts about.

19.35It is not the status of Allah to have a child. Glory be to Him! Whenever He decides something to happen, He only says to it: "Be!" and it becomes. 19.36Isa said: "Allah is my Lord and yours too, so you must worship Him. This is a path that is straight." 19.37However, the sects began to have disagreements among themselves. So, the disbelievers will be damned when they face a Terrible Day. 19.38How clearly will they hear and see on the Day when they will come Us! However, today the wrongdoers are clearly astray.

19.39O Prophet Muhammad, you should warn them of the Day of Regret when every matter will be settled, because they aren't paying any attention and just won't believe. 19.40It is We Who will inherit the earth with everyone on it, and it is Us they will be brought back to.

^{19.41}O Prophet Muhammad, **mention in the Book** the story of **Ibrahim.** He was a man of truth, a prophet. ^{19.42}Remember when he said to his foster **father:** "Dear Father! Why do you worship something that can neither hear, see, nor help you in any way at all? ^{19.43}Dear Father! Some knowledge that did not reach you has come to me, so follow me and I will guide you on a path that is smooth. ^{19.44}Dear Father! Don't worship Shaytan. He is a rebel against Allah – the Most Compassionate. ^{19.45}Dear Father! I fear you might suffer a punishment from Allah – the Most Compassionate, and become Shaytan's friend."

^{19.46}His uncle and foster father Aazar said: "Are you turning away from my gods, Ibrahim? If you don't stop, I will certainly stone you to death. Now get away from me for a long time!" ^{19.47}Ibrahim replied: "Peace be upon you. I will ask my Lord to forgive you. He has always been gracious to me. ^{19.48}For now, I will stay away from the lot of you and also from what you pray to besides Allah. I will continue to pray to my Lord. I most certainly will never be disappointed when praying to my Lord."

^{19.49}When he had left them and what they worshipped besides Allah, We gave him Is'haq and Ya'qub. We made each of them a prophet. ^{19.50}We gave them some of Our special mercy and a high mention among truthful people.

^{19.51}O Prophet Muhammad, **mention in the Book** the story of **Musa.** He was specially chosen, and was a messenger, a prophet. ^{19.52}We called to him from the right side of Mount Tur, and brought him close to Us for a secret conversation. ^{19.53}Out of Our special mercy, We gave him his brother Haroon, who was also a prophet.

¹⁹·⁵⁴**Mention in the Book** the story of **Isma'il**. He was true to his promise, and was a messenger, a prophet. ¹⁹·⁵⁵He used to tell his family to establish the ritual prayers and pay zakah, and he was most pleasing to his Lord.

¹⁹·⁵⁶**Mention in the Book** the story of **Idris (Enoch)**. He was a man of truth, a prophet. ¹⁹·⁵⁷We raised him up to a high rank.

¹⁹·⁵⁸**They're the ones,** some prophets Allah has done favours to; from the descendants of Adam, and from those We carried in the Ark with Nuh; from the descendants of Ibrahim and Ya'qub; and from those We guided and chose. When the verses of Allah – the Most Compassionate were recited to them, they would fall down prostrating and weeping. *<Prostration Point 5>*

¹⁹·⁵⁹**After them came** other generations who missed prayers and followed their own desires. They will very soon meet destruction ¹⁹·⁶⁰– but not those who repent, believe, and do good, because it is they who will enter Paradise and won't be treated unfairly in any way at all. ¹⁹·⁶¹They will live in **Gardens of Eden,** which Allah – the Most Compassionate has promised His servants in the unseen world. His promise will always come true. ¹⁹·⁶²They won't hear any foolishness there but only words of peace, and where there will be plenty of food for them morning and evening. ¹⁹·⁶³That is the Paradise We will give as inheritance to those of Our servants who are Godfearing.

¹⁹·⁶⁴**The angels say:** "We only come down at your Lord's command. Everything in front of us, behind us, and in between, belongs only to Him. Your Lord never forgets. ¹⁹·⁶⁵He is the Lord of the heavens and the earth and everything in between them. So, you must worship Him, and be steadfast in worshipping Him. Do you know of anyone equal to Him?"

¹⁹·⁶⁶The human being asks in rejection: "When I die, will I be brought out again alive?" ¹⁹·⁶⁷What? Doesn't he remember that We created him before when he was nothing at all? ¹⁹·⁶⁸O Prophet Muhammad, I swear by your Lord: We will certainly gather them together, and the evil ones too. Then We will definitely bring them around Hell, on their knees. ¹⁹·⁶⁹Then, from every group, We will certainly snatch out all those who were most rebellious against Allah – the Most Compassionate, ¹⁹·⁷⁰even though We know best those who are most deserving of being burned in Hell. ¹⁹·⁷¹You will all have to pass over it. This is a promise upon your Lord and it will be fulfilled. ¹⁹·⁷²Then We will save those who were mindful of Me, and We will leave the wrongdoers there, on their knees.

¹⁹·⁷³When Our verses are recited to them, to make things clear, the disbelievers mockingly ask the Believers: "Which of the two groups among us has the better position and finer social gatherings?" ¹⁹·⁷⁴Anyway, how many generations have We destroyed before them who had far better luxury and better things to show! ¹⁹·⁷⁵O Prophet Muhammad, say: "If anyone is astray, Allah – the Most Compassionate certainly gives them lots of chances, until, when they will see what they're being warned of – either the punishment or the Final Hour – they will realise who is in the worst position with the weakest army!"

¹⁹·⁷⁶Allah gives more guidance to those who follow it: everlasting good actions are the best in the sight of your Lord, both as a reward and as an end result.

¹⁹·⁷⁷What do you think about the one who disbelieves in Our revelations yet says: "I will certainly be given lots of wealth and children in the next life too."? ¹⁹·⁷⁸Does he know the unseen secrets,

or has he taken a promise from Allah – the Most Compassionate? ¹⁹·⁷⁹No, no! We will continue to record what he says, and We will continue to make his punishment longer and longer. ¹⁹·⁸⁰The things he talks about, We will inherit them, and he will come to Us all alone with no wealth or children.

¹⁹·⁸¹They began worshipping other gods besides Allah so they might give them glory and power. ¹⁹·⁸²Never! Their gods will reject their worship and go against them. ¹⁹·⁸³Don't you see that We have sent the evil ones to the disbelievers, who are **always inciting them** to disobey Allah? ¹⁹·⁸⁴So don't be hasty about them because **We are counting down against them** for punishment.

¹⁹·⁸⁵The Day We will gather those who are mindful of Me as an honoured **group in front of** Allah – the Most Compassionate, ¹⁹·⁸⁶and We will drive the criminals, like thirsty cattle, to Hell, ¹⁹·⁸⁷they won't be able to intercede, unless it is someone who has taken a promise from Allah – the Most Compassionate.

¹⁹·⁸⁸They claim: "Allah – the Most Compassionate has a child." ¹⁹·⁸⁹What an outrageous thing you have said! ¹⁹·⁹⁰At this lie, the skies are ready to break apart! The earth is about to split open! The mountains could come crashing down! ¹⁹·⁹¹– because they have attributed a child to Allah – the Most Compassionate?! ¹⁹·⁹²It is not the status of **Allah to have a child!**

¹⁹·⁹³Everyone in the heavens and the earth will come as a mere servant to Allah – the Most Compassionate. ¹⁹·⁹⁴He has included them and counted them exactly. ¹⁹·⁹⁵All of them will come to Him all alone on Judgement Day.

19.96Allah – the Most Compassionate will create love for those who believe and do good.

19.97O Prophet Muhammad, **We have made the Qur'an easy in your own language, so that you can give good news with it to those who are mindful** of Allah, **and give warnings to those who are quarrelsome.**

19.98How many generations have We destroyed before them! Can you sense any one of them or hear even a faint sound from them?

Surah 20. Taa Haa

Allah's name I begin with, the Most Compassionate, the Ever-Merciful

20.1*Taa Haa.*
20.2**We revealed the Qur'an to you – not to put you in any difficulty,** 20.3**but as a reminder for anyone who fears Allah,** 20.4**– as a revelation from Him Who created the earth and the high heavens.**

20.5Allah – the Most Compassionate has firmly established His authority on the Throne. 20.6Everything in the heavens and the earth belongs only to Him, and so does everything in between them, and everything under the ground too. 20.7It is up to you **if you speak out loud because He knows the secrets and anything that is even more hidden.** 20.8He is **Allah. There is no god except Him. He has the most beautiful names.**

20.9O Prophet Muhammad, **has the story of Musa reached you?** 20.10When he saw a fire, he said to his family: "Stay here. I've seen a fire. Hopefully I can bring you a burning brand from it or find a way from there."

20.11When he came to the fire, it was called out: "O Musa! 20.12I am your Lord! So take off your shoes. You are in the holy valley of Tuwa. 20.13I have chosen you, so listen carefully to what is being revealed. 20.14I am most definitely Allah. There is no god except Me, so worship Me and establish the ritual prayers to remember Me. 20.15The Final Hour is coming – I want to keep it secret – so that every person can receive their reward or punishment for the efforts they make. 20.16So you mustn't let anyone distract you from it who himself doesn't believe in it but follows his own desires, or you will also be ruined."

20.17Allah asked: "What is that in your right hand, Musa?" 20.18He replied: "It is my staff. I lean on it, I beat down leaves with it for my flocks, and I have other uses for it too." 20.19Allah said: "Throw it down, Musa." 20.20Musa threw it down, and suddenly it was a slithering snake! 20.21Allah said: "Grab hold of it! Don't be afraid. We will immediately turn it to its original form. 20.22Now, press your hand under your arm and it will come out dazzling white – free from any illness – as another sign, 20.23so We can show you some of Our greater signs. 20.24Now go to Fir'awn because he has broken all limits of rebellion."

20.25Musa prayed: "My Lord! Make my heart wide open for me; 20.26make my mission easy for me; 20.27remove the difficulty in my tongue 20.28so the people can understand clearly what I say; 20.29give me a helper from my family 20.30– my brother Haroon; 20.31give me strength through him, 20.32and let him share my mission 20.33so we both can glorify You even more 20.34and remember You even more. 20.35You have always been Ever-Watchful of us." 20.36Allah responded: "All your wishes have been granted to you, Musa."

20.37Allah added: "We have already done favours to you before 20.38when We inspired your mother, what was inspired: 20.39"Place him in the box, and the box in the river. The river will push him up the bank, where someone – who is My enemy and his – will pick him up.' I blessed you, O Musa, with special adorability from Me so you would be brought up under My watchful eye. ^{20.40}Remember when your sister went to Fir'awn's family and said, 'Shall I show you someone who can look after this child?' Then We brought you back to your mother so that her eye might be cooled in happiness and not worry. Later on, you killed a man by mistake, but We saved you from distress, and tested you in many other ways. You lived among the people of Madyan for many years. Eventually, you came because of Our fixed plan, O Musa. ^{20.41}I have prepared you for Myself."

^{20.42}Allah continued: "Go, you and your brother, with My signs, and don't be lazy in remembering Me. ^{20.43}Go, both of you, to Fir'awn, because he has broken all limits of rebellion, ^{20.44}but speak to him gently; hopefully he will learn a lesson or show some fear." ^{20.45}They said: "Our Lord! We are afraid he will harm us, or break all limits of rebellion further." ^{20.46}He replied: "Don't be afraid. I am with both of you, listening and watching everything. ^{20.47}Now go, both of you, and say, 'We are both messengers from your Lord, so let the Descendants of Ya'qub go with us, and don't oppress them. We've brought you a sign from your Lord. Peace be upon whoever follows guidance. ^{20.48}It has been revealed to us that punishment will come to anyone who calls the truth a lie and turns away from it.'."

^{20.49}Fir'awn asked: "Who then is the Lord of you two, O Musa?" ^{20.50}He replied: "Our Lord is the one Who gave everything its created form, and then gave it guidance." ^{20.51}Fir'awn asked: "So what about the previous generations of disbelievers?" ^{20.52}He replied: "Knowledge about them is with my Lord, in a record. My Lord neither makes mistakes nor forgets."

²⁰·⁵³Allah is the one **Who has made the earth spread out for you, made through it pathways for you, and sends down water from the sky. With that water, We bring out pairs of various kinds of plants.** ²⁰·⁵⁴**You yourselves may eat** them **and graze your cattle too. There are certainly signs in this for wise people.** ²⁰·⁵⁵**We created you from the earth; We will send you back into it; We will bring you out from it once again.** ²⁰·⁵⁶**We certainly showed Fir'awn Our signs – all of them, but he called the truth a lie and refused to believe.**

²⁰·⁵⁷He said: "Have you come to us to expel us from our land using your magic, O Musa? ²⁰·⁵⁸We too can certainly bring you magic just like it! So, fix a time and place between us and you, which we won't break – neither we nor you – at an open ground." ²⁰·⁵⁹Musa replied: "Your fixed time and place should be on the Day of the Festival, and the people should be assembled at mid-morning."

²⁰·⁶⁰So Fir'awn went away, put his plan of tricks together, and arrived on the fixed day. ²⁰·⁶¹Musa said to the magicians: "You are all damned! Don't make lies about Allah or He will destroy you with some punishment. Anyone who makes lies will fail." ²⁰·⁶²Then the magicians started arguing the matter among themselves and kept their discussion secret. ²⁰·⁶³They said to each other: "These two are only magicians who want to expel you from your land using their magic, and they want to end your exemplary way of life. ²⁰·⁶⁴Therefore, you magicians must put your tricks together, and then come in a queue to the arena. Whoever wins today will certainly be successful."

²⁰·⁶⁵They asked: "Musa! Either you throw, or we will be the ones to throw first?" ²⁰·⁶⁶He replied: "Rather, you throw." Suddenly, their ropes and their staffs seemed to him, by their magic, to be moving around! ²⁰·⁶⁷Musa felt some fear inside himself. ²⁰·⁶⁸We said: "Don't be afraid! Only you will win. ²⁰·⁶⁹Throw down what is in your right hand

so it can swallow up what they have faked. They have faked only a magician's trick, and a magician can never be successful no matter where he goes."

20.70 So the magicians lost and were made to fall down into prostration. They declared: "We believe in the Lord of Haroon and Musa." 20.71 Fir'awn said: "How dare you believe in Him before I give you permission! He must be your leader who taught you magic! I will definitely cut off your hands and feet from opposite sides, and I will crucify you on the trunks of palm trees, and you will certainly find out which of us can give a punishment that is more severe and lasts longer!" 20.72 They responded: "We swear by the one Who made us, we will never prefer you over the clear signs that have appeared to us. Do whatever you want. You can only decide about this worldly life. 20.73 We have believed in our Lord so that He forgives us our mistakes and also the magic you forced us to do. Allah is Best and Everlasting."

20.74 Anyone who comes back to his Lord as a criminal will suffer Hell, where he will neither die nor live. 20.75 However, anyone who comes back to Him as a Believer who has done good, it is they who will have the high ranks, 20.76 including the Gardens of Eden – that have rivers flowing beneath them, where they will remain forever. This is the reward of someone who keeps himself clean and pure.

20.77 We revealed to Musa: "Set out with My servants at night, and make a dry route for them through the sea by hitting your staff. You won't be at risk of being caught nor should you worry." 20.78 Then Fir'awn chased after them with his armies, but, as they did, the waves of the river swept over them. 20.79 Fir'awn misled his people and didn't guide them correctly.

20.80 Descendants of Ya'qub! We saved you from your enemy, made you a promise on the right side of Mount Tur, and sent manna and quails down to you. 20.81 Allah said: "You may eat from the wholesome things We've given you, but don't be rebels in it or else My anger will come down on you. Anyone My anger comes down on will certainly be ruined! 20.82 However, I am definitely Ever-Forgiving to anyone who repents, believes, does good, and then follows guidance."

20.83 Allah asked: "What has made you come to Mount Tur before your people, O Musa?" 20.84 He replied: "They are here, coming right behind me. I came to You quickly, my Lord, so You might be well-pleased." 20.85 Allah said: "We have put your people to a test after you left, and the Saamiri has misled them."

20.86 So Musa went back to his people, angry and sad. He said: "My people! Didn't your Lord make you a good promise? Was the promise too long in coming to you? Did you want anger to come down on you from your Lord and so you broke your promise to me?" 20.87 They replied: "We didn't break the promise to you of our own choice. In fact, we were loaded with the burdens of jewellery from Fir'awn's dead army, and so we threw it into the fire, and the Saamiri did the same." 20.88 Then he made for them the image of a calf that made a mooing sound. His servants said: "This is your god, and Musa's too – though he has forgotten." 20.89 Didn't they see that it couldn't speak back to them, and that it could neither help nor harm them?

20.90 Haroon had already told them before: "My people! You are being tested with this. Your Lord is Allah – the Most Compassionate; so, follow me and obey my orders!" 20.91 They replied: "We won't stop worshipping it until Musa comes back to us."

20.92Musa asked: "Haroon! When you saw them going astray, what stopped you 20.93from following me? Did you disobey my orders?" 20.94Haroon replied: "My mother's son! Don't grab my beard nor the hair of my head! I feared you would say, 'You've made division among the Descendants of Ya'qub, and didn't care about what I said!'."

20.95Musa asked: "And what were you doing, Saamiri?!" 20.96He replied: "I noticed something they didn't. So, I took a handful of dust from the hoof-print of the horse of the Messenger-Angel Jibra'il and threw it on the statue of the calf. This is what my own self tempted me to do." 20.97Musa ordered: "Go away! In this life your punishment is that you will keep saying, 'Don't touch me,' as well as another promised punishment that won't be missed out on. Now look at your false god to which you had become devoted. We will certainly burn it up and then scatter it into the river like dust! 20.98Your real god is only Allah – there is no god except Him. He surrounds everything in His knowledge."

20.99O Prophet Muhammad, in this way We tell you some of the stories of what happened before. We have given you a special Reminder (-Qur'an) from Us. 20.100Those who neglect it will carry a heavy burden of sins on Judgement Day. 20.101They will remain in that state forever. What a terrible burden they will have to carry on Judgement Day!

20.102One Day the Trumpet will be blown, and We will assemble the criminals together on that Day and they will be pale out of fear, 20.103quietly whispering to each other: "You hardly stayed for ten days in the world." 20.104We know best what they will be saying, when the wisest among them will say: "You hardly stayed for a single day!"

20.105 O Prophet Muhammad, they ask you about the mountains. So reply: "My Lord will blow them away like dust, 20.106 leaving them as a flat plain 20.107 – in which you will see neither bends nor bumps."

20.108 That Day they will follow the caller without moving away from him. All voices will be silent in front of Allah – the Most Compassionate and you won't be able to hear anything other than a very faint sound. 20.109 Intercessions will be useless on that Day, except by someone Allah – the Most Compassionate has given permission and agreed for him to speak. 20.110 Allah knows everything that happened before them and what will happen after them, but they cannot understand Him with any amount of knowledge. 20.111 All faces will be humbled to Allah – the Ever-Living, the Everlasting. Anyone who carries the burden of wrongdoing will fail. 20.112 Anyone who does good, being a Believer, won't need to fear any injustice or being deprived of reward.

20.113 In this way We've sent it down as a Qur'an in Arabic, and gave a variety of warnings in it, so that hopefully they will become mindful of Allah, or that it might give them a reminder. 20.114 Allah is most high! The real King! O Prophet Muhammad, you shouldn't hurry when reciting the Qur'an before its revelation to you is complete, but pray: "My Lord! Increase me even more in knowledge."

20.115 We had already ordered Adam long ago, but he forgot. We didn't find him to have had any intention to disobey. 20.116 When We ordered the angels: "Prostrate in front of Adam," and so they did prostrate – but not Iblees. He refused. 20.117 Then We said: "Adam, this is your enemy and your wife's too. Don't let him get you expelled from Paradise or you will experience difficulty. 20.118 You are guaranteed that you won't be hungry in Paradise nor unclothed, 20.119 nor feel thirsty, and nor suffer from the sun's heat." 20.120 However, Shaytan whispered to him an idea. He said: "Adam! Shall I show you the Tree of Immortality and a kingdom that never ends?" ²⁰·¹²¹As a result, both of them (- Adam and his wife) ate from the tree, so their private parts became visible to them, and they began to stitch together some leaves of Paradise over their bodies. Adam slipped in understanding the command of his Lord, and so he couldn't reach his aim of immortality. ²⁰·¹²²But still his Lord selected him, forgave him, and guided him.

²⁰·¹²³He ordered: "Go down from here, both of you, altogether, as enemies of each other. Whenever any guidance comes to you from Me, anyone who follows My guidance won't go astray and nor be unblessed. ²⁰·¹²⁴However, if anyone neglects to remember Me, he will have a difficult life, and We will raise him up blind on Judgement Day." ²⁰·¹²⁵He will ask: "My Lord! Why have you raised me up blind whereas I could see?" ²⁰·¹²⁶Allah will reply: "This is how it is. Our signs came to you but you ignored them, in the same way you will be ignored Today." ²⁰·¹²⁷This is how We punish anyone who goes to extremes and doesn't believe in his Lord's revelations. The punishment of the Hereafter is most severe and lasts forever.

²⁰·¹²⁸Isn't it clear to them how many generations We have destroyed before them in whose homes they now walk about? There are certainly signs in this for wise people. ²⁰·¹²⁹If it wasn't for something already fixed by your Lord, as well as an end date, the expected punishment would have come right now.

²⁰·¹³⁰So, O Prophet Muhammad, you should continue to have patience with what they say, and continue to glorify the praises of your Lord before sunrise and sunset, during the night, and at all the extremes of the day, so that you will be well-pleased. ²⁰·¹³¹Don't let your eyes desire what We've let some of their groups enjoy as the luxury of this

life. This is for Us to test them with it. However, what your Lord gives is best and lasts forever. ²⁰·¹³²Tell your family to pray and you too should remain steadfast in it. We don't ask you for any wealth because it is We Who give you. The best end will be for being mindful of Allah.

²⁰·¹³³They ask: "Why doesn't he bring us a sign from his Lord?" What? Hasn't a clear proof already come to them mentioned in the previous Books of Revelation? ²⁰·¹³⁴If We had destroyed them with a punishment before this, they would have said: "Our Lord! Why didn't You send us a messenger so we could have followed Your revelations before we were humbled and humiliated?" ²⁰·¹³⁵Reply: "Everyone is waiting to see what happens, so you must wait too. You will soon come to know who are the companions of the Smooth Path and who follow guidance."

Surah 21. Prophets (al-Anbiyaa')

[PART 17]

Allah's name I begin with, the Most Compassionate, the Ever-Merciful

²¹·¹The time for judgement of actions for people has come closer to them, yet they're turning away in neglect. ²¹·²Whenever some fresh advice comes to them from their Lord, they pretend they are listening to it while they play games; ²¹·³while their hearts are in amusement. The wrongdoers keep their private discussions secret saying: "Is he anything other than human, just like you? Will you follow magic when you can clearly see?"

²¹·⁴The Messenger Muhammad replied: "My Lord knows everything that is said in the sky and on earth. He is the All-Hearing, the All-Knowing." ²¹·⁵But they go on to say: "The Qur'an is a confused mixture

of dreams. In fact, he made it up. But no! He is just a poet. He should bring us a sign like the previous prophets were sent with." ²¹·⁶The towns We destroyed before them, none of them believed. Now, will these people believe?

²¹·⁷O Prophet Muhammad, We sent before you as messengers only men We gave revelations to. So, if you people yourselves don't know then ask the people of knowledge. ²¹·⁸We neither made them mere bodies that wouldn't eat food nor were they immortals. ²¹·⁹Eventually, We fulfilled Our promise to them and saved them, as well as others We chose, but We destroyed those who went to extremes.

²¹·¹⁰We've sent down to you people a book that has advice for you. Won't you even think? ²¹·¹¹How many towns have We destroyed that were unjust, and We raised up other communities after them! ²¹·¹²Yet, when they sensed Our punishment coming, they immediately started running away from there. ²¹·¹³"Don't run away," they were told, "come back to where you were addicted to luxuries, and to your homes, so you can be asked questions." ²¹·¹⁴They replied: "We are damned! We have been wrongdoers!" ²¹·¹⁵They continued screaming like this until We had turned them into dry stubble like mown down harvest and silent ashes.

²¹·¹⁶We didn't create the heaven and the earth and everything in between them so We could play games. ²¹·¹⁷If We had wanted to have any kind of amusement, We would have done it on Our own, if We were at all to do so. ²¹·¹⁸But no! We launch the truth against falsehood; the truth crushes it; falsehood immediately vanishes! You people are damned for what you falsely describe.

²¹·¹⁹Everyone in the heavens and the earth belongs only to Him. Those angels who are close to Him don't turn arrogantly away from

worshipping Him nor do they get tired. ²¹·²⁰They glorify Him night and day without ever pausing.

²¹·²¹Have the disbelievers made gods from the earth that can bring the dead back to life? ²¹·²²If there were besides Allah any gods in the heavens and the earth, both the heavens and the earth would have been destroyed. However, glory be to Allah – Lord of the Throne – above what they describe.

²¹·²³He cannot be questioned for what He does but they will be questioned. ²¹·²⁴Have they made other gods besides Him? O Prophet Muhammad, say: "Bring me your proof. This Qur'an is the reminder for those who are with me and for those who were before me," but most of them don't know the truth, which is why they turn away. ²¹·²⁵O Prophet Muhammad, We haven't sent any messenger before you without giving him the same revelation that, 'there is no got except Me, so worship Me.'

²¹·²⁶They also say: "Allah – the Most Compassionate has a child." Glory be to Him! Never! They are only honoured servants. ²¹·²⁷They never speak before He does and they always do what He orders. ²¹·²⁸He knows everything that happened before them and what will happen after them, they only intercede for someone He approves, and they remain anxious out of fear of Him. ²¹·²⁹If any of them says: "I am a god besides Allah," We will punish them with Hell. This is how We punish wrongdoers.

²¹·³⁰Don't the disbelievers realise that the heavens and the earth were once joined together as a unit before We split them apart? We made every living thing from water. Won't they still believe? ²¹·³¹We have placed firm mountains in the earth, in case it shakes under them, and placed wide paths as routes in it so they can find their way. ²¹·³²We

have made the sky a protected roof, but they still turn away from its signs! ²¹·³³He is the one Who created night and day, and the sun and the moon. Everything is floating in an orbit.

²¹·³⁴O Prophet Muhammad, **We did not give immortality to any human being before you. So, if you will pass away, will they live forever?** ²¹·³⁵**Everyone is going to taste death. We are testing you all with bad and good things as challenges, and then it is Us you will be brought back to.**

²¹·³⁶O Prophet Muhammad, **the disbelievers make fun of you when they see you** by saying: "Is this the one who talks against your gods?" while it is they who reject the mention of Allah – the Most Compassionate. ²¹·³⁷The human is created from haste. I will soon show you My signs, so don't ask Me to do things any quicker. ²¹·³⁸They ask: "When will this warning be fulfilled, if you are telling the truth?" ²¹·³⁹If only the disbelievers knew of the time when they won't be able to keep the Fire off their faces and their backs, and nor will they be helped! ²¹·⁴⁰In fact, it will come upon them all of a sudden and confuse them. They cannot stop it, and they won't be given any chances. ²¹·⁴¹O Prophet Muhammad, many **messengers before you were also mocked, but the punishment the mockers used to make fun of ended up punishing them.**

²¹·⁴²**Ask: "Who can keep you safe night and day from** the punishment of Allah – the Most Compassionate?" Yet they still continue to turn away from remembering their Lord. ²¹·⁴³**Do they have gods besides Us who can protect them** from the punishment? They don't have any power to even help themselves nor will they have any support from Us. ²¹·⁴⁴The truth is, We let these people and their forefathers enjoy themselves throughout their lives. Now, don't they see how We come to the land reducing it from its borders? Is it they who will win?

21.45O Prophet Muhammad, **say:** "I am giving you warnings only through revelation," but the deaf won't hear the call even when they are warned. 21.46Even if a whiff of your Lord's punishment came past them, they would definitely cry: "We are damned! We have been wrongdoers!"

21.47We will set up the scales of justice for Judgement Day so that no one will be treated unfairly in any way at all; and if there is anything someone did as little as the weight of a mustard seed, We will bring it out. We are enough to judge.

21.48**We gave** the Tawrah **to Musa and Haroon** as **a criterion** between right and wrong, **a light, and a reminder for those who are mindful** of Allah, 21.49**who fear their Lord without seeing Him, while they're also terrified of the Final Hour.** 21.50**This Qur'an is a blessed reminder We've sent down. Are you the ones who reject it?**

21.51**We gave Ibrahim his true guidance long ago as We knew him very well.** 21.52Remember **when he asked his foster father and his people:** "What are these images you are devoted to?" 21.53They replied: "We saw our fathers worshipping them." 21.54He responded: "You and your forefathers have been clearly astray." 21.55They asked: "Have you brought us the truth or are you having a joke?" 21.56He replied: "The truth is, your Lord is the lord of the heavens and the earth – Who made them, and I am one of those who testify to it." 21.57He said to himself: "By Allah, I will certainly make a plan for your idols after you've turned your backs and gone away." 21.58Then he smashed them into pieces, except their big one, so they could go to it for answers.

21.59Some of them asked: "Who did this to our gods? He must be a wrongdoer!" 21.60Others replied: "We heard a young man talking against them. He is called Ibrahim." ²¹·⁶¹They demanded: "Then bring him so people can see him, so people can be witnesses."

²¹·⁶²They asked him: "Ibrahim! Is it you who did this to our gods?" ²¹·⁶³He replied: "Actually, their big one did it. Ask *them* if they can speak." ²¹·⁶⁴So they turned to themselves and admitted: "You yourselves are the wrongdoers." ²¹·⁶⁵Then they went back to their previous mindset and said: "You very well know they cannot speak!" ²¹·⁶⁶Ibrahim asked: "So, do you worship, besides Allah, what can neither help nor harm you in any way at all? ²¹·⁶⁷Shame you and on anything you worship besides Allah! Don't you even think?" ²¹·⁶⁸They agreed: "Burn him and take revenge for your gods, if you are going to do anything!"

²¹·⁶⁹We ordered: "O fire! Be cool and calming for Ibrahim!" ²¹·⁷⁰They tried to make a dangerous plan against Ibrahim, but We made them fail badly.

²¹·⁷¹We saved him and his nephew Lut, and directed them to the land where We have placed blessings for everyone. ²¹·⁷²We gave him Is'haq and, as a grandson, Ya'qub, and We made each one of them righteous. ²¹·⁷³We made them leaders who guided by Our command, and We sent them revelations to do good, establish the ritual prayers, and pay zakah; and they always worshipped Us.

²¹·⁷⁴We gave wisdom and knowledge to Lut as well, and We saved him from the town which used to do disgusting things. They were a terrible, immoral people. ²¹·⁷⁵We took him into Our special mercy. He was one of the righteous.

²¹·⁷⁶Remember Nuh, when he called out to Us before that. So, We responded to him and saved him and his family from the great

disaster. ²¹·⁷⁷We helped him against the people who called Our revelations a lie. They were a terrible people, so We drowned them, all together.

²¹·⁷⁸Remember **Dawud and Sulayman, when** they were giving judgement about the crops into which the sheep of a certain tribe had strayed at night. We were witnessing their judgement. ²¹·⁷⁹We gave Sulayman an understanding of that case, but We gave wisdom and knowledge to them both. We made the mountains obey Dawud in glorifying Allah with him, and the birds too. We can always do this. ²¹·⁸⁰We taught him how to make body armour for you to protect you in your battles. Will you be thankful? ²¹·⁸¹We made **the fierce wind obedient for Sulayman to blow** calmly **at his command to the land where We had placed blessings. We always know everything very well.** ²¹·⁸²We made **some jinns** obey him, **that used to dive** in the sea for him and did other things too. We always kept watch over them.

²¹·⁸³Remember **Ayyub, when** He called out to his Lord: "I am suffering hardship, but You are the Most Merciful of all." ²¹·⁸⁴So We responded to him and removed everything he was suffering. We gave him back his family and more just like and as many as **them – as a special mercy from Us, and as a reminder for all** sincere **worshippers.**

²¹·⁸⁵Remember **Isma'il, Idris, and Dhu'l-Kifl (Ezekiel).** They were all from among those who had patience. ²¹·⁸⁶We took them into Our special **Mercy.** They were from among the righteous.

²¹·⁸⁷Remember **Dhu'n-Nun (Prophet Yunus), when, in anger, he left** his **community, and thought We wouldn't restrict him, but then he called out in the depths of darkness: "There is no god except You. Glory be to You! I was one of those who did wrong."** ²¹·⁸⁸So We responded to him and saved him from sadness. This is how We save the Believers.

²¹·⁸⁹Remember **Zakariyya, when he called out to his Lord: "My Lord! Don't leave me without a child even though You are the Best Inheritor of all."** ²¹·⁹⁰So We responded to him and gave him Yahya, and made his wife healthy for him. They would always rush to do good things. They used to pray to Us with hope and fear, and were humble in front of Us.

²¹·⁹¹Remember **Maryam, the lady who guarded her chastity. We breathed into her from Our spirit and made her and her son** Isa **a sign for everyone.**

²¹·⁹²This is your community – a single community, and I am your Lord, so worship Me. ²¹·⁹³However, these people have **broken their religion into pieces among themselves.** They should know that **they will all come back to Us.** ²¹·⁹⁴Anyone who is a Believer and does something good, his effort won't be rejected. We are recording it for him.

²¹·⁹⁵However, it's impossible for any town to come back after We have destroyed it ²¹·⁹⁶until the Ya'juj and Ma'juj are let loose, rushing down from every high place, ²¹·⁹⁷and the true promise of Judgement Day will come very close. That is when the eyes of the disbelievers will stare in horror and they will cry: "We are damned! We hadn't been paying attention to this. In fact, we have been wrongdoers!" ²¹·⁹⁸You disbelievers, **as well as any** idols you worship besides Allah, will all be fuel for Hell – you will all fall into it. ²¹·⁹⁹If these had really been gods, they wouldn't have fallen into it. All will remain there forever. ²¹·¹⁰⁰They will suffer screaming there and won't be able to hear anything else **in it.**

²¹·¹⁰¹Those already promised the most beautiful reward by Us, it is they who will be kept far away from Hell. ²¹·¹⁰²They won't hear even

its slightest hissing sound. They will remain forever among the things their hearts desired. ²¹·¹⁰³Even the greatest horror of Judgement Day won't worry them and the angels will welcome them saying: "This is your Day which you had been promised." ²¹·¹⁰⁴On that Day, We will roll up the sky like papers are rolled up for completed records. We will bring back creation just like We created it the first time. It is a promise binding on Us. We will certainly do this. ²¹·¹⁰⁵We have already written in the Zabur, after the reminder, that: "Only My righteous servants will inherit the earth."

²¹·¹⁰⁶In this Qur'an is a guarantee for any people who are Allah's devoted worshippers. ²¹·¹⁰⁷O Prophet Muhammad, We have sent you as a mercy for all the worlds. ²¹·¹⁰⁸Say: "It is revealed to me that your God is One God. Now, will you surrender to Him as Muslims?" ²¹·¹⁰⁹If they turn away, say: "I have made you all equally aware, but I won't guess if what you are warned about is near or far. ²¹·¹¹⁰He knows everything that is said openly and also what you hide. ²¹·¹¹¹I won't guess but this delay in being punished could be a test for you and some enjoyment for a while."

²¹·¹¹²He prayed: "My Lord! Give judgement with the truth. Our Lord is the Most Compassionate, Whose help is asked for against what you disbelievers falsely describe."

Surah 22. Pilgrimage (al-Hajj)

Allah's name I begin with, the Most Compassionate, the Ever-Merciful

²²·¹People! Be mindful of your Lord. The earthquake of the Final Hour will be a terrible thing. ²²·²The Day you will see it, every nursing woman will forget about the baby she was suckling, and every pregnant female will have a miscarriage. You will think the people

are in a drunken state though they won't be, but it is because **Allah's punishment will be so severe.**

22.3Some people, without having any knowledge, dispute about Allah and follow every rebellious devil. 22.4It is written about the Devil that he will mislead anyone who makes him his friend, and will take him to the punishment of the Blazing Fire.

22.5**People! If you are in doubt about the resurrection then** you should know that **We created you:** originally **from dust, then from a drop of semen, then from a clinging clot, then from a lump of chewed flesh (i.e. embryo), partly formed and partly unformed – so We could make things clear to you. Those We choose, We allow them to settle in the wombs for a fixed term. We eventually bring you out as babies, then** look after you **so you can reach your full strength. Some of you are those whose souls are taken away** young, **while others are left to reach the most weak old age so that, after having lots of knowledge, they know nothing at all. You see the earth is lifeless, but when We pour down water on it, it stirs to life, swells, and grows all kinds of beautiful plants in pairs.** 22.6**This** happens only **because only Allah is the truth; only He can bring the dead back to life; only He is Most Capable of anything.** 22.7**The Final Hour is coming, in which there is no doubt. Allah will bring back to life all those who are** buried in graves.

22.8**Some people dispute about Allah when they don't have any knowledge, guidance** or proof, **or a Book that enlightens,** 22.9**turning away** arrogantly **to mislead** people **away from Allah's cause. They will suffer disgrace in this world and We will make them taste the punishment of the Scorching Fire on Judgement Day.** 22.10They will be told: "This is only for the bad things you have done, because Allah doesn't treat His **servants unfairly."**

22.11Someone might worship Allah on the borderline of faith: he is satisfied if some good reaches him, but turns back if he has to face a test. He loses both this world and the next, and this is clearly the heaviest loss. 22.12Instead of Allah, they pray to something that can neither harm nor help him. That is the farthest anyone can stray. 22.13They pray to something whose harm is greater than their help. What an evil helper! What an evil companion!

22.14Those who believe and do good, Allah will enter them into gardens – that have rivers flowing beneath them. Allah does whatever He wants. 22.15Anyone who thinks Allah won't support His Prophet, in this world or the next, should stretch out a rope to the ceiling and hang himself. Then he should see if his plan will remove what angers him!

22.16In the same way We've sent the Qur'an down as clear proofs. Allah guides anyone He chooses. 22.17Those who believe as Muslims, as well as those who are Jews, Sabians, Christians, Magians, or those who made partner-gods with Allah, He will judge between them on Judgement Day. He is a Witness to everything.

22.18Don't you see that everyone in the heavens and the earth prostrates to Allah, including the sun, moon, stars, mountains, trees, animals, and many people? There are also many that deserve punishment. No one can give honour to anyone Allah disgraces. Allah does whatever He wants. *<Prostration Point 6>*

22.19These are two opposing groups who disputed with each other about their Lord. Those who disbelieved will have clothes of fire cut out and prepared for them. Boiling liquid will be poured over their heads 22.20with which everything will dissolve inside their bellies, and the outer skins too. 22.21They will be punished with iron hammers. 22.22Each time, due to agony, they try to get out of there, they will be forced back into it, and told: "Taste the punishment of the Scorching Fire!"

22.23Those who believe and do good, Allah will enter them into gardens – that have rivers flowing beneath them, where they will be adorned with gold bracelets and with pearls, and where their clothes will be of silk. 22.24They've been guided to the purest of speech and to the path of Allah – the Most Praiseworthy.

22.25Those who disbelieve and block people from Allah's cause, and from this Sacred Masjid in Makkah which We have made for all people – equally for its locals and the visitors, and those who try to abuse it with wrongdoing, We will make them taste a painful punishment.

22.26Remember when We guided Ibrahim to the site of the House – the Ka'bah in Makkah, saying: "Don't make anything a partner-god with Me; and keep My House clean and pure for those who go around it, and for those who stand, bow, and prostrate there in prayer; 22.27call the people to the pilgrimage and they will come to you on foot and mounted on every lean camel – coming from every faraway route, 22.28so they can witness the benefits they will gain, and so they can mention Allah's name during the specified days over the livestock animals He has given them to sacrifice. Then you can eat from them and feed those who are poor, needy. 22.29In the end, they should remove their dirt, fulfil their promises by completing their rites, and go around the Ancient House (- Ka'bah)."

22.30This is the command. Anyone who honours Allah's sacred commands, it will be better for him in the sight of his Lord. Livestock have been made lawful for you, except those already mentioned to you as unlawful. So stay clear of the filth of idols, and stay clear of lies too, ²²·³¹being true to Allah – never making partner-gods with Him. Anyone who makes partner-gods with Allah is like he is falling from the sky and birds snatch him up, or the wind hurls him into a place far away. ²²·³²This is the command. Anyone who honours Allah's sacred symbols, should know that it really comes from the mindfulness of the heart. ²²·³³There are benefits for you for a fixed term in the sacrificial animals, but then eventually their place of sacrifice will be near the Ancient House.

²²·³⁴We ordered a rite of sacrifice to every nation so they could mention Allah's name when slaughtering over the livestock animals He has given them. Your God is One God, so surrender to Him as Muslims. Give good news to those who are humble, ²²·³⁵whose hearts tremble with awe when Allah is mentioned, who have patience over everything they suffer, who establish the ritual prayers, and who donate from what We've given them.

²²·³⁶We made the sacrificial camels for you to be among the sacred symbols of Allah in which there is much goodness for you. So, you must mention Allah's name over them when they are standing for sacrifice with their front left legs tied up. Then, after slaughter, when they fall down on their sides, you may eat from them and feed both those who don't ask and those who do. In this way We've made them obedient to you so that hopefully you will be thankful. ²²·³⁷Their meat and blood aren't meant to reach Allah, but your mindfulness is. This is why He has made them obedient to you, for you to proclaim His greatness for the guidance He has given you. O Prophet Muhammad, give good news to those who do good.

²²·³⁸Allah will defend the Believers. He doesn't like any unthankful traitor. ²²·³⁹Permission to fight is given to those who are fought against in war because they have been oppressed. Allah is surely Most

Capable of helping them; ^{22.40}those oppressed people who have been expelled from their homes without having done anything wrong – only for saying: "Our Lord is Allah." If Allah didn't defend some people by others then monasteries, churches, synagogues, and masjids – where Allah's name is mentioned a lot, would certainly have been destroyed. Allah will definitely help those who work for Him. Allah is certainly Strong, Almighty. ^{22.41}They are those who, if We gave them control in the land, they would establish the ritual prayers and pay zakah, command what is right and forbid what is wrong. The end result of all matters is with Allah.

^{22.42}O Prophet Muhammad, if they accuse you of being a liar, so did those before them, such as: the people of Nuh, the 'Ad, and the Thamud, ^{22.43}and the people of Ibrahim and of Lut, ^{22.44}and the citizens of Madyan. Musa was also accused of being a liar. However, I gave the disbelievers more time to repent, but eventually punished them in the end. How terrifying was My punishment!

^{22.45}There are many towns We have destroyed because they were unjust, and so they're now in ruin. How many abandoned wells! How many tall palaces! ^{22.46}Don't they travel through the earth so they could think with their minds and listen with their ears? It isn't the eyes but the hearts inside the chests that go blind. ^{22.47}They want you to bring the punishment sooner, but Allah will never break His promise. A day in the sight of your Lord is like a thousand years according to your counting. ^{22.48}There are many towns I gave more time to repent even though they were unjust, but in the end I punished them. The final return will be to Me.

^{22.49}O Prophet Muhammad, say: "People! I give you clear warnings." ^{22.50}Those who believe and do good, they will have forgiveness and

some honourable wealth. ²²·⁵¹However, those who try their best to defeat Our revelations, it is they who will be the people of Hell-Fire.

²²·⁵²O Prophet Muhammad, before you, whenever We sent a messenger or a prophet, whenever he would recite anything to the people, Shaytan would throw confusions into his reciting. However, Allah would remove any confusions Shaytan threw in. Eventually, Allah would firmly establish His revelations. Allah is All-Knowing, All-Wise. ²²·⁵³All this is so He can make the confusions Shaytan throws in a test for those with sickness in their hearts and for those whose hearts have become hard. The wrongdoers are certainly in extreme hostility. ²²·⁵⁴All this is also so that those given knowledge may realise that this is the truth from your Lord, so they will believe in it and their hearts will become humble to Him. Allah guides the Believers to a path that is straight.

²²·⁵⁵The disbelievers won't stop having doubts in the Qur'an until the Final Hour will come upon them all of a sudden, or the punishment of a Desolating Day. ²²·⁵⁶Sovereignty, on that Day, will be Allah's. He will judge between them. As for those who believe and do good, they will be in Gardens of Delight. ²²·⁵⁷However, those who disbelieve and call Our revelations a lie, it is they who will suffer a humiliating punishment. ²²·⁵⁸Those who migrated in Allah's cause, and were later killed or they died, Allah will certainly give them plenty of wealth. Allah is the Best Giver of all. ²²·⁵⁹He will definitely enter them through an entrance they will be well-pleased with. Allah is certainly All-Knowing, Most Tolerant. ²²·⁶⁰This is the command. If anyone retaliates legally according to what he suffered but then he is harmed again, Allah will certainly help him. Allah is certainly Most Pardoning, Most Forgiving.

22.61That is because Allah makes the night enter into the day and the day enter into the night, and He is All-Hearing, Ever-Watchful. 22.62That is because only Allah is the truth, and anything they pray to besides Him is false. Only Allah is the Most High, the Great.

22.63Don't you see that it is Allah Who sends down water from the sky, and the earth becomes fresh and green? Allah knows all details, is Fully-Aware. 22.64Everything in the heavens and the earth belongs only to Him. Only Allah is Free of all Needs, the Most Praiseworthy. 22.65Don't you see that, by His command, Allah has made everything in the earth obedient to you, as well as the ships that sail through the sea? He holds the sky back from falling on the earth without His permission. Allah is certainly Kind, Ever-Merciful to people. 22.66He is the one Who gave you life, will give you death, and will finally give you life again. Humans are certainly unthankful.

22.67For every nation, We made a way of worship they had to follow. They mustn't argue with you about this command. So, O Prophet Muhammad, **keep inviting** people **to your Lord**, because **you are certainly following a** path **of guidance that is straight.** 22.68If they argue with you, say: "Allah knows best everything you do." 22.69Allah will judge between you on Judgement Day about the disagreements you used to have. 22.70Don't you realise that Allah knows everything there is in the sky and earth? All this is written in a record. All that is easy for Allah.

22.71Yet they worship, besides Allah, those things for which He hasn't sent down any permission, and also things they don't know anything about. The wrongdoers won't have any helper. 22.72You can notice the anger in the disbelievers' faces when Our clear verses are recited to them. It is as if they're about to attack those who are reciting Our revelations to them. O Prophet Muhammad, say: "Shall I tell you what is worse than this? The Fire! Allah has warned the disbelievers about it. What a horrible final destination!"

22.73People! An example is given, so listen to it carefully. Those idols you pray to besides Allah, they cannot create a single fly even if they all united for that purpose. And if a fly snatched anything from them, they wouldn't be able to take it back from it. How helpless are those who ask and those that are asked! 22.74They haven't appreciated Allah's true value. Allah is certainly Strong, Almighty.

22.75It is Allah Who chooses messengers from both angels and humans. Allah is All-Hearing, Ever-Watchful. 22.76He knows everything that is in front of them and behind them, and all around them, and all matters are returned to Him.

22.77Believers! You must bow and prostrate, and worship your Lord; and keep doing good so you can succeed. *<Prostration Point according to Imam ash-Shafi'i>* 22.78You must strive hard for Allah as He deserves. He has chosen you and placed on you no difficulty in faith; it is the religion of your ancestor Ibrahim. Allah has named you 'Muslims (i.e. those who peacefully surrender to Allah's commands, work for peace, and promote peace everywhere)', both previously and in this Qur'an too, so that the Messenger can be a witness for you and you can be witnesses for all people. You must establish the ritual prayers, pay zakah, and hold on strongly to belief in Allah. He is your Protector. What an excellent Protector! What an excellent Helper!

Surah 23. Believers (al-Mu'minoon)

[PART 18]

Allah's name I begin with, the Most Compassionate, the Ever-Merciful

$^{23.1}$The Believers will succeed, $^{23.2}$who are humble in their ritual prayers, $^{23.3}$who avoid all foolishness, $^{23.4}$who pay zakah, $^{23.5}$and who guard their chastity $^{23:6}$– except with their wives, or their slavewomen – in which case they cannot be criticised. $^{23.7}$However, those trying go beyond this will be overstepping the limits. $^{23.8}$Successful will be those who honour their trusts and their promises, $^{23.9}$and those who look after their prayers. $^{23.10}$It is they who will be the inheritors, $^{23.11}$who will inherit the Highest Gardens of Paradise, where they will remain forever.

$^{23.12}$We created humans originally from an extract of clay. $^{23.13}$Later, We placed him as a drop of semen in a safe place. $^{23.14}$Later still, We made that drop into a clinging clot; then of that clot We made a lump of chewed flesh (i.e. embryo); then we made the lump into bones, which We covered in flesh; then, out of that, We brought another kind of creation. So, blessed is Allah, the Best of creators. $^{23.15}$Eventually, after that, you will all certainly die. $^{23.16}$Finally, on Judgement Day, you will all be brought back to life.

$^{23.17}$We have certainly created seven paths above you, and We are never unaware of Our creation. $^{23.18}$We send down from the sky water in perfect amount, and We make it settle in the earth. We certainly have the power to take it away too. $^{23.19}$With it, We grow gardens of date-palms for you, and grapevines too – in which there are many fruits for you – from which you can eat. $^{23.20}$We also grow a tree, coming out of Mount Tur of Sinai, which gives oil and a seasoning for those who eat. $^{23.21}$There is a definite lesson of warning for you in livestock. We give you a drink from within their bodies, and there are many other benefits in them for you too. You can also eat from them. ²³·²²You can be carried on them, and on ships too.

²³·²³We sent Nuh to his people. He said: "My people! You must worship Allah. You don't have any god besides Him. So, won't you be mindful of Him?" ²³·²⁴The disbelieving leaders among his community said: "This man is only human, just like you. He wants to establish his superiority over you. If Allah had wanted, He could have sent down angels as messengers. We never heard a message like this among our ancestors. ²³·²⁵He is just a man gone mad. So, bear with him for a while and you will see what happens."

²³·²⁶Nuh prayed: "My Lord! Help me, because they've accused me of being a liar." ²³·²⁷So We revealed to him: "Build the Ark under Our watchful eyes and with Our guidance. Then, when Our command comes, and the oven overflows with water, take a pair – male and female – from each species, as well as your family – apart from those of them against whom the decision has already been made that they will stay behind. Don't pray to Me for the wrongdoers because they will be drowned." ²³·²⁸When you and those with you are settled in the Ark, say: "All praise is for Allah Who saved us from these unjust people," ²³·²⁹and pray: "My Lord! Land me at a blessed destination because You are the Best Giver of destinations." ²³·³⁰There are definitely signs in this story, and We are certainly always testing people.

²³·³¹Later, We raised up another generation after them. ²³·³²We sent them a messenger from among themselves, saying: "You must worship Allah. You don't have any god besides Him. So, won't you be mindful of Him?" ²³·³³The leaders among his community – who disbelieved and called the meeting in the Hereafter a lie, and those

We allowed to enjoy luxuries in this life – said: "This man is only human, just like you; he eats what you eat and drinks what you drink; ²³·³⁴if you obey a human who is just like you then you will certainly be losers.

²³·³⁵Is he warning you that when you die and become dust and bones, you will be brought out again alive? ²³·³⁶Nonsense! What you are being warned of is nonsense! ²³·³⁷There's nothing beyond our life in this world. We die, we live, and we won't be brought back to life. ²³·³⁸He is only a man who has made lies about Allah. However, we won't believe merely because he says so."

²³·³⁹The messenger prayed: "My Lord! Help me, because they're accusing me of being a liar." ²³·⁴⁰Allah said: "In a little while, they will certainly be regretful." ²³·⁴¹Then the Mighty Blast seized them with justice, and We turned them into filthy scum! Gone are those unjust people!

²³·⁴²Then We raised up other generations after them. ²³·⁴³No nation can go before or after its end date. ²³·⁴⁴Then We sent our messengers one after another. Each time its messenger came to a community, they accused him of being a liar. So, We destroyed them one after another, and turned them into stories of the past. Gone are those disbelieving people!

²³·⁴⁵Then We sent Musa and his brother Haroon with Our signs and a clear authority ²³·⁴⁶to Fir'awn and his ministers, but they showed arrogance. They were a cruel people. ²³·⁴⁷They said: "Should we believe merely because two humans just like us say so when their people are our slaves?" ²³·⁴⁸They accused them both of being liars, and so they ended up among those who were destroyed. ²³·⁴⁹We gave Musa the Book, so that hopefully they will follow guidance.

²³·⁵⁰**We made Isa - the Son of Maryam and his mother to be a sign**, and gave them both refuge on high ground – a place that was liveable with a flowing spring.

²³·⁵¹My honourable **Messengers! You may eat from the wholesome things and do what is good. I know perfectly well everything you do.** ²³·⁵²**This is your one and only community, and I am your Lord, so be mindful of Me.** ²³·⁵³However, in their religion, the people split up into many groups among themselves, each group happy with what little religion it had. ²³·⁵⁴So, O Prophet Muhammad, **leave them in their ignorance for a while.** ²³·⁵⁵What? Do they think that because We give them wealth and children, ²³·⁵⁶We are bringing good things to them sooner? No! They aren't even **aware** of what's coming!

²³·⁵⁷**Those: who remain anxious out of fear of their Lord,** ²³·⁵⁸who believe in their Lord's revelations, ²³·⁵⁹who don't make partner-gods with their Lord, ²³·⁶⁰who donate to charity whatever they can, yet their hearts still **tremble with awe because they will go back to their Lord** ²³·⁶¹– it is they who rush to do good things sooner, and they're always **the first to do them.**

²³·⁶²**We don't force anyone to do more than what they can. There's a record with Us that will speak the truth. They won't be treated unfairly.** ²³·⁶³The truth is, their hearts are in ignorance of this reality, and they continue to do other bad things besides this, ²³·⁶⁴until, when We will punish their elite, that is when they will cry out! ²³·⁶⁵They will be told: "Don't cry out today because you won't be helped by Us. ²³·⁶⁶My verses used to be recited to you but you used to go back in rejection, ²³·⁶⁷showing arrogance to the Qur'an, talking nonsense all night long."

23.68Don't they then think over these words, or has something new come to them that didn't come to their ancestors? 23.69Don't they recognise their Messenger, which is why they are rejecting him? 23.70Are they saying: "He has gone mad."? Never! He has brought them the truth, but most of them don't like the truth.

23.71If the truth had followed their desires, then the heavens and the earth and everyone inside them would have been ruined. In actual fact, We have brought them their Reminder (- Qur'an) but they're the ones neglecting it. 23.72Do they think you are asking them for some payment? They should know that your Lord's payment is the best. He is the Best Giver of all. 23.73You are certainly inviting them to a path that is straight, 23.74but those who don't believe in the Hereafter are staying away from it.

23.75If We were extra merciful to them and removed all harm from them, they would still choose to remain confused and wander blindly in their rebellion. 23.76We did make them suffer but they still didn't submit themselves to their Lord nor did they humble themselves, 23.77until when We will open a gate to a severe punishment for them, that is when they will lose all hope.

23.78He is the one Who created for you hearing, sight, and intelligence, yet you hardly give any thanks. 23.79He is the one Who has multiplied you throughout the earth, and it is in front of Him you will all be assembled. 23.80He is the one Who gives life and death, and to Him belongs the control of the rotation of the night and day. Won't you even think? 23.81But no! They say the same as what the previous disbelievers said.

23.82They say: "What? When we die and have become dust and bones, will we then be brought back to life? 23.83This has been promised to us before, and to our forefathers too. This Qur'an is nothing but stories made up by previous people."

23.84O Prophet Muhammad, ask: "Whose is the earth, and everyone in it? Tell me if you know." 23.85They will reply: "Allah's." Say: "Then won't you remind yourselves?" 23.86Ask: "Who is the Lord of the seven heavens and of the Mighty Throne?" 23.87They will reply: "They are Allah's." Say: "Then why aren't you mindful of Allah?" 23.88Ask: "In Whose control are the kingdoms of everything, Who gives protection but cannot be protected against? Tell me if you know." 23.89They will reply: "In Allah's." Say: "Then how are you being tricked?" 23.90In actual fact, We have brought them the truth, about which they will certainly tell lies.

23.91Allah has no child, and there is no god together with Him. If there was, each god would take away what he created, and they would have competed with each other. Glory be to Allah above what they describe. 23.92Knower of the unseen secrets and the visible, He is much higher than the partner-gods they make with Him.

23.93Pray: "My Lord! If You are going to show me the punishment they are being warned about 23.94then, my Lord, don't put me among these unjust people." 23.95O Prophet Muhammad, We can certainly show you the punishment We are warning them about. 23.96You should respond to anything bad with the best. We know very well everything they say.

23.97You should pray: "My Lord! I ask You to protect me from the temptations of the evil ones, 23.98and I ask You to protect me, My Lord, in case they come near me."

[23.99]Then, when death comes to any of them, he says: "My Lord! Send me back into the world, [23.100]so I can do the good I've missed out on." Never! They are only words he utters. There will now be a barrier behind them until the Day they will be brought back to life.

[23.101]Then, when the Trumpet will be blown, that Day there will be no more relationships between them nor will they be able to ask each other any questions.

[23.102]Those whose scales of good will be heavy, it is really they who will be successful.

[23.103]As for those whose scales will be light, it is they who have ruined themselves, and will remain forever in Hell. [23.104]The Fire will burn their faces and their lips will melt back exposing their teeth.

[23.105]It will be said to them: "My revelations used to be recited to you, didn't they? But you used to call them lies!" [23.106]They will reply: "Our Lord! Our disobedience defeated us, and we became a people gone astray. [23.107]Our Lord! Get us out of here. If we ever go back to disobeying You then we will certainly be wrongdoers." [23.108]Allah will reply: "Stay there in disgrace. Don't talk to Me! [23.109]There was a group of My servants who used to pray, 'Our Lord! We believe, so forgive us and have mercy on us, because You are the Best of those who show mercy.' [23.110]However, you disbelievers were so busy making fun of them that while you continued to laugh at them, they made you forget to remember Me! [23.111]Today, I have rewarded them because of their patience. They are the winners."

[23.112]He will ask: "In numbers of years, how long did you stay in the world?" [23.113]They will reply: "We stayed a day or part of a day, but ask those who keep count." [23.114]He will say: "You stayed for only a short while, if only you had known this before! ^{23.115}Did you really think We created you for no reason, and that you wouldn't be brought back to Us?" ^{23.116}Allah is most high. The real King! There is no god except Him – the Lord of the Honourable Throne!"

^{23.117}If someone prays, together with Allah, to any other god for which he has no proof then he should know that his judgement will be up to his Lord. The disbelievers will never be successful.

^{23.118}So pray: "My Lord! Forgive and have mercy, because You are the Best of those who show mercy."

Surah 24. Light (an-Noor)

Allah's name I begin with, the Most Compassionate, the Ever-Merciful

^{24.1}This is a surah We have revealed, made its commands obligatory, and sent down clear verses in it, so that you might remind yourselves.

^{24.2}Any woman or man who are guilty of fornication: whip each of them a hundred lashes. Don't let sympathy for them stop you from fulfilling Allah's law, if you believe in Allah and the Last Day. A group of Believers should witness them being punished.

^{24.3}A man who fornicates doesn't like to marry any woman other than a woman who fornicates or a female polytheist. A woman who fornicates, no one likes to marry her but a man who fornicates or a male polytheist. This act of fornication or adultery is unlawful for Believers.

^{24.4}Those who accuse chaste women of fornication, and then fail to bring forward four witnesses, you must whip those accusers eighty

lashes, and never ever accept their testimony. It is they who are the big sinners – {}^{24.5}except those who repent after that and correct themselves. Allah is Most Forgiving, Ever-Merciful.

{}^{24.6}Those who accuse their own wives of adultery but don't have any witnesses except themselves, the testimony of each accusing husband is to swear four times by Allah that he is definitely telling the truth, {}^{24.7}and the fifth time that Allah's curse be upon him if he is telling a lie. {}^{24.8}It would remove the punishment from the wife if she swears four times by Allah that the husband is definitely telling a lie, {}^{24.9}and the fifth time that Allah's anger be upon her if he is telling the truth. {}^{24.10}If it wasn't for Allah's grace and mercy upon you people, you would be lost. Allah accepts repentance much, is All-Wise.

{}^{24.11}Those who came up with the false accusation, they're a group of people from among you. You mustn't think of it as something bad for you because it is now good for you. Each man from among them will be punished according to what he did, and the one who played the greater part will suffer a terrible punishment.

{}^{24.12}When you heard it, why didn't you Believing men and women think well of their own people and say: "This is a blatant lie!"? {}^{24.13}Why couldn't the accusers bring forward for it four witnesses? Since they haven't been able to bring witnesses, it is really they who are liars in the sight of Allah. {}^{24.14}If it wasn't for Allah's grace and mercy upon you people, in this world and the next, you would certainly have suffered a terrible punishment because of your spreading this lie, {}^{24.15}since you were discussing the rumour on your tongues, your mouths were uttering things that you had no knowledge of, and you were taking it lightly when it was very serious in the sight of Allah. {}^{24.16}When you heard this rumour, why didn't you Believers say: "We don't have any right to talk about this," and said: "O Allah, Glory be to You. This is a serious false accusation!"? ²⁴·¹⁷Allah warns you never to repeat anything like this again, if you are true Believers. ²⁴·¹⁸Allah makes the revelations clear to you. Allah is All-Knowing, All-Wise.

²⁴·¹⁹Those who like anything shameful to spread among the Believers, they will suffer a painful punishment in this world and the next. Allah knows but you don't. ²⁴·²⁰If it wasn't for Allah's grace and mercy upon you people, you would be lost. **Allah is Kind, Ever-Merciful.**

²⁴·²¹Believers! Never follow Shaytan's footsteps. Anyone who follows Shaytan's footsteps will find that he orders shamefulness and doing bad things. If it wasn't for Allah's grace and mercy upon you people, none of you would ever have become pure of this false accusation, but it is Allah Who cleans and purifies anyone He chooses. Allah is All-Hearing, All-Knowing.

²⁴·²²Those of you who are gracious and rich, you mustn't promise not to give to those involved in this accusation from among close relatives, the needy, and those who have migrated in Allah's cause. They should forgive and ignore. Wouldn't you love it for Allah to forgive you? Allah is Most Forgiving, Ever-Merciful.

²⁴·²³Those who wrongfully accuse chaste, unsuspecting, Believing women, they will be cursed in this world and the next, and they will suffer a terrible punishment ²⁴·²⁴on the Day when their tongues, hands, and feet will testify against them for everything they used to do. ²⁴·²⁵On that Day, Allah will repay them in full what they really deserve, and they will realise that Allah is the truth Who makes everything clear.

²⁴·²⁶Bad women deserve bad men, and bad men deserve bad women; good women deserve good men, and good men deserve good women

– they are innocent of what bad people say, and they will have forgiveness and some honourable wealth.

^{24.27}Believers! Apart from your own homes, you mustn't enter other houses until you've taken permission and have greeted those who live there. This is best for you so that you might remind yourselves why. ^{24.28}If you don't find anyone inside, you mustn't enter them until you are given permission. If you are asked: "Go back," then go back. This is more virtuous for you. Allah knows perfectly well everything you do.

^{24.29}There is nothing wrong if you enter without permission a public place not used for living in and which is of benefit to you. Allah knows everything you show or hide.

^{24.30}Tell the Believing men to lower their eyes and guard their chastity. This is more virtuous for them. Allah is Fully-Aware of everything they do. ^{24.31}Tell the Believing women to: lower their eyes; guard their chastity; not show their beauty except the parts that are acceptable in view; keep their coverings over their chests and not let their beauty be seen by anyone except their husbands, fathers, husbands' fathers, own sons, husbands' sons, brothers, brothers' sons, sisters' sons, Muslim women, their slavewomen, male servants who don't have any sexual desire, or young children who don't have any sense of female private issues; and not to stamp their feet so as to draw attention to their covered beauty. Believers! Repent to Allah, all together, so you can be successful.

^{24.32}Marry off those among you who are single, as well as those of your male and female slaves who are capable of marriage. If they are poor, Allah will make them rich from His grace. Allah is All-Surrounding, All-Knowing. ^{24.33}Those who cannot find ways to marry must keep

themselves chaste until Allah makes them capable from His grace. If any of your slaves want to buy their freedom then you should make a contract with them if you know they have good in them, and you should give them some of the wealth Allah has given you. In trying to gain the temporary wealth of this world, you mustn't force your slavewomen into prostitution when they want to remain chaste, and if anyone does force them, then even after they've been forced they will find **Allah is Most Forgiving, Ever-Merciful** to them.

24.34 **We have already sent down to you** people: **revelations that make things clear, the example of those** people **who passed away before you, and a source of advice for those who are mindful** of Me.

24.35 **Allah is the Light of the heavens and the earth. An example of His Light is that of a niche in which there is a lamp: the lamp is in crystal: the crystal is like a twinkling star that is lit from a blessed olive tree – neither of the East nor of the West – whose oil glows even though no flame has touched it: light upon light! Allah guides to His light anyone He chooses. He uses examples for people, and He knows everything perfectly well.**

24.36 **This light shines through houses Allah has ordered to be honoured and His name be mentioned inside them. There, glorifying Him morning and evening,** 24.37 **are servants who won't be distracted by neither trade nor buying and selling from either remembering Allah, establishing the ritual prayers, or paying zakah. They fear the Day when hearts and eyes will turn over** in fear, 24.38 **so that Allah may give them the best reward for what they did, and increase it** even more **for them from His grace. Allah gives without limits to anyone He chooses.**

24.39The good things the disbelievers do are like a mirage in a desert which the thirsty person mistakes for water; until when he reaches it, he finds it to be nothing at all. However, he will find Allah right next to him in the Hereafter, but Allah will have repaid him his account in full in this world. Allah is quick in settling accounts. 24.40Or like the many layers of darkness in a deep ocean, that waves have covered up – above which there are more waves, above which there are clouds: depths of darkness! layer upon layer! If someone pushes his hand out of the water, he can hardly see it himself. Anyone Allah doesn't give any light, will have no light.

24.41Don't you see that everyone in the heavens and the earth glorifies Allah, as do the birds with outspread wings? Each one knows its own way of praying and glorifying Him. Allah knows perfectly well everything they do. 24.42Control of the heavens and the earth belongs to Allah, and the final return will be to Him.

24.43Don't you see that Allah gently moves the clouds, then joins them together, and then piles them up, until you see rain pouring out from within them? He sends down from the sky mountains of snow that He pours down on those He chooses and turns away from those He chooses. The flash of its lightning almost snatches away the eyesight. 24.44Allah rotates the night and day. There is a definite lesson of warning in this for those who can see.

24.45Allah created every living creature from liquid. Some of them crawl on their bellies, some walk on two legs, and some on four. Allah creates whatever He wants. He is Most Capable of anything.

24.46We have already sent down revelations that make things clear, and it is Allah Who guides anyone He chooses to a path that is straight. 24.47They say: "We believe in Allah and the Messenger

Muhammad, and we obey," but even after that a group of them turns away. They aren't really Believers. ²⁴·⁴⁸When they're invited to Allah and His Messenger so he can judge between them, some of them stay away. ²⁴·⁴⁹If the judgement was in their favour, they would come running to him and accept. ²⁴·⁵⁰Is there a sickness in their hearts, do they have doubts about Islam, or do they fear Allah and His Messenger will be unjust to them? No, no! It is really they who are unjust.

²⁴·⁵¹The response of the Believers when they're invited to Allah and His Messenger so he can judge between them is they say: "We hear and obey!". It is really they who will be successful. ²⁴·⁵²Those who obey Allah and His Messenger, and are afraid of Allah and are mindful of Him, it is they who will be the winners.

²⁴·⁵³O Prophet Muhammad, they have sworn by Allah with their strongest oaths that they would definitely go out to fight if you told them to. Say: "You don't have to swear. Your obedience is well known. Allah is Fully-Aware of everything you do." ²⁴·⁵⁴Say: "You have to obey Allah and the Messenger too. If you turn away, then you should know that the Messenger is only responsible for the duty given to him and you are responsible for the duty given to you. If you obey him, you will be following guidance. The Messenger's duty is only to deliver the message clearly."

²⁴·⁵⁵Allah has promised those of you who believe and do good that He will certainly make them successors in this world, as He did with those before them; that He will create possibilities to help them in their religion which He has chosen for them; and that He will certainly change their state of fear into that of safety. He says: "They worship Me and they don't make anything a partner-god with Me." Anyone who disbelieves after this promise then it is really they who

are disobedient. [24.56]Therefore, you must establish the ritual prayers, pay zakah, and obey the Messenger Muhammad, so you may be shown mercy. [24.57]Never think the disbelievers can escape Allah in this world. Their home will be the Fire. What a dreadful final destination!

[24.58]Believers! Your slaves, and those of you who haven't yet reached puberty, should ask your permission to come in at three times of the day: before Fajr Prayer; when you take off your outer clothes at noon; and after Isha Prayer. These are your three times of privacy. Outside of these times, there is nothing wrong for you or for them to move around visiting each other. In this way Allah makes the commands clear to you. Allah is All-Knowing, All-Wise. [24.59]However, when the children among you reach puberty, they should ask your permission like those before them have been doing. In this way Allah makes His commands clear to you. Allah is All-Knowing, All-Wise.

[24.60]The elderly women who are past childbearing age – who don't have any desire for marriage anymore, there is nothing wrong if they take off their outer clothes as long as they don't display any of their beauty. However, it is best for them to avoid this. Allah is All-Hearing, All-Knowing.

[24.61]There is no restriction on the blind, the disabled, or the sick. There is no harm if you eat in your own homes or the homes of your fathers or mothers, your brothers or sisters, your paternal uncles or aunts, your maternal uncles or aunts, or the places you own the keys to, or your friends' homes. There is nothing wrong if you eat together or separately. When you enter houses, you should greet each other with a greeting that is blessed and good from Allah. In this way Allah makes His commands clear to you so that you might think.

24.62True Believers are those who believe in Allah and His Messenger. When they're with him on a matter that is important for everyone, they wouldn't leave until after they have his permission. O Prophet Muhammad, those who ask your permission are those who truly believe in Allah and His Messenger. So, when they ask your permission to go to a private matter of theirs, you should give permission to any of them you choose, and ask Allah to forgive them. Allah is Most Forgiving, Ever-Merciful.

24.63You people are not allowed to call the Messenger among you like you call each other. Allah knows those of you who sneak away backing each other. So, those who disobey the Messenger's orders should be afraid in case they're put to a test or they suffer a painful punishment.

24.64Beware! Everything in the heavens and the earth belongs to Allah! He certainly knows the state you are in. On the Day they will all be taken back to Him, He will tell them about everything they did. Allah knows everything perfectly well.

Surah 25. Criterion (al-Furqaan)

Allah's name I begin with, the Most Compassionate, the Ever-Merciful

25.1Blessed is the one Who revealed the Criterion (- Qur'an) to His Special Servant so he could give warnings to everyone; 25.2Allah – Who has control of the heavens and the earth, Who doesn't have a child nor a partner in His Kingdom, and Who created everything and fixed due proportions for them; 25.3yet, instead of Him, they began to worship other gods: that cannot create anything but are themselves created; that don't have any power to harm nor help even themselves; that can neither control death nor life, nor bring the dead back to life.

25.4The disbelievers say: "This Qur'an is only a lie he has made up, and other people have helped him in." They've come down to injustice and dishonesty. 25.5They also claim: "These are stories made up by previous people which he has had written down for him and are read out to him morning and evening." 25.6O Prophet Muhammad, say: "The one Who revealed it knows the secrets of the heavens and the earth. He is always Most Forgiving, Ever-Merciful." 25.7They also say: "What is wrong with this Messenger? He eats food and walks about in marketplaces? Why wasn't an angel sent down to him to give warnings alongside him? 25.8Why hasn't he been given a treasure? Why doesn't he have his own orchard to eat from?" The wrongdoers say: "You are only following a man who is under a magic spell." 25.9See how they make comparisons of you! They've now gone so far astray that they'll never be able to find a way back. 25.10Blessed is the one Who, if He wanted, could make things for you that are far better than these, such as gardens – that have rivers flowing beneath them, and make for you palaces too.

25.11In fact, they've called the Final Hour a lie, but We have prepared a Blazing Fire for those who call the Final Hour a lie. 25.12When it will see them from a place far away, they will hear it raging and screaming. 25.13When they will be tied up together and thrown into it from some narrow place, it is there and then they will cry out for their own total destruction. 25.14They will be told: "Don't scream just for one total destruction today but for many total destructions!"

25.15O Prophet Muhammad, ask: "Which is better: this or the Garden of Immortality which has been promised to those who are mindful of Allah? That will be a reward for them as well as their final destination. ²⁵·¹⁶"There they will have anything they want while they will remain in it forever. It's a promise guaranteed by your Lord."

²⁵·¹⁷The Day when He will gather them together, as well as everything they worship besides Allah, He will ask: "Was it you who misguided these servants of Mine, or did they stray by themselves from the right way?" ²⁵·¹⁸They will reply: "Glory be to You! We wouldn't dare take protectors besides You, but You let them and their forefathers enjoy themselves until they forgot to remember You. They became a people who were ruined." ²⁵·¹⁹They will accuse you disbelievers of being liars in everything you say, and you won't be able to avoid the punishment nor be helped. Those of you who keep doing wrong, We will make them taste a mighty punishment.

²⁵·²⁰O Prophet Muhammad, the messengers We sent before you, they all ate food and walked about in marketplaces. We've made some of you a test for others. Will you people have patience? Your Lord is always Ever-Watchful.

[PART 19]
²⁵·²¹Those who don't expect to have a meeting with Us, they say: "Why haven't angels been sent down to us?" or, "We would believe if we could see our Lord." They've become too arrogant about themselves, and too disobedient. ²⁵·²²One Day when they see the angels, there won't be any joy for the criminals on that Day. The angels will say: "Paradise for you is absolutely forbidden." ²⁵·²³We will turn to whatever good they will have done and scatter it like dust particles. ²⁵·²⁴On that Day, the people of Paradise will have the best place to stay and the finest place to rest.

²⁵·²⁵On that Day, the sky will burst into clouds and angels will be sent down, rank upon rank. ²⁵·²⁶True Sovereignty will belong only to Allah

– the Most Compassionate on that Day. It will be a hard day for the disbelievers.

25.27On that Day, the wrongdoers will bite their own hands while crying: "Oh! If only I had followed a way with the Messenger. 25.28I am damned! If only I hadn't made close friends with so-and-so! 25.29He led me away from the Reminder after it had come to me!" Shaytan always betrays humans.

25.30The Messenger Muhammad will say: "My Lord! My people had totally abandoned this Qur'an." 25.31In this way We let every prophet have enemies from among the criminals, but your Lord is enough as Guide and Helper.

25.32O Prophet Muhammad, the disbelievers objected: "Why wasn't the Qur'an revealed to him all in one go?" This is how it is. We did this to make your noble heart strong by it, and that is also why We have recited it in slow clear stages. 25.33Whenever they raise any objection against you, We bring you the truth and the best explanation. 25.34Those who will be pushed towards Hell – falling on their faces, it is they who are worst in rank and furthest from the way to Paradise.

25.35We gave Musa the Book, and made his brother Haroon a helper alongside him. 25.36We ordered: "Go, both of you, to the people who call Our signs a lie." Then, after giving them warnings, We completely destroyed those disbelieving people.

25.37When the people of Nuh accused the messengers of being liars, We drowned them and made them a sign of warning for all people. We have prepared a painful punishment for the wrongdoers.

[25.38]We also destroyed **the 'Ad and the Thamud, and the People of the Well (- As'haab ar-Rass) too, as well as many other generations between them.** [25.39]We gave examples to each one of them, and then We wiped them out completely. [25.40]The disbelievers have certainly come across the town that was showered with deadly rain. Haven't they seen it? The truth is, they don't expect to be brought back to life.

[25.41]O Prophet Muhammad, when the disbelievers see you, they make fun of you by saying: "Is this the one Allah has sent as a messenger? [25.42]If we hadn't kept ourselves strongly devoted to our gods, he would have led us away from them." When they see the punishment, they will definitely realise who was the furthest from the right way. [25.43]What do you think of someone who makes his own desires his god? Should you then be responsible for him? [25.44]Do you think most of them cannot hear or understand? They are like cattle. In fact, they're far more astray from the right way.

[25.45]Don't you see how your Lord stretches out the shade? If He had wanted, He could have made it stand still. Then again, We made the sun its guide. [25.46]Eventually, We gently pull the shade back towards Us.

[25.47]He is the one Who made the night a covering for you, sleep for resting, and made the day a time to get up.

[25.48]He is the one Who sends the winds like good news before His mercy. We send down from the sky pure water, [25.49]with which We bring back to life a land that is dead, and give it as a drink to many animals and people We've created. [25.50]We keep distributing the water among them so they can learn lessons, yet most people reject everything **but** choose to **be unthankful.**

25.51If We had wanted, We could have sent someone to give warnings to every town. 25.52So, you must never give in to the disbelievers, but strive your hardest against them using this Qur'an.

25.53Allah is the one Who placed two seas together: one sweet and fresh, and the other salty and bitter; and He put between them a barrier that cannot be crossed. 25.54He is the one Who creates human beings from a drop of fluid, and then gives them relations through blood and marriage. Your Lord is always Most Capable. 25.55Yet, instead of Allah, they worship things that can neither help nor harm them. The disbeliever has always helped against his own Lord.

25.56O Prophet Muhammad, We have sent you to give good news and warnings. 25.57Say: "I'm not asking you any payment for it, except that whoever wants should choose a way towards his Lord."

25.58You must put your trust in Allah – the Ever-Living Who will never die, and you must glorify His praises. He is enough as being Fully-Aware of His servants' sins, 25.59Who created the heavens and the earth and everything in between them in six stages, and then established His authority on the Throne. He is the Most Compassionate – ask anyone who knows about Him.

25.60When they are told: "You must prostrate to Allah - the Most Compassionate," they reply: "What is 'the Most Compassionate'? Should we prostrate to something you order us?" and this increases their hatred of the truth. *<Prostration Point 7>*

25.61Blessed is the one Who placed in the sky: constellations, and also the sun as a lamp and a moon that gives light. 25.62He is the one Who made the night and day come after each other as a sign for anyone who wants to learn a lesson or to be thankful.

25.63The servants of Allah – the Most Compassionate are: those who walk on the earth gently, and when bad-mannered people speak to them in a rude manner, they reply with words of peace; 25.64those who spend their nights worshipping their Lord – prostrating or standing; 25.65those who pray: "Our Lord! Keep the suffering of Hell away from us, because its suffering is continuous pain. 25.66It is such a horrible place to stay and rest!" 25.67They are those who are neither wasteful nor stingy when they spend, but keeping a balance between the two; 25.68those who don't pray to any other god along with Allah, nor kill a person Allah has made sacred – except by lawful right, nor have unlawful sexual relations. Anyone who does these will face punishment. 25.69His punishment on Judgement Day will be doubled, and he will remain humiliated in Hell forever, 25.70but not someone who repents, believes, and does good, because it is they whose bad Allah will change into good. Allah is always Most Forgiving, Ever-Merciful. 25.71Someone who repents and does good has certainly turned to Allah like he should. 25.72They are those who don't bear false witness, and when they come across foolishness they pass it by with dignity; 25.73those who don't fall down deaf and blind to their Lord's revelations when they're reminded of them; 25.74and those who pray: "Our Lord! Give us coolness of our eyes in happiness through our wives and children, and make us leaders of those who are mindful of You." 25.75It is they who will be rewarded the high mansions in Paradise because of their patience, and they will be welcomed there with greetings and peace. 25.76They will remain there forever. What a wonderful place to stay and rest!

25.77O Prophet Muhammad, say to the disbelievers: "Why should My Lord care about you if you don't pray to Him? It is because you have called the truth a lie that the expected punishment will come to you very soon."

Surah 26. Poets (ash-Shu'araa')

Allah's name I begin with, the Most Compassionate, the Ever-Merciful

^{26.1}Taa Seen Meem.
^{26.2}These are the verses of the Clear Book.

^{26.3}O Prophet Muhammad, **you might end up destroying yourself with worry because they won't believe.** ^{26.4}If We had wanted, We could send down to them a sign from the sky, to which their necks would stay bowed in humility. ^{26.5}However, when a fresh reminder comes to them from Allah – the Most Compassionate, they turn away from it. ^{26.6}They have called the truth a lie, so the details of what they used to make fun of will come to them soon.

^{26.7}**Don't they look at the earth and see** all the wonderful things We grow in it? ^{26.8}There is certainly a sign in this, yet most of them won't believe. ^{26.9}Only your Lord is the Almighty, the Ever-Merciful.

^{26.10}Remember **when your Lord called out to Musa: "Go to the people who are unjust** ^{26.11}– to Fir'awn's people. Won't they be mindful of Allah?" ^{26.12}Musa replied: "My Lord! I fear they will accuse me of being a liar. ^{26.13}My heart feels tight and my speech is not fluent, so send a revelation **to Haroon.** ^{26.14}They also have a charge against me which is why I fear they will kill me." ^{26.15}Allah said: "No **they won't!** Go, both of you, with Our signs. We are with you, listening. ^{26.16}Now go to Fir'awn, both of you, and say, 'We are both messengers from Allah – the Lord of all the worlds, ^{26.17}so let the Descendants of Ya'qub go with us.'."

^{26.18}Fir'awn said: "Didn't we bring you up among us when you were a child? Didn't you spend many years of your life with us? ^{26.19}Then,

being unthankful, you did what you did." ²⁶·²⁰Musa replied: "I did it when I didn't know it would kill him. ²⁶·²¹So I ran away from you people when I feared you, but my Lord has given me wisdom and made me one of the messengers. ²⁶·²²Anyway, is this even a favour you are reminding me of when you have turned the Descendants of Ya'qub into slaves?"

²⁶·²³Fir'awn asked: "What is 'the Lord of the all the worlds'?" ²⁶·²⁴Musa replied: "He is the Lord of the heavens and the earth and everything in between them – if only you would be strong Believers." ²⁶·²⁵Fir'awn asked those around him: "Are you listening?" ²⁶·²⁶Musa added: "He is your Lord and the Lord of your ancestors too." ²⁶·²⁷Fir'awn said: "This messenger who has been sent to you must be mad!" ²⁶·²⁸Musa continued: "Allah is the Lord of the East and the West and everything in between them – if only you would think!"

²⁶·²⁹Fir'awn threatened: "If you worship any god other than me, I will definitely throw you among the prisoners!" ²⁶·³⁰Musa asked: "Even if I brought you something to make the truth clear?" ²⁶·³¹Fir'awn demanded: "Bring it then, if you are telling the truth!" ²⁶·³²So Musa threw down his staff, and it immediately became an actual large snake! ²⁶·³³And he pulled out his hand from under his collar opening, and it immediately became dazzling white to everyone who was watching!

²⁶·³⁴Fir'awn said to the ministers around him: "He is certainly an expert magician. ²⁶·³⁵He wants to expel you from your land using his magic. Now what do you advise?" ²⁶·³⁶They replied: "Give him and his brother some time while you send out marshals to the cities ²⁶·³⁷to bring you every skilful magician." ²⁶·³⁸So the magicians were brought together for the fixed time and place on a specified day. ²⁶·³⁹The

people were asked: "Will you gather together [26.40]so we can support the magicians to help them win?"

[26.41]So, when the magicians came, they asked Fir'awn: "Will there be some reward for us if we win?" [26.42]He replied: "Yes, and then you will certainly be among those nearest to me in high positions."

[26.43]Musa told them: "Throw down whatever you want to throw." [26.44]So they threw down their ropes and their staffs, and said: "By Fir'awn's might: it is we who will certainly win." [26.45]Then Musa threw down his staff, and it immediately began swallowing up what they had made through illusion.

[26.46]The magicians were made to fall down in prostration. [26.47]They declared: "We believe in Allah – the Lord all of the Worlds, [26.48]the Lord of Musa and Haroon." [26.49]Fir'awn said: "How dare you believe in Him before I give you permission! He must be your leader who taught you magic! You will very soon come to know my power. I will definitely cut off your hands and feet from opposite sides, and I will crucify the lot of you!" [26.50]They replied: "We don't care! We'll go back to our Lord. [26.51]We hope Our Lord will forgive us our sins now that we've become the first to believe."

[26.52]We revealed to Musa: "You should set out with My servants at night, though you will all be chased." [26.53]Then Fir'awn sent out marshals to the cities [26.54]announcing: "They're merely a handful of people, [26.55]yet making us very angry, [26.56]but we are all ready." [26.57]So We made Fir'awn's people leave the gardens, fountains, [26.58]treasures, and wonderful homes. [26.59]It was like that. Later, We made the Descendants of Ya'qub inheritors of those fine things.

$^{26.60}$Fir'awn's people chased after them at sunrise. $^{26.61}$When the two groups saw each other, Musa's companions said: "We will certainly be caught." $^{26.62}$Musa replied: "Never! My Lord is with me. He will guide me." $^{26.63}$Then We revealed to Musa: "Hit the sea with your staff." So the sea split itself up, and each part was like a huge mountain. $^{26.64}$We made the others – Fir'awn's army – come near that place. $^{26.65}$We saved Musa and all the people who were with him. $^{26.66}$Then We drowned the others. $^{26.67}$There is certainly a sign in this, yet most of them won't believe. $^{26.68}$Only your Lord is the Almighty, the Ever-Merciful.

$^{26.69}$You should tell them the story of Ibrahim, $^{26.70}$when he asked his foster father and his people: "What do you worship?" $^{26.71}$They replied: "We worship idols, and we are devoted to them." $^{26.72}$He asked: "Do they hear you when you call them, $^{26.73}$or can they help or harm you?" $^{26.74}$They replied: "Actually, this is what we saw our forefathers doing." $^{26.75}$He asked: "Have you people ever thought about what you've been worshipping, $^{26.76}$both you and your ancestors? $^{26.77}$They're all my enemies, except for Allah – the Lord of all the worlds: $^{26.78}$Who created me and He is the one Who guides me, $^{26.79}$He is the one Who gives me food and drink, $^{26.80}$He is the one Who cures me when I am ill, $^{26.81}$Who will give me death and then life again, $^{26.82}$and Who I hope will forgive me my mistakes on Judgement Day."

$^{26.83}$Then he prayed: "My Lord! Give me wisdom and join me with righteous people. $^{26.84}$Give me a good mention among later generations. $^{26.85}$Make me one of those who will inherit the Garden of Delight. $^{26.86}$Forgive my foster father because he is among those who go astray. $^{26.87}$Don't disgrace me on the Day when people will be brought back to life; $^{26.88}$the Day when neither wealth nor children will be of any use, $^{26.89}$but only he will be saved who comes to Allah with a heart that is pure."

²⁶·⁹⁰Paradise will be brought close to those who are mindful of Allah, ²⁶·⁹¹and Hell-Fire will be shown to those who went astray ²⁶·⁹²– and they will be asked: "Where are those you used to worship ²⁶·⁹³besides Allah? Can they help you? Can they even help themselves?"

²⁶·⁹⁴The idols will be thrown headfirst into Hell-Fire, they and also those who went astray, ²⁶·⁹⁵as well as the armies of Iblees, the lot of them! ²⁶·⁹⁶While arguing with each other, they will say: ²⁶·⁹⁷"By Allah, we were clearly astray, ²⁶·⁹⁸when we made you equals to Allah – the Lord of all the Worlds. ²⁶·⁹⁹It was the criminals who misled us, ²⁶·¹⁰⁰and now we don't have anyone to intercede for us ²⁶·¹⁰¹– not even a single loyal friend. ²⁶·¹⁰²Now, if only we had a chance to go back, we would definitely believe!" ²⁶·¹⁰³There is certainly a sign in this, yet most of them won't believe. ²⁶·¹⁰⁴O Prophet Muhammad, only your Lord is the Almighty, the Ever-Merciful.

²⁶·¹⁰⁵The people of Nuh accused the messengers of being liars. ²⁶·¹⁰⁶Remember when their brother Nuh said to them: "Won't you be mindful of Allah? ²⁶·¹⁰⁷I'm a trustworthy messenger sent to you, ²⁶·¹⁰⁸so be mindful of Allah and obey me. ²⁶·¹⁰⁹I'm not asking you any payment for it. My reward will come only from Allah – the Lord of all the worlds. ²⁶·¹¹⁰So, be mindful of Allah and follow me."

²⁶·¹¹¹They asked: "Why should we believe merely because you say so and when the lowliest kind of people are following you?" ²⁶·¹¹²He replied: "What do I know as to what they've been doing? ²⁶·¹¹³If you are aware, their judgement is up to my Lord. ²⁶·¹¹⁴I'm not going to push Believers away. ²⁶·¹¹⁵I only give clear warnings."

²⁶·¹¹⁶They threatened: "Nuh! If you don't stop, you will certainly be stoned to death." ²⁶·¹¹⁷He prayed: "My Lord! My people have accused

me of being a liar. ²⁶·¹¹⁸Now, You make a clear judgement between me and them, and save me and the Believers who are with me."

²⁶·¹¹⁹So We saved him and those with him in the fully loaded Ark. ²⁶·¹²⁰Finally, We drowned all the rest. ²⁶·¹²¹There is certainly a sign in this, yet most of them won't believe. ²⁶·¹²²O Prophet Muhammad, only your Lord is the Almighty, the Ever-Merciful.

²⁶·¹²³The 'Ad accused the messengers of being liars ²⁶·¹²⁴when their brother Hud said to them: "Won't you be mindful of Allah? ²⁶·¹²⁵I'm a trustworthy messenger sent to you, ²⁶·¹²⁶so be mindful of Allah and obey me. ²⁶·¹²⁷I'm not asking you any payment for it. My reward will come only from Allah – the Lord of all the worlds. ²⁶·¹²⁸Are you building a monument on every high place for no reason? ²⁶·¹²⁹Are you making fortresses hoping you will live forever? ²⁶·¹³⁰When you use force on people, you do it so viciously! ²⁶·¹³¹So be mindful of Allah and obey me. ²⁶·¹³²Be mindful of Him Who has given you everything you know; ²⁶·¹³³He has given you livestock, children, ²⁶·¹³⁴gardens, and fountains. ²⁶·¹³⁵I fear for you the punishment of a Dreadful Day."

²⁶·¹³⁶They replied: "It makes no difference to us if you preach to us or not. ²⁶·¹³⁷What we like doing is the custom of previous people. ²⁶·¹³⁸We won't be punished." ²⁶·¹³⁹They accused him of being a liar, so We destroyed them. There is certainly a sign in this, yet most of them won't believe. ²⁶·¹⁴⁰O Prophet Muhammad, only your Lord is the Almighty, the Ever-Merciful.

²⁶·¹⁴¹The Thamud accused the messengers of being liars ²⁶·¹⁴²when their brother Salih said to them: "Won't you be mindful of Allah? ²⁶·¹⁴³I'm a trustworthy messenger sent to you, ²⁶·¹⁴⁴so be mindful of Allah and obey me. ²⁶·¹⁴⁵I'm not asking you any payment for it. My reward will come only from Allah – the Lord of all the worlds. ²⁶·¹⁴⁶Will you be left

in peace to live with what you have here: ²⁶·¹⁴⁷among gardens and fountains, ²⁶·¹⁴⁸crops, and date-palms with delicate spathes of fruit? ²⁶·¹⁴⁹You carve homes out of mountains with great skill. ²⁶·¹⁵⁰So be mindful of Allah and obey me. ²⁶·¹⁵¹Don't obey the commands of those who go to extremes; ²⁶·¹⁵²who make trouble in the land and who don't put things right."

²⁶·¹⁵³They replied: "You are one of those who are under a magic spell. ²⁶·¹⁵⁴You're only human, just like us, so show us a sign, if you are telling the truth!"

²⁶·¹⁵⁵Salih replied: "Here is a she-camel. She has a turn for drinking, and you also have a turn for drinking – each on a specified day. ²⁶·¹⁵⁶Don't bring her any harm or the punishment of a Dreadful Day will seize you." ²⁶·¹⁵⁷But they hamstrung her, and then became regretful ²⁶·¹⁵⁸when the punishment seized them. There is certainly a sign in this, yet most of them won't believe. ²⁶·¹⁵⁹O Prophet Muhammad, only your Lord is the Almighty, the Ever-Merciful.

²⁶·¹⁶⁰The people of Lut accused the messengers of being liars ²⁶·¹⁶¹when their brother Lut said to them: "Won't you be mindful of Allah? ²⁶·¹⁶²I'm a trustworthy messenger sent to you, ²⁶·¹⁶³so be mindful of Allah and obey me. ²⁶·¹⁶⁴I'm not asking you any payment for it. My reward will come only from Allah – the Lord of all the worlds. ²⁶·¹⁶⁵Of all people, do you lustfully approach males ²⁶·¹⁶⁶and leave your wives your Lord has created for you? The truth is, you are a people overstepping the limits!"

²⁶·¹⁶⁷They threatened: "If you don't stop preaching, you will certainly be expelled." ²⁶·¹⁶⁸Lut replied: "I'm disgusted by what you do."

²⁶·¹⁶⁹He prayed: "**My Lord! Save me and my family from what they are doing.**" ²⁶·¹⁷⁰So We saved him and his family, all of them, ²⁶·¹⁷¹except an old lady from among those who stayed behind. ²⁶·¹⁷²Eventually, We destroyed everyone else. ²⁶·¹⁷³We showered them with a rain of destruction. How devastating was the shower on those who were given warnings! ²⁶·¹⁷⁴There is certainly a sign in this, yet most of them won't believe. ²⁶·¹⁷⁵O Prophet Muhammad, **only your Lord is the Almighty, the Ever-Merciful.**

²⁶·¹⁷⁶The People of the Forest accused the messengers of being liars ²⁶·¹⁷⁷when Shu'ayb said to them: "Won't you be mindful of Allah? ²⁶·¹⁷⁸I'm a trustworthy messenger sent to you, ²⁶·¹⁷⁹so be mindful of Allah and obey me. ²⁶·¹⁸⁰I'm not asking you any payment for it. My reward will come only from Allah – the Lord of all the worlds. ²⁶·¹⁸¹You must give full measure and not be of those who cause losses to people. ²⁶·¹⁸²You must weigh with an even balance. ²⁶·¹⁸³Don't cheat people out of their things nor go around making trouble in the world. ²⁶·¹⁸⁴Be mindful of Allah Who created both you and the previous generations too."

²⁶·¹⁸⁵They said: "You are one of those who are under a magic spell. ²⁶·¹⁸⁶You're only human, just like us, and we think you are a liar! ²⁶·¹⁸⁷So, make pieces of the sky fall down upon us, if you are telling the truth!" ²⁶·¹⁸⁸He replied: "My Lord knows best everything you do."

²⁶·¹⁸⁹They accused him of being a liar, so the punishment of the Day of Shadow seized them. It was the punishment of a dreadful day. ²⁶·¹⁹⁰There is certainly a sign in this, yet most of them won't believe. ²⁶·¹⁹¹O Prophet Muhammad, **only your Lord is the Almighty, the Ever-Merciful.**

26.192This Qur'an is a revelation from Allah – the Lord of all the worlds. 26.193O Prophet Muhammad, the Trustworthy Spirit (- Angel Jibra'il) has brought it down, 26.194to your noble heart so you could be one of those who give warnings, 26.195in the Arabic language that is clear. 26.196It is mentioned in the Holy Books of previous people. 26.197Isn't it a proof for the disbelievers that the scholars from the Descendants of Ya'qub know about it?

26.198If We had revealed it to someone who wasn't an Arab, 26.199and he recited it to these disbelievers, they still wouldn't have believed in it. 26.200In this way We let its rejection enter deep into the hearts of criminals. 26.201They will never believe in it until they see the painful punishment, 26.202that will come upon them all of a sudden when they least expect it. 26.203Then they will beg: "Can we be given another chance?"

26.204Are they trying to bring Our punishment sooner? 26.205What do you think: if We do let them enjoy themselves for a few years, 26.206then the punishment they've been warned about comes upon them, 26.207how will the things they used to enjoy help them? 26.208We have never destroyed any town unless it already had warners 26.209as a reminder. We are never unfair.

26.210Devils didn't come down with this Qur'an, 26.211as they're neither worthy nor capable. 26.212In fact, they are banned from even hearing it in the heavens. 26.213So, o human, You mustn't pray to any other god along with Allah or you will be among those who will be punished.

26.214O Prophet Muhammad, warn your close relatives, 26.215and be merciful to the Believers who follow you. 26.216Then if they disobey you, say: "I have nothing to do with anything you do." 26.217You must put your trust in Allah – the Almighty, the Ever-Merciful, 26.218Who sees you when you stand up to pray, ²⁶·²¹⁹and your movements among those who prostrate in prayer. ²⁶·²²⁰Only He is the All-Hearing, the All-Knowing.

²⁶·²²¹Shall I tell you the people the devils come down to? ²⁶·²²²They come down to anyone who is a disobedient liar, ²⁶·²²³pouring hearsay into his ear, and most of them tell lies.

²⁶·²²⁴As for the poets, only those who are astray will follow them. ²⁶·²²⁵Don't you see the poets wandering aimlessly in every valley? ²⁶·²²⁶They say things they don't do, ²⁶·²²⁷unless they are those who believe, do good, remember Allah a lot, and defend themselves when they are wronged. The wrongdoers will soon find out which place they will go back to after they die.

Surah 27. Ants (*an-Naml*)

Allah's name I begin with, the Most Compassionate, the Ever-Merciful

²⁷·¹*Taa Seen*. These are the verses of the Qur'an and of a Clear Book. ²⁷·²It is a guidance as well as a joy for the Believers, ²⁷·³who establish the ritual prayers, pay zakah, and they strongly believe in the Hereafter.

²⁷·⁴As for those who don't believe in the Hereafter, We have made their bad actions seem attractive to them which is why they are confused and distracted from the truth. ²⁷·⁵They're the ones who will suffer a grievous punishment, and in the Hereafter they will be the worst losers. ²⁷·⁶O Prophet Muhammad, you are receiving this Qur'an from the presence of an All-Wise, All-Knowing Lord.

27.7Remember **when Musa told his family: "I've seen a fire. I will bring you some information from it, or some flaming fire on a branch so you can warm yourselves."**

27.8**When he came to the fire, it was called out: "Blessed is the one near the fire and those around it, and glory be to Allah – Lord of all the worlds.** 27.9**Musa! It is I, Allah, the Almighty, the All-Wise!** 27.10**Throw down your staff."** When he saw it moving as if it were a snake, he turned back in retreat and didn't even look back: "Musa! Don't be afraid. Messengers shouldn't have any fear in My presence. 27.11However, if someone does wrong and then replaces something bad with good then** they will find that **I am Most Forgiving, Ever-Merciful.** 27.12**Now put your hand into your shirt front, and it will come out dazzling white – free from any illness.** These are **among the nine signs to** show **Fir'awn and his people. They have been a disobedient people."** 27.13**However, when Our signs came to them, obvious to see, they said: "This is clearly magic."** 27.14**They rejected those signs wrongly and arrogantly, even though their hearts were sure of them. Now take a look at what was the end result of the troublemakers.**

27.15**We gave** special **knowledge to Dawud and Sulayman. They both said: "All praise is for Allah Who has made us superior to many of His Believing servants."** 27.16**Sulayman was Dawud's heir. He said: "People! We've been taught the language of birds and given all kinds of things. This is certainly the most obvious grace** from Allah."

27.17**Sulayman's armies were gathered for him from jinns, humans, and birds, and they** were well organised and **marched in groups.** 27.18**They marched** until when **they came to a valley of ants, an ant said: "Ants! Get into your homes so Sulayman and his armies don't crush you as they might not notice you."** 27.19**Sulayman smiled, amused at her words, and prayed: "My Lord! Keep me strong that I continue to be** thankful for Your favours You have done to me and my parents, and that I do good with which You are well-pleased. Include me, by Your mercy, among your righteous servants."

27.20He inspected the birds and said: "Why is it that I don't see the Hoopoe? Or is he with those who are absent? 27.21Unless he brings me a good excuse, I will severely punish him, or even slaughter him!"

27.22The Hoopoe didn't stay away long. He arrived and said: "I've found out something you didn't know, and brought you some certain information from Saba' (Sheba). 27.23I saw a woman ruling over them, and she has been given all kinds of things. She also has a magnificent throne. 27.24I saw her and her people prostrating to the sun instead of Allah. Shaytan has made everything they do seem attractive to them, and has blocked them from the right way so they cannot follow guidance 27.25nor prostrate to Allah Who brings out what is hidden in the heavens and the earth and knows everything you hide or show. 27.26He is Allah. There is no god except Him – the Lord of the Mighty Throne." *<Prostration Point 8>*

27.27Sulayman said: "We will soon see if you are telling the truth or one of those who tell lies. 27.28Take this letter of mine and deliver it to them. Then stand well away from them and see how they will respond."

27.29The Queen announced: "Ministers! A noble letter has been delivered to me. 27.30It is from Sulayman, and it says, 'Allah's name I begin with, the Most Compassionate, the Ever-Merciful. 27.31Don't show me pride, but come to me in surrender.'."

27.32She said: "Ministers! Advise me in this matter of mine. I never make a final decision in any matter unless you are present with me."

²⁷·³³They replied: "We are strong people and mighty warriors but you are in command, so you should think about what orders you should give." ²⁷·³⁴She said: "When kings attack any town, they destroy it, and turn its most respectable people into the most disgraced. That is what they do. ²⁷·³⁵However, I will send him a gift and see what the messengers bring back."

²⁷·³⁶Now, when the messenger came to him, Sulayman said: "Are you trying to help me by giving me wealth? What Allah has given me is far better than what He has given you, but you are the ones who are proud of your gifts! ²⁷·³⁷Go back to your people. We will come to attack them with troops they cannot defeat, and We will expel them from there in such disgrace that they will be dishonoured."

²⁷·³⁸Sulayman asked: "Ministers! Which of you can bring me her throne before they come to me in surrender?" ²⁷·³⁹From among the jinns, a mighty one said: "I will bring it to you before you stand from your place. I am certainly strong enough for the purpose, and trustworthy too."

²⁷·⁴⁰Then, **a man who had some knowledge of the Book** said: "I will bring it to you in the twinkling of an eye." When Sulayman saw it placed firmly next to him, he exclaimed: "This is from my Lord's grace! It is to test me if I will give thanks or not. Anyone who gives thanks does so for his own good, and anyone who doesn't give thanks should know that **my Lord is Free of all Needs, Gracious!**"

²⁷·⁴¹He ordered: "Disguise her throne for her so We can see if she will recognise it or will be one of those who don't." ²⁷·⁴²Then, when she arrived, she was asked: "Is your throne like this?' She replied: "It looks like this is the one. We were already told about this and that is why **we have surrendered** as Muslims." ²⁷·⁴³What she had been

worshipping instead of Allah had blocked her from the truth because she was from a disbelieving people.

^{27.44}She was asked: "Enter the palace courtyard," but when she saw it, she thought it was a lake, and so she pulled up her clothing and uncovered her lower legs. Sulayman explained: "It is only a courtyard paved smooth with crystal." She declared: "My Lord! I have been unjust to myself, and now, with Sulayman, I surrender myself to Allah – Lord of all the worlds."

^{27.45}To the people of Thamud, We sent their brother Salih to say: "Worship Allah," but they split into two groups arguing with each other. ^{27.46}He said: "My people! Why are you rushing to do bad things before good? Why don't you ask Allah to forgive you so you may be shown mercy?" ^{27.47}They said: "We sense bad luck from you and from those with you." He replied: "The bad result of your actions is up to Allah. In fact, you are a people being tested."

^{27.48}In the city, there were nine leaders who used to make trouble in the land and wouldn't do anything good. ^{27.49}They said: "Let's swear an oath together by Allah that we will attack and kill him and his family at night, and then say to his heir, 'We didn't witness his family's murder. We are telling the truth.'." ^{27.50}They made a plot in secret and We also made a plan against them in secret without them even being aware. ^{27.51}So take a look at what was the end result of their plot! We destroyed them and their people, all together.

^{27.52}Now these are their houses lying in utter ruin because of their wrongdoing. There is certainly a sign in this for any who have the right knowledge. ^{27.53}We saved those who believed and were mindful of Allah.

27.54We also sent **Lut.** Remember when he said to his people: "Do you do something so shameful when you can see so clearly? 27.55Are you lustfully approaching men instead of women? The truth is, you are a group of people behaving ignorantly." 27.56However, the only response from his people was for them to say: "Expel Lut's family from your town. They are a people who want to remain clean and pure!" 27.57So We saved him and his family, but not his wife: We decided she should be among those who will stay behind. 27.58We showered them with a rain of destruction. How devastating was the rain on those who were given warnings!

27.59Pray: "Praise be to Allah, and peace be upon His servants He has chosen. Who is better: Allah or the partner-gods they make with Him?"

[PART 20]

27.60Well, Who is it that created the heavens and the earth, and sends down water for you from the sky? Then, with that water, We grow beautiful gardens when you couldn't even grow trees in them. Is it another god with Allah? Never! They are a people who make others equal to Him. 27.61Who is it that made the earth a place to live on, made rivers inside it, placed firm mountains in it, and placed a separating barrier between the two seas? Is it another god with Allah? Never! Most of them don't know. 27.62Who is it that listens to the distressed person when he prays to Him, removes all harm, and makes you successors in this world? Is it another god with Allah? How little you remind yourselves! 27.63Who is it that guides you through the many layers of darkness on land and sea, and sends the winds like good news before His mercy? Is it another god with Allah? Allah is much higher than the partner-gods they make with Him. 27.64Who is it that starts creating and then repeats it, and gives you from the sky and the earth? Is it another god with Allah? Say to them, O Prophet Muhammad: "Bring me your proof, if you are telling the truth."

27.65O Prophet Muhammad, say: "Apart from Allah, no one in the heavens or the earth knows the unseen secrets. They aren't even aware of when they will be brought back to life." 27.66But no! Their knowledge of the Hereafter has ended up nowhere. In fact, they're in doubt about it. The truth is, they are blind to it.

27.67The disbelievers say: "What? When we and our forefathers become dust, will we be brought out of our graves? 27.68This has been promised to us before, and to our forefathers too. This warning is nothing but stories made up by previous people." 27.69Say: "Travel through the earth and take a look at what was the end result of the criminals." 27.70Don't worry about the disbelievers nor distress yourself because of the plots they make.

27.71They also ask: "When will this warning be fulfilled, if you are telling the truth?" 27.72Reply: "Perhaps some of what you are trying to bring sooner is right behind you." 27.73Your Lord gives grace to people yet most of them don't even give thanks. 27.74Your Lord certainly knows everything their hearts are hiding as well as anything these people show. 27.75There is nothing hidden in the sky or earth except that it's in a Record that is clear.

27.76This Qur'an explains to the Descendants of Ya'qub most of the things in which they disagree. 27.77It is certainly a guidance and a mercy for the Believers. 27.78Your Lord will judge between them by His command. He is the Almighty, the All-Knowing. 27.79So, you must put your trust in Allah, because you certainly are on the clear truth. 27.80You cannot make these lifeless people listen nor make these deaf people hear the call when they have their backs turned, walking away. 27.81You won't guide these blind people out of their misguidance. You cannot make anyone listen unless they believe in Our revelations, surrendering to Allah as Muslims.

27.82When the time comes for the promise to take place against them, We will bring out for them a Creature from the Earth which will speak to them, because people didn't have strong belief in Our signs. 27.83On the Day We will gather together from every community a group of those who called Our revelations a lie, and they will be kept well organised and marched in groups 27.84until, when they come forward, Allah will ask: "Did you call My revelations a lie without understanding them with any kind of knowledge? What else were you doing?" 27.85When the promise will take place against them because of their wrongdoing, they won't be able to speak.

27.86Don't they see that We've made the night for them to rest in and the day clear to see? There are certainly signs in this for any people who believe.

27.87On the Day the Trumpet will be blown, everyone in the heavens and the earth will be horrified, except those Allah chooses. All of them will come to Him in humility. 27.88Though you know the mountains are firmly fixed right now, but you will see them floating away like clouds passing by. You see Allah's design – Who has made everything perfectly. He is Fully-Aware of everything you do.

27.89Anyone who comes with something good will have a reward better than it, and they will be safe from horror on that Day. 27.90Those who come with something bad, they will be thrown headfirst into the Fire and asked: "Should you be rewarded for anything other than what you used to do?"

27.91 O Prophet Muhammad, say: "I've been ordered to worship Allah – the Lord of this city of Makkah – Who has made it holy, and everything belongs to Him. I've been ordered to be among those who surrender to Him as Muslims 27.92 and to keep reciting the Qur'an." Anyone who accepts guidance accepts it for his own good, and whoever goes astray, say to him, O Prophet Muhammad: "I'm one of those who give warnings."

27.93 O Prophet Muhammad, say: "All praise is for Allah. He will show you His signs and you will recognise them. Your Lord isn't unaware of anything you people do."

Surah 28. Stories (al-Qasas)

Allah's name I begin with, the Most Compassionate, the Ever-Merciful

28.1 *Taa Seen Meem.*
28.2 These are the verses of the Clear Book. 28.3 O Prophet Muhammad, We will tell you truthfully some of the story of Musa and Fir'awn for any people who believe: 28.4 Fir'awn had arrogantly raised himself up in the land and divided its people into different groups, oppressing some of them and by killing their boys but keeping their women alive. He was one of the troublemakers. 28.5 We wanted to do favours to those who were oppressed in the land, and make them leaders and inheritors, 28.6 and create possibilities for them in the land, and through them show Fir'awn, Haamaan, and their armies, the very thing they were afraid of.

28.7 We inspired Musa's mother: "You may breastfeed him now, but when you fear for his safety, you should place him in the river, but don't fear or worry. We will bring him back to you and will make him one of the messengers." 28.8 Then, Fir'awn's family picked him up from the river, only for him to become an enemy and a cause of worry for them. Fir'awn, Haamaan, and their armies were mistaken.

28.9Fir'awn's wife said: "He is a coolness of the eye for my happiness and yours too. Don't kill him. He could be useful to us or we might adopt him as a son." They had no idea of who he really was.

28.10The heart of Musa's mother began to feel empty, and she almost revealed his identity if We hadn't made her heart strong so she could remain one of the true Believers in Allah's promise. 28.11She told his sister: "Follow him." So, she watched him carefully from a distance without them being aware.

28.12We didn't let him be fed by wet-nurses at first, but then his sister came and said: "Shall I show you the family of a certain house who will look after him for you and will be good to him?" 28.13So, We brought him back to his mother that her eye might be cooled in happiness, and she would be certain that Allah's promise is true, though most of them don't know this reality.

28.14When he reached his full strength and became mature enough, We gave him wisdom and knowledge. That is how We reward those who do good.

28.15One day, he entered the city at a time when its people weren't paying attention, and he found there two men fighting – one from his own group and the other from his enemy. The man from his own group cried out to him for help against the one from his enemy, and so Musa punched him and unwillingly killed him. He said: "This what I've done is from Shaytan's doing. He is an enemy who openly misleads." 28.16He prayed: "My Lord! I have done something wrong so forgive me!" and Allah did forgive him. He is the Most Forgiving, the

Ever-Merciful. ²⁸·¹⁷Musa promised: "My Lord! Because of Your favours to me, I will never support the criminals."

²⁸·¹⁸Musa, fearful, waited in the city till morning, worried what might happen, when suddenly the man who had asked him for help the previous day, cried out to him again for help. Musa criticised him: "You are definitely an obvious troublemaker!" ²⁸·¹⁹Then, when Musa tried to catch hold of the man who was their enemy, that man said: "Musa! Do you want to kill me like you killed a man yesterday? You only want to become a tyrant in the land. You don't want to be a peacemaker!"

²⁸·²⁰Then, a man came running from the far side of the city and said: "Musa! The ministers are making plans about you to kill you, so leave! I'm one of your well-wishers." ²⁸·²¹So, fearful and worried what might happen, Musa left the city. He prayed: "My Lord! Save me from these oppressive people."

²⁸·²²Then, as he made his way towards Madyan, he said to himself: "I hope my Lord will keep me guided on the straight way."

²⁸·²³When he arrived at Madyan's waters, he found there a crowd of people giving water to their animals. Away from them, he saw two women holding back their animals. He asked: "What's the matter with you two?" They replied: "We cannot give water to our animals until the shepherds take away theirs. Our father is a very old man." ²⁸·²⁴So Musa took out water for them, and then turned back to the shade and prayed: "My Lord! I am in desperate need of whatever good You will send down to me."

²⁸·²⁵Later, one of the two women came walking shyly up to him and said: "My father is calling you to reward you for taking the water out

for us." When Musa went and told him all the incidents, he replied: "Don't worry. You are now safe from those oppressive people."

$^{28.26}$One of the two women said: "Dear father! Hire him. The best person you can hire is a man who is strong and trustworthy."

$^{28.27}$He said to Musa: "I want to marry one of these two daughters of mine to you if you work for me for eight years. It will be up to you if you complete ten. However, I don't want to be hard on you. If Allah chooses, you will find me as one of the righteous people." $^{28.28}$Musa replied: "This is agreed between me and you. There shouldn't be any bad feeling against me when I've fulfilled any of the two terms. Let Allah be a Guardian over what we are saying."

$^{28.29}$Now, when Musa had fulfilled the term and was travelling with his family, he saw a fire in the side of Mount Tur. He told his family: "Stay here. I've seen a fire. Hopefully I can bring you some information from it, or a burning piece of wood so you can warm yourselves."

$^{28.30}$When he came to the fire, it was called out from a tree in the blessed ground on the right side of the valley: "Musa! I am Allah – Lord of all the worlds! $^{28.31}$Throw down your staff." When he saw it moving as if it were a snake, he turned back in retreat and didn't look back: "Musa! Come forward and don't be afraid. You are one of those who are safe. $^{28.32}$Put your hand into your shirt front, and it will come out dazzling white – free from any illness; and press your arm close to yourself to remove any fear. These are two clear proofs from your Lord to Fir'awn and his ministers. They have been a disobedient people."

$^{28.33}$Musa said: "My Lord! I've killed one of their men, and now I fear they'll kill me. $^{28.34}$As for my brother Haroon, he is more eloquent than

I am, so send him with me as a helper to support me, because I fear they will accuse me of being a liar." ²⁸·³⁵Allah replied: "We will make you strong through your brother and give you both such authority that they won't be able to harm you. With Our signs, you and those who follow you will win."

²⁸·³⁶**When Musa came** and showed Fir'awn and his people **Our clear signs,** they said: "This is only magic that is made up. We've never heard a message like this among our ancestors." ²⁸·³⁷Musa replied: "My Lord knows best who has brought guidance from Him and whose end in the Hereafter will be the best. The wrongdoers will never succeed." ²⁸·³⁸Fir'awn said: "Ministers! I don't know of any god for you other than me. So, Haamaan, light me a fire to bake bricks on clay and build me a high tower so I can climb up to Musa's God, even though I think he is telling lies."

²⁸·³⁹He and his armies behaved arrogantly on earth without having any right do so, thinking they wouldn't be brought back to Us. ²⁸·⁴⁰Then We seized him and his armies, and threw them into the sea. So, take a look at what was the end result of the wrongdoers. ²⁸·⁴¹We made them take the lead in inviting towards the Fire. On Judgement Day they won't be given any help. ²⁸·⁴²We made a curse follow after them in this world, and on Judgement Day they will be among those made ugly and damned.

²⁸·⁴³**After We had destroyed the earlier generations** of wrongdoers, **We gave Musa the Book** – as clear proofs for people, as well as guidance and mercy, so that they might remind themselves.

²⁸·⁴⁴O Prophet Muhammad, **you were neither on the western side of** the mountain **nor among the witnesses when We told Musa of his mission.** ²⁸·⁴⁵**However, We raised up many generations** after him and

many long ages passed over them. You weren't living among the people of Madyan, reciting Our revelations to them, but it is We Who have been sending out the messengers. [28.46]You weren't on the side of Mount Tur when We called out to Musa, yet what you know is a mercy from your Lord for you to give warnings to a people no warner had come to before you, so that they might remind themselves. [28.47]If they suffered a disaster because of the bad things they themselves had done, they shouldn't be saying: "Our Lord! Why didn't you send us a messenger so we could have followed your revelations and become Believers?"

[28.48]Now that the truth has come to them specifically from Us, they ask: "Why hasn't he been given something like Musa was given?" What? Didn't they disbelieve in what Musa was previously given? They claimed: "Both the Qur'an and the Tawrah are magic, supporting each other." adding: "We reject them all." [28.49]O Prophet Muhammad, say: "Then bring some other book like it from Allah, one which is a better guide than these two. I will follow it, if you are telling the truth." [28.50]However, if they cannot respond to you then you should know that they're only following their own desires. Who could be further astray than someone who follows his own desire that is not connected to any guidance from Allah? Allah doesn't let unjust people succeed.

[28.51]We kept sending them Our words so that they might remind themselves. [28.52]Those people We gave the Book before this, they believe in this Qur'an too. [28.53]When it is recited to them, they declare: "We believe in it because it is the truth from our Lord. We have been surrendering to Allah as Muslims even before this." [28.54]It is they who will be given their reward twice because of their patience, because they respond to anything bad done to them with good, and they donate from what We've given them. [28.55]When they hear foolishness, they turn away from it and say: "We are responsible for our actions and you for yours. Peace be upon you. We don't follow ignorant people."

28.56You won't be able to guide everyone you like, but Allah can guide anyone He chooses. He knows best those who follow guidance.

28.57They say: "We will be snatched away from our land if we followed guidance with you." They should think: haven't We given them control of a safe, holy place, to which resources of all kinds are brought as special gifts from Us? However, most of them don't even realise nor appreciate. 28.58How many towns have We destroyed that became arrogant because of their luxury lifestyle! Here are their mansions that have hardly been lived in after them. We are the real inheritors. 28.59O Prophet Muhammad, your Lord doesn't destroy any places until after He has sent to their main city a messenger reciting Our verses to them. We never destroy any places unless its people become wrongdoers.

28.60Anything you've been given is only the enjoyment of this life and its luxuries, whereas what is with Allah is best and lasts forever. Won't you even think? 28.61Can they be the same: someone who finds fulfilled the good promise of Paradise We have made him and someone We've allowed the good enjoyment of this life but will be among those brought forward for punishment on Judgement Day?

28.62One Day Allah will call out to them and ask: "Where are those you used to claim were My partner-gods?" 28.63Those against whom the word proved true will say: "Our Lord! These are the ones we led astray. We misled them as we ourselves had gone astray. We have left them for You. It wasn't us they used to worship." 28.64It will be said: "Pray to your partner-gods." They will pray to them who won't even respond to them, and they will see the punishment. Oh! If only they had accepted guidance!

28.65 On that Day, Allah will call out to them and ask: "How did you respond to the messengers?" 28.66 On that Day, all the details will be hidden from their sight and they won't even be able to ask each other any questions.

28.67 As for someone who repents, believes, and does good, he will certainly be among those who are successful.

28.68 Your Lord creates and chooses anything He wants, but they don't have any choice or authority in that. Glory be to Allah! He is much higher than the partner-gods they make with Him. 28.69 Your Lord knows everything their hearts hide or show. 28.70 He is Allah. There is no god except Him. All praise is for Him in this world and the next. All authority is His, and it is Him you will all be taken back to.

28.71 O Prophet Muhammad, ask: "Have you people ever thought if Allah was to make the night permanent over you – until Judgement Day, which god is there other than Allah that could bring you any light? Won't you even listen?" 28.72 Ask: "What do you think? If Allah was to make the day permanent over you – until Judgement Day, which god is there other than Allah that could bring you a night in which you could rest? Can't you even see?" 28.73 It is out of His mercy that He has made for you the night and day so you can live comfortably in it, gain some of Allah's grace, and so that you might become thankful.

28.74 On that Day, He will call out to them and ask: "Where are those you used to claim to be My partner-gods?" 28.75 We will bring out a witness from each community and demand from the polytheists:

"Bring me your proof!" They will find out that the truth is only Allah's, and that the idols and lies they made up have abandoned them.

28.76Qarun (Korah) was from among Musa's people, yet he oppressed them. We had given him so many treasures that even their keys were a heavy burden for a group of strong men to carry. When his people advised him: "Don't be snobbish. Allah doesn't like those who are snobbish, 28.77but, with everything Allah has given you, try to gain the Home of the Hereafter, not forgetting your share of this world. Be generous as Allah has been generous to you. Don't try to make trouble in the land because Allah doesn't like troublemakers." 28.78He replied: "I've been given this wealth only because of certain skills I have." Didn't he know that Allah had destroyed, before him, many generations more powerful than him and greater in gathering up wealth? Does he think those criminals won't be held responsible for their crimes?

28.79He came out to his people in his splendour. Those who wanted this worldly life cried: "Oh! If only we had something like what Qarun has been given! He is certainly a man of great fortune." 28.80But those who had been given true knowledge said to them: "You are damned! Allah's reward is best for someone who believes and does good, but only those who have patience will be given that." 28.81Then, along with his mansion, We made the ground swallow him up. He had no group to help him besides Allah nor could he even save himself.

28.82The next day, those who had wanted his position the day before began to say: "Ah! It's true that it is Allah Who can increase or restrict wealth for any of His servants He chooses. If Allah hadn't done us favours, He could have made the ground swallow us up too. Ah! It is true that disbelievers never succeed."

²⁸·⁸³That Home of the Hereafter, We give it to those who look for neither superiority in this world nor trouble. The best end in the Hereafter will be for those who are mindful of Allah. ²⁸·⁸⁴Anyone who comes with something good will receive something better than it, but anyone who comes with something bad should know that those who did bad things will be punished only for what they used to do.

²⁸·⁸⁵O Prophet Muhammad, Allah – Who has made you teach and follow the Qur'an, will certainly bring you back home to Makkah. Say: "My Lord knows best who brings guidance and who is clearly astray." ²⁸·⁸⁶You – Community of Prophet Muhammad – were never expecting to be given this Book but it has come as a special mercy from your Lord. Therefore, you should never support the disbelievers in bad things. ²⁸·⁸⁷Never let anything block you from following Allah's commands after they've been revealed to you. You should keep inviting people to your Lord and never be a polytheist. ²⁸·⁸⁸Never pray to any other god along with Allah. There is no god except Him. Everything will perish except He Himself. All authority is His, and it is Him you will all be taken back to.

Surah 29. Spider (al-'Ankaboot)

Allah's name I begin with, the Most Compassionate, the Ever-Merciful

²⁹·¹*Alif Laam Meem.*

²⁹·²Do people think that once they've said: "We believe," they'll be left alone and won't be tested? ²⁹·³We already tested those before them. Allah will certainly identify the truthful and expose the liars. ²⁹·⁴Do those who do bad things think they can beat Us? How terrible are the decisions they make!

29.5Those who've been expecting to meet with Allah should know that Allah's time to reward or punish is certainly coming. He is the All-Hearing, the All-Knowing. 29.6Anyone who strives hard does it for his own good, because Allah is certainly Free of all Needs from everyone.

29.7Those who believe and do good, We will certainly remove their sins from them and give them the best reward for what they used to do.

29.8We have ordered every person to be kind to his parents, but if they persuade you to make partner-gods with Me of things you don't know anything about then don't obey them in that. You will all come back to Me, and then I will tell you about everything you used to do. 29.9Those who believe and do good, We will certainly enter them into the company of righteous people.

29.10Some people, when they declare: "We believe in Allah," but suffer abuse in Allah's cause, they mistake this harassment by people as if it were a punishment from Allah. However, O Prophet Muhammad, if any help comes from your Lord, they will certainly start saying: "We have always been with you." Doesn't Allah know best what is in everyone's hearts? 29.11Allah will definitely identify the Believers and expose the hypocrites.

29.12The disbelievers say to the Believers: "Follow our way and we will carry the burden of your sins," but they cannot carry any of their sins at all. They are certainly liars. 29.13They will carry their own burdens of sins, as well as more burdens along with their own. They will certainly be asked on Judgement Day about the lies they used to make.

29.14We sent Nuh to his people and he lived among them for nine hundred and fifty years, until the flood took them away because they continued to do wrong. ²⁹·¹⁵We saved him and the companions of the Ark, and We made the Ark a sign for everyone.

²⁹·¹⁶We also sent Ibrahim. Remember when he said to his people: "You must worship Allah and be mindful of Him. That is best for you if you only knew. ²⁹·¹⁷You are worshipping idols besides Allah, and making up lies too. Those you worship besides Allah, they don't have the power to give you anything at all, so you must try to gain wealth from Allah, worship only Him, and be thankful to Him. It is Him you will all be taken back to. ²⁹·¹⁸If you call the truth a lie then it is no surprise because so did many communities before you. The messenger's duty is only to deliver the message clearly."

²⁹·¹⁹Don't they think about how Allah starts creating and then repeats it? All that is easy for Allah. ²⁹·²⁰Say: "You should travel through the earth and take a look at how Allah started the creation. Then, He brings out the next creation. Allah is Most Capable of anything."

²⁹·²¹He punishes or shows mercy to anyone He chooses, and it is Him you will all be taken back to. ²⁹·²²You cannot escape – neither in the earth nor in the sky – and you don't have any protector or helper besides Allah. ²⁹·²³Those who disbelieve in Allah's revelations and the meeting with Him, it is they who lose hope in My mercy, and it is they who will suffer a painful punishment.

²⁹·²⁴The only response from Ibrahim's people was for them to say: "Kill him!" or "Burn him!" but Allah saved him from the fire. There are certainly signs in this for any people who believe. ²⁹·²⁵Ibrahim warned: "Instead of Allah, you had started worshipping idols only for the sake of the friendship you have with each other in this life, but on Judgement Day you will reject and curse each other; your home will be the Fire and you won't have any helpers there."

29.26However, Lut believed him for his sake. He said: "I'm going to migrate to my Lord. Only He is the Almighty, the All-Wise."

29.27To Ibrahim, We gave Is'haq and Ya'qub, placed prophethood and the Book among his descendants, and gave him his reward in this world. In the Hereafter he will be in the company of righteous people.

29.28We also sent Lut. Remember when he said to his people: "You are doing something so shameful that no one in the world has ever done before you. 29.29Are you lustfully approaching men, robbing and kidnapping travellers, and doing immoral things in the places where you meet?" But the only response from his people was for them to say: "Bring us Allah's punishment, if you are telling the truth!" 29.30He prayed: "My Lord! Help me against these troublemaking people."

29.31When Our messenger-angels came to Ibrahim with some good news, they also said: "We are going to destroy the people of this town. Its people have been wrongdoers." 29.32Ibrahim said: "But Lut lives there!" They said: "We know best who lives there. We will certainly save him and his family, but not his wife: she is one of those who will stay behind."

29.33When Our messenger-angels came to Lut, he felt sorry and powerless for them, but the angels said: "Don't be afraid nor worry. We will save you and your family, but not your wife: she is one of those who will stay behind. 29.34We will bring down on the people of this town a punishment from the sky because they have continued to be disobedient." 29.35We've left some of that town as a clear sign for any people who think.

²⁹·³⁶To the people of **Madyan**, We sent **their brother Shu'ayb, who said:** "My people! Worship Allah, expect the coming of the Last Day, and don't go around making trouble in the land." ²⁹·³⁷But they accused him of being a liar. So the earthquake shook them, and in the morning they lay dead in their homes facing down!

²⁹·³⁸We also destroyed the 'Ad and the Thamud. Some of their homes are now visible to you. Shaytan made the bad things they were doing seem attractive to them, and blocked them from the right way, though they could see the truth clearly.

²⁹·³⁹We also destroyed Qarun, Fir'awn, and Haamaan. Musa came to them with clear signs, but they behaved arrogantly in the world, yet even they could not escape Us.

²⁹·⁴⁰We punished each of them for their crime: We sent a violent hurricane of stones upon some of them, the Mighty Blast seized some of them, We made the earth swallow up some of them, and We drowned some of them. Allah would never harm them but rather they used to harm themselves.

²⁹·⁴¹The example of those who take protectors other than Allah is that of the spider which builds a house of cobweb – the weakest of houses is the spider's house – if they only knew! ²⁹·⁴²Allah knows even the most useless thing they pray to besides Him. Only He is the Almighty, the All-Wise. ²⁹·⁴³These are the examples We give to people, but only those with knowledge can truly understand them. ²⁹·⁴⁴Allah created the heavens and the earth for a real purpose. There is certainly a sign in this for the Believers.

[PART 21]

²⁹·⁴⁵O Prophet Muhammad, **you should recite from the Book anything that is revealed to you, and establish the ritual prayers. Ritual prayers should prevent shamefulness and** from doing **anything wrong. Remembering Allah is certainly the greatest. Allah knows everything you** people **do.**

²⁹·⁴⁶You Believers should **argue with the People of the Book only in the best manner, except with the wrongdoers among them. Say: "We believe in what has been sent down to us and in what was sent down to you too; our God and your God is one** and the same; **we will remain surrendered to Him as Muslims."**

²⁹·⁴⁷O Prophet Muhammad, **in this way We revealed the Book to you. Those We previously gave the Book to, they believe in this Book too, and so do some of these** Arabs. **Only disbelievers reject Our revelations.** ²⁹·⁴⁸O Prophet Muhammad, **you didn't recite any book before this, nor did you write it with your own hand. If that was the case, the supporters of falsehood would certainly have had reasons to doubt.** ²⁹·⁴⁹**The truth is, here are the clear verses in the hearts of those given** the right **knowledge. Only wrongdoers reject Our revelations.**

²⁹·⁵⁰**They ask: "Why weren't signs sent down to him from his Lord?" Reply: "The signs come only from Allah, and I only give clear warnings."** ²⁹·⁵¹ O Prophet Muhammad, **isn't it enough for them that We have revealed to you the Book that is recited to them? There is certainly mercy in it as well as a reminder for any people who believe.** ²⁹·⁵²O Prophet Muhammad, say: **"Allah is enough as a Witness between me and you all. He knows everything in the heavens and the earth. Those who believe in falsehood and disbelieve in Allah, it is really they who are the losers."**

²⁹·⁵³They want you to bring the punishment sooner. If it hadn't been for a term that is fixed, the punishment would have already come to them. However, it will come upon them all of a sudden when they least expect it. ²⁹·⁵⁴They want you to bring the punishment sooner, but they should know that Hell will completely surround the disbelievers, ²⁹·⁵⁵on the Day when the punishment will cover them from above them and from right under their legs, and all around them, and Allah will say: "Now taste the bad things you used to do!"

²⁹·⁵⁶My Believing servants! My earth is spacious, so worship only Me. ²⁹·⁵⁷Everyone is going to taste death, and then it is Us you will all be brought back to. ²⁹·⁵⁸Those who believe and do good, We will certainly let them stay in Paradise, in high mansions – that have rivers flowing beneath them, where they will remain forever. What an excellent reward for those who do good, ²⁹·⁵⁹who have patience, and put their trust only in their Lord! ²⁹·⁶⁰There are many creatures that don't carry their own food. It is Allah Who feeds them and you too. He is the All-Hearing, the All-Knowing.

²⁹·⁶¹If you ask the disbelievers: "Who created the heavens and the earth, and made the sun and the moon obey a system?" they will certainly reply: "Allah." Then how are they being misled! ²⁹·⁶²It is Allah Who can increase or restrict wealth for any of His servants He chooses. Allah knows everything perfectly well.

²⁹·⁶³If you ask them: "Who sends down from the sky water with which He gives life to the earth after it had become dead?" they will certainly reply: "Allah." Say: "All praise is for Allah." The truth is, most of them don't even think. ²⁹·⁶⁴This life is some kind of amusement and just games, but the Home of the Hereafter is the only true life. If they only knew!

29.65 When they board a ship, they pray to Allah in sincere devotion to Him to keep them safe, but when He brings them safely back to land, that is when they start making partner-gods with Him, 29.66 being unthankful for what We've given them, and to enjoy themselves. They will very soon come to know the end result.

29.67 Don't they see that We've made the Sacred Masjid a holy place that is safe, whereas all around them people are being snatched away? Will they still believe in falsehood and disregard Allah's favour? 29.68 Who could be more unjust than someone who makes lies about Allah or calls the truth a lie when it comes to him! Isn't the place for disbelievers in Hell?

29.69 However, We will certainly guide on Our ways those who strive hard in Our cause. Allah is certainly with those who do good.

Surah 30. Romans (ar-Ruum)

Allah's name I begin with, the Most Compassionate, the Ever-Merciful

30.1 Alif Laam Meem.
30.2 The Romans were defeated 30.3 in a land nearby, but they will win, after this defeat of theirs, 30.4 within a few years. The matter is in Allah's control, both before and afterwards too. On that day, the Believers will rejoice 30.5 at Allah's help. He helps anyone He chooses, and He is the Almighty, the Ever-Merciful. 30.6 It is Allah's promise and He will never break it, but most people don't realise. 30.7 They only know the outer parts of this life but are unaware of the Hereafter.

30.8 Don't they think deeply in their own minds that Allah created the heavens and the earth and everything in between them for a real purpose and for a fixed term? However, many people still disbelieve in the meeting with their Lord. ³⁰·⁹Don't they travel through the earth and take a look at what was the end result of those before them? They were more powerful than these people, they cultivated the land and built upon it more than these people did, and their messengers also came to them with clear signs. Allah would never harm them but rather they used to harm themselves. ³⁰·¹⁰Eventually, the worst end came to the bad people because they called Allah's revelations a lie and used to make fun of them.

³⁰·¹¹It is Allah Who starts creating and then repeats it, and eventually it is Him you will all be taken back to. ³⁰·¹²On the Day the Final Hour will take place, the criminals will lose all hope. ³⁰·¹³They won't have any intercessors among the partner-gods they made with Allah, and so they will reject them.

³⁰·¹⁴On the Day the Final Hour will take place, that is the Day people will break up with each other: ³⁰·¹⁵those who believed and did good, they will be made happy in a meadow of Paradise, ³⁰·¹⁶whereas those who disbelieved and called Our revelations and the meeting in the Hereafter a lie, it is they who will be brought forward to the punishment.

³⁰·¹⁷So, say: "Glory be to Allah!" when you enter evening and morning. ³⁰·¹⁸All praise is for Him in the heavens and the earth, and at late afternoon and when you enter early afternoon.

³⁰·¹⁹He brings out the living from the dead and the dead from the living, and gives life to the earth after it had become dead. In this way you people will be brought out again from your graves.

³⁰·²⁰Among His signs is that He created you from dust, and now you are humans spreading out everywhere.

30.21 Another one of His signs is that He has created for you spouses from among yourselves so you can have a comfortable living with them, and He placed love and mercy between you. There are certainly signs in this for any people who think deeply.

30.22 Another one of His signs is the creation of the heavens and the earth, and the diversity of your languages and colours. There are certainly signs in this for those who have the right knowledge.

30.23 Another one of His signs is your going to sleep during the night and in the day, and your trying to gain some of His grace. There are certainly signs in this for any people who listen.

30.24 Another one of His signs is also that He shows you the lightning – striking fear and giving hope, and He sends down from the sky water with which He gives life to the earth after it had become dead. There are certainly signs in this for any people who think.

30.25 Another one of His signs is that the sky and the earth exist by His command. Eventually, He will call you out from the earth only once, and you will come out immediately. 30.26 Everyone in the heavens and the earth belongs to Him. Everything is devoted to Him. 30.27 He is the one Who starts creating and then repeats it, and it is most easy for Him. The best attribute in the heavens and the earth belongs to Him. He is the Almighty, the All-Wise.

30.28 He gives you examples from your own lives. From among your slaves, are any of them partners in the wealth We have given you so you can all be equal, fearing them as you fear each other? In this way We explain the signs in detail for any people who think. 30.29 The truth is, the wrongdoers, out of ignorance, will follow only their own desires. So, who can guide those Allah calls astray? They won't have any helpers.

30.30So, O Prophet Muhammad, you should put your identity truly in the religion of Islam – Allah's natural way, on which He has created all people. There is no changing Allah's creation. This is the correct religion but most people don't realise.

30.31You people must turn to Him, be mindful of Him, establish the ritual prayers, and never be polytheists 30.32– who divided their religion and split up into groups, each group happy with what it has.

30.33When any harm comes to people, they cry out to their Lord, turning to Him for help, but when He gives them a taste of some special mercy from Himself, that is when a group of them starts making partner-gods with their Lord, 30.34being unthankful for what We've given them. You may enjoy yourselves for now because you will very soon come to know the end result. 30.35Have We sent down to them any permission that talks about what they can make partner-gods with Allah?

30.36When We give people a taste of some special mercy, they rejoice in it, but when they suffer a disaster because of the bad things they've done, that is when they lose hope.

30.37Don't they see that it is Allah Who can increase or restrict wealth for anyone He chooses? There are certainly signs in this for any people who believe. 30.38So, you must give close relatives their rights, as well as to the needy, and to travellers. This is best for those who want Allah's good pleasure. It is really they who will be successful. 30.39Anything you give out on usury so it gains value among other people's wealth won't have any increase in profit in the sight of Allah.

However, what you give as zakah – desiring Allah's good pleasure, it is really they who multiply their reward.

[30.40] Allah is the one Who created you all, then gives you wealth, will give you death and then life again. Can any of your partner-gods do anything at all like that? Glory be to Him! He is much higher than the partner-gods they make with Him.

[30.41] On land and sea, corruption only spreads because of the bad things people do, and so Allah will give them a taste of some of the bad they did so that they might turn back. [30.42] O Prophet Muhammad, say: "Travel through the earth and take a look at what was the end result of those before you. Most of them were polytheists."

[30.43] O Prophet Muhammad, you should put your identity in the correct religion of Islam before comes from Allah the Day that nothing can turn away. On that Day people will split up from each other. [30.44] The disbelievers will suffer because of their disbelief, whereas those who do good are preparing places of rest in Paradise for themselves, [30.45] so that Allah can reward from His grace those who believe and do good. He doesn't like disbelievers.

[30.46] Another one of His signs is that He sends the winds: to give good news, so He can give you a taste of His mercy, so ships can sail by His command, so you can try to gain some of His grace, and so that you might become thankful.

[30.47] O Prophet Muhammad, before you, We have already sent many messengers to their communities, who came to them with clear signs, then We punished the criminals. It was Our duty to help the Believers.

30.48 Allah is the one Who sends the winds, and they stir up the clouds. Then He spreads them out in the sky as He chooses, and then brings the pieces together out of which you see drops falling. When He lets the water reach any of His servants He chooses, that is when they become happy, 30.49 though they were clearly losing hope right before it was sent down to them. 30.50 So, just take a look at the effects of Allah's mercy; how He gives life to the earth after it had become dead. It is that Allah – Who will bring the dead back to life. He is Most Capable of anything. 30.51 If We sent a hot wind from which they saw their crops turn yellow, they would still continue to disbelieve.

30.52 So, you cannot make these lifeless people listen nor make these deaf people hear the call when they have their backs turned, walking away. 30.53 You won't guide these blind people out of their misguidance. You cannot make anyone listen unless they believe in Our revelations, surrendering to Allah as Muslims.

30.54 Allah is the one Who created you in weakness, then replaced weakness with strength, then replaced strength with weakness again and old age. He creates whatever He wants. He is the All-Knowing, the Most Capable.

30.55 On the Day when the Final Hour will take place, the criminals will swear they lived no more than a moment in their graves. This is how they used to be misled. 30.56 However, those given knowledge and faith will say: "According to Allah's record, you stayed until Resurrection Day – and now this is that Resurrection Day – but you hadn't realised." 30.57 So, on that Day no excuse of the wrongdoers will benefit them nor will they be allowed to repent.

30.58 In this Qur'an, We have given every kind of example to people. However, O Prophet Muhammad, if you bring them any sign, the disbelievers would certainly say: "You prophets are fake." ³⁰·⁵⁹This is how Allah seals up the hearts of those who don't know the obvious truth. ³⁰·⁶⁰So have patience because Allah's promise is true, and don't let the doubters discourage you.

Surah 31. Luqman

Allah's name I begin with, the Most Compassionate, the Ever-Merciful

³¹·¹*Alif Laam Meem.*
³¹·²These are the verses of the Book Full of Wisdom, ³¹·³a guidance, as well as a mercy for those who do good ³¹·⁴– who establish the ritual prayers, pay zakah, and strongly believe in the Hereafter. ³¹·⁵It is they who are on guidance from their Lord and it is really they who will be successful.

³¹·⁶Out of ignorance, some people buy distracting things to lead people away from Allah's cause and to make fun of it. It is they who will suffer a humiliating punishment. ³¹·⁷When Our revelations are recited to such a person, he turns away arrogantly as if he hadn't even heard them, as if there was deafness in both his ears. So, give him warnings of a painful punishment.

³¹·⁸Those who believe and do good will have Gardens of Delight, ³¹·⁹where they will remain forever. Allah's promise is true. He is the Almighty, the All-Wise.

³¹·¹⁰He created the heavens without any pillars that you can see. He fixed firm mountains in the earth in case it shakes under you, and has scattered across it all kinds of animals. We send down water from the sky, and grow on earth all kinds of wonderful things. ³¹·¹¹This is Allah's

creation. Now show me what any others besides Him have created. The truth is, the wrongdoers are clearly astray.

[31.12]We gave wisdom to Luqman saying: "Be thankful to Allah. Anyone who gives thanks does so for his own good, and anyone who doesn't give thanks should know that Allah is Free of all Needs, Most Praiseworthy." [31.13]Remember when Luqman told his son while giving him advice: "My dear son! Never make partner-gods with Allah. Polytheism is a terrible crime."

[31.14]We've ordered every person to: "Be thankful to Me and to your parents," – his mother carried him in pregnancy with pain upon pain, and his weaning took two years. The final return will be to Me. [31.15]If they force you to make partner-gods with Me of things you don't know anything about, you mustn't obey them in that, yet even then you must stay with them in this life with kindness. You must follow the way of those who turn to Me. Eventually, you will all come back to Me and then I will tell you about everything you used to do.

[31.16]Luqman said: "My dear son! If there was anything the weight of a mustard-seed, and that too inside a rock or anywhere in the heavens or in the earth, Allah can bring it out. Allah knows all details, is Fully-Aware. [31.17]My dear son! You must establish the ritual prayers, command what is right, forbid what is wrong, and have patience over everything you suffer. This is a sign of strong will. [31.18]Don't turn your face away in pride from people nor walk on the earth with arrogance. Allah doesn't like anyone who is arrogant, showoff. [31.19]You must keep your pace moderate and your voice low. The sound most disliked is the braying of donkeys."

[31.20]Don't you people see that Allah has made everything in the heavens and the earth obey a system for you, and has showered on you His favours, both open and secret? Some people dispute about Allah when they don't have any knowledge, guidance, or a Book that enlightens. ³¹·²¹When they are told: "You must follow what Allah has sent down," they reply: "Never! We will follow what we saw our forefathers doing." What? Even if it is Shaytan inviting them to the suffering of the Blazing Fire? ³¹·²²Whoever gives up his identity to Allah as Muslim and does good has actually grabbed on to the most trusty, lasting handhold. The end result of all matters is with Allah.

³¹·²³O Prophet Muhammad, **if anyone disbelieves, you mustn't let their disbelief upset you.** They will come back to Us and then We will tell them about the things they did. Allah knows the secrets of the hearts perfectly well. ³¹·²⁴**We will let them enjoy themselves for a little while** in this world **but We will eventually force them towards the severe punishment.**

³¹·²⁵O Prophet Muhammad, **if you ask them: "Who created the heavens and the earth?" they will certainly reply: "Allah."** You should say: "All praise is for Allah," but most of them don't know. ³¹·²⁶Everything in the heavens and the earth belongs to Allah. Only He is Free of all Needs, the Most Praiseworthy. ³¹·²⁷If all the trees on earth were pens, and the ocean – with seven more oceans coming behind it adding to it – were ink, Allah's words would never come to an end. Allah is Almighty, All-Wise.

³¹·²⁸**Creating you** people **or bringing you back to life is as** easy for Him as **a single person. Allah is All-Hearing, Ever-Watchful.** ³¹·²⁹**Don't you see that it is Allah Who makes the night enter into the day and the day enter into the night?** He has made the sun and the moon obey a system – each one is running its course until a fixed term. Allah is Fully-Aware of everything you do. ³¹·³⁰That is because only Allah is the

truth, and anything they pray to besides Him is false. Only Allah is the Most High, the Great.

31.31Don't you see that the ships sail through the ocean with Allah's favour so that He can show you some of His signs? There are certainly signs in this for anyone who is very patient, very thankful. 31.32When a mountain-like wave sweeps over them, they pray to Allah in sincere devotion to Him to keep them safe, but when He brings them safely back to land, only a few of them continue to remain moderate. Only an unthankful traitor would reject Our signs.

31.33People! Be mindful of your Lord, and fear the Day when no parent will be able to help their child nor a child help its parent in any way at all. Allah's promise is true, so never let this life trick you nor let Shaytan – the Big Trickster fool you about Allah.

31.34Only Allah has knowledge of the Final Hour. He sends down gentle rain and knows what is in the wombs. No one can guess what they'll be doing tomorrow nor in which land they'll die. Allah is All-Knowing, Fully-Aware.

Surah 32. Prostration (as-Sajdah)

Allah's name I begin with, the Most Compassionate, the Ever-Merciful

32.1*Alif Laam Meem.*
32.2This is the revelation of the Book in which there is no doubt, from Allah – the Lord of all the Worlds. 32.3Are they claiming: "He (- Prophet Muhammad) made it up."? Never! O Prophet Muhammad, it is the truth from your Lord, for you to give warnings to a people no warner had come to before you, so that they might follow guidance.

32.4 Allah is the one Who created the heavens and the earth and everything in between them in six stages, and then established His authority on the Throne. You don't have any protector or helper besides Him. So, won't you remind yourselves? **32.5**He governs every affair from the heavens to the earth. Eventually, every affair will go up to Him on a Day whose timespan will be a thousand years according to your counting.

32.6 Only He is the Knower of the unseen secrets and the visible, the Almighty, the Ever-Merciful, **32.7**Who made wonderful everything He created. He started creating the first human from clay, **32.8**and then made his descendants from an extract of a humble fluid. **32.9**Finally, He gave him proportion, and breathed into him of His spirit. He gave you hearing, sight, and intelligence, yet you hardly give any thanks.

32.10 The disbelievers ask: "What? Once we have decomposed in the earth, will we be made into a new creation?" The truth is, they are disbelieving in the meeting with their Lord. **32.11**O Prophet Muhammad, say: "The Angel of Death that has been put in charge of you will take your souls away. Eventually, it is your Lord you will be taken back to."

32.12 If only you could see when the criminals will bow their heads in front of their Lord, saying: "Our Lord! We have seen and heard. So, send us back to the world and we will do good, because we now strongly believe." **32.13**If We had wanted, We could have given everyone their guidance, but the statement from Me will prove true: "I will certainly fill up Hell with jinns and humans, all together." **32.14**Now taste the punishment because you forgot the meeting of this Day of yours. We will ignore you as well. Now taste the everlasting punishment for the bad things you used to do.

³²·¹⁵When they are reminded of Our revelations, only those people truly believe in them who fall down prostrating, glorify the praises of their Lord, and don't show any arrogance. *<Prostration Point 9>* ³²·¹⁶Their limbs stay away from their beds, busy praying to their Lord in fear and hope, and donating from what We've given them. ³²·¹⁷No one can imagine what joys are kept hidden for them as a reward for the good things they used to do. ³²·¹⁸Can a Believer be compared to someone who is disobedient? They cannot be the same.

³²·¹⁹Those who believe and do good, they will have the Gardens of Residence as a place to stay for the good things they used to do, ³²·²⁰whereas the home of disobedient people will be the Fire. Each time they try to escape from there, they will be forced back into it and told: "Taste the punishment of the Fire you used to call a lie!" ³²·²¹Before the big punishment in the Hereafter, We will definitely make them taste the small punishment in this life so that they might turn back to Us. ³²·²²Who could be more unjust than someone who is reminded of his Lord's revelations yet turns away from them! We will punish the criminals.

³²·²³O Prophet Muhammad, We already gave Musa the Book and made it a guidance for the Descendants of Ya'qub, so you shouldn't be in any doubt about the meeting with Allah. ³²·²⁴We made some of them leaders, guiding by Our command, as long as they had patience. They strongly believed in Our revelations. ³²·²⁵Only your Lord will judge between them on Judgement Day about the disagreements they used to have.

³²·²⁶Isn't it clear to them how many generations We have destroyed from before them in whose homes they now walk about? There are certainly signs in this. Won't they even listen? ³²·²⁷Don't they see that

to lifeless land We drive water with which We bring out crops from which their cattle can eat and so can they? Don't they see?

32.28They ask: "When will this Decision Day take place, if you are telling the truth?" 32.29Reply: "Their becoming Believers on Decision Day won't benefit the disbelievers and they won't be given any chances." 32.30So, you should turn away from them and wait, because they are waiting too.

Surah 33. Combined Forces (al-Ahzaab)

Allah's name I begin with, the Most Compassionate, the Ever-Merciful

33.1O Prophet, you should remain mindful of Allah and never obey the disbelievers and the hypocrites. Allah is always All-Knowing, All-Wise. 33.2Follow what is revealed to you from your Lord. Allah is always Fully-Aware of everything you people do. 33.3Put your trust in Allah. He is enough as a Guardian.

33.4Allah hasn't placed two hearts in anyone's body. Your wives you divorce by comparing them to your mothers' backs, He hasn't made them your actual mothers, nor has He made your adopted children your actual children. These are merely what you say from your mouths. It is Allah Who says the truth and only He guides to the Straight Way. 33.5You must call your adopted children after their actual fathers; it is more fair in the sight of Allah. However, if you don't know who their fathers are then they are, after all, your brothers-in-faith or your friends. There is nothing wrong if you make a mistake in this, but only judged by what your hearts intend. Allah is always Most Forgiving, Ever-Merciful.

³³·⁶**The Prophet** Muhammad **is closer** and superior **to the Believers than their own selves, and his wives are their mothers. According to Allah's Book, blood relatives are closer and superior** for inheritance **than other Believers and migrants, unless you want to do your friends a favour. All this is written in the Book.**

³³·⁷Remember **when Allah took a strong promise from the prophets – from you,** O Prophet Muhammad, **and also from Nuh, Ibrahim, Musa, and Isa ibn Maryam – We took a firm promise from them all** ³³·⁸**so that Allah can ask the truthful people about their truth. He has prepared a painful punishment for the disbelievers.**

³³·⁹**Believers! Remember Allah's favour to you when many armies came to** attack **you, and We sent a wind against them as well as forces of angels you couldn't see. Allah is always Ever-Watchful of everything you do.** ³³·¹⁰**When they came to** attack **you from above and below you, and when eyes lost focus and hearts jumped into throats, and** the **hypocrites among you began having bad thoughts about Allah,** ³³·¹¹**it was there and then that the Believers were tested and deeply shaken.**

³³·¹²Remember **when the hypocrites, and those with sickness in their hearts, said: "Allah and His Messenger have promised us nothing but lies!"** ³³·¹³**and when some of them said: "People of Yathrib! You won't be able to stand** the **attack, so go back," and a group of them asked the Prophet's permission, saying: "Our homes are exposed," though they weren't. They only wanted to run away.** ³³·¹⁴**If the city had been attacked from all sides and these hypocrites were asked to rebel, they would have done it with hardly any hesitation.**

³³·¹⁵**They had already made a treaty with Allah previously that they wouldn't turn their backs** and **run. The promise made to Allah will be**

asked about. ³³·¹⁶O Prophet Muhammad, say: "Running away will never benefit you. If you do manage to run away from death or from fighting, you'll only be able to enjoy yourselves for a short while." ³³·¹⁷Say: "Who is it that can protect you from Allah if He wanted harm for you or mercy?" They won't find any protector or helper for themselves besides Allah.

³³·¹⁸Allah certainly knows those of you who block people from fighting and those who tell their brothers: "Come over to us." They themselves don't participate much in battle. ³³·¹⁹They're being stingy to you Muslims. O Prophet Muhammad, when danger comes, you see them looking to you with their eyes spinning like someone about to faint because of death. Then, once the danger is over, they abuse you with sharp tongues, being greedy to gain the spoils of war. It is they who don't really believe and so Allah lets their actions be wasted. This is always easy for Allah.

³³·²⁰They think the combined forces of the enemy haven't left. If the combined forces were to come again, these people would wish they were wandering in the deserts among the bedouins and asking for news about you. However, if they were among you, they would hardly take part in fighting the enemy.

³³·²¹You certainly have an excellent role model to follow in Allah's Messenger Muhammad, especially for someone who has hope in Allah and the Last Day, and remembers Allah a lot.

³³·²²When the Believers saw the combined forces of the enemy, they said: "This is what Allah and His Messenger had promised us, and they told us the truth." It only increased their faith and obedience.

³³·²³Some Believers are men who have been true to the treaty they made with Allah. Some of them have fulfilled their promise with martyrdom and some are still waiting. They have never changed their treaty with Allah, ³³·²⁴so that Allah can reward the truthful people for their truth and punish the hypocrites, if He chooses, or forgive them. He is always Most Forgiving, Ever-Merciful.

³³·²⁵Allah forced the disbelievers to go back in all their anger without gaining any success. Allah was enough for the Believers throughout the Battle of al-Ahzaab. Allah is always Strong, Almighty.

³³·²⁶He brought down from their strongholds those People of the Book who helped the disbelievers, and He cast awe into their hearts – allowing you to kill some in battle and take others prisoners. ³³·²⁷He made you inheritors of their lands, houses, and wealth, as well as another land you hadn't yet stepped in. Allah is always Most Capable of anything.

³³·²⁸O Prophet, tell your wives: "If you desire only this life and its luxuries, then come. I will let you enjoy yourselves and I will let you go in a beautiful manner. ³³·²⁹However, if you desire Allah and His Messenger, and the Home of the Hereafter, then you should know that Allah has prepared a huge reward for those of you who do good."

³³·³⁰Wives of the Prophet, if any of you is guilty of a shameless indecency, the punishment would be doubled for her. This is always easy for Allah.

[PART 22]

³³·³¹However, if any of you remains devoted to Allah and His Messenger, and does good, We will give her reward to her twice, and We have prepared some honourable wealth for her too.

33.32Wives of the Prophet, you aren't like any other women: if you really are mindful of Allah then you mustn't speak too softly that someone with sickness in his heart might be tempted. You should speak in a noble manner. 33.33You should stay peacefully inside your own homes, and not display your beauty like that which was done during the previous Age of Ignorance before Islam. You must continue to establish the ritual prayers, pay zakah, and obey Allah and His Messenger. Household of the Prophet, Allah wants to keep all impurities away from you and keep you completely clean and pure. 33.34You must think about Allah's revelations and the prophetic wisdom that are recited inside your homes. Allah knows all details, is Fully-Aware.

33.35Men and women who surrender to Allah as Muslims: who believe, are devoted to Him, are true, have patience, are humble, give charity, who fast, guard their chastity, and remember Allah a lot – Allah has prepared for them forgiveness as well as a huge reward.

33.36No Believing man or woman will have any choice in their matter once Allah and His Messenger have decided something. Anyone who disobeys Allah and His Messenger has certainly gone clearly astray.

33.37O Prophet Muhammad, remember when you told the man Allah had done favours to, and you had also favoured: "You must stay married to your wife Zaynab and remain mindful of Allah." However, you hid something in your heart out of modesty that Allah was going to disclose. You were afraid of the people making jokes whereas Allah has more right that you should fear Him. Then, when Zayd formally divorced her, We married her to you so that there wouldn't be any restriction on the Believers in marrying the former wives of their adopted sons when those adopted sons formally divorce them. Allah's orders have to be followed. 33.38There is no blame on the

Prophet regarding what Allah has told him to do. Allah used to do this with those who have already been and gone, and His command is always firmly fixed. [33.39]Allah used to do this with **those who deliver His messages and fear only Him** – not being afraid of anyone except Him. Allah is enough as a Reckoner.

[33.40]Muhammad isn't the father of any of your men, but rather he is Allah's Messenger and the Seal of the Prophets (i.e. the Last and Final Prophet). Allah always knows everything perfectly well.

[33.41]Believers! You must continue to remember Allah a lot, [33.42]and glorify Him morning and evening. [33.43]He is the one Who sends blessings on you, and so do His angels, to bring you out of the depths of darkness into the light. He is always Ever-Merciful to the Believers. [33.44]On the Day they will meet Him, their greetings will be: "Peace," and He has prepared an honourable reward for them.

[33.45]O Prophet, We have sent you to be a witness, and to give good news, and warnings, [33.46]and to invite to Allah by His command, and to shine like **a lamp that spreads light**. [33.47]You should give good news to the Believers that they will have immense grace from Allah. [33.48]Don't obey disbelievers and hypocrites, but ignore their abuses, and continue to put your trust in Allah. He is enough as a Guardian.

[33.49]Believers! If you marry Believing women, and then divorce them before even touching them, there won't be any waiting period on them for you to start counting. However, you must give them something as a gift and let them go in a respectful manner.

[33.50]O Prophet, We have made lawful for you: your wives you have paid their dowry to; your slavewomen from the prisoners of war Allah has given you; to marry **daughters of your paternal uncles and aunts;**

daughters of your maternal uncles and aunts – who migrated with you from Makkah; and any Believing woman who gives herself to the Prophet if he also wants to marry her – exclusively for you, O Prophet Muhammad, and not for the other Believers. We know what We've told the other Believers to do regarding their wives and their slavewomen so that there wouldn't be any blame on you. Allah is always Most Forgiving, Ever-Merciful.

33.51O Prophet Muhammad, **you may delay or bring sooner** the turn of any of your wives you choose, and it won't be wrong if you desire the one you had temporarily separated from. This makes it more likely that they will be happy and not sad, and they will be well-pleased with what you have given each of them. Allah knows what is in your hearts. He is always All-Knowing, Most Tolerant. 33.52After this, you won't be allowed to marry more women nor change them for other wives, even if the moral beauty of other women seems attractive to you, except your slavewomen. Allah is always Ever-Watchful over everything.

33.53Believers! You must never enter the Prophet's rooms unless you are given permission for a meal, and not wait around for it to be ready but only go in at the time you are invited. Once you have eaten, you should leave straight away and not hang around for casual talk. This behaviour would annoy the Prophet though he is too modest to tell you, but Allah isn't shy to tell the truth. If you ask his wives for anything, you should ask them from behind a curtain. This is purer for both your hearts and theirs. You aren't allowed to annoy Allah's Messenger nor to ever marry his wives after him. In the sight of Allah, this would be an outrageous thing! 33.54If you show anything or hide it, it doesn't matter because Allah always knows everything perfectly well.

³³·⁵⁵There is nothing wrong if the Prophet's wives are visited by: their fathers, sons, brothers; brothers' sons, sisters' sons; other women; or their slavewomen. Ladies! You must remain mindful of Allah because He is always a Witness to everything.

³³·⁵⁶Allah and His angels send blessings on the Prophet. Believers! You too must send blessings on him and greet him with lots of peace.

³³·⁵⁷Those who annoy Allah and His Messenger, Allah curses them in this world and the next, and has prepared a humiliating punishment for them. ³³·⁵⁸Those who annoy Believing men and women without them having done anything wrong, they are responsible for and guilty of false accusations and obvious sins.

³³·⁵⁹O Prophet, tell your wives, your daughters, and the wives of Believers, that when they go out they must cover themselves with their outer clothing. This will make it more likely for them to be recognised so they won't be harassed. Allah is always Most Forgiving, Ever-Merciful.

³³·⁶⁰The hypocrites, as well as those with sickness in their hearts, and those who spread rumours in the city, if they don't stop, We will let you take action against them. Then they won't be your neighbours in Madinah for long, ³³·⁶¹with a curse on them, to be lawfully arrested and mercilessly killed in punishment wherever they are found. ³³·⁶²Allah used to do this with those who have already been and gone. You won't find any change in what Allah does.

³³·⁶³O Prophet Muhammad, people ask you about the Final Hour. Say: "Only Allah knows about it." You never know, the Final Hour might be near.

³³·⁶⁴Allah has cursed the disbelievers and prepared a Blazing Fire for them, ³³·⁶⁵where they will remain forever and ever. They won't find any protector or helper to get them out. ³³·⁶⁶On the Day their faces will be continually turned upside down in the Fire, they will cry: "Oh! If only we had obeyed Allah and the Messenger!" ³³·⁶⁷They will say: "Our Lord! We followed our leaders and our elders, but they led us away from the Straight Way. ³³·⁶⁸Our Lord! Give them double the punishment and make them suffer a mighty curse."

³³·⁶⁹Believers! Don't be like those who annoyed Musa, and Allah cleared him of what they accused him of. He was honourable in the sight of Allah. ³³·⁷⁰Believers! You must continue to be mindful of Allah and say words that are straightforward, ³³·⁷¹and He will set your actions right for you and forgive you your sins. Anyone who obeys Allah and His Messenger has certainly gained a tremendous victory.

³³·⁷²We offered the responsibility of free will to the heavens, the earth, and the mountains, but they all refused to take it because they were afraid of fulfilling it, but the human took it. He was mistaken, not knowing its challenges. ³³·⁷³So Allah will punish the men and women who are hypocrites and polytheists, and He will forgive the Believing men and women. He is always Most Forgiving, Ever-Merciful.

Surah 34. Saba' (Sheba)

Allah's name I begin with, the Most Compassionate, the Ever-Merciful

³⁴·¹All praise is for Allah – Who owns everything in the heavens and the earth, and all praise will be for Him in the Hereafter too. He is the All-Wise, the Fully-Aware. ³⁴·²He knows everything that goes into the earth, that comes out of it, that comes down from the sky, and that goes up into it. He is the Ever-Merciful, the Most Forgiving.

³⁴·³The disbelievers say: "The Final Hour will never come to us." Say: "Why not! I swear by my Lord – Knower of the unseen secrets: it will certainly come to you." Not even an atom's weight is hidden from Him – in the heavens or on earth, and there isn't anything smaller or bigger than that but is in a Record that is clear, ³⁴·⁴so He can reward those who believe and do good. It is they who will have forgiveness and some honourable wealth. ³⁴·⁵Those who try their best to defeat Our revelations, it is they who will suffer a punishment of agonising pain.

³⁴·⁶O Prophet Muhammad, those given knowledge can see what is revealed to you from your Lord is the actual truth, and it guides to the path of Allah – the Almighty, the Most Praiseworthy.

³⁴·⁷The disbelievers say: "Shall we show you a man who tells you that when you've been completely decayed after death, you will be made into a new creation? ³⁴·⁸Is he making lies about Allah or has he gone mad?" In fact, those who don't believe in the Hereafter will be in punishment because they're far, far astray. ³⁴·⁹Don't they see what is in front of them or behind them, coming from the sky and the earth? If We want, We can make the earth swallow them up or pieces of sky fall upon them. There is certainly a sign in this for every servant of Allah who turns to Him.

³⁴·¹⁰We gave Dawud some special grace from Us and said: "O Mountains! Praise Me with him!" and We ordered the birds too. We made iron soft for him. ³⁴·¹¹We said: "Make full-length armour and measure the links carefully. You must all continue to do good. I am Ever-Watchful of everything you people do."

³⁴·¹²We made the wind obedient to Sulayman. Its early morning journey was a month's and its evening journey was also a month's. We made a stream of molten brass flow for him. By his Lord's permission, there were some jinns that worked in front of him, and if any of them turned away from Our command, We would make them taste some punishment of the Blazing Fire. ³⁴·¹³They made him anything he wanted, including forts, statues, basins as large as reservoirs, and fixed cauldrons. We said: "Family of Dawud, you must work in thankfulness to Allah." Only a few of My servants are thankful. ³⁴·¹⁴Then, when We brought him death, nothing made the jinns aware of his death but a termite from the earth eating away at his staff. So, when he fell down, it became clear to the jinns that if they had known the unseen secrets, they wouldn't have carried on working in that humiliating suffering.

³⁴·¹⁵There was a sign for the people of Saba' within their own homeland: two gardens – one each to the right and left. We said: "You may eat from what your Lord has given you, and you must be thankful to Him. You have a land that is good and a Lord who is Most Forgiving." ³⁴·¹⁶However, they turned away from obeying Me so We let loose on them a devastating flood, and We replaced their two gardens with two other gardens having bitter fruit, tamarisks, and only a few lote-trees. ³⁴·¹⁷In this way We punished them for being unthankful. It is only the unthankful people We punish.

³⁴·¹⁸Between them and the towns We had blessed, We had placed other towns that were visible, and had fixed the journey-stages between them. We said: "You may travel to them safely, night or day." ³⁴·¹⁹But they demanded: "Our Lord! Make distances between our journey-stages longer." They also did themselves harm, so We made them become lessons of warning and scattered them in pieces everywhere.

There are certainly signs in this for anyone who is very patient, very thankful.

34.20 Iblees had proven his opinion of them, because they all followed him, apart from a group of Believers 34.21 as he didn't have any power over them – all so We would separate those who believe in the Hereafter from those who are in doubt about it. Your Lord is the Protector of everything.

34.22 O Prophet Muhammad, **say:** "You are free to **pray to those you claimed** to be gods **besides Allah.** They don't have even **an atom's weight of power, not in the heavens or the earth** – having no share in them nor is any of them Allah's helper." 34.23 Intercession will be useless in His presence, except for someone He gives permission to. When the horror will be removed from their hearts on Judgement Day, the interceders will ask: "What did your Lord just say?" The angels will tell the truth. He is the Most High, the Great.

34.24 O Prophet Muhammad, **ask:** "Who gives you food from the heavens and the earth?" Reply: "Allah! Either we are on guidance or clearly astray, or you are." 34.25 Say: "You people won't be held responsible for what we are guilty of nor will we be held responsible for what you are doing." 34.26 Say: "Our Lord will gather us together and then decide between us with the truth. He is the Supreme Judge, the All-Knowing." 34.27 Say: "Show me those you have joined with Him as partner-gods. Beware! The truth is, He is Allah, the Almighty, the All-Wise."

34.28 O Prophet Muhammad, We've sent you to all the people to give good news and warnings, but most people don't realise. 34.29 They ask: "When will this warning be fulfilled, if you are telling the truth?"

34.30 Reply: "You have the promise of a Day which you can neither delay for even a moment nor bring any sooner."

34.31 The disbelievers say: "We will never believe in this Qur'an nor in anything which came before it." O Prophet Muhammad, if only you could see when the wrongdoers will be made to stand in front of their Lord, blaming each other with their words: those who were considered weak will say to those who showed arrogance: "We would have certainly been Believers if it wasn't for you!" **34.32** Those who showed arrogance will respond to those who were considered weak: "Did we block you from following guidance after it had come to you? The truth is, you yourselves were the criminals." **34.33** Those who were considered weak will say to those who showed arrogance: "No, no! You were making plots day and night, especially when you told us to disbelieve in Allah and make others equal to Him!" They will hide their regret when they see the punishment. We will put iron collars on the disbelievers' necks. Will they be punished for anything other than what they used to do? No.

34.34 Whenever we sent a warner to any town, its elite would say: "We reject anything you've been sent with." **34.35** They also boasted: "We have more wealth and children, so we cannot be punished." **34.36** Say: "It is my Lord Who can increase or restrict wealth for anyone He chooses, though most people don't realise."

34.37 Neither your wealth nor your children can bring you closer to Us, but only those who believe and do good. It is they who will have double the reward for the good things they did, and they will live peacefully in high mansions. **34.38** Those who try their best to defeat Our revelations, it is they who will be brought forward to the punishment.

34.39Say: "It is my Lord Who can increase or restrict wealth for any of His servants He chooses. He can replace anything you donate, because He is the Best Giver of all."

34.40On the Day when He will gather them all together and then ask the angels: "Was it you these people used to worship?" 34.41The angels will reply: "Glory be to You! You are our Protector, not them. Rather, they used to worship the jinns. Most of these people had faith in them." 34.42So today you won't have any power to help or harm each other. We will tell the wrongdoers: "Taste the punishment of the Fire that you used to call a lie!"

34.43When Our clear verses are recited to the disbelievers, they say: "This is only a man who wants to stop you from worshipping what your forefathers used to worship." They also claim: "This Qur'an is only a made-up lie." The disbelievers also say about the truth when it comes to them: "This is clearly magic." 34.44O Prophet Muhammad, We neither sent them any Holy Books to study nor anyone to warn them before you. 34.45Those before them also called the truth a lie, whereas these people haven't even reached a tenth of what wealth and power We had given them, and they too accused My messengers of being liars. So, how terrifying was My punishment!

34.46O Prophet Muhammad, say: "I am advising you one thing: stand in front of Allah, either in pairs or on your own, and think deeply. He (-Prophet Muhammad) who makes you his companions hasn't gone mad. He is giving you warnings before the coming of a severe punishment." 34.47Say: "I haven't asked you for any payment. It's yours. My reward will come only from Allah. He is a Witness to everything." 34.48Say: "My Lord – the Knower of the unseen secrets, hurls the truth forward." 34.49Say: "The truth is here, and falsehood can neither start creating nor bring back to life as it is powerless."

34.50Say: "If I go astray, I do so to my own loss; if I follow guidance, it is because of what my Lord reveals to me. He is All-Hearing, Near."

34.51If only you could see when they will be horrified! There won't be any escape and they will be snatched from a place nearby. 34.52They will cry: "Now we believe in him!" but how will they reach faith from a place far away 34.53when they had previously disbelieved in him? They used to blindly criticise from a faraway place without even trying to understand. 34.54A barrier will be put up between them and what they desire, just like it was done with their kind of people previously. They had been in serious doubt.

Surah 35. The Originator (al-Faatir)

Allah's name I begin with, the Most Compassionate, the Ever-Merciful

35.1All praise is for Allah – the Originator of the heavens and the earth, Maker of the angels as messengers with wings; two, three and four. He adds to creation as He chooses. Allah is Most Capable of anything. 35.2No one can hold back any mercy Allah opens up to people, and no one can release what He holds back after that. He is the Almighty, the All-Wise.

35.3People! Remember Allah's favour to you. Is there any creator other than Allah who gives you from the sky and the earth? There is no god except Him. So how are you being misled!

35.4O Prophet Muhammad, **if they accuse you of being a liar** then it is no surprise because **messengers before you were also accused.** All matters will be returned to Allah.

35.5 People! Allah's promise is true, so never let this worldly life trick you nor let Shaytan – the Big Trickster fool you about Allah. **35.6**Shaytan is your enemy, so treat him as an enemy. He only invites his group so they can be among the people of the Blazing Fire.

35.7 Those who disbelieve will suffer a severe punishment, but those who believe and do good will have forgiveness and a large reward. **35.8**What about someone whose bad actions have been made to seem attractive to him so he thinks they must be good? Actually, Allah lets anyone He chooses go astray and also guides whoever He wants. So, O Beloved Prophet Muhammad, you mustn't let yourself waste away in guilty feelings for them. Allah knows perfectly well everything they do.

35.9 Allah is the one Who sends the winds, and they stir up the clouds. Then We drive that cloud with its water to a land that is dead, with which We give life to the earth after it had become dead. The resurrection will be like this.

35.10 Anyone wanting glory and power should know that all glory and power belongs only to Allah. All good words rise up only to Him and He lifts up good actions. Those who plot to do bad things will suffer a severe punishment, and it is their plotting which will fail.

35.11 It is Allah Who created you originally from dust, then from a drop of semen, then made you pairs. No female becomes pregnant or gives birth without His knowledge. No elderly person can have their life lengthened nor shortened unless it's in a Record with Allah. All that is easy for Allah.

35.12 The two seas are not the same: one sweet, fresh, and pleasant to drink, and the other salty and bitter; yet from each you can eat fresh meat and bring out jewellery to wear. You can see ships cutting through it so you can gain Allah's grace and so that you might become thankful.

35.13He makes night enter into the day and day enter into the night, and made the sun and the moon obey a system – each one running its course for a fixed term. That is Allah – your Lord. All control belongs to Him. Those you people pray to besides Him cannot control even as much as the skin on a date-seed. 35.14If you call them, they cannot hear your call; if they could hear, they wouldn't be able to respond to you. On Judgement Day, they will reject your making them partner-gods with Allah. No one can tell you things like Allah – the Fully-Aware.

35.15People! You are in need of Allah, whereas Allah is Free of all Needs, the Most Praiseworthy. 35.16If He wants, He can remove all of you and bring a new creation. 35.17This isn't difficult for Allah.

35.18No one will carry someone else's burden of sins. If the carrier of a heavy burden calls out for help, nothing at all will be carried for him, even if he is a close relative. O Prophet Muhammad, you can only warn those who are afraid of their Lord without seeing Him, and they establish the ritual prayers. Anyone who purifies himself does it for his own good. The final return will be to Allah.

35.19The blind and the seeing person cannot be equal, 35.20nor the depths of darkness and light, 35.21nor the cool shade and hot sunshine. 35.22The living and the dead cannot be equal either. Allah can make anyone He chooses listen, but you, O Prophet Muhammad, cannot make those buried in graves listen.

35.23O Prophet Muhammad, you are only a warner. 35.24We have sent you with the truth to give good news and warnings. There has never been a community without a warner among them. [35.25]If they accuse you of being a liar then it is no surprise because those who lived before them also called the truth a lie, when their messengers came to them with clear signs, scriptures, and the enlightening Book. [35.26]Eventually, I punished the disbelievers. How terrifying was My punishment!

[35.27]Don't you see that Allah sends down from the sky water with which We bring out fruits of different colours? In the mountains there are streaks of white and red with a variety of shades, and jet black streaks too. [35.28]In the same way, some people, beasts, and livestock, also have different colours. Those among Allah's servants who really fear Him are the scholars. Allah is Almighty, Most Forgiving.

[35.29]Those who recite Allah's Book, establish the ritual prayers, donate secretly and openly from what We've given them, they can expect a trade that will never suffer loss, [35.30]because He will repay them their rewards in full, and give them even more from His grace. He is Most Forgiving, Most Appreciative.

[35.31]O Prophet Muhammad, what We have revealed to you from the Book, that is the truth which confirms what came before it. Allah is certainly Fully-Aware, Ever-Watchful of His servants. [35.32]Then We made Our chosen servants inherit the Book. Some of them harm themselves, some are moderate, while others advance in doing good – with Allah's command. It is that which is the immense grace.

[35.33]It is the Gardens of Eden they will enter, where they will be adorned with gold bracelets and with pearls, and where their clothes will be of silk. [35.34]They will say: "All praise is for Allah Who has removed all sadness from us. Our Lord is certainly Most Forgiving,

Most Appreciative, **35.35**Who has, from His grace, let us live in the Home of Eternal Stay, where tiredness and weariness won't have any effect on us."

35.36The disbelievers will suffer the fire of Hell. They won't be finished off so they can die nor will its punishment be reduced for them. This is how we punish anyone who is unthankful. 35.37They will be screaming in there: "Our Lord! Let us out! We will do good, not the bad things we used to do!" Didn't We let you live long enough that if someone wanted, he could have reminded himself of the truth? Besides, someone did come to give you warnings. Now taste the punishment and the wrongdoers won't have any helper.

35.38Allah knows all the unseen secrets of the heavens and the earth. He also knows the secrets of the hearts perfectly well. 35.39He is the one Who made you successors in this world. Now, anyone who disbelieves, does so to his own loss, because the disbelief of the disbelievers only makes them more hateful in the sight of their Lord, and it only increases them in loss.

35.40O Prophet Muhammad, **ask: "Have you** disbelievers **ever thought about your partner-gods you pray to besides Allah? Show me what part of the earth they created. Do they have a partnership in the heavens?"** Have We given them a Book so they would have a clear proof in it? In fact, the wrongdoers promise each other nothing but lies. 35.41It is Allah Who is holding back the heavens and the earth in case they move away. If they did move away, no one would be able to hold them back except Him. He is always Most Tolerant, Most Forgiving.

35.42The disbelievers swore by Allah with their strongest oaths that if someone did come to give them warnings, they would follow his guidance better than any other community. However, when a warner (- Prophet Muhammad) did come to them, it only increased their hatred of the truth, [35.43]showing arrogance in the land and plotting to do bad things. However, evil plots only backfire on those who make them. Now, are they waiting for something like what happened to the people of the past? You'll never find any changing or deviation in what Allah does. [35.44]Don't they travel through the earth and take a look at what was the end result of those before them? They were more powerful than these people. Nothing at all can ever defeat Allah, not in the heavens or on earth. He is always All-Knowing, All-Powerful.

[35.45]If Allah punished people immediately for the bad things they did, He wouldn't leave any creature alive on the face of the earth. However, He is giving them more time until an end date. Then, when the end of their time comes, they will find out that Allah has been Ever-Watchful of His servants.

Surah 36. Yaa Seen

Allah's name I begin with, the Most Compassionate, the Ever-Merciful

[36.1]*Yaa Seen.*
[36.2]I swear by the Qur'an Full of Wisdom: [36.3]O Prophet Muhammad, you certainly are one of the messengers, [36.4]on a path that is straight, [36.5]with a revelation sent down by Allah - the Almighty, the Ever-Merciful, [36.6]to give warnings to a people whose forefathers were not warned, which is why they're unaware of the truth.

[36.7]The command has already proven true against most of them, as they won't believe. [36.8]We have put on their necks iron collars that reach to the chins, so their heads are forced up. [36.9]We have put a barrier in front of them and also one behind them, and We've covered them up so they cannot see.

36.10 O Prophet Muhammad, it makes no difference to them if you warn them or not, they still won't believe. 36.11 You can only warn someone who follows the Reminder and is afraid of Allah – the Most Compassionate without seeing Him. So, give him the good news of forgiveness and an honourable reward. 36.12 It is We Who will bring the dead back to life, and We record everything they've done and what they leave behind. We have included everything in a Register that is clear.

36.13 O Prophet Muhammad, give them the example of the people of the town where Our messengers came. 36.14 When We at first sent them two messengers and they accused them both of being liars, We sent a third for support, and they all announced: "We have been sent to you as messengers." 36.15 The people of the town said: "You're only human, just like us, and Allah – the Most Compassionate hasn't sent down anything at all. You're only telling lies." 36.16 They replied: "Our Lord knows we have certainly been sent to you as messengers. 36.17 Our duty is only to deliver the message clearly." 36.18 The people said: "We sense bad luck from you. If you don't stop, we will certainly stone you to death and you will suffer a painful punishment from us." 36.19 The messengers replied: "Your bad luck is within yourselves. Haven't you just been reminded? The truth is, you are a people who are going to extremes."

36.20 A man came running from the far side of town and said: "My people! You must follow the messengers. 36.21 Follow those who aren't asking you for any payment, and who follow guidance.

[PART 23]

³⁶·²²Why shouldn't I worship Allah Who made me and Whom you will all be taken back to? ³⁶·²³Shall I worship other gods besides Him? If Allah – the Most Compassionate wants me any harm, their intercession won't be of any use to me at all, nor would they be able to save me. ³⁶·²⁴In that case, I would be clearly astray. ³⁶·²⁵I believe in your Lord, so please listen to me."

³⁶·²⁶It was said to him after the people murdered him: "Enter Paradise." He said: "Oh! If only my people knew, ³⁶·²⁷how my Lord has forgiven me and put me among honoured people!"

³⁶·²⁸After they had murdered him, We didn't send any army from heaven to attack them nor did We need to. ³⁶·²⁹It was only a single Mighty Blast and they immediately turned into silent ashes. ³⁶·³⁰Ah! These servants are damned! Whenever a messenger came to them, they would make fun of him. ³⁶·³¹Don't they think about the many generations We've destroyed before them who will never come back to them? ³⁶·³²Still, all of them will be brought forward in front of Us.

³⁶·³³A sign for them is the land that is dead. We gave it life and brought out from it grains, from which they can eat. ³⁶·³⁴We put orchards of date-palms and grapevines in it, and made some springs of water gush out of it, ³⁶·³⁵so they can eat of its fruit even though they didn't even work for it. So, won't they give thanks? ³⁶·³⁶Glory be to Him Who created all the pairs from the things the earth grows, from themselves, and from other things they don't even know.

³⁶·³⁷Another sign for them is the night; We peel the daylight away from it, and that is when they're left in darkness.

³⁶·³⁸The sun runs on a course fixed for it. This is the fixed plan of Allah – the Almighty, the All-Knowing. ³⁶·³⁹We have fixed some phases for

the moon too, until it goes back to looking like the old curved palm-stalk. ³⁶·⁴⁰The sun cannot catch up to the moon nor the night overtake the day. Everything is floating in an orbit.

³⁶·⁴¹Another sign for them is that We carried their forefathers in the Ark which was fully loaded. ³⁶·⁴²We have created for them similar things they can travel on. ³⁶·⁴³If We want, We can drown them and there'll be no one to hear their cries nor would they be saved, ³⁶·⁴⁴except as some special mercy from Us and some enjoyment for a while.

³⁶·⁴⁵When they are told: "Be mindful of what is in front of you or behind you so you may be shown mercy," ³⁶·⁴⁶they turn away, even when a sign of their Lord appears to them. ³⁶·⁴⁷When they are told: "Donate from what Allah has given you," they say to the Believers: "Should we feed those people Allah Himself could have fed if He wanted? You must be clearly astray."

³⁶·⁴⁸They ask: "When will this warning be fulfilled, if you are telling the truth?" ³⁶·⁴⁹What they are waiting for is a single Mighty Blast to seize them while they're busy arguing with each other. ³⁶·⁵⁰They won't be able to make a will or even to go back to their families.

³⁶·⁵¹The Trumpet will be blown a second time and that is when they will come rushing out of their graves, hurrying to their Lord. ³⁶·⁵²They will say: "We are damned! Who woke us up from our resting-place? This must be what Allah – the Most Compassionate had promised and the truth the messengers had told." ³⁶·⁵³It will be only a single Mighty Blast and that is when they, all of them, will be brought forward in front of Us. ³⁶·⁵⁴So, that Day no one will be treated unfairly in any way at all nor will you be punished except for the bad things you used to do.

36.55"Today, the people of Paradise will be busy enjoying themselves. 36.56They and their spouses will be under shades, on raised thrones, relaxing. 36.57They will have fruits there and anything they ask for. 36.58"Peace." This will be a greeting from an Ever-Merciful Lord.

36.59The bad people will be told: "Step aside Today, you criminals! 36.60Didn't I take this promise from you, humans, that You aren't allowed to worship Shaytan? He is your open enemy. 36.61You must worship Me. This is the path that is straight. 36.62Shaytan had already misled a great many of you. So, weren't you thinking? 36.63This is the Hell you were warned about. 36.64Burn in it Today because you continued to disbelieve." 36.65We will put a seal on their mouths that Day, so their hands will speak to Us and their legs will testify to the things they used to do.

36.66If We wanted, We could have easily removed their eyes, so that they might run in panic looking for the path, but how would they see? 36.67If We wanted, We could have paralysed them in their places, so they couldn't move forward or back. 36.68Anyone We give long life, we reverse them in development. Won't you even think?

36.69We didn't teach Prophet Muhammad any poetry as it isn't appropriate for him. This book is only a reminder and a Qur'an that is clear 36.70– to give warnings to anyone alive, and for the command to prove true against the disbelievers.

36.71Don't they see that, among the things We made, We created livestock for them, and now they are their owners? 36.72We made them tame for humans so they can ride on some of them and others they can eat. 36.73There are many other benefits and drinks in them for you. So, won't they give thanks?

36.74However, they started worshipping other gods besides Allah, hoping they might be helped. 36.75They're incapable of helping them. These polytheists will be brought forward for them as an army to be punished. 36.76O Prophet Muhammad, don't let their words upset you. We certainly know everything they hide or show.

36.77Doesn't the human realise that We created him from a drop of semen? Even then he challenges Us openly! 36.78He makes comparisons of Us yet forgets his own creation. He asks: "Who will give life to the bones when they have decayed?" 36.79O Prophet Muhammad, reply: "He Who created them in the first place will bring them back to life. He knows every kind of creation perfectly well; 36.80Who also gives you fire from green trees, and from that you can light more fires."

36.81He Who created the heavens and the earth, doesn't He have the power to create more people just like them? Yes, of course He does! He is the Supreme Creator, the All-Knowing. 36.82His only command, when He decides something to happen, is that He says to it: "Be!" and it becomes. 36.83So, glory be to Him in Whose control are the kingdoms of everything. You will all be taken back to Him.

Surah 37. Those in Rows (as-Saaffaat)

Allah's name I begin with, the Most Compassionate, the Ever-Merciful

37.1I swear by those angels who line up in rows, 37.2by those who are strict in duty, 37.3and by those who recite to remember 37.4that: your Lord is certainly one, 37.5Lord of the heavens and the earth and everything in between them, and Lord of all the Easts and sunrises.

37.6We have decorated the lower sky with the beauty of stars, 37.7and protected it from the reach of every rebellious devil. 37.8They cannot spy on the Highest Assembly, as they will be targeted from all sides, 37.9to be pushed away. They will suffer an everlasting punishment. 37.10Any that manages to snatch away something secretly, a shooting star of piercing brightness chases after it.

37.11O Prophet Muhammad, just ask their opinion as to which is harder to create: they or those other people and things We've created? We created humans from some sticky clay. 37.12The truth is, while you're amazed, they are making fun of these wonders. 37.13When they're reminded, they pay no attention. 37.14When they see a miracle, they start making fun of it, 37.15and they say: "This is clearly magic. 37.16What? When we die and have become dust and bones, will we then be brought back to life? 37.17And our ancestors too?" 37.18Reply: "Yes, and you will all be humiliated."

37.19It will be a single blast, and they will immediately stand and stare! 37.20They will cry: "We are damned! This is Judgement Day!" 37.21It will be announced: "This is the Decision Day you people used to call a lie! 37.22Angels! Gather together the wrongdoers, their companions, and whatever they used to worship 37.23besides Allah, and take them to the path of Hell-Fire. 37.24But make them wait. They have to be asked: 37.25'What is wrong with you? Why aren't you helping each other?'." 37.26The truth is, Today they will surrender.

37.27They will turn to each other with blame. 37.28They will say: "It was you who used to come to us from positions of authority." 37.29The accused will reply: "No! You weren't even Believers! 37.30We had no power over you. The truth is, you yourselves were a people breaking all limits of rebellion! 37.31So now our Lord's command has proven true against us. We are going to taste the punishment. 37.32We led you astray because we ourselves were astray." ³⁷·³³So, that Day, they will share the punishment. ³⁷·³⁴This is how We will deal with the criminals.

³⁷·³⁵When they were told: "There is no god except Allah," they used to show arrogance, ³⁷·³⁶and argue: "What? Should we give up our gods for the sake of a mad poet?" ³⁷·³⁷Never! He has come with the truth and has confirmed the messengers. ³⁷·³⁸You will all taste the painful punishment, ³⁷·³⁹and you will only be punished for the bad things you used to do.

³⁷·⁴⁰As for Allah's specially chosen servants, ³⁷·⁴¹it is they who will be given something well-known: ³⁷·⁴²fruits; and they will be honoured, ³⁷·⁴³in Gardens of Delight, ³⁷·⁴⁴facing each other on sofas. ³⁷·⁴⁵A cup from a flowing fountain will be passed around among them, ³⁷·⁴⁶sparkling white, delicious to those who drink, ³⁷·⁴⁷without any harm, nor will they suffer intoxication from it. ³⁷·⁴⁸There will be spouses with them, with modest gazes and wide beautiful eyes, ³⁷·⁴⁹like precious eggs that are well-protected from dust.

³⁷·⁵⁰They will turn to each other and ask questions. ³⁷·⁵¹One of them will say: "I had a close friend, ³⁷·⁵²who used to ask mockingly, 'What? Are you one of those who say it is true ³⁷·⁵³that when we die and have become dust and bones, we will be judged?'." ³⁷·⁵⁴Someone will ask: "Can you look down and see him?" ³⁷·⁵⁵He will look down and see him in the middle of Hell-Fire. ³⁷·⁵⁶He will say: "I swear by Allah: you almost ruined me! ³⁷·⁵⁷If it wasn't for my Lord's favour, I would certainly also have been among those brought forward for punishment!" ³⁷·⁵⁸Asking his friends in Paradise: "Will we never die now, ³⁷·⁵⁹except for our first death? Will we never be punished?" ³⁷·⁶⁰This is the tremendous victory. ³⁷·⁶¹Everyone should work for something like this.

37.62Which is better for hospitality: that or the Zaqqum tree? 37.63We have made it a punishment for the wrongdoers. 37.64It is a tree that grows out of the bottom of Hell-Fire. 37.65Its spathes are like the heads of devils. 37.66They will have to eat from it and fill their bellies with it. 37.67Then, on top of that, they will have to drink a mixture of boiling liquid. 37.68Eventually, they will go back to Hell-Fire again.

37.69They found their forefathers astray 37.70so they are made to come thoughtlessly rushing right behind them. 37.71Before them, most of the previous people went astray, 37.72but We sent them many warners. 37.73Now take a look at what was the end result of those who were given warnings, 37.74not including Allah's specially chosen servants.

37.75Nuh called out to Us, and how wonderfully We responded! 37.76We saved him and his family from the great disaster, 37.77and made his descendants the only survivors. 37.78We left for him praise among later generations. 37.79Peace be upon Nuh among all the people. 37.80This is how we reward those who do good. 37.81He was from among Our specially chosen servants. 37.82Then we drowned the others.

37.83Ibrahim was of the same group. 37.84He came to his Lord with a pure heart. 37.85Remember when he asked his foster father and his people: "What are you worshipping? 37.86Is it a falsehood – gods besides Allah – that you want? 37.87So, what are your thoughts about Allah – the Lord of all the worlds?" 37.88Then he took a look at the stars 37.89and said: "I'm ill." 37.90So the people turned away from him and left.

37.91Then later, he secretly went up to their gods and asked: "Don't you eat? 37.92What is wrong with you? Why don't you speak?" 37.93Then he turned on them, this time hammering with full force.

37.94Later, the people came rushing to him. 37.95He argued: "Do you worship something you yourselves have carved 37.96when it is Allah Who created you and everything you can do?" 37.97They decided: "Build him a pyre, and then throw him into the blazing fire!" 37.98They made a plot against him, but We humiliated them.

37.99Later on he said: "I am going to my Lord and He will guide me." 37.100He migrated and prayed: "My Lord! Give me a righteous child." 37.101So We gave him the good news of a forbearing son (- Isma'il). 37.102Then, when the son reached the age of running about with him, Ibrahim said: "My dear son, I dreamt that I must sacrifice you. Tell me what you think." The son replied: "Dear Father, do as you are ordered. If Allah chooses, you will find me among those who have patience." 37.103So, when they had both surrendered themselves to Allah, and Ibrahim laid his son down on his forehead, 37.104We called out to him: "Ibrahim! 37.105You have fulfilled the dream." This is how We reward those who do good. 37.106This was certainly the obvious test of faith. 37.107We ransomed Isma'il with a great sacrifice. 37.108We left for him praise among later generations: 37.109Peace be upon Ibrahim. 37.110This is how we reward those who do good. 37.111He was from among Our Believing servants. 37.112After Isma'il, We gave him the good news of Is'haq – a prophet from among righteous people. 37.113We blessed him and Is'haq too. Some of their descendants are those who do good as well as those who do obvious harm to themselves.

37.114We did favours to Musa and Haroon, 37.115and saved them and their people from the great disaster. 37.116We helped them, so they were the winners. 37.117We gave them the Book which makes guidance clear, 37.118and We guided them on the Straight Path. 37.119We left for them praise among later generations: 37.120Peace be upon Musa and Haroon. 37.121This is how we reward those who do good. 37.122Both were from among Our Believing servants.

37.123Ilyas was certainly one of the messengers. 37.124Remember when he asked his people: "Won't you be mindful of Allah? 37.125Are you praying to Ba'l (Baal, the idol) and leaving the Best of Creators 37.126– Allah, your Lord and of your ancestors too?" 37.127But they accused him of being a liar, and they will certainly be brought forward for punishment, 37.128not including Allah's specially chosen servants. 37.129We left for him praise among later generations: 37.130Peace be upon Ilyas. 37.131This is how we reward those who do good. 37.132He was from among Our Believing servants.

37.133Lut was certainly one of the messengers. 37.134Remember when We saved him and his family, all of them 37.135– except an old lady from among those who stayed behind. 37.136Finally, We destroyed everyone else. 37.137You people certainly pass them by seeing their ruins during the day 37.138and night. Don't you even think?

37.139Yunus was certainly one of the messengers. 37.140When he ran to the fully loaded ship, 37.141he took part in casting lots so they could see who did not belong there, but he lost and was thrown overboard. 37.142Then the big fish swallowed him and saved him because he was repenting. 37.143If it wasn't because he was one of those who glorify Allah, 37.144he would certainly have stayed inside its belly until the Day when people will be brought back to life. 37.145But We threw him onto the open shore while he was ill, 37.146and We grew a gourd tree over him. 37.147We sent him as a messenger to a hundred thousand people or more. 37.148They believed, so We let them enjoy themselves for a while.

37.149O Prophet Muhammad, now ask these polytheists their opinion if your Lord has daughters while they themselves have sons? 37.150Or did they witness Us creating the angels female? 37.151Beware! It is one of their lies that they say: ³⁷·¹⁵²"Allah has children." They are definitely telling lies! ³⁷·¹⁵³What? Did He choose daughters over sons? ³⁷·¹⁵⁴What is wrong with you? How are you making bad decisions? ³⁷·¹⁵⁵Won't you even remind yourselves? ³⁷·¹⁵⁶Do you have any clear proof? ³⁷·¹⁵⁷Then bring your book, if you are telling the truth. ³⁷·¹⁵⁸The disbelievers have made up a blood-relationship between Allah and the jinns too, but the jinns know they will certainly be brought forward to Allah. ³⁷·¹⁵⁹Glory be to Allah above what they describe. ³⁷·¹⁶⁰This is not the case with Allah's specially chosen servants, ³⁷·¹⁶¹because you and everything you worship, ³⁷·¹⁶²you cannot lead away from Allah ³⁷·¹⁶³anyone except those who will burn in Hell-Fire.

³⁷·¹⁶⁴Those angels say: "Each one of us has a fixed place of worship. ³⁷·¹⁶⁵We line up in rows ³⁷·¹⁶⁶and we glorify Allah."

³⁷·¹⁶⁷The disbelievers used to say: ³⁷·¹⁶⁸"If only we had a Reminder from previous people, ³⁷·¹⁶⁹we would have certainly been Allah's specially chosen servants." ³⁷·¹⁷⁰However, when it came, they rejected it. So, they will very soon come to know the end result.

³⁷·¹⁷¹Our promise to Our messenger-servants was fulfilled ³⁷·¹⁷²that only they would be helped, ³⁷·¹⁷³and that only Our army would win. ³⁷·¹⁷⁴So, O Prophet Muhammad, you should turn away from the disbelievers for a while, ³⁷·¹⁷⁵but keep watching them, because they will soon see the truth clearly. ³⁷·¹⁷⁶Do they want Our punishment to come sooner? ³⁷·¹⁷⁷When that punishment comes down in the open space in front of them, how horrible will be the morning of those who were given warnings! ³⁷·¹⁷⁸So, O Prophet Muhammad, you should turn away from them for a while, ³⁷·¹⁷⁹but keep watching, because they will soon see the truth clearly.

37.180Glory be to your Lord – Lord of glory and power – above what they describe, 37.181peace be upon the messengers, 37.182and all praise be to Allah – Lord of all the worlds.

Surah 38. Saad (The Letter *Saad*)

Allah's name I begin with, the Most Compassionate, the Ever-Merciful

38.1*Saad*. I swear by the Qur'an full of reminders: it is the Truth, 38.2but the disbelievers are stuck in arrogance and hostility. 38.3How many generations have We destroyed before them! They only cried out for mercy when there was no time left to be saved. 38.4They were surprised that a warner had come to them from among them. The disbelievers said: "This man is a magician, a complete liar! 38.5Has he turned all the gods into one God? This is a very strange thing."

38.6The leaders among them went away telling people: "Walk away and stick to your gods. This is something planned against you. 38.7We haven't heard anything like this even in the previous religion. This is a made-up lie. 38.8From among us, has the Reminder been revealed to *him*?" In fact, they are in doubt about My Reminder. The truth is, they haven't tasted My punishment yet! 38.9Do they have the treasures of your Lord's mercy, the Almighty, the Ever-Giving, 38.10or the control of the heavens and the earth and everything in between them? If so, they should climb up the pathways to the heavens.

38.11It's only an army from the combined forces of evil that will be defeated out there. 38.12Before them, the people of Nuh called the truth a lie, and so did the 'Ad, Fir'awn of the huge structures, 38.13the Thamud, the people of Lut, and the People of the Forest. They are the combined forces of evil. 38.14All of them accused the messengers of being liars, so My punishment proved true against them. 38.15Today, these people can expect a single Mighty Blast which has no delay. ³⁸·¹⁶They joke: "Our Lord! Bring us our share of punishment sooner, even before the Day of Reckoning."

³⁸·¹⁷O Prophet Muhammad, you should have patience with what they say, and remember Our servant Dawud who was very strong. He would always turn to Us. ³⁸·¹⁸We made the mountains obey a system to glorify Me with him in late afternoon and after sunrise, ³⁸·¹⁹and the birds would be gathered together too. All of them turned to him in obedience. ³⁸·²⁰We made his kingdom strong, and gave him wisdom and decisive speech.

³⁸·²¹O Prophet Muhammad, has the story reached you of those who had a dispute when they climbed over the prayer-room's wall? ³⁸·²²When they came to Dawud, and he was surprised by them, they said: "Don't be nervous. We are two people who have a dispute. One of us has wronged the other. You need to judge between us with the truth, and don't be unfair but guide us in the right decision: ³⁸·²³This man is my brother. He has ninety-nine sheep, but I have only one, yet he demands, 'Give it to me,' and puts pressure on me when he speaks." ³⁸·²⁴Dawud said: "He has certainly wronged you in demanding your one sheep to add to his flock. Many shareholders do take wrongful advantage of each other, but not those who believe and do good – but how few are they!" Dawud realised that We had tested him, so he asked his Lord to forgive him, fell down bowing in prostration, and turned to Allah in repentance. *<Prostration Point 10>* ³⁸·²⁵So We forgave him this. He is very close to Us, and will have the best destination.

³⁸·²⁶We said: "Dawud! We have made you a representative on earth. Now, you should judge between them with the truth and not follow desire, or it will lead you away from Allah's cause. Those who stray

away from Allah's cause will suffer a severe punishment for neglecting the Day of Reckoning."

38.27We haven't created the sky and the earth and everything in between them without a purpose. That is what the disbelievers think, which is why they will be damned in the Fire. 38.28Should We treat those who believe and do good like those who make trouble in the world? Should We treat those who are mindful of Allah like sinners?

38.29O Prophet Muhammad, this is a blessed Book We have revealed to you so they can think over its verses, and so that the people of understanding can remind themselves.

38.30To Dawud, We gave Sulayman. What an excellent servant! He always turned to Us. 38.31When swift horses of the highest breed were presented to Sulayman in the late afternoon, 38.32he said: "I'm in love with good things out of my Lord's remembrance," until they disappeared behind the veil. 38.33"Bring them back to me," he said, and he began fondly wiping his hand over their legs and necks.

38.34We certainly tested Sulayman: We placed on his throne a lifeless body, but then he turned to Us. 38.35He prayed: "My Lord! Forgive me, and give me a kingdom which no one will have after me. Only You are the Ever-Giving." 38.36So We made the wind obey him, blowing gently at his command to wherever he wanted; 38.37the devils among jinns too – every builder, diver, 38.38and others that were tied up in chains. 38.39Allah said: "This is Our gift. You may give to others or keep it to yourself, and no questions will be asked." 38.40He is very close to Us, and will have the best destination.

38.41Remember Our servant Ayyub. When He called out to his Lord: "Shaytan has made me suffer distress and suffering." 38.42Allah ordered him: "Stamp your foot on the ground. This here is cool water to wash and drink." ³⁸·⁴³We gave him back his family, and an equal number with them, as a special mercy from Us, and as a lesson for the people of understanding. ³⁸·⁴⁴We said: "Hold in your hand a bundle of grass and hit with that, and this way you won't break your oath." We knew he was patient. What an excellent servant! He always turned to Us.

³⁸·⁴⁵Remember Our servants: Ibrahim, Is'haq, and Ya'qub – who were very strong and intelligent. ³⁸·⁴⁶We chose them specifically to remind others of the Hereafter. ³⁸·⁴⁷They are, in Our sight, certainly among the chosen, the best. ³⁸·⁴⁸Remember Isma'il, al-Yasa', and Dhu'l-Kifl. All of them were from among the best.

³⁸·⁴⁹This is a reminder. Those who are mindful of Allah will certainly have the best destination: ³⁸·⁵⁰the Gardens of Eden, whose doors will be open for them; ³⁸·⁵¹where they will relax on sofas, calling for all kinds of fruit and drink. ³⁸·⁵²There will be spouses with them, with modest gazes and of the same age. ³⁸·⁵³This is what you are promised for the Day of Reckoning. ³⁸·⁵⁴This is what We will give and it will never end.

³⁸·⁵⁵Yes, this is for the Believers! Those who break all limits of rebellion will have the worst destination ³⁸·⁵⁶– Hell! They will burn in it. What a dreadful place! ³⁸·⁵⁷Yes, this is for the disbelievers! They will have to taste it. Some boiling liquid and pus, ³⁸·⁵⁸and a variety of other punishments of the same kind.

³⁸·⁵⁹It will be said: "Here is another crowd rushing along with you into Hell. No welcome for them. They will burn in the Fire." ³⁸·⁶⁰The newcomers will reply: "In fact, it is you! No welcome for you! You have brought this upon us. What a dreadful place to be in!" ³⁸·⁶¹They

will pray: "Our Lord! Double the punishment in the Fire for whoever brought this upon us." ³⁸·⁶²They will also say: "Why can't we see the people we used to consider were evil? ³⁸·⁶³Did we used to make fun of them or did our eyes lose sight of them?" ³⁸·⁶⁴This is certainly the truth – the people of the Fire quarrelling with each other.

³⁸·⁶⁵O Prophet Muhammad, say: "I am only giving warnings. There is no god except Allah, the One, the Dominant, ³⁸·⁶⁶the Lord of the heavens and the earth and everything in between them, the Almighty, the Ever-Forgiving."

³⁸·⁶⁷O Prophet Muhammad, say: "This is important information, ³⁸·⁶⁸yet you are neglecting it. ³⁸·⁶⁹I didn't personally have any knowledge of the Highest Assembly when the angels were having discussions. ³⁸·⁷⁰It is only revealed to me that I should give you clear warnings."

³⁸·⁷¹Remember when your Lord told the angels: "I am going to create a human from clay. ³⁸·⁷²When I have given him proportion and breathed from My spirit into him, you must all fall down prostrating in front of him." ³⁸·⁷³So the angels did prostrate, all of them, all together ³⁸·⁷⁴– but not Iblees. He showed arrogance and became a disbeliever. ³⁸·⁷⁵Allah asked him: "Iblees! What has stopped you from prostrating in front of what I created with My Own Power? Are you showing arrogance, or have you always thought you were superior to him?" ³⁸·⁷⁶Iblees replied: "I am better than he is; You created me from fire but him from clay." ³⁸·⁷⁷Allah ordered: "Get out of here! You are rejected! ³⁸·⁷⁸You will suffer My curse until Judgement Day." ³⁸·⁷⁹He pleaded: "My Lord! Then give me a chance until the Day people will be brought back to life." ³⁸·⁸⁰Allah replied: "You are among those given chances ³⁸·⁸¹until the Day of that fixed time." ³⁸·⁸²Iblees said: "Then, I swear by Your glory and power: I will lead them all astray, ³⁸·⁸³except Your specially chosen servants among them." ³⁸·⁸⁴Allah said: "Then

the truth is, as I only speak the truth, ³⁸·⁸⁵I will certainly fill up Hell with you and those of them who follow you, all together."

³⁸·⁸⁶O Prophet Muhammad, **say: "I am not asking you** people **any payment for this nor am I pretending to be someone I'm not.** ³⁸·⁸⁷This is a reminder for everyone. ³⁸·⁸⁸You will certainly come to know its truth after a short while."

Surah 39. Crowds (az-Zumar)

Allah's name I begin with, the Most Compassionate, the Ever-Merciful

³⁹·¹This Book's revelation comes from Allah, the Almighty, the All-Wise. ³⁹·²O Prophet Muhammad, **We revealed to you the Book with the truth, so worship Allah in sincere devotion to Him.** ³⁹·³Beware! Sincere devotion should only be for Allah. Those who take protectors other than Allah saying: "We worship them only so they can take us closer to Allah," Allah will judge between them about the disagreements they have. Allah doesn't let anyone succeed who tells lies and is very unthankful.

³⁹·⁴If Allah wanted to have a child, He could have chosen from His creation anything He wished. Glory be to Him! He is Allah, the One, the Dominant. ³⁹·⁵He created the heavens and the earth for a real purpose. He folds the night over the day and the day over the night. He has made the sun and the moon obey a system – each one running its course for a fixed term. Beware! He is the Almighty, the Ever-Forgiving.

³⁹·⁶He created you all from a single person. Then He made his wife from him, and also sent down eight kinds of livestock for you in pairs. He creates you inside your mothers' wombs, one stage after another,

in three layers of darkness. This is Allah – your Lord. All control belongs to Him. There is no god except Him. Then, how are you being turned away?

39.7If you are unthankful, then you should know that Allah has no need of you. He doesn't like unthankfulness from His servants. If you were thankful, He would like you for it. No one will carry someone else's burden of sins. In the end, you will all go back to your Lord, and He will tell you about everything you used to do. He knows the secrets of the hearts perfectly well.

39.8When anyone suffers harm, he prays to his Lord, turning to Him completely. Then, when Allah does him favours from Himself, that person forgets the suffering for which he prayed to Him a short while ago, and makes others equal to Allah to lead people away from Allah's cause. O Prophet Muhammad, say: "Enjoy your disbelief for a short while. You are among the people of the Fire." 39.9Is he better than someone who is devoted in worship during the night prostrating and standing, afraid of the Hereafter and hoping for his Lord's mercy? O Prophet Muhammad, ask: "Can they be the same: those who know and those who don't?" Only the people of understanding will remind themselves.

39.10O Prophet Muhammad, say: "My Believing servants! You must continue to be mindful of your Lord. Those who do good in this world will have a good reward. Allah's earth is spacious. Those who have patience will be given their reward in full without any limits." 39.11Say: "I've been ordered to worship Allah in sincere devotion to Him 39.12and to be the first to surrender to Him as Muslim." 39.13Say: "I fear the punishment of a Dreadful Day if I disobey my Lord." 39.14Say: "It is Allah I worship in my sincere devotion. 39.15You people are free to worship anything besides Him." Say: "The real losers on Judgement

Day will be those who ruin themselves and their families. Beware! It is that which is the clear loss. $^{39.16}$They will have layers of fire above them and below them – everywhere. This is what Allah is warning His servants with." My servants! You must continue to be mindful of Me.

$^{39.17}$Those people who stay clear of worshipping fake gods and they turn only to Allah, they will have joy. So, O Prophet Muhammad, give good news to My servants $^{39.18}$who listen carefully to what is said and they follow it in the best way. They're the ones Allah has guided, and it is really they who are the people of understanding. $^{39.19}$What about someone the punishment already fixed has proven true against? Will you save someone who will already be in the Fire? $^{39.20}$However, those who are mindful of their Lord will have high mansions with more high mansions made above them – that have rivers flowing beneath them. This is Allah's promise. He never breaks promises.

$^{39.21}$Don't you see that it is Allah Who sends down from the sky water and makes it run through streams in the ground? With that water He brings out crops of various colours, then they become dry and you see them turning yellow. Eventually, He makes them crumble away. There is certainly a reminder in this for people of understanding.

$^{39.22}$Someone whose heart Allah has opened to Islam, he stands in the light from his Lord. So, damned are those whose hearts are closed to remembering Allah. It is they who are clearly astray.

$^{39.23}$It is Allah Who revealed as a Book the most beautiful message that is consistent, repeating itself; the skins of those who fear their Lord shiver from it. Then, when remembering Allah, their skins and their hearts become soft. This is Allah's guidance, and He guides with it anyone He chooses. There can be no guide for someone Allah calls misguided. $^{39.24}$What will it be like for someone who tries to shield himself with his face from the grievous punishment on Judgement Day? The wrongdoers will be told: "Taste the punishment for **what you used to do!**"

[39.25]**Those before them also called the truth a lie, so the punishment came at them from where they least expected.** [39.26]**So Allah gave them a taste of humiliation in this life, but the punishment of the Hereafter will be far worse. If they only knew!**

[39.27]**In this Qur'an, We've given every kind of example to people so that they might remind themselves.** [39.28]It is **a Qur'an in Arabic without any crookedness so they can be mindful** of Him.

[39.29]**Allah gives the example of a servant serving many partners** who are **quarrelling with each other, and of another servant serving only one master. Can they be equal in comparison? All praise is for Allah. In fact, most of them don't** even **realise** what the truth is.

[39.30]O Prophet Muhammad, **you will pass away and they will die too.** [39.31]**In the end, on Judgement Day, you** people **will argue with each other in front of your Lord.**

[PART 24]

[39.32]**So, who could be more unjust that someone who lies about Allah and calls the truth a lie when it comes to him. Isn't the place for disbelievers in Hell?** [39.33]**He who brought the truth and those who confirmed it, it is really they who are mindful** of Allah. [39.34]**They will have whatever they wish from their Lord. This is the reward of those who do good,** [39.35]**so that Allah will remove even the worst things they did, and He will give them their reward according to the best things they used to do.**

39.36For His Servant, isn't Allah enough? O Prophet Muhammad, these disbelievers are trying to frighten you with those fake gods besides Him. There can be no guide for someone Allah calls misguided, 39.37and no one can mislead anyone Allah gives guidance to. Isn't Allah Almighty, Capable of Retaliation?

39.38O Prophet Muhammad, if you ask the disbelievers: "Who created the heavens and the earth?" they will certainly reply: "Allah." You should ask: "Have you people ever thought about the things you pray to besides Allah: can any of them remove the suffering Allah may want me to suffer, or hold back the mercy He may want to show me?" Say: "Allah is enough for me. Those who trust put their trust only in Him."

39.39Say: "My people! Continue working as you all are; I am also working. You will very soon come to know 39.40who will suffer a punishment that will humiliate him, and an everlasting punishment that will come down on him."

39.41We have revealed to you the Book with the truth for guiding people. Anyone who accepts guidance, does so for his own good; anyone who goes astray, does so to his own loss. You won't be held responsible for them. 39.42It is Allah Who takes away the souls of people at the time of their death, and during sleep of those who haven't yet died. He holds back the souls of those whose death He has decided and sends back the rest until an end date of their death. There are certainly signs in this for any people who think deeply.

39.43Have they taken intercessors other than Allah? Ask: "What? Even if they don't have any power at all and cannot even think?" 39.44Say: "All intercession depends on Allah if He will accept it. Control of the heavens and the earth also belongs to Him. Eventually, it is Him you will all be taken back to." ³⁹·⁴⁵When Allah is mentioned on His own, the hearts of those who don't believe in the Hereafter are filled with disgust; but when false gods other than Allah are mentioned, the disbelievers immediately become happy. ³⁹·⁴⁶O Prophet Muhammad, say: "O Allah, Maker of the heavens and the earth, Knower of the unseen secrets and the visible! Only You will judge between your servants about the disagreements they used to have."

³⁹·⁴⁷Even if the wrongdoers owned everything in the world and just as much more with it, they would want to give it up as ransom to save themselves from the grievous punishment on Judgement Day. They will be shown by their Lord something so scary they had never imagined! ³⁹·⁴⁸The bad things they did will also appear to them and the punishment they used to make fun of will end up punishing them.

³⁹·⁴⁹Now, when anyone suffers harm, he prays to Us. Then, when We do him favours from Us, he claims: "I've been given this only because of certain skills I have." Never! It is a test but most of them don't realise. ³⁹·⁵⁰Those before them said this too, but everything they achieved couldn't save them, ³⁹·⁵¹so the bad things they did made them suffer. The bad things the wrongdoers from among these people do will make them suffer too, and they won't be able to escape. ³⁹·⁵²Don't they realise that it is Allah Who can increase or restrict wealth for anyone He chooses? There are certainly signs in this for any people who believe.

³⁹·⁵³Say: "My servants who have gone to extremes against themselves, you mustn't lose hope in Allah's mercy. It is Allah Who can forgive all sins. Only He is the Most Forgiving, the Ever-Merciful. ³⁹·⁵⁴You must turn to your Lord in repentance and surrender to Him as Muslims, before the punishment comes to you – after which you won't be helped. ³⁹·⁵⁵Follow the best teachings sent down to you from your

Lord, before the punishment comes upon you all of a sudden when you least expect it, $^{39.56}$in case someone says, 'Ah! I am damned that I neglected my duty to Allah, and was one of those who mocked His revelations,' $^{39.57}$or in case he says, 'If only Allah had guided me, I would certainly have been one of those who are mindful of Him,' $^{39.58}$or in case, when he sees the punishment, he says, 'If only we had a chance to go back, I would be one of those who do good.' $^{39.59}$The reply will be: 'Never! My revelations did come to you but you called them a lie, showed arrogance, and was one of the disbelievers!'."

$^{39.60}$O Prophet Muhammad, on Judgement Day, you will see those who lied about Allah; their faces will be gloomy. Isn't the place for arrogant people in Hell? $^{39.61}$Allah will save those who were mindful of Him by giving them positions of success. They will neither suffer hardship nor will they be sad.

$^{39.62}$Allah is the Creator of every thing and also in charge of every thing. $^{39.63}$The keys of the heavens and the earth belong only to Him. Those who disbelieve in Allah's revelations, it is really they who are the losers.

$^{39.64}$O Prophet Muhammad, say: "You ignorant people! Are you telling me to worship something other than Allah?" $^{39.65}$It has already been revealed to you, as well as to the prophets before you, that: "If you made partner-gods with Allah, your good acts would certainly be wasted and you would be among the losers." $^{39.66}$In fact, it is Allah you must worship, and be among those who are thankful.

$^{39.67}$They haven't appreciated Allah's true value, when on Judgement Day, the whole world will be in His Grip of control and the heavens will be rolled up in His Right Hand of power. Glory be to Him! He is much higher than the partner-gods they make with Him.

39.68 The Trumpet will be blown the first time and everyone in the heavens and the earth will faint, except someone Allah chooses. Then it will be blown again, and they will immediately stand up, staring. 39.69 The land of the Great gathering will shine with the light of its Lord, the Record of everything will be placed open, the prophets and the witnesses will be brought forward, and judgement will be made between them with the truth. They won't be treated unfairly. 39.70 Everyone will be paid in full for what they did, and Allah knows best everything they do.

39.71 The disbelievers will be driven to Hell in crowds, until when they arrive there, its gates will be opened, and its gatekeepers will ask: "Didn't messengers come to you from among you, reciting to you Allah's revelations, and warning you of the meeting of this Day of yours?" They will reply: "Yes, of course!" but the decision of punishment will have already proven true against the disbelievers. 39.72 They will be told: "Enter the gates of Hell, to remain in it forever. What a dreadful place for arrogant people to be in!"

39.73 Those who were mindful of their Lord will be driven to Paradise in groups, until when they arrive there, its gates will be opened, and its gatekeepers will say: "Peace be upon you. You have done well. Enter it, to remain here forever." 39.74 They will reply: "All praise is for Allah Who has fulfilled His promise to us, and made us inheritors of this place. We can live in Paradise wherever we want. What an excellent reward for those who work hard!"

39.75 O Prophet Muhammad, you will see the angels surrounding the Throne on all sides, glorifying His praises. Truthful judgement will be made between the people, and it will be announced: "All praise is for Allah – Lord of all the worlds!"

Surah 40. The Forgiver (*al-Ghaafir*)

Allah's name I begin with, the Most Compassionate, the Ever-Merciful

40.1 Haa Meem.
40.2 This Book's revelation comes from Allah, the Almighty, the All-Knowing, 40.3 the Forgiver of sins, the Acceptor of repentance, the Severe in punishing, the Lord of generosity. There is no god except Him. The final return will be to Him.

40.4 O Prophet Muhammad, **only disbelievers dispute about Allah's revelations, so their free movement in all the lands mustn't trick you.** 40.5 Before them, the people of Nuh also called the truth a lie, and so did many groups after them. Every community plotted to defeat their own messenger, and they used false arguments to wipe out the truth, so I punished them. How terrible was My punishment! 40.6 In this way something already fixed by your Lord proved true against the disbelievers, that they will be the people of the Fire.

40.7 **Those** angels **who carry the Throne and also those surrounding it, they glorify the praises of their Lord, believe in Him, and beg forgiveness for the Believers** praying: "Our Lord! You surround everything in Your mercy and knowledge, so forgive those who repent and those who follow Your way, and protect them from the punishment of Hell-Fire. 40.8 Our Lord! Enter them into the Gardens of Eden You have promised them, and their righteous forefathers, spouses, and descendants too. Only You are the Almighty, the All-Wise. 40.9 **Protect them from** the punishment for **bad things. On that Day, anyone You protect from** the punishment for **bad things, You will have definitely shown him mercy. That will be the tremendous victory.**"

⁴⁰·¹⁰The disbelievers will be called out: "When you were invited to the faith of Islam and you disbelieved, Allah's displeasure with you was greater than your own hatred for yourselves Today." ⁴⁰·¹¹They will reply: "Our Lord! You gave us death twice and life twice. Now we confess our sins. Is there any way out of this punishment?" ⁴⁰·¹²This punishment is because when Allah was prayed to on His Own, you people disbelieved, and you would only believe if partner-gods were made with Him. Now, the judgement is only Allah's, the Most High, the Great. ⁴⁰·¹³He is the one Who shows you His signs and sends down for you food from the sky. However, only someone who turns to Allah can remind himself of Him.

⁴⁰·¹⁴You must all pray to Allah in sincere devotion to Him even if the disbelievers hate it. ⁴⁰·¹⁵Allah is the Raiser of ranks, the Lord of the Throne, sends the revelation by His command to any of His servants He chooses, to give warnings of the Day of Meeting on Judgement Day ⁴⁰·¹⁶– the Day they will all come out. Nothing about them at all will be hidden from Allah. It will be said: "Who has control Today? Allah, the One, the Dominant!" ⁴⁰·¹⁷Today, everyone will be rewarded according to what they did. There will be no unfairness Today. Allah is quick in settling accounts.

⁴⁰·¹⁸O Prophet Muhammad, warn them of the Day that is getting closer, when hearts will jump into throats as they suppress their sadness. The wrongdoers won't have any loyal friend or intercessor who could be listened to. ⁴⁰·¹⁹Allah knows the tricks done with the eyes and everything the hearts are hiding. ⁴⁰·²⁰Allah judges with the truth, whereas those things these people are praying to besides Him, they cannot make any judgement at all. Only Allah is the All-Hearing, the Ever-Watchful.

⁴⁰·²¹Don't they travel through the earth and take a look at what was the end result of those who lived before them? They were more powerful than these people and had greater influence in the world, yet Allah punished them because of their sins, and they had no one to save them from the punishment of Allah. ⁴⁰·²²This is because messengers used to come to them with clear proofs, but they disbelieved and that is why Allah punished them. He is Strong, severe in punishing.

⁴⁰·²³We sent Musa with Our signs and a clear authority ⁴⁰·²⁴to Fir'awn, Haamaan, and Qarun, but they called him: "A magician, a complete liar!" ⁴⁰·²⁵When he came to them with the truth from Us, they announced: "Kill the boys of those who believe with him but keep their women alive!" However, plots of disbelievers only go wrong. ⁴⁰·²⁶Fir'awn said: "Let me kill Musa, and let him call out to his Lord! I'm afraid he might change your religion or spread trouble in the land." ⁴⁰·²⁷Musa replied: "I ask my Lord and yours too to protect me from every arrogant person who doesn't believe in the Day of Reckoning."

⁴⁰·²⁸A Believing man from among Fir'awn's people, who was keeping his faith secret, said: "Are you going to kill a man merely because he says, 'My Lord is Allah,' when he has come to you with clear signs from your Lord? If he is a liar, then his lies will be to his own loss; if he is truthful then you will suffer as much as he is warning you. Allah doesn't let anyone succeed who goes to extremes, or is a complete liar. ⁴⁰·²⁹My people! Today, you are in power; you are ruling over the land, but who will save us from Allah's punishment if it comes to us?" Fir'awn said: "I only tell you what I think, and I'm only showing you the right way."

⁴⁰·³⁰Then that Believer said: "My people! I fear for you something like the day of disaster of the previous communities ⁴⁰·³¹– something like

what happened to the people of Nuh, the 'Ad, the Thamud, and those who came after them. Allah doesn't want any unfairness coming to His servants. [40.32]My people! I fear for you the Day of Crying Out [40.33]– the Day you will all turn your backs running away. You won't have anyone to defend you from the punishment of Allah. There can be no guide for someone Allah calls misguided.

[40.34]Yusuf has already been to you long ago, with clear signs, but you didn't stop having doubts in what guidance he brought you. Eventually, when he passed away, you people said: 'Allah won't send any messenger after him.' In this way, Allah lets doubting extremists go astray, [40.35]who dispute about Allah's revelations without any authority given to them. This behaviour is terribly hateful in the sight of Allah and the Believers. In this way Allah seals up the hearts of every arrogant tyrant."

[40.36]Fir'awn ordered: "Haamaan! Build me a high tower so I can reach the pathways [40.37]– the pathways to the heavens, so I can climb up to Musa's God, even though I think Musa is a liar." This is how the bad things Fir'awn was doing were made to seem attractive to him, and he was blocked from knowing the right way. Fir'awn's plot only led to his own destruction.

[40.38]Then that Believer said: "My people! Follow me and I will lead you to the right way. [40.49]My people! This life is only temporary enjoyment whereas the Hereafter is the real home to stay in forever. [40.40]Anyone who does something bad will be punished only one equal to it. Any male or female Believer who does anything good, it is they who will enter Paradise where they will be given without limits. [40.41]My people! Why is it that I'm calling you to success yet you're calling me to the Fire? [40.42]You are calling me to disbelieve in Allah and make partner-gods with Him of things I don't know anything about, whereas I'm calling you to Allah – the Almighty, the Ever-Forgiving. ⁴⁰·⁴³There's no doubt that the things you are calling me to aren't even worth calling to, neither in this world nor the next. Our return will be to Allah. Those who go to extremes will really be the people of the Fire. ⁴⁰·⁴⁴You people will remember what I'm telling you now. I give up my affair to Allah. He is Ever-Watchful of His servants." ⁴⁰·⁴⁵Then Allah protected him from the bad things they had plotted, and the grievous punishment ended up punishing Fir'awn's own people.

⁴⁰·⁴⁶They will be brought in front of the Fire morning and evening. The Day when the Final Hour will take place, it will be ordered: "Force Fir'awn's people into the harshest punishment!" ⁴⁰·⁴⁷When they will be arguing with each other in the Fire, the weak followers will say to those leaders who showed arrogance: "We used to be your followers, so will you remove any part of the Fire from us?" ⁴⁰·⁴⁸Those who showed arrogance will say: "We're all being punished in it! Allah has already judged between the servants."

⁴⁰·⁴⁹Those in the Fire will plead to Hell's gatekeepers: "Pray to your Lord to reduce the punishment for us even for a day." ⁴⁰·⁵⁰They will ask: "Didn't your messengers used to come to you with clear signs?" They will reply: "Yes, of course." The gatekeepers will say: "Then you yourselves pray!" However, the disbelievers' prayer will be of no use.

⁴⁰·⁵¹We certainly help our messengers, and the Believers too, both in this life and also on the Day when witnesses will stand to testify ⁴⁰·⁵²– the Day when the wrongdoers' excuses won't help them. They'll be cursed and will have a dreadful home.

⁴⁰·⁵³We gave Musa the guidance and made the Descendants of Ya'qub inheritors of the Book ⁴⁰·⁵⁴– which is a guidance and a reminder for people of understanding.

⁴⁰·⁵⁵O Prophet Muhammad, **you should continue to have patience because Allah's promise is true. You should ask forgiveness for a fault** that it does not come **from you, and glorify the praises of your Lord evening and morning.** ⁴⁰·⁵⁶Those who dispute Allah's revelations without any authority given to them, they have only greed in their hearts for a greatness they will never achieve. So, you should ask Allah to protect you. Only he is the All-Hearing, the Ever-Watchful.

⁴⁰·⁵⁷Creating the heavens and the earth is far greater than creating humans, but most people don't know.

⁴⁰·⁵⁸The blind and the seeing person cannot be equal, nor can those who believe and do good be equal to evildoers. How little you remind yourselves! ⁴⁰·⁵⁹The Final Hour, in which there is no doubt, will certainly come, but most people don't believe.

⁴⁰·⁶⁰Your Lord says: "Pray to Me and I will respond to you. Those who turn arrogantly away from worshipping Me will soon enter Hell humiliated."

⁴⁰·⁶¹Allah is the one Who made the night for you to rest in and the day clear to see. Allah gives grace to people yet most of them don't even give thanks. ⁴⁰·⁶²That is Allah – your Lord, the Creator of everything. There is no god except Him. So how are you being misled! ⁴⁰·⁶³In this way those who reject Allah's revelations are being misled.

⁴⁰·⁶⁴Allah is the one Who made the earth for you people to live in, and the sky a structure, shaped you in the womb and gave you a beautiful form, and gave you wholesome things. That is Allah – your Lord. So, blessed is Allah – Lord of all the worlds. ⁴⁰·⁶⁵He is the Ever-Living.

There is no god except Him, so pray to Him in sincere devotion to Him. All praise is for Allah – Lord of all the worlds.

40.66O Prophet Muhammad, say: "I am forbidden to worship those you pray to besides Allah because clear signs have appeared to me from my Lord. I've been ordered to surrender as Muslim to Allah – the Lord of all the worlds." 40.67He is the one Who created you originally from dust, then from a drop of semen, then from a clinging clot; then brought you out as a baby then nourished you so you could reach your full strength, and so you could become old – though some of you have your souls taken away sooner – so you can reach an end date of your death, and because of that you might think. 40.68He is the one Who gives life and death, and whenever He decides something to happen, He only says to it: "Be!" and it becomes.

40.69Don't you see those who dispute Allah's revelations? How are they being turned away from the truth? 40.70Those who called the Book a lie, and also everything We sent Our messengers with, they will very soon come to know the end result, 40.71when there will be iron collars on their necks, and chains too. They will be dragged away 40.72into the boiling liquid, then into the Fire to be burned as fuel. 40.73Then they will be asked: "Where are those you used to make partner-gods 40.74besides Allah? They will reply: "They've abandoned us! Actually, we never worshipped anything before." This is why Allah calls the disbelievers astray. 40.75They will be told: "This punishment is because you used to rejoice in the world for the wrong reasons, and because you used to show arrogance. 40.76Now enter the gates of Hell, to remain in it forever. What a dreadful place for arrogant people to be in!"

40.77O Prophet Muhammad, you should continue to have patience because Allah's promise is true. It doesn't matter if We show you some of that punishment we are warning them of or We take away your soul before that, because it is Us they will be brought back to. ⁴⁰·⁷⁸We already sent messengers before you; some We have told you about and others We haven't. It was never the duty of any messenger to show a sign without Allah's permission. Finally, when Allah's command arrives, it will be decided with the truth, and the supporters of falsehood will lose there and then.

⁴⁰·⁷⁹Allah is the one Who made livestock for you so you can ride on some and others you can eat. ⁴⁰·⁸⁰There are many benefits in them for you; you can reach on them destinations you desire in your hearts. You can be carried on them and on boats too. ⁴⁰·⁸¹He shows you His many signs. So, which of Allah's signs will you reject?

⁴⁰·⁸²Don't they travel through the earth and take a look at what was the end result of those before them? They were more than these people in number, more powerful than them, and had greater influence in the world, yet nothing they achieved could save them. ⁴⁰·⁸³Whenever their messengers came to them with clear signs, they showed pride in any knowledge and skills they already had. However, the punishment they used to make fun of ended up punishing them. ⁴⁰·⁸⁴So, when they saw Our punishment, they cried: "We believe in Allah, the One, and we reject anything we used to make partner-gods with Him." ⁴⁰·⁸⁵Now that they will have seen Our punishment, their belief isn't going to help them. Allah used to do this with His servants in the past. The disbelievers will lose there and then.

Surah 41. (Verses) Explained in Detail (*Fussilat*)

Allah's name I begin with, the Most Compassionate, the Ever-Merciful

41.1 Haa Meem.

41.2 This is a revelation from Allah – the Most Compassionate, the Ever-Merciful, 41.3 – a Book whose verses are explained in detail, a Qur'an in Arabic for any people who have the right knowledge, 41.4 giving good news and warnings, yet most of them turn away so they cannot hear. 41.5 They say: "Our hearts are under covers from what you are inviting us to, and deafness in our ears too, as well as a barrier between us and you. So, continue working; we are also working."

41.6 O Prophet Muhammad, say: "I'm only human, just like you, but it is revealed to me that your God is One God. Therefore, you people must stay strong on the path towards Him and beg Him to forgive you." The polytheists are damned, 41.7 who don't give charity, and it is they who disbelieve in the Hereafter. 41.8 Those who believe and do good will have a never-ending reward.

41.9 Ask: "Do you disbelieve in Him Who, in two stages, created the earth? Are you making others equal to Him? He is the Lord of all the worlds." 41.10 He has placed in the earth firm mountains towering above it, and He has blessed it, and placed its sustenance with due proportion inside it – all in four stages. This sustenance is equal for those who look for it. 41.11 Then He focussed on the sky when it was smoke and He ordered it and the earth too: "With pleasure or with force, you must both come into My obedience." Both replied: "We will come with pleasure." 41.12 Then He turned the sky into seven heavens in two stages, and gave each its duty. We decorated the lowest heaven with stars and to protect against. That's the fixed plan of Allah – the Almighty, the All-Knowing.

[41.13]Now, if the disbelievers turn away, say: "I have warned you of a thunderbolt like that which struck the 'Ad and the Thamud." [41.14]When messengers came to them from in front of them and behind them – everywhere, saying: "Don't worship anyone except Allah," they replied: "If our Lord had wanted, He would certainly have sent down angels. So, we disbelieve in what you've been sent with." [41.15]The 'Ad behaved arrogantly on earth without having any right to do so, and they bragged: "Who can be more powerful than us?" What? Didn't they see that Allah, Who created them, is far more powerful than them? But they would still reject Our revelations! [41.16]So, during days of disaster, We sent against them a furious wind to make them taste a punishment of humiliation in this life, but the punishment of the Hereafter will be far more humiliating, and they simply won't be helped.

[41.17]As for the Thamud, We gave them guidance, but they preferred being blind to it, so the thunderbolt of a disgracing punishment seized them for the bad things they used to do. [41.18]We saved those who believed and were mindful of Us.

[41.19]The Day Allah's enemies will be pushed towards the Fire, they will be kept well organised and marched in groups, [41.20]until, when they reach the Fire, their ears, eyes, and skins will testify against them about the bad things they used to do. [41.21]They will ask their skins: "Why are you testifying against us?" who will reply: "Allah, Who gives speaking power to everything, has let us speak. He created you the first time and it is Him you are all being taken back to." [41.22]You couldn't hide yourselves in a way that your ears, eyes, and skins wouldn't be able to testify against you, but thought that Allah wouldn't know much of what you were doing. [41.23]This evil thought of yours which you had about your Lord is what ruined you, and so you became losers. ⁴¹·²⁴Even if they have patience now, the Fire will still be their place to stay. They won't be among those who had Allah's good pleasure even if they try their best to earn it.

⁴¹·²⁵We let them have some close friends who made what was in front of them and behind them – everywhere seem attractive to them. The same command proved true against them as that against communities of humans and jinns who had been and gone before them. They were losers.

⁴¹·²⁶The disbelievers say: "Don't listen to this Qur'an, but drown it out with noises and interruption so you can win." ⁴¹·²⁷However, We will certainly make the disbelievers taste a severe punishment, and We will certainly punish them for the worst they used to do. ⁴¹·²⁸This is the punishment of Allah's enemies: the Fire! It'll be an everlasting home for them, as a punishment for rejecting Our revelations. ⁴¹·²⁹The disbelievers will cry: "Our Lord! Show us those jinns and humans who misled us so we can crush them under our feet, so they will be humiliated."

⁴¹·³⁰Those who declare: "Our Lord is Allah," and then stay strong, angels descend upon them saying: "Don't be afraid nor worry, but be happy in the good news of the Paradise that you've been promised. ⁴¹·³¹We are your friends and protectors in this life and the next. You can have there whatever you desire, and you will receive anything you ask for, ⁴¹·³²as a special place to come and stay, from a Most Forgiving, Ever-Merciful Lord."

⁴¹·³³Whose words could be better than someone who invites to Allah, does good, and says: "I'm of those who surrender to Allah as Muslims." ⁴¹·³⁴Good and evil can never be the same. Respond to evil with something better, in which case if there was any hatred between

you and someone, he will become a loyal friend. ⁴¹·³⁵This goodness is only given to those who have patience and who are people of great fortune. ⁴¹·³⁶O human! If a suggestion from Shaytan tempts you, ask Allah to protect you. Only He is the All-Hearing, the All-Knowing.

⁴¹·³⁷Among His Signs are the night and day, and the sun and moon. You mustn't prostrate to the sun or the moon but to Allah Who created them if you worship Him only. ⁴¹·³⁸However, it makes no difference if the disbelievers are too arrogant to worship Him because those in your Lord's presence glorify Him night and day without getting tired. <Prostration Point 11>

⁴¹·³⁹Among His Signs is also that you see the earth is dry, but when We send down water to it, it stirs to life and swells. The one Who gives it life can certainly bring the dead back to life too because He is Most Capable of anything. ⁴¹·⁴⁰Those who abuse Our verses aren't hidden from Us. Who is better: someone who is thrown into the Fire or someone who comes through safely on Judgement Day? You are free to do whatever you want. He is Ever-Watchful of everything you do. ⁴¹·⁴¹Those who reject the Reminder after it has come to them should know that it is certainly a mighty Book. ⁴¹·⁴²Falsehood cannot challenge it from neither in front of it nor behind it nor anywhere. It is a revelation from an All-Wise, Most Praiseworthy Lord.

⁴¹·⁴³O Prophet Muhammad, nothing new is said to you that wasn't said to messengers before you. Your Lord is certainly the Master of forgiveness and He is the Master of painful punishment too. ⁴¹·⁴⁴If We had sent this as a Qur'an in a language that wasn't Arabic, the disbelievers would have certainly asked: "Why aren't its verses explained clearly? What? A Book in a language that isn't Arabic and a Prophet who is an Arab?" O Prophet Muhammad, say: "It is a guidance and a healing for the Believers. Those who don't believe,

they have deafness in their ears, and it is blindness for them too. It's as if they are being called out from a place far away."

41.45 We already gave Musa the Book but disagreements arose about it. If it wasn't for something already fixed by your Lord, the matter would have been settled immediately between them. They are in serious doubt about the Qur'an.

41.46 Anyone who does good, does it for his own benefit; anyone who does bad, does so to his own loss. Your Lord doesn't treat His servants unfairly.

[PART 25]
41.47 Knowledge of the Final Hour is referred only to Him. No fruit comes out of its husk, and no female becomes pregnant or gives birth without Him knowing. On that Day, Allah will call out to the disbelievers: "Where are My partner-gods?" The polytheists will reply: "We declare to You that none of us can testify." 41.48 Those idols they used to previously pray to will abandon them, and they'll realise there's no way out for them.

41.49 The human being doesn't get tired of praying for good, but when he suffers harm, he becomes disappointed and begins to lose hope. 41.50 If We give him a taste of some special mercy from Us after he had suffered some hard times, he will certainly say: "I deserve this. I don't think the Final Hour will come. Even if I was taken back to my Lord, I will deserve the best from Him." However, We will certainly tell the disbelievers about what they did, and make them taste some severe punishment. 41.51 When We do him favours, he turns away and moves to the side far from Us, but when he suffers harm, he makes lengthy prayers to get closer to Us.

41.52O Prophet Muhammad, ask: "Have you people ever thought if this Qur'an really is from Allah and yet you reject it, who could be further astray than someone who is in extreme hostility?" 41.53We will soon show them Our signs in the world's furthest regions and within themselves too until it becomes clear to them that this is the truth. Isn't your Lord enough as He is a Witness to everything?

41.54Beware! These people are in doubt about the meeting with their Lord. Beware! He completely surrounds everything.

Surah 42. Consultation (ash-Shooraa)

Allah's name I begin with, the Most Compassionate, the Ever-Merciful

42.1Haa Meem,

42.2'Ayn Seen Qaaf.

42.3O Prophet Muhammad, this is how Allah – the Almighty, the All-Wise, has been sending revelations to you and those before you. 42.4Everything in the heavens and the earth belongs only to Him. He is the Most High, the Most Great. 42.5The heavens are about to burst apart above each other, but the angels glorify the praises of their Lord and ask forgiveness for those on earth. Beware! Only Allah is the Most Forgiving, the Ever-Merciful.

42.6O Prophet Muhammad, those who take protectors other than Allah should know that He is watching them, and you aren't responsible for them. 42.7In this way We revealed to you a Qur'an in Arabic, so you can warn the Mother of Cities (- Makkah) and everyone around it, and give warnings of the Day of Gathering in which there is no doubt, when a group will be in Paradise and a group in the Blazing Fire. 42.8If Allah had wanted, He could have made them all a single community, but He only takes into His special mercy anyone He chooses. The wrongdoers won't have any protector or helper. ⁴²·⁹What? Have they taken besides Him other protectors? Only Allah is the Protector, and only He brings the dead back to life, because He is Most Capable of anything.

⁴²·¹⁰Whatever you disagree about, its decision is eventually with Allah. That is Allah – my Lord. I put my trust only in Him, and I turn only to Him ⁴²·¹¹– the Maker of the heavens and the earth. He has made for you pairs from among yourselves, and pairs among livestock too. He multiplies you by this pairing. There is nothing like Him. He is the All-Hearing, the Ever-Watchful. ⁴²·¹²The keys of the heavens and the earth belong only to Him. He can increase or restrict wealth for anyone He chooses. He knows everything perfectly well.

⁴²·¹³He has made for you people the same religion He fixed for Nuh – as well as what We revealed to you, O Prophet Muhammad – and what We fixed for Ibrahim, Musa, and Isa, commanding: "Stick to the true religion and don't break up with each other in it. What you are inviting the polytheists to is unbearable for them. Allah selects for Himself anyone He chooses and guides to Himself anyone who turns to Him." ⁴²·¹⁴It was only after knowledge had come to them that they broke up with each other because they were jealous of each other. If it wasn't for something already fixed by your Lord until a set term, the matter would have been settled immediately between them. However, those who were made inheritors of the Book after them are really in serious doubt about it.

⁴²·¹⁵So, you should continue to invite to this true religion, stay strong as you've been ordered, and not follow their desires. You should say: "I believe in what Allah has revealed from any Book, and I've been ordered to do justice between you. Allah is our Lord and yours too. We are responsible for our actions and you for yours. There is no need

for any argument between us and you. Allah will gather us together and the final return will be to Him."

$^{42.16}$"Those who dispute about the religion of Allah after it has been accepted, their arguing is pointless in the sight of their Lord. They will have anger upon them and will suffer a severe punishment. $^{42.17}$Allah is the one Who has revealed the Book with the truth, and the Balance of justice. What will explain to you that the Final Hour might be near? $^{42.18}$Those who don't even believe in it want it to come sooner, whereas the Believers are terrified of it; they know that it is the truth. Beware! Those who are in doubt about the Final Hour are clearly astray.

$^{42.19}$Allah is Gentle to His servants, giving to anyone He chooses. He is also the Strong, the Almighty. $^{42.20}$Anyone who wants the harvest of the Hereafter, We will increase it for him; anyone who wants the harvest of this world, We will give it to him, but he won't have any share in the Hereafter.

$^{42.21}$What? Do they have partner-gods who made for them some religion for which Allah hasn't given any permission? If it wasn't for something decisive already fixed, the matter would have been settled immediately between them. The wrongdoers will suffer a painful punishment.

$^{42.22}$O Prophet Muhammad, you will see the wrongdoers terrified because of what they did, as the punishment will come down on them. Those who believe and do good will be in the Gardens of Paradise: they will have whatever they wish from their Lord. This is the immense grace. $^{42.23}$This is the good news Allah promises His servants who believe and do good. O Prophet Muhammad, say: "I'm not asking you any payment for this guidance but love for close relatives." Anyone who does something good, We will increase its good effect for him. Allah is Most Forgiving, Most Appreciative.

42.24What? Are they saying: "He has made a lie about Allah."? If Allah wants, He can put a seal of protection on your noble heart. Allah deletes falsehood and proves the truth with His words. He knows the secrets of the hearts perfectly well.

42.25He is the one Who accepts repentance from His servants and forgives sins, knowing everything you people do. 42.26He responds to those who believe and do good, and increases them in His grace. The disbelievers will suffer a severe punishment.

42.27If Allah increased wealth for all His servants, they would certainly make trouble on earth, and so He sends it down in perfect amount as He chooses. He is Fully-Aware, Ever-Watchful of His servants. 42.28He is the one Who sends down gentle rain even after the people have lost hope, and spreads His mercy. He is the Protector, the Most Praiseworthy.

42.29Among His signs is the creation of the heavens and the earth, and all kinds of animals He has scattered in them. He is Most Capable of gathering them together whenever He wants. 42.30Whatever disaster you people suffer, it's because of what you did, though He forgives a lot of sins. 42.31You cannot escape in this world. You don't have any protector or helper besides Him.

42.32Among His signs are also the ships like mountains in the sea. 42.33If He wants, He can make the wind stop and the ships would stand still on its surface. There are certainly signs in this for anyone who is very patient, very thankful. 42.34He could even wreck the ships for the bad things its people did, but He forgives a lot of sins. 42.35Those who dispute about Our revelations should know that there's no way out for them.

⁴²·³⁶Anything you've been given is only the enjoyment of this life, whereas what is with Allah is best and lasts forever – given to those who believe and put their trust only in their Lord, ⁴²·³⁷and to those who stay clear of the big sins and anything shameful, and forgive even when they're angry, ⁴²·³⁸and to those who respond to their Lord, and establish the ritual prayers; whose matters are decided through consultation between themselves; and they donate from what We've given them, ⁴²·³⁹and to those who defend themselves when they're oppressed.

⁴²·⁴⁰The punishment for something bad might be just as bad. However, if someone forgives and puts things right, his reward will come from Allah. Allah doesn't like wrongdoers. ⁴²·⁴¹Those who defend themselves after being wronged won't be blamed. ⁴²·⁴²In fact, blame is on those who oppress people and spread unjust aggression in the world. It is they who will suffer a painful punishment. ⁴²·⁴³Someone who has patience and forgives, now surely this is a sign of strong will.

⁴²·⁴⁴Anyone Allah allows to go astray will have no protector after that. O Prophet Muhammad, when the wrongdoers see the punishment, you'll see them saying: "Is there any way back to the world?" ⁴²·⁴⁵You'll see them brought in front of Hell, humble out of disgrace, glancing secretly at it. The Believers say: "The real losers are those who will ruin themselves and also their families on Judgement Day." Beware! The wrongdoers will be in an everlasting punishment. ⁴²·⁴⁶They won't have any protectors to help them besides Allah. Anyone Allah calls misguided will have no way to escape.

⁴²·⁴⁷**You** people **must respond to your Lord before comes a Day when there'll be no turning back from Allah. There'll be no place of refuge for you that Day and no possibility for you to disagree** about your sins.

⁴²·⁴⁸O Prophet Muhammad, **if they still turn away then** they should know that **We haven't sent you to be watching over them. Your duty is only to deliver the message. When We give humans a taste of some special mercy from Us, they rejoice in it, but when they suffer a disaster because of the bad things they've done, humans become unthankful.**

⁴²·⁴⁹**Control of the heavens and the earth belongs to Allah. He creates whatever He wants. He gives daughters or sons to anyone He chooses,** ⁴²·⁵⁰**or He gives them both sons as well as daughters, and leaves anyone He chooses unable to have children. He is All-Knowing, Most Capable.**

⁴²·⁵¹**It isn't normal for any human that Allah should speak to him directly but by revelation, or from behind a screen, or by sending a messenger-angel to reveal – with His permission – what He decides. He is Most High, All-Wise.** ⁴²·⁵²O Prophet Muhammad, **this is how We revealed to you a Spirit (- the Qur'an) by Our command. You knew the details of neither the Book nor faith but We have made it a light by which We guide any of Our servants we choose. You certainly do guide to a path that is straight** ⁴²·⁵³**– the Path to Allah, Who owns everything in the heavens and the earth. Beware! All matters return to Allah.**

Surah 43. Decorations of Gold (*az-Zukhruf*)

Allah's name I begin with, the Most Compassionate, the Ever-Merciful

43.1*Haa Meem.*

43.2I swear by the Clear Book: 43.3We have made it a Qur'an in Arabic so that you might think. 43.4It is high in status, full of wisdom – in the Master Record with Us.

43.5Should We take this Reminder away from you people, without concern for you, simply because you're a people going to extremes? 43.6How many prophets have We sent among the previous people! 43.7Whenever a prophet came to them, they would make fun of him, 43.8so We destroyed those – who were even more powerful than these disbelievers of Makkah. The example of previous people has already been mentioned.

43.9O Prophet Muhammad, if you ask them: "Who created the heavens and the earth?" they will certainly reply: "Allah – the Almighty, the All-Knowing created them;" 43.10– Who made the earth spread out for you and made pathways for you through it so you can find your way; 43.11– Who sends down from the sky water in perfect amount, with which We bring back to life a land that is dead. This is how you people will be brought out again alive. 43.12– Who created all kinds of things, and made for you ships and livestock on which you ride, 43.13so that you can sit firmly on their backs, then you can remember your Lord's favour when you are sitting firmly on them, and say: "Glory be to Him Who has made it obey us because we couldn't have done it on our own. 43.14We will certainly go back to our Lord."

43.15The polytheists made some of Allah's servants a part of Him in divinity. Humans are openly unthankful. 43.16What? Has He chosen from what He has created daughters for Himself and preferred sons for you people? ⁴³·¹⁷When good news of a daughter born to him is given to any of them of what he ascribes to Allah - the Most Compassionate, his face turns gloomy as he tries to hide his anger. ⁴³·¹⁸Would Allah have as a child someone brought up in finery and unable to make clear arguments? ⁴³·¹⁹They describe the angels as females, who themselves are servants of Allah - the Most Compassionate. Did these people witness them being created? Their statements will be recorded, and they will be questioned.

⁴³·²⁰They say: "If Allah - the Most Compassionate had wanted, we wouldn't have worshipped them." They don't know anything about this! They are only guessing! ⁴³·²¹What? Have We given them before this any Holy Book which they follow as an authority? ⁴³·²²In fact, they say: "We saw our forefathers following a certain religion, and so we're following right behind them in guidance." ⁴³·²³O Prophet Muhammad, in the same way, whenever we sent a warner to any town, its elite would say: "We saw our forefathers following a certain religion, and so we're right behind them in their leadership." ⁴³·²⁴That warner asked: "What? Even that I've brought you better guidance than what you saw your forefathers doing?" They replied: "We disbelieve in what you prophets have been sent with." ⁴³·²⁵So We punished them. Now take a look at what was the end result of those who called the truth a lie.

⁴³·²⁶Remember when Ibrahim said to his foster father and his people: "I have nothing to do with what you worship, ⁴³·²⁷other than Him Who made me, and He will certainly guide me." ⁴³·²⁸He left this declaration as a statement to continue among his descendants so they'd keep turning back to Allah.

$^{43.29}$In fact, I let them, and their forefathers, enjoy themselves until there came to them the truth as well as a Messenger who makes things clear. $^{43.30}$However, when the truth did come to them, they said: "This is magic and we disbelieve in it." $^{43.31}$They also asked: "Why isn't this Qur'an revealed to a man who is high-ranking in the two cities (of Makkah and Ta'if)?" $^{43.32}$O Prophet Muhammad, is it they who distribute your Lord's mercy? We distribute their livelihood among them in this world and raise some of them above others in ranks so they can help each other in work. Your Lord's mercy is far better than the wealth they gather together.

$^{43.33}$If it wasn't for the possibility that people might become one community of disbelievers, We would have made for the homes of the disbelievers in Allah – the Most Compassionate: silver roofs, silver stairs they could climb, $^{43.34}$silver doors for their homes, silver thrones on which they could relax, $^{43.35}$and decorations of gold. All this might be the enjoyment of this life but the Hereafter with your Lord will be for those who are mindful of Him.

$^{43.36}$Anyone who turns away from remembering Allah – the Most Compassionate, We let a devil stick with him as his close friend. $^{43.37}$These devils block them from the right way while they falsely think they're following guidance. $^{43.38}$Finally, when he comes to Us, he will say to his devil friend: "Oh! If only there had been between me and you the distance of East and West. What an evil close friend you were!" $^{43.39}$This arguing won't help you Today because you all did wrong and that's why you will share the punishment together.

$^{43.40}$O Prophet Muhammad, will you make these deaf people listen, or guide those who are blind to the truth, and those who are clearly astray? $^{43.41}$Even if We took you away from this world, We would still punish them, $^{43.42}$or We will show you the punishment that We have warned them, because We have perfect control over them. ⁴³·⁴³So, keep a strong hold of what's been revealed to you. You're on a path that is straight. ⁴³·⁴⁴This Qur'an is certainly a great honour for you and your community. You'll all be asked about it. ⁴³·⁴⁵O Prophet Muhammad, ask those of Our messengers We sent before you if We made any gods to be worshipped besides Allah – the Most Compassionate.

⁴³·⁴⁶We sent Musa with Our signs to Fir'awn and his ministers, and he said: "I am a messenger from Allah – the Lord of all the worlds." ⁴³·⁴⁷However, when he came to them with Our signs, they began laughing at them. ⁴³·⁴⁸Any sign We showed them was far greater than the one before it, and We punished them each time so that they might turn back to guidance. ⁴³·⁴⁹They pleaded: "Magician! Pray for us to your Lord about the promise He made you and then we will follow guidance." ⁴³·⁵⁰However, when We removed the punishment from them, they immediately broke their promise.

⁴³·⁵¹Fir'awn made an announcement among his people. He said: "My people! Isn't the control of Egypt mine, as well these streams flowing beneath me? Can't you see? ⁴³·⁵²Tell me, aren't I better than this Musa, who is nothing and can barely speak clearly? ⁴³·⁵³Why hasn't he been given gold bracelets of kingship? Why haven't angels come with him in rows?" ⁴³·⁵⁴So, Fir'awn fooled his people and they obeyed him. They were a sinful people. ⁴³·⁵⁵When they provoked Us, We punished them: We drowned them, all together. ⁴³·⁵⁶We made them a thing of the past and an example for later generations.

⁴³·⁵⁷O Prophet Muhammad, when Isa ibn Maryam is given as an example, your people begin to laugh mockingly at it. ⁴³·⁵⁸They ask: "Who is better: our gods or he?" They mention him to you only to have an argument, because the truth is they are a quarrelsome

people. ⁴³·⁵⁹He was only a servant We did favours to, and made a model for the Descendants of Ya'qub. ⁴³·⁶⁰If We want, We can make angels from among you succeed you on earth. ⁴³·⁶¹Isa will be a sign for the Final Hour, so you people mustn't doubt it but keep following the guidance sent by Me. This is the path that is straight. ⁴³·⁶²Don't let Shaytan block you; he is your open enemy.

⁴³·⁶³When Isa came with clear signs, he said: "I've come to you with wisdom, and to make clear to you some of your disagreements. So, be mindful of Allah and obey me. ⁴³·⁶⁴Allah is the one Who is my Lord and yours too, so worship Him. This is a path that is straight." ⁴³·⁶⁵Then, various groups started having disagreements with each other, which is why the wrongdoers will be damned with the punishment of a Painful Day! ⁴³·⁶⁶Are they waiting to see if the Final Hour will come to them all of a sudden when they least expect it?

⁴³·⁶⁷On that Day, even close friends will be enemies of each other, except those who are mindful of Allah, ⁴³·⁶⁸who will be told: "My servants! You won't have anything to fear Today and you won't be sad. ⁴³·⁶⁹You are those who believed in Our revelations and had surrendered to Us as Muslims. ⁴³·⁷⁰Enter Paradise, you and your kinds; you will be delighted." ⁴³·⁷¹Gold trays and drinking cups will be passed around among them, and there'll be everything the hearts desire and the eyes enjoy watching. You will remain there forever. ⁴³·⁷²That is the Paradise you'll be made inheritors of because of the good things you used to do in this life. ⁴³·⁷³There'll be lots of fruit there for you to eat.

⁴³·⁷⁴The criminals will remain forever in the punishment of Hell ⁴³·⁷⁵that won't be reduced for them, and they'll remain there without any hope. ⁴³·⁷⁶It wasn't Us who harmed them but rather they themselves were the wrongdoers. ⁴³·⁷⁷They will cry out to the guard of Hell: "Maalik! Your Lord should finish us off!" He will reply: "You

will stay here forever." $^{43.78}$We brought you the truth but most of you hated it.

$^{43.79}$What? Have the disbelievers of Makkah made a final decision? We are also making a final decision. $^{43.80}$Do they think We cannot hear their secrets and their private discussions? Why not! Even Our messenger-angels are with them, recording. $^{43.81}$O Prophet Muhammad, say: "If Allah – the Most Compassionate had a child then I would be the first to worship." $^{43.82}$Glory be to the Lord of the heavens and the earth – Lord of the Throne – above what they describe. $^{43.83}$So leave them to joke about and play games until they meet that Day of theirs which they are being warned about.

$^{43.84}$He is the one Who is God in the sky and God on earth too. He is the All-Wise, the All-Knowing. $^{43.85}$Blessed is the one Who has control of the heavens and the earth and everything in between them. Only Allah has knowledge of the Final Hour. It is Him you will all be taken back to. $^{43.86}$Those they pray to besides Allah don't have any power of intercession; only those who testify to the truth have the power of intercession, and they know it.

$^{43.87}$O Prophet Muhammad, if you asked them who created them, they will certainly reply: "Allah!" So how are they being misled! $^{43.88}$I swear by Prophet Muhammad's words: "My Lord! These are a people who just won't believe!"

$^{43.89}$O Prophet Muhammad, you should turn away from them in forgiveness and say: "Peace." They will very soon come to know the end result.

Surah 44. Smoke (ad-Dukhaan)

Allah's name I begin with, the Most Compassionate, the Ever-Merciful

44.1Haa Meem.

44.2I swear by the Clear Book: 44.3We sent it down on a blessed night, though We have always been giving warnings. 44.4However, in this night, every wise matter is decided, 44.5as a command coming from Us. We have always sent messengers, 44.6as a mercy from your Lord. Only He is the All-Hearing, the All-Knowing, 44.7the Lord of the heavens and the earth and everything in between them – if only you would strongly believe! 44.8There is no god except Him. He gives life and death. He is your Lord and of your ancestors too. 44.9Yet they're in doubt, playing games.

44.10O Prophet Muhammad, so keep watching for the Day when the sky will show smoke clearly visible, 44.11sweeping over the people. They will cry: "This is a painful punishment. 44.12Our Lord! Remove this punishment from us. Now we believe!" 44.13How will they accept the message now when a Messenger has already come to them to make things clear 44.14but they turned away from him and said: "He must've been taught by others! Mad!" 44.15We can remove the punishment for a short while but you people will repeat your crimes. 44.16One Day We will grab firmly; on that Day We will give out punishment.

44.17Before them, We tested Fir'awn's people, when there came to them an honourable messenger 44.18saying: "Hand over to me Allah's servants. I'm a trustworthy messenger sent to you. 44.19Don't think you are greater than Allah. I've come to you with a clear authority. 44.20I have asked my Lord and yours too to protect me so you don't stone me to death nor abuse me. 44.21If you aren't going to believe because I say so then just leave me alone." ⁴⁴·²²Then he prayed to his Lord: "These are a criminal people."

⁴⁴·²³We said: "You should set out with My servants at night, though you will all be chased. ⁴⁴·²⁴Leave the sea divided and still after you have crossed it, because they are an army that will be drowned."

⁴⁴·²⁵How many gardens and fountains the disbelievers had to leave, ⁴⁴·²⁶and also crops and wonderful homes too, ⁴⁴·²⁷as well as the luxuries they used to enjoy! ⁴⁴·²⁸It was like that. Later We made other people inheritors of those things. ⁴⁴·²⁹Neither heaven nor earth cried for them, nor were they given any more chances.

⁴⁴·³⁰We saved the Descendants of Ya'qub from that humiliating suffering, ⁴⁴·³¹from Fir'awn. He was arrogant, from among those who go to extremes. ⁴⁴·³²We deliberately chose the Descendants of Ya'qub above all the people of their time, ⁴⁴·³³and gave them some signs in which there was an obvious test.

⁴⁴·³⁴These disbelievers of Makkah are saying: ⁴⁴·³⁵"There is nothing except for our first death, and we won't be brought back to life. ⁴⁴·³⁶Bring back our forefathers, if you are telling the truth."

⁴⁴·³⁷Who is better: they or the people of Tubba' and those before them? We destroyed them all. They were criminals. ⁴⁴·³⁸We didn't create the heavens and the earth and everything in between them so We could play games. ⁴⁴·³⁹We created them for a real purpose, yet most disbelievers don't realise. ⁴⁴·⁴⁰Decision Day is the time fixed for them all, ⁴⁴·⁴¹a Day when no friend will be able to save any friend in any way at all, and they simply won't be helped, ⁴⁴·⁴²except those Allah has mercy on. He is the Almighty, the Ever-Merciful.

⁴⁴·⁴³The Zaqqum tree ⁴⁴·⁴⁴will be the food of disobedient people, ⁴⁴·⁴⁵like molten brass that will bubble in the bellies ⁴⁴·⁴⁶like the bubbling of boiling liquid. ⁴⁴·⁴⁷It will be ordered: "Grab him and drag him into the middle of Hell-Fire ⁴⁴·⁴⁸then pour over his head the punishment of some boiling liquid." ⁴⁴·⁴⁹It will be said to him: "Have a taste! In the world you acted mighty, honourable. ⁴⁴·⁵⁰This is what you disbelievers used to have doubts about!"

⁴⁴·⁵¹Those who are mindful of Allah will be in a place that is safe, ⁴⁴·⁵²among gardens and fountains, ⁴⁴·⁵³dressed in fine silk and heavy brocade; they'll be facing each other. ⁴⁴·⁵⁴It will be like that. We will marry them to beautiful wide-eyed spouses of Paradise. ⁴⁴·⁵⁵There, they can peacefully call for every kind of fruit. ⁴⁴·⁵⁶They won't taste death there, except for the first death in this life, and Allah will protect them from the suffering of Hell-Fire ⁴⁴·⁵⁷– as grace from your Lord. That will be the tremendous victory.

⁴⁴·⁵⁸O Prophet Muhammad, We have made this Qur'an easy in your own language so that they might remind themselves. ⁴⁴·⁵⁹So keep waiting; they will be waiting too.

Surah 45. Kneeling (al-Jaathiyah)

Allah's name I begin with, the Most Compassionate, the Ever-Merciful

⁴⁵·¹Haa Meem.
⁴⁵·²This Book's revelation comes from Allah, the Almighty, the All-Wise.

⁴⁵·³In the heavens and the earth there are certainly signs for the Believers. ⁴⁵·⁴In the creation of yourselves and the animals He scatters everywhere, there are signs for any people who strongly believe. ⁴⁵·⁵In

the rotation of the night and day, and the water, food, and everything Allah sends down from the sky – with which He gives life to the earth after it had become dead, and in the changing of the winds, there are signs for any people who think. ⁴⁵·⁶O Prophet Muhammad, these are Allah's signs that We are truthfully telling you about. Then what message will they believe in after rejecting Allah and His signs?

⁴⁵·⁷Every disobedient liar is damned, ⁴⁵·⁸who hears Allah's revelations recited to him but continues to be arrogant as if he didn't even hear them. Warn him of a painful punishment. ⁴⁵·⁹If he gets to know some of Our revelations, he starts to make fun of them. It is they who will suffer a humiliating punishment. ⁴⁵·¹⁰Hell will be right behind them. Nothing they did will be able to help them in any way at all, nor will the protectors they took besides Allah. They will suffer a terrible punishment. ⁴⁵·¹¹This Qur'an is guidance. Those who disbelieve in their Lord's revelations will suffer a punishment of agonising pain.

⁴⁵·¹²Allah is the one Who has made the sea obey a system for you, so that ships can sail through it by His command, and so that you can gain Allah's grace and might become thankful. ⁴⁵·¹³He has made everything obey a system for you in the heavens and everything in the earth too, all coming from Him. There are certainly signs in this for any people who think deeply.

⁴⁵·¹⁴O Prophet Muhammad, tell the Believers to ignore those who don't expect Allah's Days of punishment to ever come, because Allah will reward or punish any people for what they used to do. ⁴⁵·¹⁵Anyone who does good, does it for his own benefit; anyone who does bad, does so to his own loss. Eventually, it is your Lord you will all be taken back to.

⁴⁵·¹⁶We certainly gave the Descendants of Ya'qub the Book, authority, and prophethood. We gave them wholesome things and made them superior to all the people of their time. ⁴⁵·¹⁷We gave them clear commands in religious affairs. It was only after knowledge had come to them that they disagreed with each other because they were jealous of each other. Your Lord will judge between them on Judgement Day about the disagreements they used to have.

⁴⁵·¹⁸O Prophet Muhammad, then We put you on the open way of religion. You should follow this way and not the desires of those who don't know. ⁴⁵·¹⁹They won't be able to save you from the punishment of Allah in any way at all. The wrongdoers are protectors of each other, but Allah is the Protector of those who are mindful of him. ⁴⁵·²⁰These verses are clear proofs for all people, as well as guidance and mercy for any people who strongly believe.

⁴⁵·²¹What? Do those who do bad things think We will make them like those who believe and do good, so that they will be equal in their worldly life and after they die? How terrible are the judgements they make! ⁴⁵·²²Allah created the heavens and the earth for a real purpose, and for people to be rewarded or punished for what they did without them being treated unfairly.

⁴⁵·²³What do you think: if someone makes his desire his god and Allah deliberately lets him go astray, seals up his hearing and his heart, and puts a blindfold over his eyes, then who can guide him after Allah? Won't you even remind yourselves?

⁴⁵·²⁴They claim: "There's nothing beyond our life in this world. We die, we live, and we won't be brought back to life; nothing kills us but time." They don't know anything about this. They are only guessing. ⁴⁵·²⁵When Our clear verses are recited to them, their only argument is

to say: "Bring back our forefathers, if you are telling the truth!" 45.26O Prophet Muhammad, **say: "It is Allah Who gives you life, will then give you death, and then gather you together for Judgement Day in which there is no doubt, but most people don't know."**

45.27Control of the heavens and the earth belongs to Allah. The supporters of falsehood will be the real losers on the Day when the Final Hour will take place. 45.28You will see every community kneeling. They will be called to their record and told: "Today you will be rewarded or punished for the things you used to do. 45.29This is Our record and it will speak truthfully about you. We have been recording everything you used to do."

45.30Those who believed and did good, their Lord will take them into His special mercy. That will be the clear victory. 45.31However, those who disbelieved will be asked: "Weren't My verses recited to you? Instead, you showed arrogance and were a criminal people. 45.32When it was said, 'Allah's promise is true, and there is no doubt about the Final Hour,' you used to say, 'We don't know what the Final Hour is. We think it's only an idea. We aren't sure.'." 45.33The punishments of the bad things they did will appear to them, and what they used to make fun of will end up punishing them.

45.34It will also be said: "We will ignore you Today just like you forgot the meeting of this Day of yours. Your home will be the Fire, and you won't have any helpers. 45.35This is because you used to make fun of Allah's revelations, and the worldly life tricked you." From Today, they will neither be taken out of there nor allowed to repent.

45.36So, all praise is for Allah – Lord of the heavens, of earth, and of all the worlds! 45.37Greatness is His in the heavens and the earth. He is the Almighty, the All-Wise.

Surah 46. Sand Dunes (al-Ahqaaf)

[PART 26]

Allah's name I begin with, the Most Compassionate, the Ever-Merciful

46.1 Haa Meem.

46.2 This Book's revelation comes from Allah, the Almighty, the All-Wise. 46.3 We didn't create the heavens and the earth and everything in between them except for a real purpose and for a fixed term. The disbelievers are neglectful of what they've been warned about.

46.4 O Prophet Muhammad, say: "Have you people ever thought about those idols you pray to besides Allah? Show me what they've created from the earth, or if they have a share in the heavens. Bring me any Book revealed before this or any trace of knowledge, if you are telling the truth." 46.5 Who could be further astray than someone who prays to besides Allah those who will never respond to him until Judgement Day, and are even unaware of their prayers! 46.6 When the people will be gathered together on Judgement Day, those they prayed to will be their enemies and will reject their worship.

46.7 When Our clear verses are recited to them, the disbelievers say about the truth when it comes to them: "This is clearly magic," 46.8 or they say: "He made it up." O Prophet Muhammad, you should reply: "If I have made it up then you cannot save me from the punishment of Allah in any way at all. He knows best what you are busy saying about it. He is enough as a Witness between me and you all. He is the Most Forgiving, the Ever-Merciful."

46.9 Say: "I am not the first messenger ever sent nor do I know from myself what will be done to me or you. I only follow what is revealed to me. I'm only giving clear warnings."

⁴⁶·¹⁰O Prophet Muhammad, **ask: "Have you** people **ever thought if this** Qur'an really **is from Allah, and you reject it,** what will happen? A witness from among the Descendants of Ya'qub testified to something like this and so he believed whereas you people are being arrogant. Allah doesn't let unjust people succeed."

⁴⁶·¹¹About the Believers, the disbelievers say: "If Islam was something good, these Muslims wouldn't have beaten us to it." Now, since they don't follow its guidance, they will claim: "This is an old lie." ⁴⁶·¹²Before this was the Book of Musa, sent as a guide and a mercy. This Book is confirming it in the Arabic language so it can give warnings to the wrongdoers and be a joy for those who do good.

⁴⁶·¹³Those who say: "Our Lord is Allah," and then stay strong on the truth, they won't have anything to fear and will never be sad. ⁴⁶·¹⁴It is they who will be the people of Paradise, where they will remain forever as a reward for the good things they used to do.

⁴⁶·¹⁵We have ordered every person to be kind to his parents. His mother carried him in pregnancy with difficulty and gave birth to him with difficulty. His carrying and his weaning took thirty months. When he reaches his full strength, and reaches forty years of age, he prays: "My Lord! Keep me firm that I continue to be thankful for Your favours You have done to me and my parents, and that I do good with which You are well-pleased. Make my descendants righteous for me. I repent to You and I am among those who surrender to You as Muslims." ⁴⁶·¹⁶They're the ones whose good that they do We accept and whose sins We forgive – who will be among the people of Paradise. It is a promise of truth they've been given.

⁴⁶·¹⁷Anyone who disbelieves and says to his parents: "Ugh! Are you threatening me that I will be brought out again alive, when generations have been and gone before me and weren't brought back to life?" Both the parents ask Allah for help warning their child: "You will be damned! Have some faith! Allah's promise is true." He replies: "This Qur'an is nothing but stories made up by previous people." ⁴⁶·¹⁸They're the ones against whom has proven true the punishment among the communities of jinns and humans that have been and gone before them. They were all losers.

⁴⁶·¹⁹Each person will have ranks according to what they did, so Allah can repay them in full for what they've done without them being treated unfairly. ⁴⁶·²⁰The Day the disbelievers will be brought in front of the Fire, they will be told: "You spent your wholesome things in your worldly life and enjoyed them well, but Today you will be given a punishment of humiliation because you used to behave arrogantly in the world without having any right to do so, and because you used to disobey."

⁴⁶·²¹O Prophet Muhammad, remember Hud, the brother of the 'Ad, when, in the sand dunes of south-eastern Arabia, he warned his people, though many warners had been and gone before him and many came after him saying: "You mustn't worship anyone except Allah. I fear for you the punishment of a Dreadful Day." ⁴⁶·²²They argued: "Have you come to turn us away from our gods? So bring down on us the punishment you keep threatening us with, if you are telling the truth." ⁴⁶·²³He replied: "Only Allah knows about it. I will keep delivering to you what I've been sent with even though I can see that you are a people behaving ignorantly."

⁴⁶·²⁴Then, when they saw the punishment coming like a storm cloud towards their valleys, they said happily: "This is a storm cloud that

will give us rain." Hud replied: "No, no! It's that punishment which you people wanted to bring sooner. It's a sandstorm carrying painful punishment. {46.25}It will destroy everything by its Lord's command." Then, in the morning, nothing could be seen except the ruins of their homes. In this way We punish criminal people.

{46.26}Makkans! We had given those people of Hud more power on earth than We've given you. We had also given them hearing, sight, and intelligence, but neither their hearing, sight, nor intelligence could save them in any way at all since they continued to reject Allah's revelations. The punishment they used to make fun of ended up punishing them. {46.27}We have already destroyed many towns that used to exist around you, and We varied Our signs so the people might turn back to Us. {46.28}Why then did those they worshipped as gods besides Allah, hoping to get closer to Him, not help them? In fact, those gods abandoned them. That was their lie and what they used to make up.

{46.29}O Prophet Muhammad, when We turned a group of jinns to you, listening carefully to the Qur'an, when they came near it, they said to each other: "Keep quiet." Then, when the reading had ended, they went back to their community to give warnings. {46.30}They said: "Our community! We have heard a Book revealed after Musa, confirming what came before it, guiding to the truth and to a path that is straight. {46.31}Our community! Respond to the one who is inviting to Allah, and believe in him. Allah will then forgive you of your sins and save you from a painful punishment. {46.32}Anyone who doesn't respond to the one inviting to Allah won't be able to escape Allah in this world nor will he have any protectors besides Him. It is they who are clearly astray."

{46.33}Don't they see that Allah, Who created the heavens and the earth – and creating them didn't tire Him out – has the power to bring the dead back to life? Yes, of course! He is Most Capable of anything. ⁴⁶·³⁴The Day when the disbelievers will be brought in front of the Fire and asked: "Isn't this life after death real?" They will reply: "Yes, of course! We swear by our Lord!" Allah will say: "Now taste the punishment because you used to disbelieve."

⁴⁶·³⁵O Prophet Muhammad, you should continue to have patience, like the messengers of strong will did, and don't try to bring the punishment any sooner for the disbelievers. The Day when they will see the punishment they're being warned about, it will seem to them as if they had lived in this world for hardly a single hour of a day. A warning! Will anyone be destroyed other than the disobedient people?!

Surah 47. Muhammad

Allah's name I begin with, the Most Compassionate, the Ever-Merciful

⁴⁷·¹Those who disbelieve and block people from Allah's cause, Allah will let their actions be destroyed. ⁴⁷·²However, those who believe and do good, and believe in what was revealed to Muhammad – and it is the truth from their Lord, He will remove their sins from them and improve their condition. ⁴⁷·³This is because the disbelievers are following falsehood whereas the Believers are following the truth from their Lord. In this way Allah gives people their examples.

⁴⁷·⁴Therefore, when you meet the hostile disbelievers in battle, strike their necks. Then, when you've dominated them, tie them up firmly. After that, you may either release them in generosity or for ransom. Fight until war lays down its weapons. That is an order! However, if Allah chooses, He can certainly take revenge on them Himself, but He is testing some of you by others. Those who are killed in Allah's cause,

He will never let their actions be destroyed. ⁴⁷·⁵He will guide them to Paradise and improve their condition, ⁴⁷·⁶and eventually enter them into the Paradise He has identified for them.

⁴⁷·⁷Believers! If you help in the way of Allah, He will help you and will keep your footing strong. ⁴⁷·⁸The disbelievers will fall flat on their faces in failure and Allah will let their actions be destroyed; ⁴⁷·⁹that is because they hate what Allah has revealed, and so He lets their actions be wasted. ⁴⁷·¹⁰Don't they travel through the earth and take a look at what was the end result of those before them? Allah brought total destruction on them, and these disbelievers will suffer something similar. ⁴⁷·¹¹That is because Allah is the Protector of Believers, while the disbelievers have no protector.

⁴⁷·¹²Allah will enter those who believed and did good into gardens – that have rivers flowing beneath them. The disbelievers may enjoy themselves for a while and eat like animals in this world, but the Fire will be their place to stay.

⁴⁷·¹³O Prophet Muhammad, there are many cities We have destroyed with no one to help them, though they were more powerful than yours which made you leave. ⁴⁷·¹⁴Can they be the same: someone who is on a clear proof from his Lord and someone whose bad action is made to seem attractive to him and they follow their own desires?

⁴⁷·¹⁵The description of the Paradise promised to those who are mindful of Allah is that: it has rivers of water that always remains fresh; rivers of milk whose taste never changes; rivers of wine – delicious to those who drink; and rivers of pure honey. They will have all kinds of fruits there as well as forgiveness from their Lord. Can they be like those who will remain forever in the Fire, given a boiling liquid to drink that will rip their insides apart?

47.16O Prophet Muhammad, **some of them** only pretend to **listen to you,** but when they go away from you, they ask those given knowledge: "What did he say just now?" They're the ones whose hearts Allah has sealed up and who follow their own desires. **47.17**Those who follow guidance, Allah increases them in guidance, and gives them mindfulness of Him. **47.18**Are they waiting only for the Final Hour when it will come upon them all of a sudden? Anyway, its signs have already appeared. What use will its reminder be to them when the Final Hour really does come to them?

47.19O Prophet Muhammad, **you should know that there is no god except Allah, and you should ask forgiveness for a fault** that it does not come **from you, and for all Believing men and women. Allah knows the places where you** people **move about** for work, etc., **and where you rest.**

47.20 The Believers ask: "Why wasn't a surah revealed about fighting in defence?" But when a clear surah is revealed in which fighting is mentioned, you see those people with a sickness in their hearts staring at you like someone about to faint because of death. It's better for them **47.21**to obey and speak in a noble manner. Then, once the matter is decided, it would have been best for them if they were true to Allah. **47.22**So if you hypocrites **turn away** and go back from fighting now, **you will end up making trouble in the world, and you will break your family relations too. 47.23**These hypocrites **are the ones Allah has cursed. He has made them deaf and blinded their eyes. 47.24**Don't they then think over the Qur'an, or do the hearts have their locks activated?

47.25 Those who turn back after guidance has become clear to them, it is Shaytan who has fooled them and filled them with false **hopes.**

⁴⁷·²⁶This is because they said to those who hate what Allah has revealed: "We will obey you in only some matters." Allah knows their secret dealings. ⁴⁷·²⁷But what is it like when the angels take away their souls, smashing their faces and backs with hammers! ⁴⁷·²⁸That is because they followed what displeases Allah, and they didn't want Him to be pleased with them, so He let their actions be wasted.

⁴⁷·²⁹Do those with a sickness in their hearts think Allah will never expose their grudges? ⁴⁷·³⁰O Prophet Muhammad, if We had wanted, We could have shown them to you and you would have recognised them by their appearances. However, you will certainly recognise them by the way they speak. Allah knows what you people do.

⁴⁷·³¹We will certainly test you people until We prove those of you who strive hard and those who have patience. We will test the reports about you too.

⁴⁷·³²Those who disbelieve, block people from Allah's cause, and go against the Messenger after guidance has become clear to them, they cannot harm Allah in any way at all. He will let their actions be wasted.

⁴⁷·³³Believers! You have to obey Allah and the Messenger too, and don't ruin your actions. ⁴⁷·³⁴Those who disbelieve, block people from Allah's cause, then die as disbelievers, Allah will never forgive them. ⁴⁷·³⁵So, you Believers must never show weakness nor cry out for peace because you will be the winners. Allah is with you. He will never let your actions go to waste.

⁴⁷·³⁶This life is just games and some kind of amusement. However, if you believe and be mindful of Allah, He will give you your full rewards and not ask you to donate your wealth. ⁴⁷·³⁷If He did ask you for all

your wealth and put you under pressure to give, you would be stingy, and He would expose your grudges. ⁴⁷·³⁸Yet here you are, being asked to donate in Allah's cause, but some of you are being stingy. Anyone who is stingy does so to his own loss. Allah is Free of all Needs and it is you that are poor. If you turn away, He will replace you with other people, and they won't be like you.

Surah 48. Victory (al-Fath)

Allah's name I begin with, the Most Compassionate, the Ever-Merciful

⁴⁸·¹O Prophet Muhammad, **We have given you a clear victory** ⁴⁸·²**so Allah will forgive the past and future sins** of your community **for you, complete His favour to you, keep you on a path that is straight,** ⁴⁸·³**and so that He can give you some mighty help.** ⁴⁸·⁴**He is the one Who sent down tranquillity into the Believers' hearts for their faith to grow even more. The forces of the heavens and the earth all belong to Allah. Allah is always All-Knowing, All-Wise.** ⁴⁸·⁵**All** this so **He can enter the Believing men and women into gardens – that have rivers flowing beneath them, where they will remain forever; and to remove their sins from them. In the sight of Allah, that is a tremendous victory.** ⁴⁸·⁶**All** this so **He can punish the men and women who are hypocrites and polytheists who have bad thoughts about Allah. May the disasters of devastation be upon them! Allah is angry with them, and He has cursed them and prepared for them Hell. What a horrible final destination!** ⁴⁸·⁷**The forces of the heavens and the earth all belong to Allah. Allah is always Almighty, All-Wise.**

⁴⁸·⁸O Prophet Muhammad, **We have sent you to be a witness, and to give good news, and warnings,** ⁴⁸·⁹**so** you people **will believe in Allah and His Messenger – and assist him and honour him – and glorify Allah morning and evening.**

⁴⁸·¹⁰O Prophet Muhammad, **those who swear loyalty to you are actually swearing loyalty to Allah; Allah's Hand** of mercy is over their hands. Anyone who breaks his oath, does so to his own loss; but anyone who is faithful to the oath he has made with Allah, He will give him a huge reward.

⁴⁸·¹¹**Those desert Arabs who had** chosen to be **left behind will apologise to you:** "Our wealth and families kept us busy, so ask forgiveness for us." They say with their tongues what isn't in their hearts. Ask them: "So, who has the power to save you from Allah in any way at all if He wants to harm or help you? The truth is, Allah is always Fully-Aware of everything you do. ⁴⁸·¹²In fact, you thought the Messenger and the Believers would never come back to their families alive. This thought was made to seem attractive to your hearts, but you had bad thoughts, and you became a people who will be ruined." ⁴⁸·¹³Anyone who does not believe in Allah and His Messenger, We have prepared for those disbelievers a Blazing Fire. ⁴⁸·¹⁴Control of the heavens and the earth belongs to Allah. He can forgive or punish anyone He chooses, though **Allah is always Most Forgiving, Ever-Merciful.**

⁴⁸·¹⁵**Believers! When you go out to collect the spoils of war, those who had** chosen to be **left behind will say:** "Let us come with you." They want to change Allah's command. Say: "You will never come with us. This is what Allah has said before." Then they will say: "Actually, you are jealous of us." The truth is, they hardly understand.

⁴⁸·¹⁶**Say to those desert Arabs who had** chosen to be **left behind:** "You will soon be called to face some mighty warriors; either you will fight them or they will surrender to Allah as Muslims. If you obey, Allah will give you a good reward, but if you turn back as you did before, He will make you suffer a painful punishment."

⁴⁸·¹⁷There's no blame on the blind, the lame, or the sick if they cannot join the fighting. However, anyone who obeys Allah and His Messenger, Allah will enter him into gardens – that have rivers flowing beneath them. Anyone who turns back, Allah will make him suffer a painful punishment.

⁴⁸·¹⁸Allah is well-pleased with the Believers when they swore loyalty with you under the tree. He knows what is in their hearts. He sent down tranquillity on them, and He rewarded them with a speedy victory; ⁴⁸·¹⁹and the many spoils of war that you collected. Allah is always Almighty, All-Wise. ⁴⁸·²⁰Allah has promised you many spoils you will win, He has brought this victory early for you, and He has kept people's hands off you – all this so it would be a sign of future victory for the Believers and to keep you guided on a path that is straight ⁴⁸·²¹– as well as other achievements beyond your power, but which Allah can give you. Allah is always Most Capable of anything.

⁴⁸·²²If the disbelievers fought against you, they would certainly turn their backs and run. In the end, they won't find any protector or helper. ⁴⁸·²³Allah used to do this in times already been and gone long ago. You won't find any change in what Allah does.

⁴⁸·²⁴He is the one Who held back their hands from you and yours from them in the valley of Makkah even after He made you dominant over them. Allah is always Ever-Watchful of everything you do. ⁴⁸·²⁵They're the ones who disbelieved and blocked you from the Sacred Masjid, and the sacrificial animals were prevented from reaching their place of sacrifice. We would have allowed you to march through if it wasn't for the Believing men and women in Makkah you didn't know you would trample down and cause harm to without knowing. This was so Allah would take into His special mercy anyone He chose. If those

Believers and disbelievers **had separated themselves, We would certainly have made the disbelievers among them suffer a painful punishment.**

⁴⁸·²⁶When the disbelievers had filled their hearts with pride – the pride of the Ignorance before Islam – Allah sent down His special tranquillity on His Messenger and on the Believers. He let them strongly uphold the declaration of faith because they were entitled to it and worthy of it. Allah always knows everything perfectly well.

⁴⁸·²⁷Allah made the vision for His Messenger come true in reality. If Allah chooses, you will always enter the Sacred Masjid in peace – heads shaved or hair cut short, and having no fear. He knew what you didn't, and gave you besides this another speedy victory. ⁴⁸·²⁸He is the one Who sent His Messenger with guidance and the True Religion, to make him dominant over every other religion. Allah is enough as a Witness.

⁴⁸·²⁹Muhammad is Allah's Messenger. Those with him are strong against the disbelievers but merciful among each other. You can see them bowing and prostrating in prayer, trying to gain Allah's grace and good pleasure. The glowing appearance in their faces comes from the effects of prostrating. This is their description in the Tawrah and in the Injeel. They are like crops which bring out their shoots and make them strong. Then they become thick and stand straight on their stems, making the planters happy but only to make the disbelievers burn with rage at them. To those of them who believe and do good, Allah has promised forgiveness and a huge reward.

Surah 49. Private Apartments (al-Hujuraat)

Allah's name I begin with, the Most Compassionate, the Ever-Merciful

49.1Believers! Don't put yourselves ahead of Allah and His Messenger, but remain mindful of Allah. Allah is All-Hearing, All-Knowing.

49.2Believers! Never raise your voices above the Prophet's voice, nor speak to him loudly like you sometimes do with each other, in case your actions go wasted without you even being aware. 49.3Those who lower their voices in the presence of Allah's Messenger, it is they whose hearts Allah has refined for piety. They will have forgiveness and a huge reward.

49.4O Prophet Muhammad, those who call out to you from outside your private apartments, most of them don't even think. 49.5It would be best for them if only they waited patiently until you came out to them. However, Allah is Most Forgiving, Ever-Merciful.

49.6Believers! If a bad person comes to you with any information, you should investigate it in case you unknowingly harm others and then later regret what you did. 49.7Remember that Allah's Messenger is among you. If he accepted many of your suggestions then you would only suffer, but Allah has made faith dear to you and made it beautiful in your hearts, and made you hate disbelief, disobedience, and sin. It is really they who follow true guidance. 49.8All this is a grace and a favour from Allah. Allah is All-Knowing, All-Wise.

49.9If two groups of Believers start fighting each other, you must all put things right between them. If one does something wrong to the other then you must fight against the offender until he comes back to following Allah's command. Once he comes back then you must put things right between them both with justice, and be fair. Allah loves those who are fair. ⁴⁹·¹⁰Believers are siblings to each other. So, you must all keep things right between your siblings, and be mindful of Allah so you may be shown mercy.

⁴⁹·¹¹Believers! No group of people should make fun of any other group; perhaps that group might be better than them, nor should any women make fun of other women; those women might be better than them. Don't look for mistakes in each other nor call each other by offensive nicknames. How terrible is it to call someone 'sinful' after they become Believers! Those who don't repent, it is really they who are the wrongdoers. ⁴⁹·¹²Believers! Stay mostly well clear of suspicions because some suspicions are sins. Also, don't spy or backbite each other: would any of you like to eat his dead brother's flesh? You would hate it! So, you must remain mindful of Allah. Allah accepts repentance much, is Ever-Merciful.

⁴⁹·¹³People! We created you from a male and a female, and made you into nations and tribes so you could recognise each other. The most honoured among you in the sight of Allah is the most mindful among you. Allah is All-Knowing, Fully-Aware.

⁴⁹·¹⁴The desert Arabs say: "We believe." O Prophet Muhammad, reply: "You haven't believed yet, so you should say, 'We have surrendered to Allah as Muslims.' Belief hasn't fully gone into your hearts. If you obey Allah and His Messenger, He won't reduce anything at all from the good things you do. Allah is Most Forgiving, Ever-Merciful." ⁴⁹·¹⁵True Believers are those who believe in Allah and His Messenger, and they have no doubts. They strive hard with their wealth and their lives in Allah's cause. It is really they who are truthful.

^{49.16}O Prophet Muhammad, ask: "What? Are you trying to teach Allah your religion? Allah already knows everything in the heavens and the earth. He knows everything perfectly well."

^{49.17}O Prophet Muhammad, they think they've done you a favour by becoming Muslim. Say: "Don't think you have done me a favour by becoming Muslim. The truth is, Allah has done you a favour that He has guided you to the true faith, if you are sincere to it."

^{49.18}Allah knows all the unseen secrets of the heavens and the earth. Allah is Ever-Watchful of everything you do.

Surah 50. Qaaf (The Letter *Qaaf*)

Allah's name I begin with, the Most Compassionate, the Ever-Merciful

^{50.1}*Qaaf*. I swear by the Glorious Qur'an that: you, dear Muhammad, are a messenger. ^{50.2}However, they were surprised that a warner had come to them from among them. The disbelievers say: "This is something strange. ^{50.3}Is there life after when we die and become dust? That coming back is impossible!" ^{50.4}We already know how much of them the earth eats away after they die. We also have a Record that is well preserved. ^{50.5}However, they called the truth a lie whenever it came to them, and so they are now in a confused state.

^{50.6}Don't they look at the sky above them as to how We have built it and made it beautiful with no cracks in it? ^{50.7}As for the earth, We've stretched it out, fixed firm mountains in it, and made all kinds of beautiful plants grow there, ^{50.8}to be observed and used as a reminder for every servant who turns to Allah. ^{50.9}We send down from the sky blessed water with which We grow gardens, and grain for harvesting, ^{50.10}and tall palm trees, with spathes in heavy layers over each other,

⁵⁰·¹¹all as food for Allah's servants. With this water, We bring back to life a land that is dead. The coming out of the graves will be like this.

⁵⁰·¹²Before these disbelievers of Makkah, the people of Nuh also called the truth a lie, and so did the People of the Well, the Thamud, ⁵⁰·¹³the 'Ad, Fir'awn, the people of Lut, ⁵⁰·¹⁴the People of the Forest, and the people of Tubba'. They all accused the messengers of being liars. So, My warning proved true.

⁵⁰·¹⁵Did We become tired when creating the first time around? No, no! They themselves are confused about a new kind of creation. ⁵⁰·¹⁶We created the human being, and We know what bad things his own desires urge him to do. We are nearer to him than his jugular vein. ⁵⁰·¹⁷It is because the two receiving-angels are recording, on the right and on the left ⁵⁰·¹⁸that there is always a watcher with him ready to record anything he says. ⁵⁰·¹⁹The trance of death will really come to them: "This is what you were trying to escape!"

⁵⁰·²⁰The Trumpet will be blown a second time. That will be the Day of the Warning you were given. ⁵⁰·²¹Everyone will come with an angel pushing them forward, and a witness too. ⁵⁰·²²It will be said: "You've been in neglect of this, so We have removed you of your veil, and Today your eyesight is sharp." ⁵⁰·²³And his close angel-companion will say: "Here is your record that I have ready me." ⁵⁰·²⁴It will be said: "Both of you throw into Hell any stubborn disbeliever ⁵⁰·²⁵who forbade what was good, broke the law, caused doubts; ⁵⁰·²⁶who made up another god with Allah! Both of you throw him into the severe punishment!"

⁵⁰·²⁷His close devil-companion will say: "Our Lord! I didn't make him do bad things. In fact, he had already gone far, far astray." ⁵⁰·²⁸Allah will say: "Don't argue in front of Me when I had already given you

warnings in advance. ⁵⁰·²⁹The command with Me won't be changed, and I don't treat My servants unfairly." ⁵⁰·³⁰On that Day We will ask Hell: "Are you full yet?" and it will reply: "Are there any more?"

⁵⁰·³¹Paradise will be brought close to those who were mindful of Allah; not far at all. ⁵⁰·³²They will be told: "This is what you were promised; it's for anyone who turns to Allah, protecting his faith, ⁵⁰·³³who fears Allah - the Most Compassionate without seeing Him, and comes with a heart that turns to Him. ⁵⁰·³⁴Enter Paradise in peace. This is the Day of Eternity." ⁵⁰·³⁵They will have there whatever they wish, and there will be even more blessings coming from Us.

⁵⁰·³⁶How many generations have We destroyed before these disbelievers of Makkah! They were more powerful than these people. They roamed about throughout the lands, but could they find any way out? ⁵⁰·³⁷There is a lesson in this for anyone who has a good heart or listens carefully as a witness to the truth.

⁵⁰·³⁸We created the heavens and the earth and everything in between them in six stages, and tiredness didn't have any effect on Us. ⁵⁰·³⁹So, O Prophet Muhammad, you should have patience with what they say, and continue to glorify the praises of your Lord before sunrise and sunset. ⁵⁰·⁴⁰Glorify Him at night and after the prostrations of the ritual prayers too.

⁵⁰·⁴¹Listen carefully for the Day when the caller will call out from a place that is near, ⁵⁰·⁴²the Day when they will really hear the Mighty Blast. That will be the Day of coming out of graves. ⁵⁰·⁴³It is We Who give life and death, and the final return will be to Us. ⁵⁰·⁴⁴The Day when the earth will split apart around them and they will come rushing out, that gathering together is easy for Us.

⁵⁰·⁴⁵O Prophet Muhammad, **We know best what they're saying. You aren't forcing them. So, you should keep reminding with the Qur'an anyone who fears My warnings.**

Surah 51. Winds That Scatter (adh-Dhaariyaat)

Allah's name I begin with, the Most Compassionate, the Ever-Merciful

⁵¹·¹**I swear by the winds that blow and scatter,** ⁵¹·²**that carry heavy loads,** ⁵¹·³**that speed along smoothly,** ⁵¹·⁴**and that distribute work:** ⁵¹·⁵**what you people have been promised is certainly true.** ⁵¹·⁶**Judgement will definitely take place.**

⁵¹·⁷**I swear by the sky full of waves** and paths: ⁵¹·⁸**you people certainly have different tones of voice.**

⁵¹·⁹**Anyone who is already misled will be tricked away from the truth.** ⁵¹·¹⁰**Cursed are those who spread fake news,** ⁵¹·¹¹**those who are lost in crowds and ignorance,** ⁵¹·¹²**asking: "When is Judgement Day?"** ⁵¹·¹³**On that Day they will be punished in the Fire,** ⁵¹·¹⁴**and told: "Taste your punishment! This is what you wanted to come sooner."**

⁵¹·¹⁵**Those who are mindful of Allah will be among gardens and fountains,** ⁵¹·¹⁶**enjoying whatever their Lord will give them. They used to do good in the past;** ⁵¹·¹⁷**sleeping very little at night,** ⁵¹·¹⁸**begging for Allah's forgiveness before dawn,** ⁵¹·¹⁹**and a share of their wealth used to be for beggars and poor people.**

⁵¹·²⁰**There are signs on earth for strong believers,** ⁵¹·²¹**and in yourselves too. Can't you see?** ⁵¹·²²**What you need is in the sky and so is what you are promised.** ⁵¹·²³**So, I swear by the Lord of sky and earth: this is**

certainly the truth as much as the fact that you can speak clearly to each other.

51.24O Prophet Muhammad, has the story of Ibrahim's honoured guests reached you? 51.25When they came to him and greeted with words of peace, he replied: "Peace." Then he thought to himself: "This is a group of strangers.". 51.26Then he swiftly went to his family and came back with a fat roasted calf, 51.27and placed it near them. He asked: "Won't you eat?" 51.28They didn't, and so he felt afraid of them. They said: "Don't be afraid," and gave him the good news of a knowledgeable son. 51.29Then his wife Sara came forward frowning in amazement. She clasped her forehead and said: "A baby from an old woman who cannot have children?" 51.30They replied: "This is how it will be. Your Lord has said it. Only He is the All-Wise, the All-Knowing."

[PART 27]

51.31Ibrahim asked: "Then what is your mission, O Messenger-Angels?" 51.32They replied: "We have been sent to a criminal people, 51.33to shower down on them stones of baked clay, 51.34that come marked from your Lord for those who go to extremes."

51.35So, We evacuated any Believers who were there, 51.36though We found there only one house of Muslims (- of Lut and his two daughters). 51.37We left there a sign as a lesson of warning for those who fear the painful punishment.

51.38There are also signs in the story of Musa, when We sent him to Fir'awn with a clear authority. 51.39However, Fir'awn turned away arrogant because of his power, and said: "He must be a magician or a madman!" 51.40So We seized him and his armies, and threw them into the sea. He was guilty.

⁵¹·⁴¹There are also signs in the destruction of **the 'Ad. When We sent against them the desolating wind,** ⁵¹·⁴²it reduced to dust whatever it came across.

⁵¹·⁴³There are also signs in the destruction of **the Thamud. When they were told: "You may enjoy yourselves for a while,"** ⁵¹·⁴⁴they arrogantly disobeyed their Lord's command, so a thunderbolt struck them, and they could only stare in shock. ⁵¹·⁴⁵**They could neither stand nor defend themselves.**

⁵¹·⁴⁶**The people of Nuh** were destroyed long ago. They had been a disobedient people. ⁵¹·⁴⁷We built the universe with power and We make things spacious. ⁵¹·⁴⁸We spread out the earth. How excellent We are at levelling out! ⁵¹·⁴⁹We created pairs of everything so that you might remind yourselves. ⁵¹·⁵⁰So, you must all run to Allah; I am sent by Him to give you clear warnings. ⁵¹·⁵¹**Don't make another god with Allah;** I am sent by Him to give you clear warnings.

⁵¹·⁵²In the same way, whenever a messenger came to the people before them, they said: "He must be **a magician or a madman!"** ⁵¹·⁵³Did they advise each other to do this? The truth is, they were a people who broke all limits of rebellion. ⁵¹·⁵⁴O Prophet Muhammad, **you should turn away from them. You won't be blameworthy.** ⁵¹·⁵⁵However, you should keep reminding, because reminders do help the Believers.

⁵¹·⁵⁶I created jinns and humans only so they worship Me. ⁵¹·⁵⁷Neither do I want any food from them nor that they should feed Me. ⁵¹·⁵⁸Only Allah is the Great Provider, Lord of Power, Mighty.

⁵¹·⁵⁹These wrongdoers will have shares of punishments **similar to** those of their companions-in-sin from the past. So, they shouldn't ask

Me to bring those punishments any sooner. ⁵¹·⁶⁰The disbelievers will be damned on that Day of theirs which they've been warned about.

Surah 52. Mount Tur (*at-Tur*)

Allah's name I begin with, the Most Compassionate, the Ever-Merciful

⁵²·¹I swear by Mount Tur, ⁵²·²and a Book that is written ⁵²·³on pages that are open, ⁵²·⁴and I swear by the House that is much visited by the angels, ⁵²·⁵and the ceiling of the sky that is raised high, ⁵²·⁶and the ocean that is filled up: ⁵²·⁷O Prophet Muhammad, your Lord's punishment will certainly take place ⁵²·⁸– nothing can stop it ⁵²·⁹– on the Day when the sky will shake violently, ⁵²·¹⁰and the mountains will move swiftly away.

⁵²·¹¹Then, damned on that Day will be those who call the truth a lie, ⁵²·¹²who are playing silly games. ⁵²·¹³On that Day they will be shoved into the Fire ⁵²·¹⁴and told: "This is the Fire that you people used to call a lie. ⁵²·¹⁵Now, is all of this magic or is it you who cannot see? ⁵²·¹⁶Burn in it! It makes no difference to you now if you have patience or not, because you will still be punished for the bad things you used to do."

⁵²·¹⁷Those who are mindful of Allah will be in Gardens and in delights, ⁵²·¹⁸enjoying themselves with what their Lord will give them. Their Lord will protect them from the suffering of Hell-Fire. ⁵²·¹⁹They will be told: "You may eat and drink with enjoyment because of the good things you used to do." ⁵²·²⁰They'll be relaxing on sofas arranged in rows. We will marry them to beautiful wide-eyed spouses of Paradise. ⁵²·²¹The Believers and their descendants who followed them in faith, We will join them with their descendants, and We won't reduce anything at all from the reward of their good works. Everyone will be held responsible for what they did. ⁵²·²²We will keep giving them any

fruit and meat they desire. ⁵²·²³They will grab on to cups there from each other of holy drinks, **neither** hearing, saying, or doing **any foolishness** there nor anything leading to sin. ⁵²·²⁴Serving them will be young servants – like pearls all covered up.

⁵²·²⁵**They will turn to each other and ask questions.** ⁵²·²⁶**They will say:** "Before this, we were among our families and terrified of Allah's punishment, ⁵²·²⁷but He did us a favour and saved us from the suffering of the Hot Wind of Hell. ⁵²·²⁸We used to pray only to Him before. He is the Kind, the Ever-Merciful."

⁵²·²⁹**So, O Prophet Muhammad, you should keep reminding, because, by your Lord's blessing, you are neither a fortune-teller nor a madman;** ⁵²·³⁰**or are they saying** about you: "A poet! We are waiting for something bad to happen to him." ⁵²·³¹**You should reply:** "**Then keep waiting; I will wait with you among those who are waiting** to see what happens." ⁵²·³²**Are their thoughts telling them these things, or are they a people who are breaking all limits of rebellion?** ⁵²·³³**Are they saying:** "He made the Qur'an up himself."? **The truth is, they just won't believe.** ⁵²·³⁴**So, they should bring a message like it, if they are telling the truth.**

⁵²·³⁵**Were they created without a creator or are they themselves the creators?** ⁵²·³⁶**Did they create the heavens and the earth? In fact, they don't have any strong beliefs.** ⁵²·³⁷**Do they have your Lord's treasures or are they in control?** ⁵²·³⁸**Do they have a ladder on which they can climb up and spy** on the heavenly secrets? **Then their listening-spy should bring a clear proof.** ⁵²·³⁹**Does Allah have daughters while you yourselves have sons?** ⁵²·⁴⁰O Prophet Muhammad, **are you asking them for a payment** for this guidance **so they are weighed down with debt?** ⁵²·⁴¹**Do they have** knowledge of **the unseen secrets that they write down?** ⁵²·⁴²**Do they want to play tricks? The disbelievers are**

themselves tricked. ⁵²·⁴³Do they have a god apart from Allah? Glory be to Allah above the partner-gods they make with Him.

⁵²·⁴⁴If they saw a piece of the sky falling, they would say: "It's only a cloud piled up." ⁵²·⁴⁵So, leave them until they meet their Day in which they will be knocked down ⁵²·⁴⁶– the Day when their trickery will be of no use to them at all and they simply won't be helped. ⁵²·⁴⁷Before that, there is another punishment for the wrongdoers in this world, but most of them don't know.

⁵²·⁴⁸O Prophet Muhammad, wait patiently for your Lord's command – as you are under Our watchful eyes – and you should continue to glorify the praises of your Lord as you stand, ⁵²·⁴⁹and glorify Him during the night, and also when the stars are fading away.

Surah 53. Star (an-Najm)

Allah's name I begin with, the Most Compassionate, the Ever-Merciful

⁵³·¹I swear by the star (Prophet Muhammad) when it came back down: ⁵³·²he (– Prophet Muhammad) who makes you his companions was never astray and never failed to reach his aim.

⁵³·³He doesn't speak from his own desire. ⁵³·⁴It's a revelation given to him. ⁵³·⁵Allah – the Lord of Mighty Powers has taught him, ⁵³·⁶the Lord of Wisdom. He unveiled Himself ⁵³·⁷when Prophet Muhammad was on the highest horizon. ⁵³·⁸Then Allah came close and then even closer, ⁵³·⁹and the distance left was only a small space of two bow-lengths away or even less than that. ⁵³·¹⁰Then Allah revealed to His Servant whatever it was He revealed. ⁵³·¹¹His noble heart did not doubt what he saw with his eyes.

⁵³·¹²Are you arguing with him about what he saw? ⁵³·¹³He certainly saw Allah when he came down the second time, ⁵³·¹⁴at the Lote-Tree of the Final Frontier ⁵³·¹⁵with the Garden of Residence next to it ⁵³·¹⁶when something amazing was covering up the Lote-Tree. ⁵³·¹⁷The eyesight never lost focus nor overstepped the limit. ⁵³·¹⁸He certainly saw some of his Lord's greatest signs.

⁵³·¹⁹Have you people ever thought about the idols Laat and 'Uzzaa, ⁵³·²⁰and another, that third idol, Manaat? ⁵³·²¹What? Do you polytheists have sons and Allah has daughters? ⁵³·²²In that case, this would be such an unfair distribution! ⁵³·²³These are only names you and your forefathers have given these idols for which Allah hasn't sent down any permission. They're only following suspicion and what they themselves want, even though guidance has already come to them from their Lord.

⁵³·²⁴Does a person get everything he wants? ⁵³·²⁵Both the Hereafter and this world belong only to Allah. ⁵³·²⁶There are many angels in the heavens whose intercessions will be of no use at all – except after Allah gives permission to anyone He chooses and approves.

⁵³·²⁷Those who don't believe in the Hereafter are giving female names to the angels. ⁵³·²⁸They don't know anything. They're only following suspicion, and it cannot replace the truth in any way at all. ⁵³·²⁹So stay away from anyone who turns away from remembering Us and only wants this worldly life. ⁵³·³⁰That is the level their knowledge only reaches. Your Lord knows best anyone who strays from His cause and who follows guidance.

⁵³·³¹Everything in the heavens and the earth belongs to Allah, so He can punish those who did bad for what they did and reward those who did good with the most beautiful reward, ⁵³·³²those who stay clear

of the big sins and anything shameful, making only unintended small mistakes. O Prophet Muhammad, your Lord is generous in forgiving. He knows you humans best since He created you from the earth, and since you were foetuses inside your mothers' wombs. So, don't think you are clean and pure. Only He knows best which person is mindful of Him.

[53.33]Have you seen someone who turns away from the truth, [53.34]gives only a little, and then stops giving? [53.35]What? Does he have knowledge of the unseen secrets so that he can see? [53.36]Hasn't he been told of what is in the Books of Revelation given to Musa [53.37]and to Ibrahim – who completely fulfilled his duty? [53.38]Hasn't he been told that no one will carry someone else's burden of sins, [53.39]that every person will receive only according to the effort he makes, [53.40]and that his efforts will soon be shown? [53.41]Eventually, he will be given full reward or punishment.

[53.42]Hasn't he been told that the Final Destination is with your Lord; [53.43]that only He gives reasons to laugh and cry, [53.44]that only He gives death and life, [53.45]that He creates the genders: male and female, [53.46]from a drop of semen when it is ejaculated; [53.47]that it is upon Him to bring to life again; [53.48]that only He makes people rich or satisfied, [53.49]that only He is the Lord of the star Sirius, [53.50]that it was Him Who destroyed the first people of 'Ad [53.51]and the Thamud – leaving no survivors, [53.52]and previously, the people of Nuh. These were the most unjust worst criminals. [53.53]He destroyed the overturned cities (- where Lut lived) [53.54]and covered them up with whatever did cover them up. [53.55]So which blessings of your Lord will you argue about?

[53.56]This Prophet Muhammad is a warner from the line of previous warners. [53.57]The Approaching Judgement Day has come nearer. [53.58]Only Allah can reveal it. [53.59]Do you people ever wonder at these words of the Qur'an? ⁵³·⁶⁰Are you laughing and not crying? ⁵³·⁶¹Are you being careless? ⁵³·⁶²Instead, you must all prostrate to Allah and worship Him. *<Prostration Point 12>*

Surah 54. Moon (al-Qamar)

Allah's name I begin with, the Most Compassionate, the Ever-Merciful

⁵⁴·¹The Final Hour has come nearer, and the moon split apart, ⁵⁴·²yet when these disbelievers see a sign, they turn away and say: "This is same old continuous magic." ⁵⁴·³They call the truth a lie and follow their own desires, but every matter will be settled.

⁵⁴·⁴There have already come to them news with plenty of warnings ⁵⁴·⁵full of perfect wisdom, but still the preachings of the warners have been of no use to them. ⁵⁴·⁶So, O Prophet Muhammad, turn away from them. One Day the caller-angel will make the call to something terrible; ⁵⁴·⁷with their eyes looking down, they will come out of their graves like swarms of locusts, ⁵⁴·⁸rushing towards the caller-angel. The disbelievers will say: "This is a difficult Day."

⁵⁴·⁹Before them, the people of Nuh called the truth a lie. They accused Our servant of being a liar, and said: "He must be mad!" He was given threats. ⁵⁴·¹⁰Then he finally prayed to his Lord: "I am defeated. Help!" ⁵⁴·¹¹So We opened the sky's floodgates with water pouring out, ⁵⁴·¹²and made springs of water gush out of the ground. The waters joined together for the reason already fixed. ⁵⁴·¹³We carried him on that Ark made of planks and nails, ⁵⁴·¹⁴floating under Our watchful eyes. All this was as a punishment to help someone who was rejected. ⁵⁴·¹⁵We have certainly left this as a sign, but will anyone take advice? ⁵⁴·¹⁶So, how dreadful were My punishment and warnings! ⁵⁴·¹⁷We've certainly made the Qur'an easy to understand, but will anyone take advice?

⁵⁴·¹⁸The 'Ad also called the truth a lie, so how dreadful were My punishment and warnings! ⁵⁴·¹⁹We sent upon them a furious wind during a day of endless disaster, ⁵⁴·²⁰snatching people out as if they were trunks of palm trees ripped up from the ground. ⁵⁴·²¹So, how dreadful were My punishment and warnings! ⁵⁴·²²We've certainly made the Qur'an easy to understand, but will anyone take advice?

⁵⁴·²³The Thamud also accused the warners of being liars. ⁵⁴·²⁴They said: "What? Are we supposed to follow a human from among us? In that case, we would be astray and crazy. ⁵⁴·²⁵From among us all, has the Reminder been given to him only? No, no! He is a complete liar, an arrogant one." ⁵⁴·²⁶Tomorrow, they will find out who really is the liar, the arrogant one! ⁵⁴·²⁷We will send the she-camel as a test for them. So, O Salih, keep watching them and have patience. ⁵⁴·²⁸Tell them that the water has been divided between them and the she-camel. Each one will drink in turn. ⁵⁴·²⁹Then they called their companion (- Qidar), and he attacked the she-camel with a sword and hamstrung her. ⁵⁴·³⁰So, how dreadful were My punishment and warnings! ⁵⁴·³¹We sent upon them a single Mighty Blast, and they became like reeds and dry trampled twigs of fence-builders. ⁵⁴·³²We've certainly made the Qur'an easy to understand, but will anyone take advice?

⁵⁴·³³The people of Lut also accused the warners of being liars. ⁵⁴·³⁴We sent a violent hurricane of stones upon them, apart from Lut's family – We saved them before dawn, ⁵⁴·³⁵as a special favour from Us. In this way We reward anyone who gives thanks. ⁵⁴·³⁶Lut did warn them of Our punishment, but they disputed the warnings. ⁵⁴·³⁷They had even tried to snatch his guests away from him, but We blinded their eyes, and said to them: "Now taste my punishment and warnings!" ⁵⁴·³⁸In the early morning, an everlasting punishment had hit them. ⁵⁴·³⁹It was

said: "Now taste my punishment and warnings!" ⁵⁴·⁴⁰We've certainly made the Qur'an easy to understand, but will anyone take advice?

⁵⁴·⁴¹Warners did come to Fir'awn's people too. ⁵⁴·⁴²However, Fir'awn's people called all Our signs lies, so We made them suffer the punishment of Allah the Almighty Who has perfect control.

⁵⁴·⁴³Disbelievers of Makkah! Are your disbelievers any better than those people who were destroyed, or do you have immunity from punishment in the Holy Books? ⁵⁴·⁴⁴Do they say: "We are united to defend ourselves."? ⁵⁴·⁴⁵They will soon be defeated together and will turn their backs and run. ⁵⁴·⁴⁶In fact, the Final Hour is the time they've been warned about. That Hour will be most terrible and most bitter. ⁵⁴·⁴⁷Those criminals are astray and crazy. ⁵⁴·⁴⁸One Day they will be dragged on their faces into the Fire and told: "Taste the burning touch of the Scorching Fire!"

⁵⁴·⁴⁹We have created everything in perfect measure. ⁵⁴·⁵⁰Our command comes once, in the blink of an eye. ⁵⁴·⁵¹We have already destroyed many of your groups, but will anyone take advice? ⁵⁴·⁵²Everything they did is in records with Allah. ⁵⁴·⁵³Everything small or big is taken note of.

⁵⁴·⁵⁴Those who are mindful of Allah will be among gardens and rivers, ⁵⁴·⁵⁵at a seat of honour in the presence of a King Who has perfect control.

Surah 55. The Most Compassionate (*ar-Rahmaan*)

Allah's name I begin with, the Most Compassionate, the Ever-Merciful

55.1It is Allah – the Most Compassionate 55.2Who taught the Qur'an. 55.3He created the human being, 55.4and taught him how to communicate.

55.5The sun and the moon move with accuracy, 55.6the herbs and trees prostrate in surrender to Him, 55.7and He raised the sky up and set up the balance, 55.8so you wouldn't cheat the balance. 55.9You must weigh with fairness and not make the balance show less.

55.10He laid out the earth for all creatures. 55.11There is fruit in it, as well as palm trees full of blossoms, 55.12chaff-covered grain, and sweet-smelling plants: 55.13*So, O humans and jinns, which blessings of your Lord will you call a lie?*

55.14He created the first human from clay – that gives a sound like pottery, 55.15and jinns from a smokeless flame of fire: 55.16*So, which blessings of your Lord will you call a lie?*

55.17He is the Lord of both Easts and sunrises and both Wests and sunsets: 55.18*So, which blessings of your Lord will you call a lie?*

55.19He made two seas flow, joining with each other, 55.20yet there is between them a barrier they cannot cross: 55.21*So, which blessings of your Lord will you call a lie?* 55.22Out of both seas come pearls and corals: 55.23*So, which blessings of your Lord will you call a lie?*

55.24The ships – raised up in the sea like mountains – are His: 55.25*So, which blessings of your Lord will you call a lie?*

⁵⁵·²⁶Everything on earth will die, ⁵⁵·²⁷but your Lord Himself, Master of Majesty and Honour, will remain: *⁵⁵·²⁸So, which blessings of your Lord will you call a lie?*

⁵⁵·²⁹Everyone in the heavens and the earth need Him; every moment He is in a glorious state: *⁵⁵·³⁰So, which blessings of your Lord will you call a lie?*

⁵⁵·³¹We will soon deal with you, you two groups of humans and jinns! *⁵⁵·³²So, which blessings of your Lord will you call a lie?* ⁵⁵·³³O assembly of jinns and humans! If you can pierce through the boundaries of the heavens and the earth then do it! You cannot pierce through without My permission. *⁵⁵·³⁴So, which blessings of your Lord will you call a lie?* ⁵⁵·³⁵Smokeless flames of fire will be sent against both of you and smoke too, and you won't be able to defend yourselves: *⁵⁵·³⁶So, which blessings of your Lord will you call a lie?*

⁵⁵·³⁷Wait for when the sky will split apart and become rosy like burnt oil or red leather: *⁵⁵·³⁸So, which blessings of your Lord will you call a lie?* ⁵⁵·³⁹That Day there will be no need for any human or jinn to be asked about his sin: *⁵⁵·⁴⁰So, which blessings of your Lord will you call a lie?*

⁵⁵·⁴¹The criminals will be recognised by their appearances, and they will be grabbed by their forelocks and feet: *⁵⁵·⁴²So, which blessings of your Lord will you call a lie?* ⁵⁵·⁴³They will be told: "This is the Hell that the criminals used to call a lie!" ⁵⁵·⁴⁴Here they will wander about lost between Hell and some boiling liquid: *⁵⁵·⁴⁵So, which blessings of your Lord will you call a lie?*

⁵⁵·⁴⁶Anyone who fears standing in front of his Lord will have two gardens: *⁵⁵·⁴⁷So, which blessings of your Lord will you call a lie?* ⁵⁵·⁴⁸Both

have plants and shrubs of **thick branches:** [55.49]*So, which blessings of your Lord will you call a lie?* [55.50]Both have two fountains flowing in them: [55.51]*So, which blessings of your Lord will you call a lie?* [55.52]Both have two types of every kind of fruit: [55.53]*So, which blessings of your Lord will you call a lie?* [55.54]They will be relaxing on sofas with inner linings of heavy brocade, and the fruits of both gardens will be hanging low for them: [55.55]*So, which blessings of your Lord will you call a lie?* [55.56]In them will be spouses with modest gazes – no human or jinn has touched before them: [55.57]*So, which blessings of your Lord will you call a lie?* [55.58]They are like rubies and pearls: [55.59]*So, which blessings of your Lord will you call a lie?* [55.60]Is the reward for doing good anything but good? [55.61]*So, which blessings of your Lord will you call a lie?* [55.62]And besides these two, there are two more gardens: [55.63]*So, which blessings of your Lord will you call a lie?* [55.64]Both are lush green: [55.65]*So, which blessings of your Lord will you call a lie?* [55.66]There are two fountains gushing out in these two as well: [55.67]*So, which blessings of your Lord will you call a lie?* [55.68]There are fruits, palm trees and pomegranates in both of them: [55.69]*So, which blessings of your Lord will you call a lie?* [55.70]There will be pious, beautiful companions in all the gardens: [55.71]*So, which blessings of your Lord will you call a lie?* [55.72]They are the spouses of Paradise, living in tall tents: [55.73]*So, which blessings of your Lord will you call a lie?* [55.74]No human or jinn has touched them before the people of Paradise: [55.75]*So, which blessings of your Lord will you call a lie?* [55.76]The Believers will be relaxing on green cushions and fine carpets. [55.77]*So, which blessings of your Lord will you call a lie?*

[55.78]Blessed is the Name of your Lord, Master of Majesty and Honour.

Surah 56. Event (al-Waaqi'ah)

Allah's name I begin with, the Most Compassionate, the Ever-Merciful

[56.1] **When the Occurring Event** of Judgement Day **will take place,** [56.2] – **there is no doubt it will take place** [56.3] – **it will lower** some people, **raise** others up. [56.4] **When the earth will be violently shaken,** [56.5] **and the mountains will be crumbled to pieces** [56.6] **and become dust particles scattered about;** [56.7] **and you** people **will be divided into three groups,** [56.8] **The** good **Companions of the Right Hand – what people they are!** [56.9] **The** bad **Companions of the Left Hand – what people they are!**

[56.10] **However, a third group is of those ahead** in faith, and **they will be right at the front.** [56.11] **These will be nearest** to Allah, [56.12] **in Gardens of Delight:** [56.13] **many from previous generations** [56.14] **and a few from later generations,** [56.15] **on sofas decorated** with gold, [56.16] **relaxing on them, facing each other.** [56.17] **Eternal youths will go around** serving them [56.18] **with pots and jugs, and a cup from a flowing fountain.** [56.19] **They won't suffer any headache from it nor any loss of senses.** [56.20] **They will have any fruit they want,** [56.21] **and any bird-meat they desire;** [56.22] **and there will be beautiful wide-eyed spouses of Paradise,** [56.23] **like pearls that are all covered up;** [56.24] **as a reward for the good things they used to do.** [56.25] **They won't hear any foolishness there nor anything leading to sin,** [56.26] **but only the calming greetings of peace.**

[56.27] **The** good **Companions of the Right Side – what people they are!** [56.28] **They will be among thornless lote-trees,** [56.29] **and bunches of bananas,** [56.30] **in shades that are spread out,** [56.31] **continuously flowing water,** [56.32] **and lots of fruit** [56.33] – **unlimited and unrestricted,** [56.34] **relaxing on sofas that are raised high.** [56.35] **We've created the spouses of Paradise as a special creation,** [56.36] **and made them virgins** [56.37] – **loving, of the same age,** [56.38] **for the good Companions of the Right**

Side: ⁵⁶·³⁹many from previous generations, ⁵⁶·⁴⁰and many from later generations.

⁵⁶·⁴¹The bad Companions of the Left Side – what people they are! ⁵⁶·⁴²They will be in the Hot Wind of Hell and in a boiling liquid, ⁵⁶·⁴³in the shade of black smoke ⁵⁶·⁴⁴– neither cool nor pleasant. ⁵⁶·⁴⁵Before this, they used to enjoy luxuries in the world, ⁵⁶·⁴⁶but continued living in the greatest sin of disbelief and polytheism. ⁵⁶·⁴⁷They used to ask: "What? When we die and have become dust and bones, will we then be brought back to life? ⁵⁶·⁴⁸And our ancestors too?" ⁵⁶·⁴⁹Reply: "Of course! The previous and later generations too! ⁵⁶·⁵⁰Everyone altogether will certainly be gathered for the promised time on a fixed Day. ⁵⁶·⁵¹Then surely, O you who went astray! O you who called the truth a lie! ⁵⁶·⁵²You will certainly eat from the Zaqqum tree! ⁵⁶·⁵³You will fill your bellies with it, ⁵⁶·⁵⁴and drink some boiling liquid on top of that: ⁵⁶·⁵⁵drinking like thirsty camels!" ⁵⁶·⁵⁶This will be their hospitality on Judgement Day. ⁵⁶·⁵⁷It is We Who created you, so why don't you believe in the resurrection?

⁵⁶·⁵⁸Have you people ever thought about the semen you ejaculate? ⁵⁶·⁵⁹Who creates it: you or We? ⁵⁶·⁶⁰It is We Who placed death among you, and We cannot be stopped ⁵⁶·⁶¹from changing your forms and making you grow into something you don't even know. ⁵⁶·⁶²You already know about the first form of creation, so won't you even remind yourselves?

⁵⁶·⁶³Have you people ever thought about what you sow in the ground? ⁵⁶·⁶⁴Who makes it grow: you or We? ⁵⁶·⁶⁵If We had wanted, We could certainly make it crumble away, and you would be left wondering: ⁵⁶·⁶⁶"We are in definite loss! ⁵⁶·⁶⁷In fact, we've been deprived!"

56.68Have you people **ever thought about the water you drink?** 56.69**Who brings it down from the clouds: you or We?** 56.70If We had wanted, We could make it bitter. So, why don't you be thankful?

56.71**Have you people ever thought about the fire you light up?** 56.72**Who grows its tree** for fuel: **you or We?** 56.73It is We Who made it a reminder of Hell-Fire **as well as a convenience for travellers.**

56.74So, O Prophet Muhammad, **continue to glorify the Name of your Lord, the Supreme!**

56.75I swear by the positions of the stars 56.76– and this definitely is, if you realise, a mighty oath: 56.77that this is certainly an honourable Qur'an, 56.78in a Record that is well covered. 56.79Only purified people are allowed to touch it. 56.80Its revelation comes from Allah – the Lord of all the Worlds. 56.81Do you think this Message isn't important? 56.82Are you making your living by calling it a lie?

56.83So what is it like when the soul of the dying person **reaches the throat,** 56.84while you people **can only watch?** 56.85Even then, **We are nearer to him than you are, though you cannot see.** 56.86Now, if you are not restricted by Allah, 56.87you should be able to bring the soul back, if you're telling the truth.

56.88So, if the dying person is from those nearest to Allah 56.89then he will enjoy comfort and sweet-smelling foods, as well as a Garden of Delight. 56.90If he is one of the good Companions of the Right Side, 56.91then it will be said: "Peace be to you from the Companions of the Right Side." 56.92However, if he is of those who called the truth a lie, who go astray, 56.93then he will suffer a welcome of boiling liquid 56.94and will end up burning in Hell-Fire. 56.95This is the absolute truth.

^{56.96}So, O Prophet Muhammad, **continue to glorify the Name of your Lord, the Supreme!**

Surah 57. Iron (*Hadeed*)

Allah's name I begin with, the Most Compassionate, the Ever-Merciful

^{57.1}Everything in the heavens and the earth glorifies Allah. He is the Almighty, the All-Wise. ^{57.2}Control of the heavens and the earth belongs to Him. He gives life and death. He is Most Capable of anything. ^{57.3}He is the First and the Last, the Outer and the Inner, and He knows everything perfectly well. ^{57.4}He is the one Who created the heavens and the earth in six stages, and then established His authority on the Throne. He knows everything that goes into the earth, that comes out of it, that comes down from the sky, and that goes up into it. He is with you wherever you are. Allah is Ever-Watchful of everything you do. ^{57.5}Control of the heavens and the earth belongs to Him. All matters will be returned to Allah. ^{57.6}He makes the night enter into the day and the day enter into the night. He knows the secrets of the hearts perfectly well.

^{57.7}You must all believe in Allah and His Messenger, and donate from what He has made you successors of. Those of you who believe and donate will have a large reward.

^{57.8}Disbelievers! **What is wrong with you? Why won't you believe in Allah when the Messenger is inviting you to believe in your Lord? Allah has already taken a strong promise from you if you are true Believers.** ^{57.9}He is the one Who reveals clear verses to His Servant to bring you out of the depths of darkness into the light. Allah is certainly Kind, Ever-Merciful to you.

⁵⁷·¹⁰**What is wrong with you? Why won't you donate in Allah's cause?** The heritage of the heavens and the earth belongs to Allah anyway. Those of you who donated and fought before the Victory in Makkah are higher in rank than those who donated and fought afterwards. They aren't the same. However, Allah has promised the most beautiful reward to all. Allah is Fully-Aware of everything you do. ⁵⁷·¹¹**Who is it that will give Allah a generous loan which Allah will multiply for him? He will also have an honourable reward.**

⁵⁷·¹²O Prophet Muhammad, **one Day, when you will see the Believing men and women with their light moving quickly in front of them and on their right sides,** it will be said to them: "**The joy for you Today are the gardens – that have rivers flowing beneath them, where** you will remain forever. This is the tremendous victory."

⁵⁷·¹³On that Day, the hypocrite men and women will beg the Believers: "Wait for us so we can have some of your light." They will be told: "Go back to your past and look there for some light." Then a wall with a door in it will be raised up between them: there will be mercy inside the wall and its outside will be facing punishment. ⁵⁷·¹⁴They will call out to the Believers: "Weren't we with you?" They will reply: "Yes, of course! However, you led yourselves astray, you waited to see what would happen to us, **you doubted, and** false **hopes tricked you until Allah's command** of your death **arrived; when** Shaytan – the Big Trickster fooled you about Allah. ⁵⁷·¹⁵Today, ransom won't be accepted – neither from you hypocrites nor from the disbelievers. Your home will be the Fire. It will be your companion. What a dreadful final destination!"

⁵⁷·¹⁶Isn't it about time for the Believers' hearts to become humble: to remember Allah and for the truth which has come down? They shouldn't be like those previously given the Book and a long time

passed over them so their hearts became hard. Many of them are still disobedient.

⁵⁷·¹⁷You should all know that it is Allah Who gives life to the earth after it had become dead. We've made the signs clear to you so that you might think.

⁵⁷·¹⁸The men and women who give charity and who give Allah a generous loan will have it multiplied for them, and they will also have an honourable reward. ⁵⁷·¹⁹Those who believe in Allah and His messengers, it is really they who are sincere and are witnesses to the truth in the sight of their Lord. They will have their reward and their special light. Those who disbelieved and called Our revelations a lie, it is they who will be the people of Hell-Fire.

⁵⁷·²⁰You must all know that this life is just games, some kind of amusement, luxury, showing off to each other, and trying to gain more wealth and children than each other. It is like rain that causes plants to grow, which excites the farmers. Then the plants become dry and you see them turning yellow. Then they crumble away. In the Hereafter there will be either severe punishment for those who disobey or forgiveness from Allah and His good pleasure for those who obey. This life is only fake enjoyment. ⁵⁷·²¹You should race each other to get forgiveness from your Lord, and for a garden as vast as the sky and earth put together, prepared for those who believe in Allah and His messengers. This is Allah's grace; He gives it to anyone He chooses. Allah gives tremendous grace.

⁵⁷·²²Any disaster that takes place in the world or in your lives, it is mentioned in a Record before We make it happen. All that is easy for Allah. ⁵⁷·²³We are telling you this so you don't lose hope over what you miss out on nor boast about what He gives you. Allah doesn't like

anyone who is arrogant, showoff, ⁵⁷·²⁴those who are themselves stingy or tell others to be stingy. Anyone who turns away from giving should know that Allah is Free of all Needs, the Most Praiseworthy.

⁵⁷·²⁵We sent Our messengers with clear signs, and We revealed with them the Book as well as the balance of justice, so people can be fair. We sent down iron, in which there is a lot of hardness and many other benefits for people, and so Allah can prove who it is that would help Him and His messengers without seeing. Allah is Strong, Almighty.

⁵⁷·²⁶We sent Nuh and Ibrahim, and placed prophethood and the revealed Book among their descendants, which is why some of them follow guidance even though many of them are disobedient.

⁵⁷·²⁷Then We sent many messengers in succession following right behind them, and then We sent Isa ibn Maryam right behind them and gave him the Injeel, and We placed kindness and mercy in his followers' hearts. They themselves made up monasticism only to try and gain Allah's good pleasure, because We hadn't prescribed it for them, but they couldn't properly maintain it. So we gave the faithful among them their reward, but many of them are disobedient.

⁵⁷·²⁸Believers! You must continue to be mindful of Allah and continue to believe in His Messenger, and He will give you a double share of His special mercy, give you a special light to walk in, and also forgive you. Allah is Most Forgiving, Ever-Merciful. ⁵⁷·²⁹This is mentioned so that the People of the Book will realise they don't have any power over any of Allah's grace, and that all grace is in Allah's control; He gives it to anyone He chooses. Allah gives tremendous grace.

Surah 58. Dispute (*al-Mujaadalah*)

[PART 28]

Allah's name I begin with, the Most Compassionate, the Ever-Merciful

58.1 O Prophet Muhammad, Allah has heard the words of the woman who was arguing with you about her husband and complaining to Allah. Allah hears your conversation. Allah is All-Hearing, Ever-Watchful.

58.2 Those of your men who divorce their wives by saying they're like their own mothers' backs should know that their wives cannot be their mothers. Their mothers are only those who have given birth to them. They are saying something wrong and false, yet Allah is certainly Most Pardoning, Most Forgiving. 58.3 Those who try to divorce their wives by saying they're like own mothers' backs, but then want to go back on what they said, they must free a slave before they can even touch each other. This is what you've been told to do. Allah is Fully-Aware of everything you do. 58.4 If the husband cannot do this, he must fast for two months in a row before they can touch each other. If he cannot do this as well then he must feed sixty needy people. This is for you to prove your belief in Allah and His Messenger. These are the limits set by Allah. The disbelievers will suffer a painful punishment.

58.5 Those who go against Allah and His Messenger will be humiliated like those before them were. We've sent down some clear revelations. The disbelievers will suffer a humiliating punishment. 58.6 On the Day when Allah will bring them all back to life, He will tell them what they did. Allah has recorded it but they've forgotten it. Allah is a Witness to everything.

⁵⁸·⁷O Prophet Muhammad, **don't you see that Allah knows everything in the heavens and in the earth?** Whenever there is a private discussion between three, He is the fourth among them; between five, and He is the sixth among them; between less than that number or more, He is with them wherever they are. Then on Judgement Day, He will tell them what they did. Allah knows everything perfectly well.

⁵⁸·⁸**Haven't you seen those who were forbidden from having private discussions, but then they went back to doing what they were told not to?** They secretly discuss doing bad things, being hostile, and disobeying the Messenger. O Prophet Muhammad, when they come to you, they greet you using bad words unlike Allah greets you, and they ask each other: "Why isn't Allah punishing us for what we are saying?" Hell will be enough for them. They will burn in it. What a dreadful final destination!

⁵⁸·⁹**Believers! When you discuss privately, you mustn't discuss doing bad things, being hostile, nor disobeying the Messenger,** but you can privately discuss being righteous and mindful. You must remain mindful of Allah in front of Whom you will all be assembled. ⁵⁸·¹⁰**Harmful** private discussions are inspired by Shaytan to make the Believers sad. Without Allah's permission, he cannot harm them in any way at all. True Believers must put their trust only in Allah.

⁵⁸·¹¹**Believers! When you are told: "Make room in gatherings", you should do so;** Allah will make room for you. When you are told: "Stand up from your place," you should do so; Allah will raise high in ranks the faithful among you and those given knowledge. Allah is Fully-Aware of everything you do.

⁵⁸·¹²Believers! When you want to have any private discussion with the Messenger, you should give charity before your discussion with him. This is better for you and purer. If you cannot do this then you should know that Allah is Most Forgiving, Ever-Merciful. ⁵⁸·¹³Are you afraid of giving in acts of charity before your private discussion with him? If you don't, and Allah forgives you, then you should continue to establish the ritual prayer, pay zakah, and obey Allah and His Messenger. Allah is Fully-Aware of everything you do.

⁵⁸·¹⁴Haven't you seen those who took as their protectors the people Allah is angry with? They're neither of you nor of them, and they deliberately swear false oaths. ⁵⁸·¹⁵Allah has prepared a severe punishment for them. How terrible is what they've been doing! ⁵⁸·¹⁶They have made their oaths a shield, and so they block others from Allah's cause, which is why they will suffer a humiliating punishment. ⁵⁸·¹⁷All their wealth and their children won't be able to save them from the punishment of Allah in any way at all. It is they who will be the people of the Fire. They will remain in it forever! ⁵⁸·¹⁸On the Day when Allah will bring them all back to life, they will swear to Him as they swear to you, and they think they're on the Right Path. In fact, they themselves are telling lies. ⁵⁸·¹⁹Shaytan has taken control of them and made them forget to remember Allah. It is they who are Shaytan's group. Beware! It is Shaytan's group that will lose! ⁵⁸·²⁰Those who go against Allah and His Messenger, it is they who are among the lowest of all.

⁵⁸·²¹Allah has decided: "I and My messengers will certainly win." Allah is Strong, Almighty.

⁵⁸·²²You won't find any people who believe in Allah and the Last Day loyal to those who go against Allah and His Messenger, even if they are their parents, children, siblings, or relatives. Allah has made faith

strong in their hearts and supported them with some special help from Himself. He will enter them into gardens – that have rivers flowing beneath them, where they will remain forever. Allah is well-pleased with them and they are well-pleased with Him. It is they who are Allah's group. Beware! It is Allah's group that will be successful.

Surah 59. Gathering (al-Hashr)

Allah's name I begin with, the Most Compassionate, the Ever-Merciful

[59.1] Everything in the heavens and the earth glorifies Allah. He is the Almighty, the All-Wise. [59.2] He is the one Who made the disbelievers among the People of the Book leave their homes during the first gathering and banishment. You didn't think they would leave, and they thought their fortresses would save them from the punishment of Allah. However, punishment from Allah came to them from where they had never imagined. He cast awe into their hearts. They destroyed their own homes with their own hands and the Believer's hands. So, you who can see must learn a lesson of warning! [59.3] If Allah hadn't written exile for them, He would have certainly punished them in this world. In the Hereafter, they will suffer the punishment of the Fire. [59.4] That is because they went against Allah and His Messenger. Anyone who goes against Allah should know that He is severe in punishing.

[59.5] Any palm trees you had cut down or left standing on their roots, it was by Allah's permission, so He could humiliate those who were disobedient. [59.6] Whatever property Allah gave back to His Messenger from them, you Muslims used neither horses nor camels to reach it, but it is Allah Who gives power to His messengers over anyone He chooses. Allah is Most Capable of anything.

⁵⁹·⁷The wealth Allah has given His Messenger taken from the people of the towns, it belongs to Allah, His Messenger, his close relatives, orphans, the needy, and travellers; so that this wealth doesn't go around only within the rich people among you. You must take anything the Messenger gives you and stay away from anything he forbids you. You must continue to be mindful of Allah. Allah is severe in punishing. ⁵⁹·⁸Some is for the poor migrants who were expelled from their homes and property. They're trying to gain Allah's grace and good pleasure, and they're helping in the way of Allah and His Messenger. It is really they who are truthful. ⁵⁹·⁹Some is for those who live in Madinah and had embraced the faith of Islam before them. They love those who have migrated to them, and feel no need in their hearts for what those migrants have been given. In fact, they prefer them to themselves even if they themselves are in desperate need. Those who are protected from their own selfishness, it is really they who are successful.

⁵⁹·¹⁰Those who came after them, they pray: "Our Lord! Forgive us and our brothers who embraced the faith of Islam before us. Don't let our hearts hold any grudge against the Believers. Our Lord! You are Kind, Ever-Merciful."

⁵⁹·¹¹Haven't you seen the hypocrites saying to their disbelieving brothers among the People of the Book: "If you are expelled, we will leave with you, and will never obey anyone against you. If you are attacked, we will help you." Allah is Witness that they are certainly telling lies. ⁵⁹·¹²The truth is, if the disbelievers are expelled, the hypocrites won't leave with them; if they are attacked, the hypocrites won't help them; if they do come to help them, they will eventually turn their backs and run. Then, they won't be helped at all.

⁵⁹·¹³**There is more fear in their hearts for you** Muslims **than for Allah. This is because they are a people who don't understand.** ⁵⁹·¹⁴**Even united they won't fight you, unless they're in well-protected areas, or** they will attack you **from behind walls. Their violence between themselves is intense. You might think they are united, but their hearts are split apart. This is because they are a people who don't think.** ⁵⁹·¹⁵They are **like those recently before them who tasted the terrible result of their behaviour. They will suffer a painful punishment.**

⁵⁹·¹⁶Hypocrites are **like Shaytan when he tells someone: "Disbelieve!" but when that person disbelieves, Shaytan says: "I have nothing to do with you. I fear Allah – Lord of all the worlds."** ⁵⁹·¹⁷**The end result of both will be that they'll end up in the Fire where they will remain forever. That is the punishment of the wrongdoers.**

⁵⁹·¹⁸**Believers! You must continue to be mindful of Allah, and everyone should look carefully at what he does for tomorrow. You must continue to be mindful of Allah. Allah is Fully-Aware of everything you do.** ⁵⁹·¹⁹**You mustn't be like those who forget Allah that He makes them forget themselves. It is really they who are disobedient.** ⁵⁹·²⁰**The people of the Fire and the people of Paradise can never be the same. It's the people of Paradise who are the real winners.**

⁵⁹·²¹**If We had sent down this Qur'an on a mountain, you would have certainly seen it humble itself, crumble to pieces from the fear of Allah. These are the examples We give to people so that they might think deeply.**

⁵⁹·²²**He is Allah, as there is no god except Him – the Knower of the unseen secrets and the visible. He is the Most Compassionate, the Ever-Merciful.** ⁵⁹·²³**He is Allah, as there is no god except Him – the real**

King, the Most Pure, the Most Perfect, the Giver of Peace, the Guardian, the Almighty, the Highest Authority, the Supremely Great. Glory be to Allah above the partner-gods they make with Him. [59.24]He is Allah – the Creator, the Maker, the Shaper. He has the most beautiful names. Everything in the heavens and the earth glorifies Him. He is the Almighty, the All-Wise.

Surah 60. Tested Woman (al-Mumtahanah)

Allah's name I begin with, the Most Compassionate, the Ever-Merciful

[60.1]Believers! You mustn't take My enemies and your enemies as protectors by showing them your love when they have disbelieved in the truth that has come to you. They've expelled the Messenger and you too only because you believe in Allah – your Lord. If you've come out to strive hard in My cause and trying to gain My good pleasure, but you're hiding your love for them – though I know everything you hide or show – should know that anyone among you who does that has certainly strayed away from the Straight Way. [60.2]The truth is, if they ever gain control over you, they will become your enemies and will try to harm you physically and verbally, and they would love it if you disbelieved. [60.3]Neither your family relations nor your children will be able to help you, on Judgement Day, as Allah will cause separation between you and them. Allah is Ever-Watchful of everything you do.

[60.4]You certainly have an excellent role model to follow in Ibrahim and those with him, when they told their people: "We have nothing to do with you nor with anything you worship besides Allah. We reject you, and that is why enmity and hatred has forever come between us and you – unless you believe in Allah, the One." However, Ibrahim said to his foster father: "I will pray for your forgiveness even though I cannot give you anything at all from Allah." Then he prayed: "Our Lord! We put our trust only in You. We turn only to You in repentance. The final return will be to You. ⁶⁰·⁵Our Lord! Don't make us a target for the disbelievers, but forgive us, our Lord! Only you are the Almighty, the All-Wise." ⁶⁰·⁶You certainly have a perfect example to follow in them, especially for someone who has hope in Allah and the Last Day. However, anyone who turns away should know that only Allah is Free of all Needs, the Most Praiseworthy.

⁶⁰·⁷Perhaps Allah will later place goodwill between you and those of them who are now your enemies. Allah is Most Capable. Allah is Most Forgiving, Ever-Merciful.

⁶⁰·⁸Allah doesn't stop you from being good and fair to those who neither fight you because of religion nor expel you from your homes. Allah loves those who are fair. ⁶⁰·⁹Allah only stops you from taking as your protectors those who fight you because of religion, expel you from your homes, and help others in expelling you. Those who take them as their protectors, it is really they who are the wrongdoers.

⁶⁰·¹⁰Believers! When Believing women come to you as emigrants, you should test them. Allah knows best about their faith. Once you are sure that these women really are Believers then don't send them back to the disbelievers, because neither are they lawful as wives for them nor the disbelievers lawful as husbands for them. Pay the disbelievers what they spent on their dowry. There is nothing wrong for you to marry them if you pay them their dowry. You mustn't hold on to marriage with disbelieving women. You can ask for what you've spent on their dowry, and the disbelievers can also ask for what they spent on the Believing women who have left them. This is Allah's command. He judges between you. Allah is All-Knowing, All-Wise.

⁶⁰·¹¹If any of your wives leaves you and goes to the disbelievers, and you gain spoils in war, then pay to those whose wives have left them the amount they paid on their dowry. You must continue to be mindful of Allah as you believe in Him.

⁶⁰·¹²O Prophet, when Believing women come to you to swear loyalty to you that they won't make anything at all a partner-god with Allah; and that they won't: steal, have unlawful sexual relations, kill their children, make lies about who has fathered their children; and that they won't disobey you in anything good, then you should accept their swearing of loyalty, and ask Allah to forgive them. Allah is Most Forgiving, Ever-Merciful.

⁶⁰·¹³Believers! You mustn't take as your protectors the people Allah is angry with. They've already lost hope in the Hereafter just like the disbelievers have lost hope in those who are buried in graves to come back.

Surah 61. Rows (as-Saff)

Allah's name I begin with, the Most Compassionate, the Ever-Merciful

⁶¹·¹Everything in the heavens and the earth glorifies Allah. He is the Almighty, the All-Wise.

⁶¹·²Believers! Why do you say the things you don't do? ⁶¹·³It is terribly hateful in the sight of Allah for you to say the things you don't do. ⁶¹·⁴Allah loves those who fight in His cause, in rows as if it were a wall made solid with molten lead.

⁶¹·⁵Remember when Musa said to his people: "My people! Why are you abusing me when you know that I am Allah's messenger sent to you?"

Then, when they lost focus of the truth, Allah let their hearts lose focus too. Allah doesn't let disobedient people succeed.

61.6 Remember when Isa ibn Maryam said: "Descendants of Ya'qub! I am Allah's messenger sent to you, confirming the Tawrah which came before me, and giving the good news of a Messenger Muhammad who will come after me – whose heavenly name is Ahmad. However, when he (Ahmad, i.e. Muhammad) came to them with clear proofs, they said: "This is clearly magic." 61.7 Who could be more unjust than someone who makes lies about Allah when he is being invited to Islam! Allah doesn't let unjust people succeed.

61.8 They want to blow out Allah's light with their mouths, but Allah will complete the revelation of His light even if the disbelievers hate it. 61.9 He is the one Who sent His Messenger with guidance and the True Religion, to make him dominant over every other religion, even if the polytheists hate it.

61.10 Believers! Shall I show you a bargain that will save you from a painful punishment? 61.11 You should believe in Allah and His Messenger, and strive hard in Allah's cause with your wealth and your lives. This is best for you if you only knew. 61.12 He will also forgive you your sins, and enter you into gardens – that have rivers flowing beneath them, and into beautiful mansions in the Gardens of Eden. That will be the tremendous victory. 61.13 You will also have something else that you like: help from Allah and a speedy victory. O Prophet Muhammad, give this good news to the Believers.

61.14 Believers! You should be helpers in the religion of Allah, just like Isa ibn Maryam asked the disciples: "Who will be my helpers in guiding others to Allah?" "We will be the helpers in the religion of Allah," they replied. So, a section of the Descendants of Ya'qub believed while another disbelieved. Then We helped the Believers against their enemy, so they ended up winning.

Surah 62. Friday Congregation (al-Jumu'ah)

Allah's name I begin with, the Most Compassionate, the Ever-Merciful

$^{62.1}$Everything in the heavens and the earth is glorifying Allah, the real King, the Most Pure, the Almighty, the All-Wise.

$^{62.2}$He is the one Who raised up within the people who have no Book a Messenger from among them, who recites Allah's revelations to them, cleans and purifies them, and teaches them the Book and wisdom, while, before that, they had been clearly astray. $^{62.3}$He also teaches and purifies those of them who haven't already joined them. Allah is the Almighty, the All-Wise. $^{62.4}$This is Allah's grace; He gives it to anyone He chooses. Allah gives tremendous grace.

$^{62.5}$The example of those who were made to carry the commands of the Tawrah and then failed to act upon it is that of a donkey carrying books. How evil is the example of those who call Allah's revelations lies! Allah doesn't let unjust people succeed.

$^{62.6}$O Prophet Muhammad, say: "Jews! If you claim that you out of all the people are the only friends of Allah then you should wish for death, if you are telling the truth." $^{62.7}$But they won't wish for death because of the bad things they've done. Allah knows the wrongdoers perfectly well. $^{62.8}$Say: "The death you're running away from will soon catch up with you. Then you will be taken back to Allah – the Knower of the unseen secrets and the visible, and He will tell you about everything you used to do."

⁶²·⁹Believers! When on Friday the call for prayer is made, you must hurry to Allah's remembrance, and leave everything, including buying and selling. That is best for you if you only knew. ⁶²·¹⁰When the ritual prayer is finished, you can spread out in the land, try to gain some of Allah's grace, and remember Allah a lot so that you might be successful.

⁶²·¹¹However, when some unwise people see a bargain or an opportunity for amusement, they rush to it and leave you standing all alone. Say: "What is with Allah is better than this amusement and bargain. Allah is the Best Giver of all."

Surah 63. Hypocrites (al-Munafiqoon)

Allah's name I begin with, the Most Compassionate, the Ever-Merciful

⁶³·¹O Prophet Muhammad, when the hypocrites come to you, they say: "We testify that you certainly are Allah's Messenger." Allah knows that you certainly are His Messenger, but He is also witness that the hypocrites are definitely liars. ⁶³·²They've made their oaths a shield, and so they block others from Allah's cause. How terrible is what they are doing! ⁶³·³That is because they believed on the outside, then disbelieved on the inside, which is why their hearts are sealed up so now they don't understand what to do.

⁶³·⁴When you see them, their looks impress you. When they speak, you listen to what they say. However, they're like pieces of wood made to lean against a wall. They think every loud noise is raised against them. They're the enemy, so beware of them. May Allah ruin them! How are they being misled!

63.5When they're told: "Come! Allah's Messenger will pray for your forgiveness," they shake their heads aside and you see them arrogantly staying away. 63.6O Prophet Muhammad, it makes no difference to them if you pray for their forgiveness or not. Allah will never forgive them. Allah doesn't let disobedient people succeed.

63.7They're the ones who say: "Don't spend on those who are with Allah's Messenger so they will scatter away from him." However, the treasures of the heavens and the earth belong only to Allah, but the hypocrites won't understand. 63.8They say: "If we go back to Madinah, the respectable ones will expel the disgraced ones from there." However, glory and power belong only to Allah and His Messenger, and to the Believers, but the hypocrites don't realise.

63.9Believers! You mustn't let your wealth or your children make you forget to remember Allah. Those who do that, it is they who are the real losers. 63.10Donate from what We've given you before death comes to any of you and he says: "My Lord! If you give me a little more time, I will give charity and be one of the righteous."

63.11However, Allah will never give more time to anyone when the end of their time comes. Allah is Fully-Aware of everything you people do.

Surah 64. Being Defeated (*at-Taghaabun*)

Allah's name I begin with, the Most Compassionate, the Ever-Merciful

64.1Everything in the heavens and the earth is glorifying Allah. All control belongs to Him. All praise is for Him. He is Most Capable of anything. 64.2He is the one Who created you all: some of you are disbelievers while others are Believers. Allah is Ever-Watchful of everything you do. ⁶⁴·³He created the heavens and the earth for a real purpose, shaped you in the womb and gave you a beautiful form, and the final return will be to Him. ⁶⁴·⁴He knows everything in the heavens and the earth, and everything you people hide or show. Allah knows the secrets of the hearts perfectly well.

⁶⁴·⁵Hasn't the news reached you of those who disbelieved previously? They tasted the evil result of what they did, and they will suffer a painful punishment. ⁶⁴·⁶That was because though their messengers used to come to them with clear proofs, but they said: "What? Is it human beings who will guide us?" So they disbelieved and turned away, but Allah didn't need them. Allah is Free of all Needs, Most Praiseworthy.

⁶⁴·⁷The disbelievers claim they won't be brought back to life. O Prophet Muhammad, say: "Why not! I swear by my Lord that: you will definitely be brought back to life, and then you will be told about everything you did. All that is easy for Allah." ⁶⁴·⁸So, you must believe in Allah and His Messenger, and the Light (- Qur'an) We have revealed. Allah is Fully-Aware of everything you do. ⁶⁴·⁹One Day He will gather you all together for the Day of Gathering; that will be the Day of defeat to each other. Those who believe in Allah and do good, Allah will remove their sins from them and enter them into gardens – that have rivers flowing beneath them, where they will remain forever and ever. That will be the tremendous victory. ⁶⁴·¹⁰Those who disbelieve and call our revelations lies, it is they who will be the people of the Fire, where they will remain forever. What a dreadful final destination!

⁶⁴·¹¹Disaster can only take place with Allah's permission. Allah will guide the heart of anyone who believes in Him. Allah knows everything perfectly well. ⁶⁴·¹²You have to obey Allah and the

Messenger too. If you turn away it is your loss because Our Messenger's duty is only to deliver the message clearly. ⁶⁴·¹³He is Allah. There is no god except Him. True Believers must put their trust only in Allah.

⁶⁴·¹⁴Believers! Among your wives and your children there are some who are your enemies, so beware of them. However, if you pardon, ignore, and forgive, then Allah too is Most Forgiving, Ever-Merciful. ⁶⁴·¹⁵Your wealth and your children are only a test, and from Allah will come a huge reward. ⁶⁴·¹⁶So, you must continue to be mindful of Allah as much as you can. You must listen and obey, and donate in His cause. It is best for you. Those who are protected from their own selfishness, it is really they who are successful. ⁶⁴·¹⁷If you give Allah a generous loan, He will multiply it for you, and He will forgive you too. Allah is Most Appreciative, Most Tolerant, ⁶⁴·¹⁸Knower of the unseen secrets and the visible, the Almighty, the All-Wise.

Surah 65. Divorce (*at-Talaaq*)

Allah's name I begin with, the Most Compassionate, the Ever-Merciful

⁶⁵·¹O Prophet, tell the Muslims: When you divorce your wives, then do so keeping in mind their waiting period – and keep count of it. Continue to be mindful of Allah, your Lord. Don't force them to leave their homes nor should they themselves leave, unless they do something clearly shameful. These are the limits set by Allah. Whoever oversteps the limits set by Allah does wrong to himself. You never know, Allah might change the situation after that.

⁶⁵·²When they reach near the end of their waiting period, you must decide either to keep them with respect or separate them with honour. It's better if you make witnesses of two men from among you

who are completely fair, and you must establish the witnessing for Allah's sake. This is the advice given to someone who believes in Allah and the Last Day. Anyone who is mindful of Allah, He will make a way out for him, [65.3] and will give him in ways he could never imagine. Allah is enough for anyone who puts his trust in Him. Allah always achieves what He wants to do. He has already fixed a measure for everything.

[65.4] Those of your women who have passed the age of menstruation, if you are in doubt then their waiting period is three months – and also for those who have never menstruated. The waiting period for pregnant women is when they reach the end of their pregnancy. Anyone who is mindful of Allah, He will make his situation easy for him. [65.5] This is Allah's command which He has sent down to you all. Anyone who is mindful of Allah, He will remove his sins from him and increase the reward for him.

[65.6] Let your divorced wives live as and where you live, according to your means. Don't annoy them to make them suffer. If they are pregnant then you should spend on them until they reach the end of their pregnancy. If they breastfeed a child for you then you should give them their payment. You should continue to discuss matters in a good way with each other. If you are experiencing difficulties then another woman can breastfeed the child for him. [65.7] A rich person should spend from his wealth, but someone whose wealth is limited by poverty should spend from what little Allah has given him. Allah doesn't force anyone to do more than what He has given them. Soon after any difficulty, Allah will give ease.

[65.8] There are many towns which disobeyed the command of their Lord and His messengers, so We judged them severely, and made them suffer a dreadful punishment. [65.9] Then they tasted the evil result of what they did, whereas the end result of what they did was total loss. ⁶⁵·¹⁰Allah has prepared a severe punishment for them. Therefore, you must remain mindful of Allah, O people of understanding who believe! Allah has sent down to you a reminder ⁶⁵·¹¹– a Messenger who recites to you Allah's verses that make things clear, to bring those who believe and do good out of the depths of darkness into the light. Anyone who believes and does good, Allah will enter him into gardens – that have rivers flowing beneath them, where they will remain forever and ever. Allah will give him beautifully.

⁶⁵·¹²Allah is the one Who created seven heavens and the same of the earth. The command comes down between them for you to realise that Allah is Most Capable of anything, and that it is He Who fully covers everything in His knowledge.

Surah 66. Prohibition (*at-Tahreem*)

Allah's name I begin with, the Most Compassionate, the Ever-Merciful

⁶⁶·¹O Prophet, why do you avoid what Allah has made lawful for you because you want to please your wives? Allah is Most Forgiving, Ever-Merciful.

⁶⁶·²Allah has already shown you Muslims how to free yourselves from your unfulfilled oaths. Allah is your Master, and only He is the All-Knowing, the All-Wise.

⁶⁶·³When the Prophet secretly said something to one of his wives and she told it to someone else, and Allah let him know about it, the Prophet reminded her of some of it and left out a part. When he told her about it, she asked: "Who told you this?" He replied: "Allah – the All-Knowing, the Fully-Aware told me."

⁶⁶·⁴You should both repent to Allah as your hearts have already moved to repent. However, if you help each other against him then you should know that **Allah is his Protector, as well as Jibreel, and the righteous Believers.** Besides them, all the angels are his helpers too. ⁶⁶·⁵If he divorced you all, perhaps Allah will give him wives who are better than you – who will be surrendering to Allah as Muslims, believing, devoted, repenting, worshipping, fasting, previously married and virgins.

⁶⁶·⁶Believers! Save yourselves and your families from a Fire whose fuel is people and stones, over which are there angels who are strict and harsh, who never disobey what Allah orders them, but do as they are told. ⁶⁶·⁷Disbelievers! Stop making excuses today! You're only being punished for the bad things you used to do.

⁶⁶·⁸Believers! Repent to Allah sincerely. Perhaps your Lord will remove your sins from you and enter you into gardens – that have rivers flowing beneath them, on the Day when Allah won't humiliate the Prophet or those who believe with him. Their light will be moving quickly in front of them and on their right sides. They will pray: "Our Lord! Perfect our light for us, and forgive us. You are Most Capable of anything."

⁶⁶·⁹O Prophet, you should continue to strive hard against the disbelievers and the hypocrites, and be firm with them. Their home will be Hell. What a horrible final destination!

⁶⁶·¹⁰ To the disbelievers, Allah gives the example of Nuh's wife and Lut's wife. Both were married to two of Our pious servants but betrayed them. So, their husbands won't save them from the

punishment of **Allah in any way at all. Both women will be told:** "Enter the Fire along with the others!"

66.11"To the Believers, Allah gives the example of Fir'awn's wife, when she prayed: "My Lord! Build me a house near You in Paradise, and save me from Fir'awn and the bad things he does. Save me from these wrongdoing people." 66.12Another example is **Maryam, the daughter of Imran, who guarded her chastity, so We breathed from Our spirit into her shirt opening. She truly believed in her Lord's commandments and His Books, and she was one of those who are devoted** to the truth.

Surah 67. All Control (al-Mulk)

[PART 29]

Allah's name I begin with, the Most Compassionate, the Ever-Merciful

67.1Blessed is the one Who holds all control. He is Most Capable of anything 67.2– Who created death and life so He can test which of you does the best. He is the Almighty, the Most Forgiving, 67.3Who created the seven heavens in harmony on top of each other. You won't see any disharmony in the creation of Allah – the Most Compassionate. Keep looking around: can you see any defect? 67.4Again, keep looking around, again and again. Your sight will come back to you tired and frustrated.

67.5We've certainly decorated the lowest heaven with stars and celestial objects like **lamps, and We use them as something to hit the devils with. We have prepared for them the punishment of the Blazing Fire.**

⁶⁷·⁶Those who disbelieve in their Lord will suffer the punishment of Hell. What a dreadful final destination! ⁶⁷·⁷When they will be flung into it, they will hear its roar as it boils over, ⁶⁷·⁸almost bursting with rage. Each time a group is thrown into it, Hell's gatekeepers will ask them: "Did no one come to warn you?" ⁶⁷·⁹They will reply: "Yes, of course. Someone did come to give us warnings but we accused him of being a liar and said, 'Allah hasn't sent down anything. You are greatly astray.'." ⁶⁷·¹⁰They will also say: "If we had listened and thought carefully, we wouldn't be among the people of the Blazing Fire Today." ⁶⁷·¹¹They will then confess their sins, but the people of the Blazing Fire will be far from Allah's mercy.

⁶⁷·¹²Those who fear their Lord without seeing Him, they will have forgiveness and a large reward.

⁶⁷·¹³Whether you people speak secretly or openly, Allah knows the secrets of the hearts perfectly well. ⁶⁷·¹⁴He Who created everything, how wouldn't He know? He knows all details, the Fully-Aware. ⁶⁷·¹⁵He is the one Who made the earth tame for you, so you may walk along its slopes and eat from what He gives. The resurrection will be to Him.

⁶⁷·¹⁶Do you feel safe that Allah – the Lord of the sky won't make the earth swallow you up when it shakes? ⁶⁷·¹⁷Do you feel safe that the Lord of the sky won't send a violent hurricane of stones upon you? That is when you will realise how serious My warning was! ⁶⁷·¹⁸Those before them also rejected My warning. So, how terrifying was My punishment!

⁶⁷·¹⁹Don't they see the birds above them, spreading out their wings and folding them in? Only Allah – the Most Compassionate is holding them up. He is Ever-Watchful of everything. ⁶⁷·²⁰Is there an army that can help you against Allah – the Most Compassionate? The

disbelievers are only being tricked. ⁶⁷·²¹Is there anyone who can give you food from Allah if He holds it back from you? They continue to remain in disobedience and in hatred of the truth. ⁶⁷·²²Who follows guidance better: someone who walks falling down flat on his face or someone who walks upright along a path that is straight?

⁶⁷·²³O Prophet Muhammad, say: "He is the one Who created you, and gave you hearing, sight, and intelligence, yet you hardly give any thanks." ⁶⁷·²⁴Say: "He is the one Who has multiplied you throughout the earth, and it is in front of Him you will all be assembled." ⁶⁷·²⁵They ask: "When will this warning be fulfilled, if you are telling the truth?" ⁶⁷·²⁶Reply: "Its knowledge is only with Allah. I am only giving clear warnings." ⁶⁷·²⁷When they see it very close, the disbelievers' faces will be worried, and it will be said: "This is the warning you were asking for!"

⁶⁷·²⁸O Prophet Muhammad, ask: "What do you think: if Allah gives me death and also to those with me, or even if He has mercy on us, who will save the disbelievers from a painful punishment?" ⁶⁷·²⁹Say: "He is the Most Compassionate Lord. We believe in Him and put our trust only in Him. You will soon come to know who is clearly astray." ⁶⁷·³⁰Say: "What do you think: if your water sinks deep underground then who could bring you running water?"

Surah 68. Pen (al-Qalam)

Allah's name I begin with, the Most Compassionate, the Ever-Merciful

⁶⁸·¹*Nuun.* I swear by the Pen and everything they write: ⁶⁸·²O Prophet Muhammad, by your Lord's blessing, you aren't a madman. ⁶⁸·³You will definitely have a never-ending reward. ⁶⁸·⁴You certainly have outstanding manners.

⁶⁸·⁵Soon, you will see and so will they, ⁶⁸·⁶as to which of you is really mad. ⁶⁸·⁷It is your Lord Who knows best anyone who strays away from His cause and also those who follow guidance.

⁶⁸·⁸So, you shouldn't listen to those who call the truth a lie. ⁶⁸·⁹They'd like you to compromise the truth, so they would make compromises too. ⁶⁸·¹⁰You mustn't obey any despicable person who: swears lots of oaths, ⁶⁸·¹¹makes false accusations, goes around spreading lies, ⁶⁸·¹²strictly forbids good, breaks the law, a sinner, ⁶⁸·¹³violent, and above all that, of doubtful birth; ⁶⁸·¹⁴merely because he has lots of wealth and children. ⁶⁸·¹⁵When Our verses are recited to him, he says: "These are stories made up by previous people." ⁶⁸·¹⁶Soon, We will mark him on the snout!

⁶⁸·¹⁷We will test them like We tested the owners of a certain garden: when they swore they would definitely pick its fruit in the morning ⁶⁸·¹⁸but will make no exception for the poor. ⁶⁸·¹⁹Then, as they slept, a disaster from your Lord hit the garden, ⁶⁸·²⁰and, in the morning, it had turned it into something like a field that had been cut down.

⁶⁸·²¹Then, as they entered the morning, they began calling out to each other: ⁶⁸·²²"Leave early for your land if you want to do the picking." ⁶⁸·²³So they set off whispering quietly to each other: ⁶⁸·²⁴"Today, no needy person is allowed to enter the garden with you." ⁶⁸·²⁵They left early, confident in their plan. ⁶⁸·²⁶But when they saw their garden, they cried: "We must have lost our way. ⁶⁸·²⁷In fact, we have been deprived!"

⁶⁸·²⁸A sensible man among them said: "Didn't I tell you, 'Why don't you glorify Allah?'." ⁶⁸·²⁹They replied: "Glory be to our Lord! It is we who have been wrongdoers." ⁶⁸·³⁰Then they turned to each other, blaming

each other. ⁶⁸·³¹They cried: "We are damned! We used to break all limits of rebellion. ⁶⁸·³²Perhaps our Lord will give us something better than this garden. We turn in hope to our Lord." ⁶⁸·³³This is the punishment in this world, but the punishment of the Hereafter will be far worse. If only they knew!

⁶⁸·³⁴Those who are mindful of Allah will have Gardens of Delight with their Lord. ⁶⁸·³⁵Those who surrender to Us as Muslims, will We treat them like criminals? ⁶⁸·³⁶What is wrong with you? How are you making bad decisions? ⁶⁸·³⁷Do you have a Book in which you read ⁶⁸·³⁸that it contains everything you like? ⁶⁸·³⁹Do you have any oaths from Us continuing until Judgement Day that you can have anything you decide? ⁶⁸·⁴⁰Ask them which of them can guarantee that. ⁶⁸·⁴¹Do they have any partners? Then they must bring their partners, if they are telling the truth.

⁶⁸·⁴²On the Day when the horror becomes real, and they're invited to prostrate, they won't be able to do so. ⁶⁸·⁴³Their eyes will be looking down with humiliation covering them. They were invited to prostrate in the world when they were healthy but they refused. ⁶⁸·⁴⁴O Prophet Muhammad, then leave Me to deal with those who call this Message (- Qur'an) a lie. We will let them gradually fall into ruin in ways they won't even realise. ⁶⁸·⁴⁵I am giving them more time, but My plan is set and powerful. ⁶⁸·⁴⁶Are you asking them for a payment for this guidance so they are weighed down with debt? ⁶⁸·⁴⁷Do they have knowledge of the unseen secrets that they're writing down?

⁶⁸·⁴⁸You should have patience with your Lord's command, and not be like the Man in the Whale (- Prophet Yunus) – when he called out to Allah in distress. ⁶⁸·⁴⁹If the favour from his Lord hadn't helped him, he would have certainly been thrown onto the open shore and left there,

and only he would have been blamed. ⁶⁸·⁵⁰However, his Lord selected him and made him one of the righteous people.

⁶⁸·⁵¹O Prophet Muhammad, the disbelievers almost kill you with their angry looks when they hear the Reminder, and they say: "He must be mad!" ⁶⁸·⁵²They should know that this Qur'an is a reminder for everyone.

Surah 69. Truthteller (al-Haaqqah)

Allah's name I begin with, the Most Compassionate, the Ever-Merciful

⁶⁹·¹The Truth-Revealer! ⁶⁹·²What is the Truth-Revealer? ⁶⁹·³What will explain to you what the Truth-Revealer is?

⁶⁹·⁴The Thamud and the 'Ad called the Great Smash of Judgement Day a lie. ⁶⁹·⁵The Thamud - they were destroyed by the Deafening Blast, ⁶⁹·⁶and the 'Ad - they were destroyed by a furious, roaring wind; ⁶⁹·⁷Allah punished them with it for seven nights and eight days continuously. You could see the people lying dead in its path as if they were hollow trunks of palm trees. ⁶⁹·⁸Do you think any of them survived? ⁶⁹·⁹Fir'awn, and those before him, and those of the overturned cities (of Sodom and Gomorrah), did bad things, ⁶⁹·¹⁰and they disobeyed their Lord's messenger, so Allah punished them severely.

⁶⁹·¹¹When the water of Nuh's Flood began to overflow, We carried you all in the floating Ark, ⁶⁹·¹²to make it a reminder for you, and for retentive ears to remember it.

⁶⁹·¹³Then, when the Trumpet will be blown one blast, ⁶⁹·¹⁴and the earth and mountains will be lifted up and smashed in one go, ⁶⁹·¹⁵that is the

Day the Occurring Event will take place. ⁶⁹·¹⁶The sky will split apart because it will be weak on that Day, ⁶⁹·¹⁷and angels will be positioned at its edges. Eight will be carrying your Lord's Throne above them on that Day. ⁶⁹·¹⁸On that Day, you will all be brought forward. None of your secrets will remain hidden.

⁶⁹·¹⁹Anyone given his record in his right hand will happily say: "Here! Read my record! ⁶⁹·²⁰I was sure I would reach my account easily." ⁶⁹·²¹Then he will be in a life of happiness, ⁶⁹·²²in a magnificent garden, ⁶⁹·²³whose fruit-clusters will be hanging low. ⁶⁹·²⁴He will be told: "You may eat and drink with enjoyment because of the good things you did before in the days that have past."

⁶⁹·²⁵Anyone given his record in his left hand will sadly cry: "Oh! If only I had not been given my record! ⁶⁹·²⁶If only I had not known about my account. ⁶⁹·²⁷Oh! If only death had been the end of me. ⁶⁹·²⁸Even my wealth cannot save me. ⁶⁹·²⁹My power and authority has gone from me." ⁶⁹·³⁰It will be ordered: "Grab hold of him and put an iron collar around his neck, ⁶⁹·³¹then burn him in Hell-Fire, ⁶⁹·³²then tie him up tightly with a chain that is seventy cubits long! ⁶⁹·³³He wouldn't believe in Allah – the Supreme! ⁶⁹·³⁴nor encourage others to give food to the needy. ⁶⁹·³⁵This is why he will have no loyal friend here Today, ⁶⁹·³⁶nor any food apart from filthy pus ⁶⁹·³⁷that only bad people will eat."

⁶⁹·³⁸I swear by what you people can see ⁶⁹·³⁹and also what you cannot see ⁶⁹·⁴⁰that: this Qur'an is certainly the command of an honourable Messenger ⁶⁹·⁴¹and not the word of any poet. How little you believe! ⁶⁹·⁴²It isn't the word of any fortune-teller. How little you remind yourselves! ⁶⁹·⁴³It's a revelation from Allah – the Lord of All the Worlds.

⁶⁹·⁴⁴If he had made up a lie about Us, ⁶⁹·⁴⁵We would have grabbed him by the right hand ⁶⁹·⁴⁶and cut off the main vein to his heart, ⁶⁹·⁴⁷and none of you could stop Us from doing that.

⁶⁹·⁴⁸This Qur'an is certainly a reminder for those who are mindful of Allah. ⁶⁹·⁴⁹We certainly know some of you call the Qur'an's truth a lie, ⁶⁹·⁵⁰but it will definitely be a matter of regret for the disbelievers. ⁶⁹·⁵¹This Qur'an is the absolute truth. ⁶⁹·⁵²So, O Prophet Muhammad, continue to glorify the Name of your Lord, the Supreme.

Surah 70. Pathways to Heaven (al-Ma'aarij)

Allah's name I begin with, the Most Compassionate, the Ever-Merciful

⁷⁰·¹Someone asked about the punishment which will take place ⁷⁰·²on the disbelievers; nothing can stop it. ⁷⁰·³It will come from Allah, Lord of the Pathways going up to Heaven.

⁷⁰·⁴The angels and the Holy Spirit (- Angel Jibra'il) go up to Him on a Day whose timespan is fifty thousand years. ⁷⁰·⁵So, O Prophet Muhammad, you should have patience – wonderful patience. ⁷⁰·⁶They think that Day is far away ⁷⁰·⁷but We know it is near.

⁷⁰·⁸On that Day, the sky will be like molten brass, ⁷⁰·⁹the mountains will be like wool, ⁷⁰·¹⁰and no loyal friend will ask about his loyal friend ⁷⁰·¹¹– even though they will be shown to each other. All criminals would love to ransom themselves from that Day's punishment by their children, ⁷⁰·¹²their spouse and siblings, ⁷⁰·¹³their family who gave them safety, ⁷⁰·¹⁴and everyone on earth – just to save themselves.

[70.15]But no! It's a Flaming Fire [70.16]that will rip flesh off bones! [70.17]It is calling to those who turned their backs and moved away from the truth, [70.18]and gathered wealth and stored it away.

[70.19]The human being has been created impatient and greedy; [70.20]becoming distressed when he suffers bad things, [70.21]and stingy when good things come to him [70.22]- but not those who pray, [70.23]who are regular in their ritual prayers; [70.24]and in whose wealth there's a fixed share [70.25]for beggars and poor people; [70.26]and those who truly believe in Judgement Day; [70.27]and those who are terrified of their Lord's punishment [70.28]- because there's no safety from their Lord's punishment; [70.29]and those who guard their chastity, [70.30]except with their wives, or their slavewomen – in which case they cannot be criticised. [70.31]However, those trying go beyond this will be overstepping the limits.

[70.32]Successful are those who fulfil their trusts and their promises, [70.33]and those who stay firm in their witnessing, [70.34]and those who look after their prayers. [70.35]It is they who will be honoured in the Gardens of Paradise.

[70.36]Now what is wrong with the disbelievers? O Prophet Muhammad, they're rushing towards you to make fun of you [70.37]from the right and the left – everywhere, in crowds. [70.38]Does every one of them hope to be entered into the Garden of Delight? [70.39]Never! They know well what substance We've created them from. [70.40]So, I swear by Allah – the Lord of the Easts and sunrises and the Wests and sunsets that: We certainly have the power [70.41]to replace them with people better than them, and We cannot be stopped. [70.42]So leave them to joke about and play games until they meet that Day of theirs which they are being warned about. [70.43]The Day when they will come rushing out of their graves as if running to a target, [70.44]their eyes will be looking down and humiliation covering them. That's the Day they've been warned about.

Surah 71. Nuh (Noah)

Allah's name I begin with, the Most Compassionate, the Ever-Merciful

71.1We sent Nuh to his People telling him: "Warn your people before a painful punishment comes to them." 71.2He said: "My people! I am giving you clear warnings 71.3that you must worship Allah and be mindful of Him, and obey me. 71.4He will forgive you some of your sins and give you chances to do good until the end time that is fixed. Normally, when the end time fixed by Allah comes, chances are not given, if you only knew!"

71.5He said: "My Lord! I have preached to my people night and day 71.6but my preaching only made them run further away from the truth. 71.7Each time I invited them so You could forgive them, they would thrust their fingers into their ears, cover themselves with their clothes, continue in disbelief, and show a lot of arrogance. 71.8Then I called them out loud, 71.9and I spoke to them in both public and private, 71.10and I said, 'You must beg your Lord to forgive you. He is Ever-Forgiving. 71.11He will send you plenty of rain; 71.12and give you lots of wealth and children; and grow for you gardens and make rivers flow for you. 71.13What is wrong with you? Why don't you believe in Allah's majesty? 71.14He has created you through different stages.

71.15Don't you see how Allah created the seven heavens in harmony on top of each other, 71.16made the moon to be a light within them, and the sun to be a lamp? 71.17It is Allah Who makes you grow like plants from the earth, 71.18into which He will send you back, and then bring you out again. ⁷¹·¹⁹It is Allah Who made the earth spread out for you, ⁷¹·²⁰so you could travel through it along its routes that are wide paths.'."

⁷¹·²¹Finally, Nuh cried: "My Lord! They've disobeyed me. They follow those people whose wealth and children have increased them only in loss. ⁷¹·²²They've made big evil plans. ⁷¹·²³They said to the people, 'Never leave your gods. Never leave your idols Wadd and Suwa', nor Yaguth, Ya'uq, or Nasr.' ⁷¹·²⁴They've misguided many, so dear Lord, let the wrongdoers increase only in straying further." ⁷¹·²⁵Because of their sins, they were drowned in the flood and thrown into the Fire, and they couldn't find themselves any helpers against Allah.

⁷¹·²⁶Nuh said: "My Lord! Don't leave even a single disbeliever to live on this land. ⁷¹·²⁷If You do leave them alive, they will keep on misguiding Your servants and giving birth to sinful, very unthankful people. ⁷¹·²⁸My Lord! Forgive me, my parents, anyone who enters my house as a Believer, and all Believing men and women; and let the wrongdoers increase only in destruction."

Surah 72. Jinns (al-Jinn)

Allah's name I begin with, the Most Compassionate, the Ever-Merciful

⁷²·¹O Prophet Muhammad, say: "It has been revealed to me that a group of jinns listened to my Qur'an recitation. They went back and said, 'We have heard a wonderful recitation. ⁷²·²It leads to true guidance so we believed in it: we will never make anyone a partner-god with our Lord. ⁷²·³Our Lord, His majesty is high, has neither a wife nor a child. ⁷²·⁴Only a fool among us would utter outrageous things about Allah, ⁷²·⁵and We thought humans and jinns would never tell lies about Him!

⁷²·⁶Some human men started asking jinn men to protect them, and in this way they increased the arrogance of the jinn men. ⁷²·⁷Those humans thought like you jinns think, that Allah won't bring anyone back to life. ⁷²·⁸We touched the sky but found it filled with strict guards and shooting stars. ⁷²·⁹We used to sit at certain positions there to eavesdrop. If anyone tries to eavesdrop now, he will find a shooting star waiting in ambush for him. ⁷²·¹⁰We don't know if something bad is intended for those on earth, or if their Lord intends to lead them to true guidance. ⁷²·¹¹There are some among us who are righteous and others who aren't; we've always followed many different paths. ⁷²·¹²We are sure that we can never defeat Allah in this world nor escape Him by running away. ⁷²·¹³We believed in the guidance as soon as we heard it. Anyone who believes in his Lord will neither fear any loss nor oppression. ⁷²·¹⁴There are some among us who surrender to Allah as Muslims and others who are wrongdoers. Those who surrendered to Allah as Muslims, it is they who are looking for true guidance, ⁷²·¹⁵but the wrongdoers will be fuel for Hell.'."

⁷²·¹⁶If they had stayed strong on the right path, We would certainly have given them plenty of food and water ⁷²·¹⁷so We could test them with it. However, anyone who turns away from remembering his Lord, Allah will put him into a punishment of increasing difficulty.

⁷²·¹⁸All places of worship are Allah's, so you people mustn't worship anyone with Him. ⁷²·¹⁹However, when Allah's special servant – Prophet Muhammad stood to pray to Him, they began to gather tightly around him. ⁷²·²⁰O Prophet Muhammad, say: "I pray only to my Lord without making anyone a partner with Him." ⁷²·²¹Say: "I don't have any power from myself to harm or guide you." ⁷²·²²Say: "No one can save me from the decision of Allah, nor will I ever find any refuge except in Him, ⁷²·²³but my duty is only to deliver the truth from Allah,

and His messages too. Anyone who disobeys Allah and His Messenger will suffer the fire of Hell, where they will remain forever and ever."

^{72.24}"Finally, when they see what they are being warned about, they will realise whose helpers are weaker and whose numbers are fewer. ^{72.25}O Prophet Muhammad, say: "I won't guess if what you are warned about is near or if my Lord has fixed a longer time for it."

^{72.26}Allah is the **Knower of the unseen secrets** – not telling anyone about them ^{72.27}apart from any messenger He chooses. Then He puts protectors in front of him and behind him – everywhere, ^{72.28}**to prove they have delivered their Lord's messages. He already knows everything about them, and has kept count of everything.**

Surah 73. Wrapped in His Clothes (al-Muzzammil)

Allah's name I begin with, the Most Compassionate, the Ever-Merciful

^{73.1}**O you** Beloved Prophet Muhammad **wrapped up in your clothes,** ^{73.2}**You should stand to pray at night, but not too long** ^{73.3}– **a half of it, or make it a little less than that,** ^{73.4}**or even a little more than that; and recite the Qur'an in slow clear stages.** ^{73.5}**We will soon send down some heavy words to you.**

^{73.6}**Getting up to pray at night is more effective in controlling the self and in paying attention to the words.** ^{73.7}**You are busy for long periods during the day,** ^{73.8}**but you should remember your Lord's Name, and devote yourself to Him completely.** ^{73.9}He is the Lord of the East and the West. There is no god except Him. So, make Him your Guardian.

^{73.10}**You should have patience with what they say, and avoid them in a good way.** ^{73.11}**Leave Me to deal with those enjoying luxury who call**

the truth a lie, and give them a little more time. ⁷³·¹²We have chains with Us, and Hell-Fire too, ⁷³·¹³as well as food that gets stuck in the throat, and also a painful punishment, ⁷³·¹⁴prepared for the Day the earth and the mountains will shake violently, and the mountains will become heaps of shifting sand.

⁷³·¹⁵We have sent you people a Messenger to be a witness over you, just like we sent a messenger to Fir'awn. ⁷³·¹⁶However, Fir'awn disobeyed the messenger, so We punished him heavily. ⁷³·¹⁷If you disbelievers keep on disbelieving, how will you protect yourselves on a Day which will turn children's hair grey ⁷³·¹⁸– when even the sky will break apart because of it? Allah's promise is bound to happen. ⁷³·¹⁹This Qur'an is a reminder, so anyone who wants can find a way to his Lord.

⁷³·²⁰O Prophet Muhammad, your Lord knows that you, and some of those with you, regularly stand to pray for nearly two-thirds of the night, and maybe sometimes a half or a third of it. It is Allah Who fixes the lengths of night and day, and He knows you people won't be able to cover it, so He has excused you all. Therefore, you may recite as much of the Qur'an that is easy for you. He knows that some of you who will be ill, and others who will be travelling through the earth trying to gain some of Allah's grace, and some who will be fighting in His cause. Therefore, you may recite as much of it that is easy for you, establish the ritual prayers, pay zakah, and give Allah a generous loan. Anything good you do for yourselves, you will find it with Allah as something far better and of a greater reward. So, keep begging Allah to forgive you. Allah is Most Forgiving, Ever-Merciful.

Surah 74. Wrapped in His Cloak (*al-Muddaththir*)

Allah's name I begin with, the Most Compassionate, the Ever-Merciful

74.1**O you** Beloved Prophet Muhammad **wrapped up in your cloak,** 74.2**Stand and give warnings,** 74.3**proclaim the greatness of your Lord,** 74.4**keep your clothes clean and pure,** 74.5**stay away from idols,** 74.6**don't do favours merely to gain more for yourself,** 74.7**and have patience for your Lord's sake.**

74.8**Then, when the Trumpet will be blown** a second time, 74.9**that Day will be a hard Day,** 74.10**not at all easy for the disbelievers.**

74.11**Leave Me,** to deal **with what I alone created** 74.12– **and gave lots of wealth to,** 74.13**as well as children to be present with him,** 74.14**and also gave** all the things **openly** 74.15– **yet he hopes I give** him **more.** 74.16**Never! He was stubborn against Our revelations.** 74.17**I will soon make the punishment increasingly difficult for him.**

74.18**He thought and plotted.** 74.19**May he be cursed! How he plotted!** 74.20**Again, may he be cursed! How he plotted!** 74.21**Then he looked again,** 74.22**then he frowned and scowled,** 74.23**then he turned his back to the truth and showed arrogance.** 74.24**Eventually, he said: "This** Qur'an **is only magic transmitted** from the past. 74.25**It is only the words of a human being."** 74.26**Soon will I burn him in the Scorching Fire.** 74.27**What will explain to you what the Scorching Fire is?** 74.28**It neither lets anything live nor leaves it to die.** 74.29**It repeatedly scorches the skin.** 74.30**There are nineteen** angels guarding **over it.**

74.31**We have made guards of the Fire only angels. We've set their number only as a test for the disbelievers: so that the People of the Book can be certain and the Believers can increase in faith; so that the People of the Book and the Believers would have no doubts; and so that those with sickness in their hearts, and the disbelievers too, may ask: "What does Allah mean by giving this example?" In this way Allah lets anyone He chooses go astray and also guides anyone He wants. Only your Lord knows His armies. This mention of Hell is only a reminder for people.

74.32Of course! I swear by the moon, 74.33and the night as it goes away, 74.34and the morning as it brightens: 74.35Hell is one of the biggest disasters 74.36– giving warnings to humans, 74.37for any of you who want to get ahead in doing good or fall behind in doing bad.

74.38Everyone will be held responsible for what they did, 74.39except the good Companions of the Right Side 74.40– in Gardens, asking each other 74.41about the criminals: 74.42"What made you enter the Scorching Fire?" 74.43They will reply: "We neither performed the ritual prayers 74.44nor fed the needy, 74.45but joked about with those who did useless things. 74.46We used to call Judgement Day a lie, 74.47until that death which is certain came upon us." 74.48Now, any requests of intercessors will be useless for them.

74.49So what is wrong with them that they're turning away from the Reminder, 74.50like they were panicked wild donkeys 74.51running from a lion! 74.52The truth is, each of them wants books of revelation laid open and given to them directly. 74.53Never! In fact, they don't even fear the Hereafter. 74.54Beware! This Qur'an is a reminder. 74.55So, anyone who wants may remember it. 74.56However, they will only remember if Allah allows. Only He should be feared and only He is the Lord of Forgiveness.

Surah 75. Resurrection (*al-Qiyaamah*)

Allah's name I begin with, the Most Compassionate, the Ever-Merciful

[75.1]I swear by Judgement Day, [75.2]and I swear by the self-criticising soul: [75.3]does the human being think We won't put his bones back together? [75.4]Why not! We even have the power to perfectly restore his fingertips.

[75.5]However, the human being wants to continue doing bad things even in the time ahead of him. [75.6]He asks mockingly: "When is Judgement Day?" [75.7]When eyes will be dazzled, [75.8]the moon will become dark, [75.9]and the sun and moon will be joined together, [75.10]that Day the human being will cry: "Where is the place to escape?" [75.11]Beware! There is no place of safety. [75.12]On that Day, the only place to stay in safety will be with your Lord. [75.13]On that Day, the human being will be told about what he did as an investment for the next world and what he left behind as an effect in this world. [75.14]In fact, every human knows about himself [75.15]but he will still offer his excuses.

[75.16]O Prophet Muhammad, **you shouldn't rush your** noble **tongue in reciting the Qur'an to try and speed up** memorising it. [75.17]**We are responsible for collecting it** in your noble heart **and making sure it is recited.** [75.18]So, you should follow its recitation when We recite it through Angel Jibra'il. [75.19]Moreover, it is also Our responsibility to explain it.

[75.20]**The truth is, you** people **love this available world** [75.21]**and you leave aside the Hereafter.**

75.22On that Day, some faces will be bright 75.23– looking towards their Lord, 75.24and some will be gloomy 75.25– thinking that some back-breaking disaster is about to be dropped on them.

75.26Beware! When the leaving soul reaches the collar-bone, 75.27and it is asked: "Is there someone? A healer to save him?" 75.28and he realises that now is the time to leave, 75.29and one leg clings to the other, 75.30your soul will be moving towards your Lord on that Day.

75.31However, the disbeliever neither confirmed the truth nor performed the ritual prayers, 75.32but called the truth a lie and turned away. 75.33Then he arrogantly went off to his people. 75.34You are damned, you arrogant disbeliever, and damned again! 75.35Again, you are damned, and damned again!

75.36Does a person think he will be left alone without being judged? 75.37Wasn't he a drop of ejaculated semen? 75.38Then it became a clinging clot that Allah created into another form and gave proportion to. 75.39From that He made the two genders: male and female. 75.40Doesn't He have the power to bring the dead back to life?

Surah 76. Human Being (al-Insaan)

Allah's name I begin with, the Most Compassionate, the Ever-Merciful

76.1There was certainly a time when a person was nothing worthy of mention. 76.2We created the human being – from a mixed drop of fluid – to test him, which is why We made him capable of hearing and seeing. 76.3We gave him guidance to Our way, so now he can choose to be thankful or unthankful.

⁷⁶·⁴We have prepared for the disbelievers chains, iron collars, and a Blazing Fire! ⁷⁶·⁵Pious people will drink from cups blended with camphor ⁷⁶·⁶– a fountain from which Allah's servants will drink, making it gush out freely as they wish. ⁷⁶·⁷They fulfil their promises in this world and fear a Day whose destruction will be widespread.

⁷⁶·⁸Out of the love for Allah, they give food to the needy, to orphans, and to prisoners, ⁷⁶·⁹saying: "We feed you for Allah's good pleasure. We want neither any payment nor any thanks from you. ⁷⁶·¹⁰We fear from our Lord a dreadfully distressful Day." ⁷⁶·¹¹However, Allah will protect them from that Day's destruction, and will give them freshness on their faces and happiness in their hearts.

⁷⁶·¹²He will reward them with a garden in Paradise and clothes of silk because of their patience, ⁷⁶·¹³where they will be relaxing on raised thrones, neither experiencing burning sun nor freezing cold. ⁷⁶·¹⁴The garden's shades will be close above them, and its fruit-clusters will also be made to hang low. ⁷⁶·¹⁵Silver dishes will be passed around among them, and drinking cups of crystal ⁷⁶·¹⁶– crystalline silver, which they will fill with perfect measure. ⁷⁶·¹⁷There they'll be given to drink from cups blended with ginger, ⁷⁶·¹⁸from a fountain there called Salsabeel. ⁷⁶·¹⁹Eternal youths will go around serving them. When you see those youths, you would think they were pearls scattered about. ⁷⁶·²⁰When you look around, you will see delights and a huge kingdom all around. ⁷⁶·²¹They will be wearing green clothing of fine silk and heavy brocade, and they will be adorned with silver bracelets, and their Lord will give them a drink that is pure and purifies. ⁷⁶·²²They will be told: "This is your reward, and your hard work has been appreciated."

⁷⁶·²³O Prophet Muhammad, We revealed the Qur'an to you in stages, ⁷⁶·²⁴so wait patiently for your Lord's command, and don't obey anyone

among them who is a sinner or an unthankful person. ⁷⁶·²⁵Continue to remember your Lord's Name morning and evening. ⁷⁶·²⁶Prostrate to Him in some part of the night, and glorify Him for a long time during the night that is long.

⁷⁶·²⁷These people love this available world and are leaving aside the Difficult Judgement Day coming behind them. ⁷⁶·²⁸It is We Who created them and made their joints strong, and We can completely replace them with others like them whenever We want. ⁷⁶·²⁹This Qur'an is a reminder, so anyone who wants can choose a way to his Lord. ⁷⁶·³⁰You can only have something if Allah allows. Allah is always All-Knowing, All-Wise.

⁷⁶·³¹He takes into His special mercy anyone He chooses, and for the wrongdoers He has prepared a painful punishment.

Surah 77. Those Sent Forwards (*al-Mursalaat*)

Allah's name I begin with, the Most Compassionate, the Ever-Merciful

⁷⁷·¹I swear by those breezes that are sent one after the other, ⁷⁷·²then by those strong winds that blow violently, ⁷⁷·³and those that scatter things everywhere; ⁷⁷·⁴then by those that separate things from each other, ⁷⁷·⁵then by those that deliver a reminder ⁷⁷·⁶– as a proof or a warning: ⁷⁷·⁷what you've all been promised will certainly happen.

⁷⁷·⁸Then, when light from the stars will be taken away, ⁷⁷·⁹the sky cracked open, ⁷⁷·¹⁰the mountains blown away as dust, ⁷⁷·¹¹and the messengers brought together at the time and place that is fixed ⁷⁷·¹²– until which Day have these been set? ⁷⁷·¹³For Decision Day! ⁷⁷·¹⁴What will explain to you what Decision Day is? ⁷⁷·¹⁵On that Day, those who call the truth a lie will be damned!

⁷⁷·¹⁶Didn't We destroy the previous disbelievers? ⁷⁷·¹⁷We will also make the later ones follow them in destruction. ⁷⁷·¹⁸This is how We deal with the criminals. ⁷⁷·¹⁹*On that Day, those who call the truth a lie will be damned!*

⁷⁷·²⁰Didn't We create you from a humble fluid? ⁷⁷·²¹We placed it in a safe place ⁷⁷·²²until a time that is fixed. ⁷⁷·²³Then We fix its development. How excellent We are at developing! ⁷⁷·²⁴*On that Day, those who call the truth a lie will be damned!*

⁷⁷·²⁵Haven't We made the earth bring together ⁷⁷·²⁶the living and the dead? ⁷⁷·²⁷We placed tall firm mountains in it and gave you sweet water to drink. ⁷⁷·²⁸*On that Day, those who call the truth a lie will be damned!*

⁷⁷·²⁹They will be told: "Move on to what you used to call a lie! ⁷⁷·³⁰Move on to Hell's shadow rising in three columns, ⁷⁷·³¹neither giving any shade nor protecting from the blazing flames. ⁷⁷·³²It is throwing up sparks as huge as castles, ⁷⁷·³³as if they were yellow camels!" ⁷⁷·³⁴*On that Day, those who call the truth a lie will be damned!*

⁷⁷·³⁵This is a Day when they cannot speak ⁷⁷·³⁶and aren't allowed to offer any excuses. ⁷⁷·³⁷*On that Day, those who call the truth a lie will be damned!*

⁷⁷·³⁸This is Decision Day. We will bring you together with the previous people. ⁷⁷·³⁹Now, try and trick Me if you have any plan! ⁷⁷·⁴⁰*On that Day, those who call the truth a lie will be damned!*

⁷⁷·⁴¹Those who are mindful of Allah will be among shades, fountains, ⁷⁷·⁴²and all the fruits they desire. ⁷⁷·⁴³It will be said to them: "You may eat and drink with enjoyment because of the good things you used to

do." ⁷⁷·⁴⁴This is how we reward those who do good. ⁷⁷·⁴⁵On that Day, those who call the truth a lie will be damned!

⁷⁷·⁴⁶Disbelievers! You can eat and enjoy yourselves for only a short while in this world. You are criminals. ⁷⁷·⁴⁷On that Day, those who call the truth a lie will be damned!

⁷⁷·⁴⁸When they're told: "You must bow to Allah," they don't. ⁷⁷·⁴⁹On that Day, those who call the truth a lie will be damned!

⁷⁷·⁵⁰Now, what revelation after this Qur'an will they believe in?

Surah 78. News (an-Naba')

[PART 30]

Allah's name I begin with, the Most Compassionate, the Ever-Merciful

⁷⁸·¹What are they asking each other about? ⁷⁸·²It's about the important news of Judgement Day ⁷⁸·³in which they disagree. ⁷⁸·⁴Beware! They will soon know. ⁷⁸·⁵Again, beware! They will soon know.

⁷⁸·⁶Haven't We made the earth a resting place, ⁷⁸·⁷and the mountains to pegs? ⁷⁸·⁸We created you in pairs, ⁷⁸·⁹made your sleep for resting, ⁷⁸·¹⁰the night a covering, ⁷⁸·¹¹and the day to earn a living.

⁷⁸·¹²We built seven strong skies over you, ⁷⁸·¹³made the sun a shining lamp,⁷⁸·¹⁴sent down water heavily from the squeezing rainclouds, ⁷⁸·¹⁵so We could bring out with it grains and plants, ⁷⁸·¹⁶and dense gardens too.

⁷⁸·¹⁷Decision Day is a time that is fixed; ⁷⁸·¹⁸it is the Day the Trumpet will be blown and you will come in crowds. ⁷⁸·¹⁹The sky will be opened

up and become gateways; [78.20]and the mountains will be moved away and become only a mirage.

[78.21]Hell is as a place of ambush [78.22]– a home for those who break all limits of rebellion [78.23]– where they will live for ages. [78.24]There they'll taste neither coolness nor anything to drink, [78.25]apart from some boiling liquid and pus, [78.26]as an appropriate punishment.

[78.27]This is because they weren't expecting any judgement, [78.28]and called Our signs absolute lies. [78.29]We have put everything in a record. [78.30]Now have a taste, because We will keep increasing the punishment for you!

[78.31]Those who are mindful of Allah will have a position of success: [78.32]orchards and grapevines, [78.33]companions of the same age, [78.34]and overflowing cups. [78.35]O Prophet Muhammad, there they'll hear neither any foolishness nor any lies [78.36]– as a reward from your Lord, as an appropriate gift [78.37]– from the Lord of the heavens and the earth and everything in between them, Allah – the Most Compassionate. They won't dare speak to Him.

[78.38]On the Day when the Holy Spirit (- Angel Jibra'il) and the angels will stand in rows, none will speak except someone Allah – the Most Compassionate will allow and had said the right thing in this life. [78.39]That will be the Day of Truth. So, anyone who wants should make his destination with his Lord.

[78.40]We have warned you of a punishment coming soon – the Day when every person will see what they did, and every disbeliever will cry out: "Oh! If only I were dust!"

Surah 79. Soul-Snatchers (*an-Naazi'aat*)

Allah's name I begin with, the Most Compassionate, the Ever-Merciful

79.1 I swear by those angels who snatch out souls aggressively, 79.2 who draw out souls gently, 79.3 and who glide through swiftly, 79.4 then by those who overtake quickly, 79.5 then by those who manage every affair: 79.6 you must be prepared for the Day when the first blast will shake violently, 79.7 followed by another blast.

79.8 On that Day, many hearts will be pounding in horror 79.9 when their eyes will be looking down. 79.10 They ask: "What? Will we really be brought back to our previous state 79.11 even when we've become rotten bones?" 79.12 They even say: "In that case, it will be a losing return!" 79.13 It will be a single blast the second time, 79.14 and they will suddenly be in the open ground.

79.15 O Prophet Muhammad, has the story of Musa reached you? 79.16 When his Lord called to him in the holy valley of Tuwa 79.17 and told him: "Go to Fir'awn because he has broken all limits of rebellion, 79.18 and say, 'Do you want to become pure 79.19 and let me guide you to your Lord? Then you should fear Him.'." 79.20 Then, Musa showed him the great sign, 79.21 but Fir'awn called it a lie and disobeyed. 79.22 Then, moving quickly, he turned his back to the truth, 79.23 gathered the people and started calling out. 79.24 "I am your greatest lord!" he said, 79.25 but Allah punished him with a lesson of warning both in the next life and in this life too. 79.26 There is a definite lesson in this for anyone who fears Allah.

79.27 Which is harder to create: you people or the sky? Allah built it. 79.28 He raised its ceiling high, then gave it proportion. 79.29 He made its night to be dark, and brought out its morning brightness. 79.30 After that He spread out the earth. ⁷⁹·³¹He brings out from it its water and its fresh green pasture too, ⁷⁹·³²and has firmly fixed the mountains in it, ⁷⁹·³³all for you and your livestock to enjoy.

⁷⁹·³⁴Therefore, when the Great Overwhelming Calamity of Judgement Day will come, ⁷⁹·³⁵it will be the Day when every person will remember the efforts they had made, ⁷⁹·³⁶and Hell-Fire will be shown to those who will see. ⁷⁹·³⁷Someone who broke all limits of rebellion ⁷⁹·³⁸and preferred this life, ⁷⁹·³⁹Hell-Fire will be the home for him. ⁷⁹·⁴⁰As for someone who feared to stand before his Lord, and stopped himself from following sinful desires, ⁷⁹·⁴¹then Paradise will be the home for him.

⁷⁹·⁴²O Prophet Muhammad, they ask you about the Final Hour: "When will it be?" ⁷⁹·⁴³Why should you mention it? ⁷⁹·⁴⁴It will end with your Lord. ⁷⁹·⁴⁵You can only give warnings to someone who fears it. ⁷⁹·⁴⁶On the Day when they will see it, it will seem to them as if they had hardly lived for an evening or its morning.

Surah 80. He Frowned ('Abasa)

Allah's name I begin with, the Most Compassionate, the Ever-Merciful

⁸⁰·¹He frowned and turned away, ⁸⁰·²because the blind man came to him and interrupted him. ⁸⁰·³O Prophet Muhammad, you never know, he might have become even more pure ⁸⁰·⁴or learnt a lesson, and the advice might benefit him.

⁸⁰·⁵Someone who thinks he doesn't need anything, ⁸⁰·⁶you pay more attention to him that he might accept the truth, ⁸⁰·⁷even though you won't be blamed if he doesn't purify himself by not becoming Muslim. ⁸⁰·⁸As for someone who came to you making an effort to learn, ⁸⁰·⁹while

fearing Allah, ⁸⁰·¹⁰you turn away from him. ⁸⁰·¹¹Be careful! These verses are a reminder. ⁸⁰·¹²So, anyone who wants may remember it. ⁸⁰·¹³It is written in pages that are honoured, ⁸⁰·¹⁴raised high in status, kept pure, ⁸⁰·¹⁵by the hands of those who write ⁸⁰·¹⁶– who are honourable, pious.

⁸⁰·¹⁷May the disbelieving human be cursed for being so unthankful! ⁸⁰·¹⁸From what has Allah created him? ⁸⁰·¹⁹From a drop of semen! He created him, gave him his proportion, ⁸⁰·²⁰then made the path of life easy for him. ⁸⁰·²¹Then He will let him die and place him in a grave. ⁸⁰·²²Eventually, when He chooses, He will bring him back to life. ⁸⁰·²³Beware! He still hasn't completed what Allah told him to do.

⁸⁰·²⁴So, the human should just take a look at his food and think deeply ⁸⁰·²⁵because: We pour down lots of water, ⁸⁰·²⁶then split the earth open, ⁸⁰·²⁷then make grain grow in it, ⁸⁰·²⁸as well as grapes, vegetables, ⁸⁰·²⁹olives, date-palms, ⁸⁰·³⁰dense orchards, ⁸⁰·³¹fruits, and fodder, ⁸⁰·³²all for you and your livestock to enjoy.

⁸⁰·³³Then, when the Deafening Blast will come, ⁸⁰·³⁴it will be the Day when every person will run from their own siblings, ⁸⁰·³⁵mother, father, ⁸⁰·³⁶spouse, and children! ⁸⁰·³⁷On that Day, every one of them will be concerned only about themselves.

⁸⁰·³⁸On that Day, many faces will be bright, ⁸⁰·³⁹cheerful, feeling happy. ⁸⁰·⁴⁰On that Day, many faces will also have dust on them, ⁸⁰·⁴¹gloom covering them. ⁸⁰·⁴²It is really they who are the disbelievers, the sinners.

Surah 81. Folding Up (*at-Takweer*)

Allah's name I begin with, the Most Compassionate, the Ever-Merciful

[81.1]When the sun will be folded up, [81.2]when the stars will fall, [81.3]when the mountains will be moved away, [81.4]when the ten-month pregnant she-camels will be neglected, [81.5]when the wild beasts will be herded together, [81.6]when the seas will be made to boil over, [81.7]when the souls will be paired with their bodies, [81.8]when the infant girls buried alive will be asked [81.9]for what crime they were killed, [81.10]when the records of what people did will be laid open, [81.11]when the sky will be stripped away, [81.12]when Hell-Fire will be made to blaze, [81.13]and when Paradise will be brought near: [81.14]that is when each person will find out what achievements he has brought along.

[81.15]So, I swear by the heavenly bodies that go back [81.16]gliding, hiding; [81.17]by the night when it slowly turns away, [81.18]and the morning when it breathes gently and brightens: [81.19]this Qur'an is certainly the command of an honourable Messenger [81.20]who has power, a high status with Allah - the Lord of the Throne, [81.21]obeyed there too, trustworthy. [81.22]He (- Prophet Muhammad) who makes you his companions isn't a madman, [81.23]as he has seen Him on the clear horizon.

[81.24]Prophet Muhammad isn't stingy in telling about the unseen secrets. [81.25]This Qur'an isn't the words of any rejected devil. [81.26]So where are you people going? [81.27]This Qur'an is a reminder for everyone, [81.28]especially for anyone among you who wants to stay strong on the right path, [81.29]but you can only have something if Allah allows, and He is the Lord of all the worlds.

Surah 82. Breaking Apart (*al-Infitaar*)

Allah's name I begin with, the Most Compassionate, the Ever-Merciful

82.1When the sky will break apart, 82.2when the stars will fall away, 82.3when the seas will be made to overflow, 82.4and when graves will be turned inside out: 82.5each person will find out what he did as an investment for the next world **and what he left behind** as an effect in this world.

82.6O human! What has tricked you against your Gracious Lord? 82.7He created you, gave you proportion, and then composure. 82.8He put you together in any form He wanted. 82.9Of course! However, you humans call the Judgement a lie, 82.10when there certainly are guardian-angels over you 82.11– honourable, always recording, 82.12knowing everything you do.

82.13Pious people will certainly be in delights, 82.14and the sinful will be in Hell-Fire 82.15– where they will burn on Judgement Day, 82.16unable to get away from it.

82.17What will explain to you what Judgement Day is? 82.18Again, what will explain to you what Judgement Day is? 82.19It'll be the Day when no one will be able to do anything for anyone else in any way at all, and the command that Day will entirely be Allah's.

Surah 83. Those Who Cheat (*al-Mutaffifeen*)

Allah's name I begin with, the Most Compassionate, the Ever-Merciful

83.1Damned are those who cheat in measuring and weighing, 83.2who, when they take by measure from people, they take full, 83.3but when they give them by measure or weight, they give less. [83.4]What? Don't these people think they'll be brought back to life [83.5]on a Dreadful Judgement Day [83.6]– the Day when people will stand in front of Allah – the Lord of all the Worlds?

[83.7]Beware! The record of sinners is in Sijjeen. [83.8]What will explain to you what Sijjeen is? [83.9]It's a register that is written.

[83.10]On that Day, those who call the truth a lie will be damned [83.11]– especially those who call Judgement Day a lie. [83.12]No one would call it a lie except any disobedient lawbreaker. [83.13]When Our revelations are recited to him, he says: "These are stories made up by previous people." [83.14]No, no! The truth is, the bad things they used to do have rusted their hearts. [83.15]Beware! They will certainly be veiled from seeing their Lord on that Day. [83.16]Then, they will burn in Hell-Fire. [83.17]They'll be told: "This is that punishment which you used to call a lie!"

[83.18]Beware! The record of pious people is in Illiyyoon. [83.19]What will explain to you what Illiyyoon is? [83.20]It's a register that is written. [83.21]Those angels nearest to Allah can witness it.

[83.22]Pious people will certainly be in delights [83.23]– on raised thrones, gazing. [83.24]You will recognise the freshness of delight on their faces. [83.25]To drink, they'll be given the best holy wine, sealed. [83.26]Its aftertaste is musk. That is what the competitors should be competing for! [83.27]Its blend is with Tasneem [83.28]– a fountain from which only those nearest to Allah will drink.

[83.29]The criminals used to laugh at the Believers, [83.30]winking at each other whenever they passed them by, [83.31]and on their way back to their own people, they used to go back joking about the Believers,

83.32saying: "These are the ones gone astray," whenever they saw them, 83.33though they hadn't been sent to watch over them.

83.34Now, Today, at the disbelievers, the Believers are laughing 83.35– on raised thrones, watching.

83.36So, have the disbelievers now been punished for the bad things they used to do!

Surah 84. Splitting Apart (al-Inshiqaaq)

Allah's name I begin with, the Most Compassionate, the Ever-Merciful

84.1When the sky will crack and split apart, 84.2and will obey its Lord, as it must; 84.3and when the earth will be stretched, 84.4and will throw out everything inside it and become empty, 84.5and will obey its Lord, as it must: 84.6O human! You are working painfully hard to reach your Lord. You will eventually meet Him.

84.7As for someone given his record in his right hand, 84.8he will very soon be judged in an easy way, 84.9and will go back happy to his people. 84.10As for someone given his record from behind his back, 84.11he will very soon cry out for his own total destruction, 84.12and will burn in a Blazing Fire. 84.13He used to be happy among his people, 84.14thinking he would never go back to Allah. 84.15Of course he will! His Lord is always Ever-Watchful of him.

84.16So, I swear by the twilight glow, 84.17and the night and everything it covers, 84.18and the moon when it becomes full: 84.19you will definitely ride along from stage to stage. 84.20Then what is wrong with them? Why won't they believe?

[84.21]When the Qur'an is recited to them, they won't prostrate? <Prostration Point 13> [84.22]Instead, the disbelievers are calling the truth a lie, [84.23]but Allah knows best what they are hiding in their minds. [84.24]So, O Prophet Muhammad, warn them of a painful punishment, [84.25]but not for those who believe and do good, because they will have a never-ending reward.

Surah 85. Constellations (al-Burooj)

Allah's name I begin with, the Most Compassionate, the Ever-Merciful

[85.1]I swear by the sky full of constellations, [85.2]and by the Promised Day, [85.3]and by the witness and the one who will be witnessed: [85.4]cursed are the trench-diggers, [85.5]who lit the fire full of fuel [85.6]when they sat beside it [85.7]and they themselves witnessed what they were doing to the Believers. [85.8]They only hated the Believers because they believed in Allah, the Almighty, the Most Praiseworthy, [85.9]Who has control of the heavens and the earth. Allah is a Witness to everything.

[85.10]Those who oppress the Believing men and women, and then they don't repent, they will suffer the punishment of Hell, and specifically the punishment of the Scorching Fire. [85.11]Those who believe and do good, they will have gardens – that have rivers flowing beneath them. That will be the great victory.

[85.12]O Prophet Muhammad, your Lord's grip is certainly severe. [85.13]It is He Who starts creating and will bring back to life. [85.14]He is the Most Forgiving, the Most Loving, [85.15]Lord of the Throne, the Glorious, [85.16]does absolutely whatever He wants.

85.17Has the story of the armies reached you 85.18– of Fir'awn and Thamud? 85.19Yet the disbelievers are calling the truth a lie, 85.20while Allah completely surrounds them from all sides.

85.21Of course, this is a Glorious Qur'an, 85.22written on a Tablet that is well-preserved.

Surah 86. Night-Comer (*at-Taariq*)

Allah's name I begin with, the Most Compassionate, the Ever-Merciful

86.1I swear by the sky and by the night-comer. 86.2What will explain to you what the night-comer is? 86.3It's the star of piercing brightness.

86.4Every person has a guardian watching over them. 86.5So, the human should think about what he was created from. 86.6He was created from some spurting fluid 86.7which comes out from between the sacrum and the ribs.

86.8Allah has the power to bring him back to life 86.9on the Day when all secrets will be disclosed. 86.10Then the human will have neither any strength nor any helper.

86.11I swear by the sky that recycles itself, 86.12and the earth that splits open: 86.13this Qur'an is certainly a decisive command. 86.14It is no joke!

86.15They are plotting schemes, 86.16and I am making a plan too. 86.17Therefore, O Prophet Muhammad, give the disbelievers some time: let them relax a short while.

Surah 87. Most High (al-A'laa)

Allah's name I begin with, the Most Compassionate, the Ever-Merciful

87.1O Prophet Muhammad, glorify the Name of your Lord, the Most High; 87.2Who creates, then makes perfect; 87.3Who gives proportion, then guides; 87.4Who brings out fresh green pasture, 87.5then turns it into dark filthy scum.

87.6O Prophet Muhammad, We will teach you to recite that you will never forget, 87.7except what Allah chooses. He knows everything that is open or hidden. 87.8We will make the smooth path of Islam easy for you. 87.9So, you should keep reminding, if it helps.

87.10Someone who fears Allah will learn lessons; 87.11but the wretched person will avoid it 87.12– who will then burn in the Biggest Fire, 87.13where he will be neither dead nor alive.

87.14Successful will be the one who becomes pure, 87.15mentions his Lord's Name, and prays. 87.16However, you people are choosing this life, 87.17even though the Hereafter is best and lasts forever.

87.18All this is written in the previous Books of Revelation 87.19– those given to Ibrahim and Musa.

Surah 88. Overwhelming Event (al-Ghaashiyah)

Allah's name I begin with, the Most Compassionate, the Ever-Merciful

88.1Has the news of the Overwhelming Event reached you? 88.2On that Day, many faces will be looking down, 88.3worn out, tired. 88.4They will burn in an Intense Fire 88.5and forced to drink from a boiling spring.

88.6They will have no food apart from some dry, thorny, bitter, poisonous shrub, 88.7which neither nourishes nor satisfies hunger.

88.8On that Day, many faces will be glowing, 88.9well-pleased with their efforts, 88.10in a magnificent garden, 88.11where they won't hear any foolishness. 88.12There'll be a flowing fountain in that garden, 88.13and sofas raised high, 88.14with cups placed in order, 88.15cushions arranged in rows, 88.16and rugs spread out.

88.17Don't people think about: the camels – how they've been created; 88.18the sky – how it's been raised high; 88.19the mountains – how they've been fixed in place; 88.20and the earth – how it's been spread out? 88.21So, O Prophet Muhammad, keep reminding them, because you are a reminder 88.22– and no, you're not being forceful with them. 88.23However, if someone turns away and disbelieves, 88.24Allah will make him suffer the worst punishment.

88.25Their return will be to Us, 88.26then, it will be upon Us to judge them.

Surah 89. Dawn (al-Fajr)

Allah's name I begin with, the Most Compassionate, the Ever-Merciful

89.1I swear by the dawn, 89.2the ten holy nights, 89.3the even and odd, 89.4and the night as it moves on: 89.5isn't there an oath in this for those who can understand?

89.6O Prophet Muhammad, don't you see how your Lord dealt with: the 'Ad 89.7of Iram, of the tall pillars, 89.8whose like hasn't been created in any of the lands; 89.9the Thamud, who carved homes in rocks in the valley; 89.10and Fir'awn, of the huge structures? 89.11They were those who broke all limits of rebellion in the lands they controlled, ⁸⁹·¹²and spread a lot of trouble there. ⁸⁹·¹³So, your Lord unleashed a scourge of punishment on them. ⁸⁹·¹⁴Your Lord is Watching closely.

⁸⁹·¹⁵Now, as for the human, when his Lord tests him by giving him honour and blessings, he says: "My Lord has honoured me." ⁸⁹·¹⁶However, when He tests him by restricting his wealth for him, he then protests: "My Lord has humiliated me!" ⁸⁹·¹⁷No, no! The truth is, you people don't even honour the orphans, ⁸⁹·¹⁸nor encourage each other to give food to the needy. ⁸⁹·¹⁹You greedily eat up all the inheritance belonging to others, ⁸⁹·²⁰and you love wealth so dearly!

⁸⁹·²¹Guess what! When the earth will be smashed up into dust, ⁸⁹·²²and your Lord brings His command, and His angels appear row after row, ⁸⁹·²³and Hell is brought forward that Day, that will be the Day the human will remind himself, but what good will that reminding be to him then? ⁸⁹·²⁴He will cry out: "Oh! If only I had prepared for this life of mine!" ⁸⁹·²⁵On that Day, no one can punish like Allah will, ⁸⁹·²⁶and no one can tie up like He will.

⁸⁹·²⁷Allah will say to the Believers: "O you satisfied soul! ⁸⁹·²⁸Come back to your Lord well-pleased with Him and well-pleasing to Him. ⁸⁹·²⁹Now join My servants ⁸⁹·³⁰and enter My Paradise."

Surah 90. City (al-Balad)

Allah's name I begin with, the Most Compassionate, the Ever-Merciful

⁹⁰·¹I swear by this city of Makkah ⁹⁰·²because you, O Beloved Prophet Muhammad, are living in it; ⁹⁰·³and I swear by every parent and child ⁹⁰·⁴that: We have created humans to struggle.

[90.5]Does anyone really think no one can have power over him? [90.6]He arrogantly says: "I've spent lots of wealth!" [90.7]Does he think no one saw him? [90.8]Haven't We given him two eyes, [90.9]a tongue, and two lips; [90.10]and shown him the two ways of good and evil?

[90.11]However, he hasn't even attempted the steep path yet! [90.12]What will explain to you what the steep path is? [90.13]It is: to free a slave, [90.14]giving food on a day of starvation [90.15]to the closely-related orphan, [90.16]or to the needy – homeless and down in the dust. [90.17]He will also have to be of those who believe and encourage patience and mercy among themselves. [90.18]It is they who are the good Companions of the Right Hand.

[90.19]However, those who disbelieve in Our signs, they are the bad Companions of the Left Hand. [90.20]It is upon them that the Fire will be closed over.

Surah 91. Sun (ash-Shams)

Allah's name I begin with, the Most Compassionate, the Ever-Merciful

[91.1]I swear by the sun and its morning brightness, [91.2]and the moon as it comes after it, [91.3]and the day as it displays it, [91.4]and the night as it covers it; [91.5]and I swear by the sky and what Allah built, [91.6]and the earth and what He stretched out, [91.7]and the soul and what He gave proportion to, [91.8]then inspired it to know what is sinful or mindful for it: [91.9]anyone who purifies his soul will succeed, [91.10]but whoever corrupts it will fail.

[91.11]The Thamud accused their Prophet Salih of being a liar by their rebellion, [91.12]when the most wretched of them was prepared to kill the she-camel. [91.13]So Allah's messenger Salih warned them: "Be careful with Allah's she-camel and her turn to drink!" 91.14But they accused him of being a liar and hamstrung her. So, their Lord crushed them because of their crime, and then totally flattened them! 91.15He doesn't fear what happens because of it.

Surah 92. Night (al-Layl)

Allah's name I begin with, the Most Compassionate, the Ever-Merciful

92.1I swear by the night as it covers up the light, 92.2and the day as it appears bright, 92.3and I swear by the males and females He created: 92.4your efforts are certainly of different kinds.

92.5So, someone who donates, and is mindful of Allah, 92.6and truthfully accepts the most beautiful guidance, 92.7We will put him on the smooth path of Islam. 92.8As for someone who is stingy, and thinks he doesn't need anything, 92.9and calls the most beautiful guidance a lie, 92.10We will put him on the difficult path to punishment; 92.11his wealth won't help him when he falls into ruin.

92.12It is certainly Our duty to guide, 92.13and the Hereafter and this world are both Ours. 92.14So, I've warned you of a Fire blazing fiercely, 92.15in which only the most wretched people will burn 92.16– especially someone who calls the truth a lie and turns away. 92.17The most mindful people of Allah will be kept away from it 92.18– especially someone who donates his wealth to become pure in heart and soul, 92.19and not to return a favour to anyone, 92.20but only to gain the good pleasure of their Lord, the Most High. 92.21Such a person will soon be well-pleased.

Surah 93. Mid-Morning Light (ad-Duhaa)

Allah's name I begin with, the Most Compassionate, the Ever-Merciful

[93.1] I swear by the increasing mid-morning light, [93.2] and the night as it silently spreads over: [93.3] O Prophet Muhammad, your Lord neither abandoned you nor is He displeased. [93.4] Every next moment is better for you than the previous. [93.5] Very soon your Lord will give you so much that you will be well-pleased.

[93.6] Didn't He have you, then through you gave shelter to the orphans? [93.7] He had you, then through you guided those astray. [93.8] He had you, then through you gave to those in need.

[93.9] So, as for orphans, you shouldn't be strict with them, [93.10] and as for beggars, don't turn them away. [93.11] As for your Lord's favours, speak openly about them.

Surah 94. Opening the Heart (al-Inshiraah)

Allah's name I begin with, the Most Compassionate, the Ever-Merciful

[94.1] O Prophet Muhammad, haven't We made your noble chest wide open for you, [94.2] and taken away from you your burden [94.3] which was becoming heavy on your noble back?

[94.4] We have raised high and increased your honour for you.

[94.5] So, along with every difficulty there is ease: [94.6] along with this difficulty there is more ease.

94.7Therefore, when you are free, you should keep making tiring efforts, 94.8and keep turning to your Lord.

Surah 95. Fig (at-Teen)

Allah's name I begin with, the Most Compassionate, the Ever-Merciful

95.1I swear by the fig and the olive, 95.2and Mount Tur of Sinai, 95.3and this peaceful city of Makkah 95.4that: We certainly created the human in the most beautiful form.

95.5Then We pushed him down to be the lowliest of the low, 95.6but not those who believe and do good; they will have a never-ending reward.

95.7Then, after knowing this, who can accuse you of lying about the Judgement after death? 95.8Isn't Allah the Greatest of Judges?

Surah 96. That Which Clings (al-'Alaq)

Allah's name I begin with, the Most Compassionate, the Ever-Merciful

96.1O Prophet Muhammad, recite in the Name of your Lord Who created everything. 96.2He created humans out of something that clings. 96.3Recite, as your Lord is Most Generous, 96.4Who taught by the pen 96.5– taught humans what they never knew.

96.6Beware! The disobedient human certainly breaks all limits of rebellion 96.7when he thinks he doesn't need anything nor cares for it. 96.8However, the return of everyone will be to your Lord.

96.9What you do think of someone who stops 96.10a servant of Allah when he prays? 96.11Imagine if he himself was on guidance, 96.12or he told others to be mindful of Allah? ⁹⁶·¹³What do you think: does he call the truth a lie and turn away? ⁹⁶·¹⁴Doesn't he know that Allah is watching? ⁹⁶·¹⁵Beware! If he doesn't stop, We will certainly drag him by the forelock ⁹⁶·¹⁶– that lying, sinful forelock! ⁹⁶·¹⁷Then, he can even call his friends, ⁹⁶·¹⁸because We will call the angel-guards of Hell! ⁹⁶·¹⁹No, no! O Prophet Muhammad, you shouldn't obey him; but prostrate to Me, and bring yourself even closer to Me. <Prostration Point 14>

Surah 97. Great Value (al-Qadr)

Allah's name I begin with, the Most Compassionate, the Ever-Merciful

⁹⁷·¹We revealed the Qur'an on the Night of Great Value. ⁹⁷·²What will explain to you what the Night of Great Value is? ⁹⁷·³The Night of Great Value is better than a thousand months, ⁹⁷·⁴in which the angels and the Holy Spirit (- Angel Jibra'il) come down for all matters by their Lord's command. ⁹⁷·⁵It is peace until the rising of dawn.

Surah 98. Clear Proof (al-Bayyinah)

Allah's name I begin with, the Most Compassionate, the Ever-Merciful

⁹⁸·¹The disbelievers from among the People of the Book, and the polytheists too, would never stop disbelieving unless there would come to them the clear proof: ⁹⁸·²a Messenger (- Muhammad) from Allah, reciting pages of the Qur'an kept pure, ⁹⁸·³that have firm commands written inside them.

⁹⁸·⁴It was only after the clear proof had come to them that the People of the Book broke up with each other, ⁹⁸·⁵even though the only orders they were given were to worship Allah in sincere devotion to Him, be

true, establish the ritual prayers, and pay zakah; and that is the correct religion.

⁹⁸·⁶The disbelievers from among the People of the Book, and the polytheists too, will be in the fire of Hell, where they will remain forever. It is they who are the worst of creation.

⁹⁸·⁷Those who believe and do good, it is they who are the best of creation. ⁹⁸·⁸Their reward, with their Lord, will be Gardens of Eden – that have rivers flowing beneath them, where they will remain forever and ever. Allah is well-pleased with them and they are well-pleased with Him. This reward will be for anyone who fears his Lord.

Surah 99. Earthquake (*az-Zilzaal*)

Allah's name I begin with, the Most Compassionate, the Ever-Merciful

⁹⁹·¹When the earth will be shaken violently with its final earthquake, ⁹⁹·²and throws out all its burdens, ⁹⁹·³and humans will ask: "What's happening to it?" ⁹⁹·⁴On that Day it will tell all its experiences ⁹⁹·⁵because your Lord will order it to.

⁹⁹·⁶On that Day people will go out in separate groups to be shown what they had done in this life: ⁹⁹·⁷anyone who does even an atom's weight of good will see it, ⁹⁹·⁸and whoever does even an atom's weight of bad will also see it.

Surah 100. Charging Warhorses (al-'Aadiyaat)

Allah's name I begin with, the Most Compassionate, the Ever-Merciful

100.1I swear by the charging warhorses panting heavily, 100.2striking sparks with their hooves, 100.3making sudden raids at dawn, 100.4where they raise dust clouds, 100.5and they altogether dash straight into the centre of the enemy ranks! 100.6The human is certainly very unthankful to his Lord, 100.7and he definitely knows it. 100.8He is extreme in his love for wealth.

100.9What? Doesn't he know that when everything in the graves will be turned inside out, 100.10and when the secrets inside the hearts will be exposed, 100.11that their Lord is Fully-Aware of them, even to that Day?!

Surah 101. Crashing Shudder (al-Qaari'ah)

Allah's name I begin with, the Most Compassionate, the Ever-Merciful

101.1The Crashing Shudder! 101.2What is the Crashing Shudder? 101.3What will explain to you what the Crashing Shudder is?

101.4On the Day when people will be like scattered moths 101.5and the mountains will be like tufts of coloured wool: 101.6anyone whose scales of good are heavy, 101.7he will be in a life of happiness; 101.8but as for someone whose scales are light, 101.9his home will be the Bottomless Pit. 101.10What will explain to you what that is? 101.11It's a bottomless pit of intense fire!

Surah 102. Competing for More (*at-Takaathur*)

Allah's name I begin with, the Most Compassionate, the Ever-Merciful

[102.1] **Competing in having more** in this world will keep distracting you from Allah, [102.2] **until you enter the graves.** [102.3] **Beware! You will very soon come to know** the reality of this world. [102.4] **Again, beware! You will very soon find out.** [102.5] **Beware! If only you knew with certain knowledge!**

[102.6] **You will definitely see Hell-Fire;** [102.7] **you will definitely see it with true vision.** [102.8] **Then, on that Day, you will certainly be questioned about** your worldly **pleasures.**

Surah 103. Passing of Time (*al-'Asr*)

Allah's name I begin with, the Most Compassionate, the Ever-Merciful

[103.1] I swear by the passing of time: [103.2] humans are certainly in loss, [103.3] except those who believe, do good, and encourage truth and patience among themselves.

Surah 104. False Accuser (*al-Humazah*)

Allah's name I begin with, the Most Compassionate, the Ever-Merciful

[104.1] Damned is every false accuser, faultfinder, [104.2] who gathers wealth and keeps on counting it. [104.3] He thinks his wealth will make him live forever. [104.4] Never! He will most certainly be thrown into the Crushing Fire!

¹⁰⁴·⁵Anyway, what will explain to you what the Crushing Fire is? ¹⁰⁴·⁶It is Allah's Fire set ablaze, ¹⁰⁴·⁷which rises over the hearts and minds. ¹⁰⁴·⁸It will be closed down on them ¹⁰⁴·⁹in outstretched pillars of flames.

Surah 105. Elephant (al-Feel)

Allah's name I begin with, the Most Compassionate, the Ever-Merciful

¹⁰⁵·¹O Prophet Muhammad, haven't you seen how your Lord dealt with the companions of the Elephant? ¹⁰⁵·²Didn't He turn their plans into panic? ¹⁰⁵·³He sent against them flocks of birds from all directions ¹⁰⁵·⁴that were striking them with small stones of hard-baked clay, ¹⁰⁵·⁵with which He turned them into what looked like hay – chewed up and swallowed.

Surah 106. Quraysh (Quraysh Tribe)

Allah's name I begin with, the Most Compassionate, the Ever-Merciful

¹⁰⁶·¹For placing love in the Quraysh ¹⁰⁶·²– placing in them love for the Winter and Summer trade journeys: ¹⁰⁶·³this is why they must worship Allah – the Lord of this House (– the Ka'bah), ¹⁰⁶·⁴Who has fed them in hunger and protected them from fear.

Surah 107. Small Necessities (al-Maa'oon)

Allah's name I begin with, the Most Compassionate, the Ever-Merciful

¹⁰⁷·¹What do you think of someone who calls the Judgement a lie? ¹⁰⁷·²He is the one who violently pushes the orphan away, ¹⁰⁷·³and doesn't encourage others to give food to the needy.

[107.4]So, damned are those who pray [107.5] but who are careless about their prayers, [107.6]who only show off, [107.7]and they don't lend even small items of need.

Surah 108. Abundance (al-Kawthar)

Allah's name I begin with, the Most Compassionate, the Ever-Merciful

[108.1]O Prophet Muhammad, We have given you lots of everything. [108.2]So, continue to pray to your Lord and make sacrifice. [108.3]It is only your enemy who will be cut off.

Surah 109. Disbelievers (al-Kaafiroon)

Allah's name I begin with, the Most Compassionate, the Ever-Merciful

[109.1]O Prophet Muhammad, say: "Disbelievers! [109.2]I don't worship what you worship, [109.3]and You don't worship what I worship. [109.4]I won't worship what you worship, [109.5]and you won't worship what I worship. [109.6]You have your religion and I have mine."

Surah 110. Help (an-Nasr)

Allah's name I begin with, the Most Compassionate, the Ever-Merciful

[110.1]When Allah's help and victory comes, [110.2]and you see people entering Allah's religion in crowds, [110.3]then glorify the praises of your Lord and ask forgiveness from Him. He always accepts repentance much.

Surah 111. Flame (al-Lahab)

Allah's name I begin with, the Most Compassionate, the Ever-Merciful

^{111.1}May Abu Lahab's hands be destroyed! May he himself be devastated! ^{111.2}Neither his wealth nor what he earned will help him. ^{111.3}He will burn in a Fire of blazing flames. ^{111.4}His wife too! That firewood-carrier! ^{111.5}Around her neck here will be a rope of twisted palm-fibre.

Surah 112. Sincerity (al-Ikhlaas)

Allah's name I begin with, the Most Compassionate, the Ever-Merciful

^{112.1}O Prophet Muhammad, **say: "He is Allah – the One and Only;** ^{112.2}**Allah – the independent, eternal and absolute.** ^{112.3}**He has never had children and nor was He born.** ^{112.4}**Nothing can be equal to Him."**

Surah 113. Daybreak (al-Falaq)

Allah's name I begin with, the Most Compassionate, the Ever-Merciful

^{113.1}O Prophet Muhammad, **say: "I ask for protection with Allah – the Lord of daybreak** ^{113.2}**from the harms of everything He has created;** ^{113.3}**from the harms of the dark night when it spreads over,** ^{113.4}**from the harms of witches who blow magic spells on knots,** ^{113.5}**and from the harms of an envier when he envies."**

Surah 114. People (*an-Naas*)

Allah's name I begin with, the Most Compassionate, the Ever-Merciful

[114.1]O Prophet Muhammad, say: "I ask for protection with Allah – the Lord of all people, [114.2]King of all people, [114.3]God of all people: [114.4]from the harms of the sneaky whisperer, [114.5]who whispers evil into people's hearts and minds, [114.6]whether he is from jinns or from people."

❧ Ends ❧

Printed in Great Britain
by Amazon